W9-APY-956

TOWARDS SOCIALISM

TOWARDS
SOCIALISM

Perry Anderson * Thomas Balogh
Robin Blackburn * Ken Coates
Richard Crossman * André Gorz
Tom Nairn * Richard Titmuss
John Westergaard * Raymond Williams

Edited for the New Left Review *by*
Perry Anderson and Robin Blackburn

Introduction to the American Edition
by Andrew Hacker

Cornell University Press

ITHACA, NEW YORK

Library of Congress Catalog Card Number: 66-13810

PRINTED IN THE UNITED STATES OF AMERICA
BY VALLEY OFFSET, INC.
BOUND BY VAIL-BALLOU PRESS, INC.

INTRODUCTION TO
THE AMERICAN EDITION

The time spent in reading this book is an investment—
which may or may not pay off. There is no way of knowing which ones among the countless political tracts published each year will be memorialized by subsequent
generations. The *Fabian Essays,* the *Communist Manifesto,*
and the *Federalist Papers* all appeared as essays for their
times: their intended purpose was to spur a head-on confrontation with the critical issues of their day. That these
volumes are reprinted and remembered is not only testimony to the lasting insights found on their pages but is
also evidence that events of history have vindicated the
arguments of the original authors.

Shaw and the Webbs, Marx and Engels, Hamilton and
Madison, may have been special pleaders rather than objective scholars. But the current political shape of Great
Britain, the Soviet Union, and the United States shows
the imprint of the ideologies espoused in this political literature. Whether the writings of Marx and Madison and the
Webbs actually had a direct effect on political and social
arrangements is a matter to be argued by those who are
attracted to debates unsusceptible of yielding answers. No
one can prove that a book or a pamphlet had had an influence
on the behavior of a society. What can be said is that some
books, by chance or prescience, argue for changes which
then happen to take place at a later time. Such books are
counted the winners, or at least remain as the survivors, in
the bibliographies of politics. They become what some
scholars like to think of as the "tradition" of a political
system, and the texts are as often as not used to lend a
historic authority to a regime that is no longer a contender
for power and is now an established concern.

Towards Socialism speaks of and for a society, both socialist and democratic, that may not be realized in our own or anyone's lifetime. Here are ten socialists, plainspokenly dissatisfied with both the pace and outlook of the party and movement that constitutes their political home. All are sympathetic to the Labour Party of Great Britain, and none show any desire to defect to a doctrinaire splinter group that might offer greater ideological purity. They realize that the kind of Britain they want to create will only come about through the ministrations of a government and party capable of mustering impressive majority support. If they are critics of Labour, they are loyal and sympathetic in their criticism. And their vantage point is substantially to the Left of the already Left-leaning center of British politics.

It is necessary, even if wearisome, to point out that there is a Marxian overlay to these essays. But it is a Marxism informed by a sophisticated understanding of the structure of modern society: if some of the old categories of the dialectic are utilized, many others have been discarded because they simply are no longer relevant to our time. No one suggests that there have not been important changes in the century since Marx wrote. Yet it must also be noted that there have been significant patterns to society that have persisted amidst those changes. The economy is still largely capitalist in organization and purpose; classes and social disparities continue to exist; power in society remains unequally distributed and is deployed without having to secure popular consent.

The chief focus of *Towards Socialism* centers, not surprisingly, on the distribution of power in a capitalist society. Almost immediately the question arises as to whether one can still call the British—or the American—system a "capitalist" one and still have an analysis that is useful and realistic. The majority of established economists, sociologists, and political scientists would have us believe that things are no longer as they once were. How can one fail to distinguish the grim mills of Manchester from the computerized palaces of the air-conditioned corporation? The property-owning bourgeoisie of the nineteenth century has, we are told, been replaced by a revolving and talented managerial stratum not unconscious of its social responsibilities. And the exploited and demoralized proletariat have been transformed into well-organized and well-paid trade unionists, with an increasing proportion of the working force consisting of white-collar employees now ensconced in the middle class. Even government enters the economy to provide services and subventions in a variety of expanding areas and ensures, through regulations and controls, that business is accountable to the public interest. This, at all events, is the standard interpretation. It is one that is rejected on these pages.

For talk of a welfare state, of a mixed economy, even of a managerial revolution, is of limited utility. For the fact remains that major decisions in the economy are private. They are made within the confines of closed circles, and public agencies may not intrude in any effective way. Corporate capitalism of course differs from classical capitalism, but the transformation has been only in the adjective—not the noun. This is why discussion of reform is so difficult. Can the private managers of corporate capital be made institutionally responsible to the public? After all the tergiversations of assorted pundits, the answer seems to be that accountability is impossible of achievement in either the British or the American frameworks. Experience has thus far shown that governmental bodies set up to regulate private enterprise are soon brought to a close sympathy with the industries they are supposed to be regulating. This should occasion no surprise. Corporations are powerful, and they will use their resources to maintain a favorable climate for themselves. While in the realm of pure logic a Federal Power Commission in Washington might tell Standard Oil of California what it might or might not do, in actual fact such an agency is less powerful than the corporation it is theoretically able to control. Similarly our ideology permits us to rest happy in the thought that the

Monopolies Commission in London could, if it so desired, "break up" Unilever or Imperial Chemical Industries into congeries of separate companies. The fact of power, however, is that this has not, cannot, and will not be done, because government is weaker than the corporate institutions purportedly subordinate to it. This is the politics of capitalism. It is not at all expressive of a conspiracy but rather a harmony of political forms and economic interests on a plane determined by the on-going needs of corporate institutions.

The problem for British socialists—and, with variations, it is the problem of American radicals and reformers—is how to produce a political ferment in a society that is generally affluent and most of whose members are content with things pretty much as they are. While it may still be argued that there continues to exist a propertyless proletariat, regardless of whether its members wear white collars or blue collars, this majority does not feel itself seriously aggrieved by poverty or exploitation or the concentration of economic power in giant institutions. Such citizens will often favor the redistribution of wealth on a piecemeal basis and the gradual introduction of new social legislation; but they simply are not persuaded by the argument that the society in which they live is irrational or unjust or in need of fundamental reconstruction.

At the same time it is common knowledge that affluence, while widespread, has not reached everyone in society. Here, it might be thought, is a constituency for socialism. The problem is that those who are really dispossessed are exceedingly difficult to mobilize and are usually uncomprehending of the political system in which they are supposed to play a part. Old people, mothers with families of fatherless children, and the lowly-paid who are ignored by trade union organizers tend to be non-voters, non-joiners, and so submerged that they are incapable of coalescing into a party of protest. While there are occasional, almost random, outbursts of dissatisfaction from members of this class, for all intents and purposes they remain a modern *lumpenproletariat* far removed not only from socialist overtures but from political life and thought in any form.

As for the working class with steady jobs and union cards, it is now well above the poverty line not so much owing to the services provided by a welfare state as to the fortuitous prosperity of the postwar years. While these skilled and semi-skilled workers are never happy with their wage level, their resentments are not so intense as to make them systematic opponents of capitalism. Indeed all they seem to want are larger slices of the very appetizing pies they see all around them.

Thus the contemporary working class, no longer exploited and no longer at a subsistence level, has been a grave disappointment to socialists and radicals. This may be termed "the betrayal of the proletariat"—and by this it is not intended to mean that the working class itself has been betrayed by anyone or anything. On the contrary, the once-exploited and once-submerged have themselves acted to betray those who in an earlier day held out great hopes and expectations for them. What has happened, of course, is that those who were once depressed Welsh miners are now the owners of cars and payers of school taxes; the migrant Okies are now Los Angeles suburbanites anxious to keep lesser breeds within the population from invading their well-manicured neighborhoods. These ex-proletarians are currently sitting in front of television sets, beer can in hand, waiting for a sirloin steak that is broiling on the outdoor barbeque pit. Is this what all the fervent protest of the 1930's was for?

The socialist and radical tendency, as often as not unacknowledged, is to believe that those oppressed by capitalism are possessed of an ethical purity and a great potentiality for esthetic and intellectual development. If these capabilities long remained unfulfilled it was because material deprivation was the chief fact of working-class existence. Once the shackles of poverty were removed, it was assumed the working man would emerge to appreciate and pursue a quality of life far higher than that known by anyone before. But no such thing has happened: the graduates of yesterday's proletariat have adopted most of the habits and prejudices of the tasteless middle class. And in so doing they have betrayed the socialists and radicals who worked so earnestly to help them in an earlier and unhappier day.

It would appear that those on the Left, themselves usually middle class in origins and occupation, feel the need to romanticize the people to whom they extend a helping hand. If the 1930's saw the working class so glorified, in the late 1960's the object of celebration is the Negro. Because they suffer from oppression and discrimination, Negroes are seen as possessing such sterling qualities of character and conscience that few whites have managed to achieve. Thus when it is shown that some Negroes are deficient in their social attainments, these lacks are ascribed to the social barriers that have held their race back. (This is clearly true in many cases. However most Negroes, like most whites, are not very bright and not very ambitious. Most people, in other words, are quite average.) Once again the cycle will be repeated: as Negroes are permitted to ascend to the middle class and share in the society's prosperity, they too will aspire to suburban homes and color television and wall-to-wall carpeting. And, once again, this will be marked as a "betrayal" of the good-hearted middle-class whites, who will discover that their contribution to the civil rights protests of the 1960's were not only unappreciated but in the end self-defeating.

To be sure it may be said, and with truth, that the proletariat has been corrupted by the bounty and the perverted morality of capitalism. Poverty and oppression may have been alleviated in the postwar years, but this was due not to political action but because of a historic interlude which permitted capitalism to prosper sufficiently to cut the working class in on its benefits. Thus the working class moved up the economic ladder on capitalism's own terms, all the time accepting the values of property ownership and middle-class materialism and suburban respectability.

This, it should be remarked in passing, is not the least reason why Marx and Lenin spoke of violence and underlined the imperative need for smashing the bourgeois state and economy. They wished to destroy a corrupt and irrational system because such a system was capable of bribing, enticing, and otherwise seducing the workers. They desired, in a word, to remove the capitalist alternative. For they knew that the values of capitalism are a standing temptation; they knew that not many, so lured, would be able to turn their backs on what the prosperity of free enterprise is able to offer.

Who are the socialists? Who, in particular, are the socialists at a time when capitalism seems able to provide high employment and widespread affluence?

What emerges is that today's socialists are no longer exclusively preoccupied with economic injustice. There is now a concern with the quality of life, moral and esthetic, that persists on a dismayingly low level despite the fact of prosperity. There is anxiety over the effects of popular culture and the passive role of the millions who imbibe it; there is frequent discussion of education at all levels and the fact that learning is easily adjusted to the needs of agencies outside the academy; and there is heightened awareness of conditions such as alienation and anomie, with attention drawn to the fact that individuals are searching for an identity in a system where human relationships are tenuous and transient. The entire population, especially the middle class now inflated with millions of new recruits, is seen as having an aimless character; if individuals have no sense of purpose or being, it is because their society is based on no ethical premises and is possessed by no rationale to explain its current behavior or its goals for the future.

Socialists, in short, find themselves gazing on fellow citizens who are reluctant to accept the diagnosis being applied to them. They seem happy, they feel they are free, and they have no desire to give up the creature comforts and the new opportunities in life that have recently opened to them. They are not critical of concentrations of power in large organizations, and they are not repelled by the artifacts of mass culture. There seems, in short, to be consensus and consent to the operations of modern capitalism. And if there are occasional misgivings on the part of the public about such problems as crime, delinquency, dishonesty, and amorality, there is at the same time a refusal to see those malfunctionings as the consequence of capitalist life and values.

At this time democratic socialism stands as an ethic without a significant constituency. The Labour Party in Great Britain polls impressive votes, but its supporters are content to have it be a party of welfare not unlike the Democratic Party in the United States. If its leadership speaks less of nationalization of industry, as a means of rendering powerless institutions dedicated to the pursuit of private profit, this stance is based on the knowledge that that electorate is simply unconcerned with economic power or even political principles. Those who adhere to the socialist persuasion and who embrace the socialist vision are not those at the bottom of the economic ladder but rather a small and selective segment of the upper middle class. Democratic socialism is a subtle and sophisticated outlook, as the essays on the pages that follow testify, and it takes some intellectual commitment to accept its ethical and empirical premises. There has to be not simply the conviction that it is possible to order a society in a just and rational manner but also the understanding that democratic processes are compatible with a wide degree of public ownership.

Given that those with a meaningful and more than transitory attachment to socialism are few in number, how will a socialist society be achieved? The answer lies not in conspiracy or *coup d'état* but in waiting patiently until such time as a substantial number of citizens are ready for recruitment into the socialist movement. This will not depend on political education but is rather a function of economic conditions. Socialist ranks are augmented at such time as capitalism swings into a serious, if not devastating, downturn that proves incapable of remedy through the techniques of modern government and the tools of fiscal planning. If millions who have been steadily employed find themselves without jobs, there can develop a loss of faith in the system of private enterprise that may produce a wide receptivity for socialist programs. But those who turn in this direction, it must be reiterated, are not led there by a conversion to socialist ideals as much as they are by the pressure of economic insecurity. Thus it may not be possible to renew the socialist mandate at such time as prosperity is again achieved by socialist means. If this is so, then the historic contribution of socialism will ultimately lie in its continuing critique of capitalism rather than in its ability to establish an enduring social order in its own right.

ANDREW HACKER

Ithaca, New York
January 1966

CONTENTS

ACKNOWLEDGEMENTS

We wish to thank the *New Statesman* for kind permission to reprint Richard Crossman's essay 'The Lessons of 1945' which was first published in the *New Statesman*, April 19th, 1963. André Gorz's essay 'Work and Consumption' is drawn from his *Strategie Ouvrière et Neo-Capitalisme*, by permission of Editions du Seuil. Richard Titmuss's essay 'Goals of Today's Welfare State' is based on a lecture delivered to the Hebrew University of Jerusalem. Raymond Williams's essay 'Towards a Socialist Society' derives in part from the last chapter of *The Long Revolution*, and we wish to thank the publishers of this book, Chatto and Windus, for kind permission to reprint the excerpts in question.

CONTRIBUTORS

PERRY ANDERSON is Editor of the *New Left Review*, and author of *Portugal et La Fin de l'Ultra-Colonialisme*.

THOMAS BALOGH is a Fellow of Balliol College, Oxford, and author of *Unequal Partners*. He is at present economic adviser to the Prime Minister.

ROBIN BLACKBURN formerly worked in the Economist Intelligence Unit. He is a member of the editorial committee of the *New Left Review*.

KEN COATES is Chairman of the Nottingham Labour Party and one of the editors of the *International Socialist Journal*.

RICHARD CROSSMAN, M.P. is Minister of Land and Housing. He is author of *Plato Today*.

ANDRÉ GORZ is on the editorial committee of *Les Temps Modernes*. He is author of *Strategie Ouvrière et Neo-Capitalisme*.

TOM NAIRN was formerly Fellow in Philosophy at the University of Birmingham. He is a member of the editorial committee of the *New Left Review*.

RICHARD TITMUSS is Professor of Social Administration at the London School of Economics, and author of *Income Distribution and Social Change*.

JOHN WESTERGAARD is Lecturer in Sociology at the London School of Economics.

RAYMOND WILLIAMS is Lecturer in English Literature at the University of Cambridge, and author of *Culture and Society* and *The Long Revolution*.

INTRODUCTION

This volume of essays tries to explore some of the fundamental problems facing British socialism today. The authors, who are responsible only for their own contributions, represent a variety of standpoints and idioms. No attempt has been made to give their essays an artificial unity. The structure of the book, however, offers certain common themes.

The first part of the book examines the nature of the crisis in British society today, and the character of the neo-capitalism which bids to succeed it. Studies of the situation and history of the Labour Party logically follow this analysis. The second part of the book is concerned with a strategy for socialism. Successive essays suggest the concrete aims which the socialist movement should set itself in the years ahead – aims based on a coherent analysis of British capitalism and a critique of it as a human society. We have deliberately departed from tradition by including in this section a major contribution from a continental socialist; we have done so because we are convinced that one of the pre-conditions of creative socialist thought in the present decade is a real internationalism.

Two basic ideas run through all the contributions to this volume. The first is that the advent of political democracy in Britain has not created a true equality of power in British society – and that any serious socialist strategy must start from a recognition of this root fact. This is the theme of 'hegemony' – of the enduring political supremacy of one class, under conditions of universal suffrage. The second common idea in these essays is that socialism in rich societies of the West must move beyond the traditional preoccupations of the labour movement, towards a political programme which conceives men in their entirety, and tries to liberate them in their whole social life. This is the theme of a 'socialism of abundance'. It is explored in different ways in all the concluding essays in the book.

This book is intended to open discussion, not to close it. We hope that it will contribute to a debate which socialists everywhere are initiating today.

NEW LEFT REVIEW

7 Carlisle St., London w.1

PART ONE

ORIGINS OF THE PRESENT CRISIS

Perry Anderson

British society is in the throes of a profound, pervasive but cryptic crisis, undramatic in appearance, but ubiquitous in its reverberations. So much everyone agrees. But what kind of crisis is it? What kind of outcomes to it are likely? Anyone who looks for an answer to these questions in the flood of recent books on the 'condition of England' is likely to be disappointed. By and large, these offer not an analysis of the crisis, but simply an account of its symptoms.

These works – by Shonfield, Hartley, Sampson, Shanks, MacRae[1] – are ephemeral in the most literal sense: they have no historical dimension. Shonfield, whose book is the earliest and best of the genre, devotes five pages out of three hundred to an explanation of the secular decline of the British economy he discusses in the rest of his book; and he is unique in offering any structural explanation at all.

If one turns to socialist critics of the right or the left, the same central blankness is striking. Crosland's *Conservative Enemy* is in many ways an eloquent and intelligent work; it is certainly far more serious than the vulgar run of books whose theme – the 'stagnation' of Britain – is the same. Yet Crosland, too, attacks 'conservatism' in every reach and level of British society without providing a single line of explanation of the malady he denounces. No socialist writer stands in greater contrast to Crosland than Raymond Williams, whose *Culture and Society* and *The Long Revolution* undoubtedly represent the major contribution to socialist thought in England since the war. Apparently, *Culture and Society* is a historical work; in

[1] *British Economic Policy since the War; A State of England; Anatomy of Britain; The Stagnant Society; Sunshades in October.* See also the *Encounter* symposium, *Suicide of a Nation?*

reality, for all its merits, it is so in a strictly limited sense. It is, in fact, a purely immanent ideological critique, consciously abstracted from the effective movement of history. The title of *The Long Revolution* promises a directly historical perspective, but, despite crucial insights, the achievement of the book is theoretical rather than historical. The concluding discussion of 'Britain in the Sixties' starts *ex nihilo*, after the philosophical and cultural analysis which precedes it. The unity of the book deliberately lies elsewhere. Yet it is surely significant that neither the 'technical' (Crosland, Shonfield) nor the 'ethical' (Williams) criticisms of British society today are founded historically.

Does the available corpus of history and sociology make this unnecessary? Nothing could be farther from the truth. We must be unique among advanced industrial nations in having *not one single structural* study of our society today; but this stupefying absence follows logically from the complete lack of any serious global history of British society in the twentieth century. The limits of our sociology reflect the nervelessness of our historiography. Marxist historians, whose mature works are only now beginning to emerge and consolidate each other, have so far nearly all confined themselves to the heroic periods of English history, the seventeenth and early nineteenth centuries: most of the eighteenth and all of the twentieth remain unexplored. Thus no attempt has ever been made at even the outline of a 'totalizing' history of modern British society. Yet until our view of Britain today is grounded in some vision of its full, effective past, however misconceived and transient this may initially be, we will continue to lack the basis for any understanding of the dialectical movements of our society, and hence – necessarily – of the contradictory possibilities within it which alone can yield a strategy for socialism. The present conjuncture, which offers such opportunities to the Labour Party, was neither created nor foreseen by it. If the Left is to take advantage of the present situation, the first prerequisite is a serious attempt to analyse its real nature. To do this involves a consideration of the distinctive total trajectory of modern British society, since the emergence of capitalism. The remarks which follow will inevitably be extremely simplified and approximate notations, but their essential focus – *the global evolution of the class structure* – must be the anchorage of any socialist theory of contemporary Britain. The present crisis can, in effect, only be understood in terms of the differential formation and development of British capitalist society since the seventeenth century. The crude schema offered below is intended only to start discussion at the point where it should properly begin.[1]

A. *History and Class Structure: Trajectory*

Capitalist hegemony in England has been the most powerful, the most durable and the most continuous anywhere in the world. The reasons for this lie in the *cumulative constellation* of the fundamental moments of modern English history.

1. *England had the first, most mediated, and least pure bourgeois revolution of any major European country.* The Civil War of 1640–49 remains the most obscure and controversial of all the great upheavals which led to the creation of a modern, capitalist Europe. Never was the ultimate effect of revolution more transparent, and its immediate agents more enigmatic. The view that the conflict of the 1640s was a simple struggle between a rising bourgeoisie and a declining aristocracy is clearly untenable. The current alternatives – that the Civil War was the work of a *fronde* of discontented squires or that it was a sudden, transcendant condensation of 'faith and freedom' (puritan and constitutional) in the clear air of Stuart England – are still less convincing; the one is trivial, the other naïve. Who made the Revolution? What kind of a Revolution was it? It can, perhaps, be said that it was a clash between two segments of a land-owning class, neither of which were *direct* crystallizations of opposed economic interests, but rather were *partially* contingent but *predominantly* intelligible lenses into which wider, more radically antagonistic social

[1] To avoid making the text unwieldy, all substantiating references, in the form of footnotes, etc., will be omitted.

forces came into temporary and distorted focus. Furthermore, the ideological terms in which the struggle was conducted were largely religious, and hence still more dissociated from economic aspirations than political idioms normally are. Thus, although its outcome was a typically bourgeois rationalization of state and economy, and its major direct beneficiary was a true bourgeoisie, it was a 'bourgeois revolution' only by proxy. The main protagonists on both sides were a rural, not an urban class. The conflict between them revolved round the economic, political, and religious role of the monarchy. It is clear that the inefficient, would-be feudal Stuart monarchy was threatening by its economic exactions to cripple the expansion of the rationalized agrarian and commercial capitalism which had been maturing in England for a century before 1640. It is probable, but not proved that a majority of those landowners who were dynamic and investment-oriented sided with Parliament, and that a majority of routine and rentier landlords sided with the King; it is, however, certain that the most economically progressive regions of England were Parliamentarian, and the most backward Royalist. At the same time, the nature of the allies flanking each side magnified and clarified the logic of the division between them. Taking extremes – on the one side, the archaic clan society of northern Scotland, on the other mercantile capital, particularly in the City of London; this last formed a crucial component in the bloc which finally won the Civil War, providing the indispensable financial reserves for the victory. The Revolution, once under way, followed a classic course of radicalization. When military victory was won, the artisans and yeomen recruited to the New Model Army increasingly intervened to inflect the Army to the left, thus effectively severing it from the Parliamentary Right; but when their pressure began to threaten the franchise privileges of the landowning class itself, the landed officer élite crushed them. The military apparatus was thereafter alone in a void. The Revolution had overshot the political intentions of its agrarian initiators (execution of the King, etc.), but had been halted immediately it threatened their economic interests. It was in this ambiguous vacuum that mercantile capital, the only truly bourgeois kernel of the revolution, inherited the fruits of victory. The economic policy of the Commonwealth did more for its interests than for that of any other group. This anomalous outcome was the culminating product of the complexly refracted and mediated character of the Revolution. Because it was primarily fought *within* and not *between* classes, while it could and did destroy the numerous institutional and juridical obstacles of feudalism to economic development, it could not alter the basic property statute in England. (There was not even a serious attempt at 'political' confiscation of Royalist estates.) But it could do so – decisively – abroad. The immense, rationalizing 'charge' of the Revolution was detonated overseas. The decisive economic legacy of the Commonwealth was imperialism (Navigation Acts, Dutch and Spanish Wars, seizure of Jamaica, etc.). Mercantile capital was its beneficiary. When political anarchy threatened after Cromwell's death, it was the City that triggered the Restoration – and a general settlement that confirmed it in its enhanced position.

The six decades from 1640 through 1688 to the end of the century saw the stabilization and progressive consolidation of the gains of the Revolution: essentially, the development of a dynamic capitalist agriculture and the rise of a mercantile imperialism, in a period of great economic boom.

Thus the three crucial idiosyncrasies of the English Revolution, which have determined the whole of our subsequent history, can be summed up as follows. First, the Revolution shattered the juridical and constitutional obstacles to rationalized capitalist development in town and country: monopolies, arbitrary taxation, wardships, purveyance, restraints on enclosure, etc. The immediate effect of this was a dramatic quickening of the whole economy, from 1650 onwards. In this sense, it was a supremely successful *capitalist* revolution. At the same time, however, it left almost the entire social structure intact.

Second, it achieved this by profoundly transforming the *roles* but not the *personnel* of the ruling class. No social group was evicted or displaced by the Revolution;[1] rather one section of a class fought another and by its victory converted the whole class to a new type of production. For the next hundred years the British aristocracy proceeded to perfect the ruthless and richly rewarding triad system of capitalist landlord, tenant farmer and landless agricultural labourer, which destroyed the English peasantry and made Britain the most agriculturally efficient country in the world. But no career open to talents, no enlarged franchise, no weakening of the principles of heredity and hierarchy, followed this. Landed aristocrats, large and small, continued to rule England.[2]

At the same time, mercantile capital expanded on a new, imperial basis. It had not been the main military or political force in the Revolution; it was its main economic inheritor. But it was never subsequently able to constitute itself as an internally compact and autarchic political force. Despite their rapidly increasing wealth, bankers and merchants remained a subaltern group within the ruling system, an 'interest' and not a class. There was a constant haemorrhage of its profit and pioneers towards the countryside, as successful merchants abandoned their background, investing in estates and becoming members of the landed class. Conversely, landowners had from the outset of the Revolution (and earlier) participated in colonial and trading ventures (Pym, Hampden). There was thus a *permanent partial interpenetration* of the 'moneyed' and 'landed' interests, which simultaneously maintained the political and social subordination of merchant capital, and gave the City the aristocratic coloration it has retained to this day.

Finally, the ideological legacy of the Revolution was almost nil. Its most militant creed, radical Puritanism, was the great loser from the Restoration Settlement. Henceforth it went into a profound spiritual recession, losing its fiery intramundane

[1] A section of the smaller Royalist landowners, who did not regain their estates after the Restoration, forms the only exception.

[2] Throughout this essay, the term 'aristocracy' is used to designate, not the nobility, but the landowning class as a whole. This use blurs the important distinction between the large agrarian magnates and the gentry, but space precludes discussion of this secondary division here.

activism and becoming the repressed private creed of a dis-established minority. The religious beliefs which had seen divine intervention justifying Rebellion when it was successful, saw it also – and irrevocably – condemning it when the Revolution collapsed and the monarchy was restored. Because of its 'primitive', pre-Enlightenment character, the ideology of the Revolution founded no universal tradition in Britain. Never was a major revolutionary ideology neutralized and absorbed so completely. Politically, Puritanism was a useless passion.

The eighteenth century sailed forward into an era of un-paralleled stability. The landed aristocracy had, after a bitter internecine struggle, become its own capitalist class. The mercantile bourgeoisie was contained and decanted into an honourable ancillary status. No ferment of ideas or memories remained. By a classic process of psychological suppression, the Civil War was forgotten and its decorous epilogue, the Glorious Revolution of 1688, became the official, radiant myth of creation in the collective memory of the propertied class.

2. *England experienced the first industrial revolution, in a period of international counter-revolutionary war, producing the earliest proletariat when socialist theory was least formed and available, and an industrial bourgeoisie polarized from the start towards the aristocracy.* The Revolution of 1640 had made possible the transformation of the body of landowners into a basically capitalist class with powerful mercantile auxiliaries. It was precisely this 'mix' which, after a hundred years maturation, set off the industrial revolution: agrarian capitalism provided the economic and human surplus for industrialization, depopulating the countryside to provide investment and labour for the towns. Mercantile imperialism, dominating Asia, Africa and Latin America, provided the markets and raw materials. The cotton industry, based squarely on control of the world market, from India (calico) to West Africa (slaves), to the Caribbean (raw cotton), launched the take-off. The colossal industrial concatenation which followed inevitably produced its own, new bourgeoisie – the manufacturing middle class of Manchester and the North. *Yet the condition of its*

appearance in England was the prior existence of a class which was also capitalist in its mode of exploitation. There was thus from the start no fundamental, antagonistic contradiction between the old aristocracy and the new bourgeoisie. English capitalism embraced and included both. The most important single key to modern English history lies in this fact.

A period of intense political conflict between the nascent industrial bourgeoisie and the agrarian élite was, of course, inevitable once the manufacturers began to aspire towards political representation and power. But this clash itself was profoundly affected, and attenuated, by the context in which it occurred. The French Revolution and Napoleonic expansion froze propertied Europe with terror. For twenty panic-stricken years the new English manufacturing class .allied to the aristocracy; in that time it developed habits and attitudes it has never lost. A whole era of war against the French abroad and repression against the working class at home marked the years of its maturation. Two decades after the fall of Bastille, it celebrated its entry into history by cutting down working-class demonstrators at Peterloo.

When the fear of the early years of the nineteenth century finally receded, the industrial bourgeoisie at last began to mass its strength to secure incorporation into the political system. It was almost overtaken by a radicalized working class which had developed in isolation from it during the pitiless years of reaction. But with considerable belated skill, it forced an extension of the franchise which nakedly demarcated the new ruling bloc, including itself and excluding the proletariat. By the same stroke, the Reform Bill of 1832 secured precisely that change which the merchants and bankers of the seventeenth and eighteenth centuries had never managed – or needed – to effect. The traditional mercantile bourgeoisie had never achieved direct political representation in Parliament; because of its peculiar situation and composition it had always been content to delegate its 'interest' to a section of the (Whig) aristocracy. It now entered Parliament for the first time, behind its industrial successor, in the breach the latter had made.

The next – and last – victory of the new middle class was the

Repeal of the Corn Laws in 1846. Convinced that cereal protection favoured landowners at its expense by contracting both
internal and external markets for manufacturers, the industrial
bourgeoisie mounted a second triumphant campaign for its
abolition. This sectional conflict was the last moment at which
the industrial middle class played an independent role in
British history. It was its – brief and inglorious – high-water
mark. The aftermath was illuminating. Fired by the success
of the Anti-Corn Law League, its greatest spokesman, Cobden,
launched a campaign against 'the eleventh commandment',
primogeniture, the basic device securing aristocratic control of
the land. The call for 'free trade not only in corn but in land'
aimed directly at the root power position of the aristocracy.
The bourgeosie refused to follow it. Its courage had gone.
Henceforth it was bent exclusively on integrating itself into the
aristocracy, not collectively as a class, but by individual vertical
ascent.

Even after 1832, it was noticeable that the new middle-class
used its vote to elect members of Parliament not from among
its own ranks, but from those of the aristocracy, thus reproduc-
ing the exact relationship between its predecessor and the
landed élite even *after* it had won the power to do otherwise: as
late as 1865, over 50 per cent of the House of Commons
formed a single, intricately extended kinship group. Thus for
a period one can speak of a delegation of power by one distinct
social class to another. But this phase was relatively short. It
was followed by a *deliberate, systematized symbiosis of the two
classes*. This unique fusion was effected, above all, by creating
common educational institution, the new public schools, which
were designed to socialize the sons of the – new or old – rich in
a distinctive, uniform pattern, which henceforth became the
fetichized criterion of the 'gentleman'. The reforms of the universities, and more particularly, of the Civil Service (1854),
instituting a rationalized but rigidly hierarchic recruitment
based on prior induction into the public schools, complemented
this central mechanism of assimilation. Meanwhile, as industrial accumulation proceeded and the relative weight of the
agrarian sector declined, an increasing horizontal imbrication

of landed, commercial and industrial capital took place. Agrarian magnates opened up mines and invested in railways, manufacturing tycoons purchased estates and formed special relationships with merchant bankers. The end result of these convergent mutations was the eventual creation of a *single hegemonic class, distinguished by a perpetually recreated virtual homogeneity and actual – determinate – porousness*.[1] The second generation of any parvenu bourgeois family could henceforward automatically enter the 'upper class' via the regulating institutions of assimilation. Thus it was that by a unique paradox, in the supremely capitalist society of Victorian England, the aristocracy became – and remained – the vanguard of the bourgeoisie.

For the first five decades of the century – the heroic age of the English proletariat – the working class evolved in a diametrically opposite direction to that of the middle class. Counter-revolutionary war abroad was accompanied by social siege at home (more troops mobilized to suppress the Luddites than to fight the concurrent Peninsular War, etc.). Repression circumscribed the working class and cut it off from the rest of society. Plunged in its own racked and famished world, it fought bitterly for an alternative human order for itself. It was the first proletariat ever to suffer industrialization: it had to invent everything – tactics, strategy, ideas, values, organization

---

[1] i.e. exactly what Sartre calls a 'detotalized totality'. The dominant bloc in England can be envisaged as a narrow, highly-structured hegemonic class, with, beneath it, a large, diffuse, polymorphous reservoir – the entrepreneurial, professional and salaried 'middle classes'. The rigorous structure of the one radically destructures the other, as access is always open to the select few from the 'middle' to the 'upper' class: thus the middle classes in England have never produced institutions and culture of anything like a comparable distinctiveness and density to those of the 'upper' or for that matter, working class. The device of the two-party system has, of course, also powerfully acted to inhibit the emergence of a clear, corporate identity in the middle class, by denying it expression at the political level. It is striking that England has never known an independent political movement of the petty-bourgeoisie of any serious dimensions, in contrast to all other major West European countries. The special nature of the dominant bloc in England has undoubtedly contributed to preventing this.

– from the start. It achieved no victories, but its defeats were astonishing. In 1819 it organized the first national political campaign of the post-war period, so scaring both the bourgeoisie and aristocracy that it provoked a massacre and exceptional legislation. In 1831–2 it formed the great heaving swell of the Reform Movement, constantly threatening to capsize the bourgeois groupings adroitly navigating on its surface. From 1829–34 it produced in Owenism the first, mass socialist movement of the century. When this was crushed by 1836, it rose again in an independent working-class movement for Reform: Chartism, its final, supreme effort, lasted for a decade. Wrecked by its pitifully weak leadership and strategy, in the end it collapsed without a fight. With it disappeared for thirty years the *élan* and combativity of the class. A profound caesura in English working-class history supervened.

The tragedy of the first proletariat was not, as has so often been said, that it was immature; it was rather that it was in a crucial sense *premature*. Its maximum ardour and insurgency coincided with the minimum availability of socialism as a structured ideology. Consequently it paid the price of the forerunner. For simple technical–educational reasons, the development of socialist thought in the nineteenth century had to be overwhelmingly the work of non-working-class intellectuals. (The utopian socialism of Owen was, of course, just this.) Thus, everywhere, it came to the proletariat from outside. But it took fifty years of the experience of industrialization over a whole continent for it properly to form, and the timing of its impact has been crucial. It is no accident that the youngest proletariats, of Italy and Japan, have been the most thoroughly won to Marxism; or that the oldest, those of England and Belgium, have rather similar political parties and consciousness. In England, in contrast to countries that industrialized afterwards, Marxism came too late: the *Communist Manifesto* was written just two months before the collapse of Chartism.

3. *By the end of the nineteenth century, Britain had seized the largest empire in history, an empire qualitatively distinct in its immensity from all its rivals, which saturated and 'set' British*

society in a matrix it has retained to this day. Late nineteenth-century imperialism was the intoxicated climax of three centuries of plunder and annexation. It was the most self-conscious and belligerent phase of British imperialism; but it was not the most profoundly formative for British society. The mercantile imperialism of the seventeenth and eighteenth centuries, which provided the pre-conditions for the economic take-off of the early nineteenth century, and the diplomatic-industrial imperialism of the mid-nineteenth century, whose enforcement of international Free Trade had created British world economic supremacy, were both more decisive. The lasting contours of British society were already visible before the rise of the military-industrial imperialism of the 1880s.[1] Yet it was this apparent apotheosis of British capitalism which gave its characteristic *style* to a whole society, consecrating and fossilizing to this day its interior space, its ideological horizons, its diffused and intimate sensibility. It is, above all, from this period that the suffocating 'traditionalism' of English life dates.

The multiform impact of militant imperialism on the economy and society of Britain can only be suggested here. It is clear that the existence, maintenance and constant celebration of the Empire affected all classes and institutions in Britain; it could not have done otherwise. Equally obviously, its effects varied enormously in kind from group to group. The main single effect of the new imperialism in the period from 1880–1914 was probably its definitive consolidation of the praeternaturally hierarchical character of the total social order and in particular of its typical *model of leadership*. It has been argued that the imperialist expansion of this epoch (scramble for Africa, partition of China, etc.) was an 'atavistic' phenomenon, the product of 'pre-capitalist', aristocratic, agrarian and military residues in the industrialized states of

[1] By 'diplomatic-industrial imperialism' is meant the economic subjugation of other nations, usually secured by the threat of force, rather than by outright annexation. 'Military-industrial imperialism' proceeded by straight conquest; it was a product of the fear of rival European imperialisms, in particularly of Germany, whose shadow haunted the extreme patriots of the period. It thus marks the moment at which British world supremacy was no longer unquestioned.

Europe. This view is manifestly inadequate; imperialism was, of course, the inevitable climax of pre-Keynesian capitalism, the product of a massive investment surplus and a limited internal market. But Schumpeter's imaginary cause was a true effect. The reflux of imperialism at home not merely preserved but reinforced and sanctified the already pronounced personality type of the governing class: aristocratic, amateur, and 'normatively' agrarian. Originally this metaphysic was naturally secreted by an agrarian aristocratic class. But by the second half of the nineteenth century the English aristocracy was rapidly becoming as factually 'bourgeois', as the English bourgeoisie was becoming 'aristocratic'. Moreover, with the agrarian depression of 1870s, the traditional economic base of the landowning class collapsed. Thus, just at the moment when the 'atavistic' values of the landed aristocracy appeared mortally threatened, imperialism rescued and reinforced them. In doing so, it bequeathed to twentieth-century England the governing class which has at length found its final, surreal embodiment in the fourteenth Earl of Home.[1]

The major impact of imperialism was almost certainly on the character and ethos of the ruling bloc. But its feed-back was not limited to this. A general internalization of the prestations and motifs of Empire undoubtedly occurred. Its most prominent manifestation was, of course, the new supercharged religion of monarchy which marked the late Victorian era – inaugurated, inevitably, by the creation for the Queen of the title of Empress of India. The Durbar, and its domestic derivative the Jubilee, became the symbol of a whole society present to itself, celebrating its own plenitude. The 'manifest' function of the monarchy was (by assertion) to unify to the nation; its 'latent' function was (by example) to stratify it. The two were equally important. Probably at no period in peace-time history was English society so suffused with chauvinism and so glutted with rank.

These implicit normative patterns were probably the lasting imprint of imperialism on English life. Its explicit ideological expressions, although extremely virulent at the time, were

[1] For a further discussion of this point, see below.

ultimately more transient. Their omnipresence in this period
merely serve to suggest how deeply acclimatized English culture became to the ambience of empire. All political groups
– Conservatives, Liberals and Fabians – were militantly imperialist in aims; each differed only in its programme of implementation. The nascent socialist movement shared in the
general jingoism. Webb, Hyndman, and Blatchford – Fabian,
'Marxist' and I.L.P.-supporter – respectively the most influential, the most 'advanced' and the most popular spokesmen
of the Left, were all in their different ways vocal imperialists.
This did not necessarily mean that the working class became in
any direct sense committed to imperialism. To start with it is
very doubtful whether the working class of this period benefited materially from colonial exploitation, although it did indirectly, of course, from the difference in productivity between
the British economy and its overseas possessions. Politically,
colonial emigration, which drained off many of the most
vigorous and independent members of the working class and
forestalled an explosive population pressure, was probably
throughout the nineteenth century a more important safety-
valve for English capitalism than its colonial super-profits.
However, the primary impact of imperialism on the working
class – as throughout English society – was at the level of
consciousness. The British working class was not in any profound sense mobilized *for* imperialism; to this extent, the
options of many of its leaders were ineffective and insignificant. But it was, undeniably, deflected *from* undistracted confrontation with the class exploiting it. This was the real –
negative – achievement of social-imperialism. It created a
powerful 'national' framework for social contradictions which
at normal periods insensibly mitigated them and at moments
of crisis transcended them altogether. The enthusiastic participation of most of the Left in the holocaust of the First World
War was only the most spectacular product of decades of
national-imperial mystification.

However, for the working class too, the zenith of imperialism
saw in essence only a consolidation of morphological changes
which had occurred long before it.

The shattering fiasco of Chartism finally broke the morale of the early proletariat; a period of intense shock and retreat followed. For thirty years the English working-class movement went through a kind of prolonged catatonic withdrawal. The most insurgent working class in Europe became the most numbed and docile. Ambitious attempts to create single national unions, audacious schemes for an autarchic co-operative economy, mass campaigns for universal suffrage – gave way to cautious, *bien-pensant* insurance clubs and wavering support for the Liberal Party. The formal goal of Chartism, votes for the working man, was partially granted by a Conservative Government in 1867. But far from being an autonomous victory of the working class, this tactical manœuvre of Disraeli's in a sense only revealed its absorption and defeat. The vote was granted to the working class precisely because there was no longer any danger that it would use it as some of the Chartists had threatened to – for the transformation of the entire social system. The Conservative Government's attention was almost purely devoted to outflanking the Liberal opposition; it cared so little about the substance of its bill that it let it be amended indefinitely by a handful of radicals in Parliament.

No significant change followed the 1867 Reform Bill. The working class continued for well over another decade to play an innocuous and subordinate role in the British political system. Artisans and home-industry workers increasingly gave way to a factory proletariat. The rapidly increasing surplus of the economy, after the first period of capital accumulation, allowed substantial increases in wage-levels to be granted by employers; this provided the economic basis of the reformism of the period. It was not until the 1880s that the working class really began to recover from the traumatic defeat of the 1840s. By then the world had moved on. In consciousness and combativity, the English working class had been overtaken by almost all its continental opposites. Marxism had missed it. Mature socialist theory was developed in precisely the years of the British proletariat's amnesia and withdrawal. In France, in Germany, in Italy, Marxism took root in the working class. In

England, everything was against it: the wounds of the past, the diffidence of the present, the national culture of past and present. In 1869 the German Social-Democratic Party was founded; in 1876 the Parti Ouvrier in France; in 1884 the Socialist Party in Italy; in 1889 the Social-Democratic Party in Sweden. In England, the first socialist *sect*, the Social Democratic Federation, was only formed in 1884 – and the first working-class *party*, the Labour Representation Committee, only in 1900; over twenty years later than in France or Germany. The S.D.F. did not succeed in making a major lasting ideological impact on the labour movement. The Labour Party, itself created primarily as a defensive measure to reverse the effects of the Taff Vale decision, included no major Marxist component from its early years onwards. The remarkable lateness of its formation was a striking index of the degree of subordination of the working-class movement within British capitalist society. It was, then, in this sense that the crescendo of imperialism which coincided with the rise of the modern labour movement only confirmed changes which had preceded it.

4. *Alone of major European nations, England emerged undefeated and unoccupied from Two World Wars, its social structure uniquely untouched by external shocks or discontinuities.* The victories of 1918 and 1945 were the last of the special graces granted by history to English bourgeois society. War and invasion have been perhaps the greatest single catalysts of change in modern Europe – even the only armed revolution modern England has ever known was precipitated by the Scottish invasion of 1640. Collapse on the Eastern Front in 1917 set in motion the Russian Revolution; defeat and invasion in 1918 produced the Spartakist rising in Germany, the Bavarian Communist Government, and Social-Democratic dominance in the Weimar Republic; the occupation of France in 1940 and the military campaigns in Italy from 1943–5 produced politicized resistance movements (of a mass character in Italy) with pronounced socialist-communist majorities. In each case the advance of the Left was checked or

reversed – by Fascism after 1930, and by Anti-Communism after 1947. But at some point the whole social order had been radically fissured and challenged, and the restabilization which followed, brought about by the world cataclysms of the Depression and the Cold War rather than by internal changes, was qualitatively different from the *status quo ante*.

No comparable crisis of disruption or transformation disturbed the placid waters of British social history. Even won, however, the two World Wars were the only serious forcing-periods of social change in English history in the twentieth century. The outbreak of the 1914–18 war providentially aborted a potentially explosive situation in Britain, when the propertied class was deeply split (on an imperial issue, Ireland) and working-class militancy threatened to escape the control of a faltering and reactionary trade union leadership (syndicalism). The long-term effect of the war, however, was to increase the weight and strength of working-class organizations. Between 1914 and 1919 T.U.C. membership doubled and the Labour vote quintupled. The Labour Party, previously a small pressure group on the flank of the Liberal Party, emerged after the war as the main opposition party and five years later as a (minority) government. Simultaneously, the classical political formations of amalgamated ruling bloc underwent a permanent mutation. The vortex of the war smashed the flimsy barriers between Conservative and Liberal Parties, temporarily producing a fluctuating disorder, out of which eventually emerged the unified political organization of the Right – the Conservative Party. The survival of the Conservative rather than the Liberal Party was conditioned both by factional divisions within the Liberal Party and by the obvious desuetude of Free Trade doctrines in the Depression years. But in a more important sense, it revealed the continuing ascendancy of the aristocratic segment within the dominant social bloc. It was in the logic of the previous fifty years. Neither party had ever been a simple crystallization of distinct strata within this bloc—precisely because its nature precluded sharply differentiated levels or layers within it. But the Liberal Party had always tended towards a greater proportionate

bourgeois, and the Conservative Party a greater proportionate aristocratic, admixture. The ideologies of the two
parties, had usually, although not always, over-expressed this
difference. The eclipse of the one and the triumph of the other
signified the final 'feudalization' of the ideology and internal
protocol of the dominant bloc.[1] The Liberal Party, despite
the initial advantage of a greater proximity to the centre of
gravity of future parliamentary politics, lost because its identity
was finally so much weaker. Necessarily so: when real danger
threatened and a single party of the Right became imperative,
proto-reformist velleities were no match for centuries of
aureoled tradition.

By the twenties, the parliamentary system had for the first
time in its long and *trompe l'oeil* history become the arena of
a genuine class confrontation. Under post-war conditions the
Labour Party swiftly rose in strength and attractive power.
Its seats in the House of Commons increased from 60 in 1919
to 191 in 1924, when it formed its short-lived first minority
government, and then – after losses in the election of that
year – to 287 in 1929, when it formed its second government,
also in a minority but this time as the strongest party. Within
two years this Labour Government collapsed – more completely and ignominiously than any other Social-Democratic
government has ever done. Vast Conservative majorities
dominated the whole of the next decade. The first cycle of the
Labour Party's history was brought to an end by the outbreak
of the Second World War.

The 1939–45 War opened the second cycle, which reproduced with remarkable similarity the timing and movement of
the first. Again the tremendous pressures of the war effected a
sudden, qualitative leap forward in British history. For the
first and only time in this century, an appreciable redistribution of income took place, secondary education was generalized,
and the foundations of the Welfare State were laid. The 1945
election confirmed these changes, when the Labour won a large
absolute majority. This time, both its electoral strength and its
legislative achievements (creation of the National Health Ser-

[1] 'Feudal' only metaphorically, of course.

vice, socialization of fuel and transport, etc.) were much greater than those of its ephemeral governments after the First World War. Its development was thus more accurately spiral, rather than truly cyclical. But at a higher level, almost exactly the same sequence was repeated. The period of upsurge was brief and rapidly dissipated. The Labour Government fell in 1951, on the twentieth anniversary of the disaster of 1931, in analogous circumstances of economic crisis, political division and ideological demoralization. The result was, once again, an uninterrupted decade of Conservative rule. In fifty years, such was the total change since the advent of political democracy, in a country where the manual working class constitutes an overwhelming sociological majority of the population.

The distinctive facets of English class structure, as it has evolved over three centuries, can thus be summed up as follows. After a bitter, cathartic revolution, which transformed the structure but not the superstructures of English society, a landed aristocracy, underpinned by a powerful mercantile affinal group, became the first dominant capitalist class in Britain. This dynamic agrarian capitalism expelled the English peasantry from history. Its success was economically the 'floor' and sociologically the 'ceiling' of the rise of the industrial bourgeoisie. Undisturbed by a feudal state, terrified of the French Revolution and its own proletariat, mesmerized by the prestige and authority of the landed class, the bourgeoisie won two modest victories, lost its nerve and ended by losing its identity. The late Victorian era and the high noon of imperialism welded aristocracy and bourgeoisie together in a single social bloc. The working class fought passionately and unaided against the advent of industrial capitalism; its extreme exhaustion after successive defeats was the measure of its efforts. Henceforward it evolved, separate but subordinate, within the apparently unshakeable structure of British capitalism, unable, despite its great numerical superiority, to transform the fundamental nature of British society.

B. *History and Class Consciousness: Hegemony*

I

The preceding schema is a crude and preliminary attempt to pose some of the developmental problems of British capitalism. It remains to complete its arguments with some consideration of the structural order produced by this distinctive history. Again, the subject is of such magnitude and complexity that only the most general suggestions can be made here. But even extremely partial and inexact definitions are perhaps better than none, since they invite correction and discussion.

The power structure of English society today can be most accurately described as an immensely elastic and all-embracing hegemonic order. Hegemony was defined by Gramsci as the dominance of one social bloc over another, not simply by means of force or wealth, but by a social authority whose ultimate sanction and expression is a profound cultural supremacy. This imperative order not merely sets external limits to the actions and aims of the subordinated bloc, it structures its intimate vision of itself and the world, imposing contingent historical facts as the necessary co-ordinates of social life itself. The hegemonic class is the primary determinant of consciousness, character and customs throughout the society. This tranquil and unchallenged sovereignty is a relatively rare historical phenomenon. In England, however, the unparalleled temporal continuity of the dominant class has produced a striking example of it. The peculiar morphology of this class has resulted in apparently bizarre and absurd, but in reality effective and explicable, forms of hegemony:

1. *Social Relations.* British society is notoriously characterized by a seemingly 'feudal' hierarchy of orders and ranks, distinguished by a multiplicity of trivial but ceremonial insignia – accent, vocabulary, diet, dress, recreation, etc. This hierarchy corresponds neither to the primary reality of a society divided into economically-based classes, nor even to the secondary reality of limited individual mobility within this system. It is, however, the projective image of society naturally

held and propagated by a landowning class. The pattern of
social relations in the countryside at the height of this class's
economic power, compounded of rank, deference and tradition,
became the fundamental model of social relations in English
society as a whole – even after industrialization – because of
the continued political leadership of this class. After the industrial revolution, the mythology of rank-order seduced and
so subjugated the nascent bourgeoisie, producing the famous
social-climbing of the middle class, its craving for titles, etc.
It also acted as a powerful mystification of real social relations
for the working class as well. For although the working class
itself continued instinctively to use a bipolar language ('us' and
'them') to describe its situation, leaders of the working-class
movement, who existed in an overlapping zone in constant
contact with representatives and institutions of the dominant
bloc, tended to absorb false, 'feudal' consciousness. Hence the
protests in *The Future Labour Offers You, etc.*, against 'outdated social distinctions', 'snobbery' as a major social evil. In
this way, that divorce between relations of production and
social consciousness which is everywhere essential to a capitalist
society, percolates into the declared opponents of the system.
In general, the hierarchical, pseudo-feudal coloration of
English society, expression and instrument of the hegemony of
an (ancestrally agrarian) aristocracy, operates as perhaps the
most successful of all camouflages of class structure: by *simultaneously intensifying and displacing* class-consciousness, it
tends to render it politically inoperative and socially self-
perpetuating.

2. *Ideology*. The hegemony of the dominant bloc in England
is not articulated in any systematic major ideology, but is rather
diffused in a miasma of commonplace prejudices and taboos.
The two great chemical elements of this blanketing English
fog are 'traditionalism' and 'empiricism': in it, visibility – of
any social or historical reality – is always zero. Traditionalism
– veneration for the monarchy, the Church, the Peerage, the
City, etc. – was the natural ideological idiom of the landed
class as soon as its pure monopoly of political power was

challenged. It emerges, in fact, with Burke, just at the moment
of the great bourgeois revolution in France, at the end of the
eighteenth century. Empiricism, on the other hand, faithfully
transcribes the fragmented, incomplete character of the English
bourgeoisie's historical experience. It did not have to overthrow a feudal state in the nineteenth century, and it did not
succeed in becoming sole master of the new industrial society.
Thus it never went through a truly egalitarian phase and so
never struck at the ideological rationale of the aristocracy.
Traditionalism and empiricism henceforward fuse as a single
legitimating system: traditionalism sanctions the present by
deriving it from the past, empiricism shackles the future by
riveting it to the present. A comprehensive, coagulated conservatism is the result, covering the whole of society with a
thick pall of simultaneous philistinism (towards ideas) and
mystagogy (towards institutions), for which England has justly
won an international reputation.

3.   *Leadership*. As already suggested, the major sociological
legacy of imperialism was its definitive consecration of the
style of leadership peculiar to the hegemonic class. The administration of an empire comprising a quarter of the planet
required – notoriously – its own special skills. Imperialism
automaticaly sets a premium on a patrician political style: as
a pure system of alien domination, it always, within the limits
of safety, seeks to *maximize the existential difference* between
the ruling and ruled race, to create a magical and impassable
gulf between two fixed essences. This need everywhere produces a distinctive colonial ceremonial and a colonial vice-
regency. Domestic domination can be realized with a 'popular'
and 'egalitarian' appearance, alien domination never. There
can by definition be no plebeian pro-consuls. In an imperial
system, the iconography of power is necessarily aristocratic: it
is a pure *presence*. The aristocrat is defined not by acts which
denote skills but by gestures which reveal quintessences: a
specific training or aptitude would be a derogation of the impalpable essence of nobility, a finite qualification of the in-
finite. The famous *amateurism* of the English 'upper class' has

its direct source in this ideal. Traditionally contemptuous of exclusive application to 'trade' or 'culture', the businessman or the intellectual, the rulers of England were also – uniquely – neither professional politicians nor bureaucrats nor militarists. They were at different times all of these, and so finally and magnificently none of them.

4. *Rejects.* The industrial bourgeoisie of the nineteenth century did produce one authentic, articulated ideology with universal claims: utilitarianism. This played an extremely important role in the early decades of industrialization, as a militant, single-minded creed of capital accumulation and cultural nihilism. But it never achieved a truly hegemonic status. In part, of course, this was due to the historic inability of the class which was its vector to win political dominance. In part, however, its failure was due to its own intrinsic limitations: its fanatically bleak materialism *ipso facto* precluded it from creating that cultural and value system which is the mark of a hegemonic ideology. It finally became simply a sectional rationale of the workings of the economy. It never penetrated the legitimation of the system as a whole. A slightly later product of the rise of the bourgeoisie was liberalism as such, both a refinement and an enfeeblement of the original virulence of utilitarian doctrine. A more contradictory, limited and occasional phenomenon, it inspired the sporadic enthusiasm for good causes abroad which distinguished the bourgeoisie of the time (Cobden). But, despite the distinction of some of its spokesmen (Mill), it was prevented from becoming a serious claimant for ascendancy by the objective structure of empire and economy, which negated all its avowed norms. Hence its tendency to seek refuge in altruistic international campaigns.

II

Capitalist hegemony bears crucially on the working class in a specific, historically determined way. A combination of structural and conjunctural factors in the nineteenth century produced a proletariat distinguished by *an immovable corporate class-consciousness and almost no hegemonic ideology.* This paradox is the most important single fact about the English working class. If a hegemonic class can be defined as one *which imposes its own ends and its own vision on society as a whole,* a corporate class is conversely one which *pursues its own ends within a social totality whose global determination lies outside it.* A hegemonic class seeks to transform society in its own image, inventing afresh its economic system, its political institutions, its cultural values, its whole 'mode of insertion' into the world. A corporate class seeks to defend and improve its own position within a social order accepted as given. The English working class has since the mid-nineteenth century been essentially characterized by an extreme disjunction between an intense consciousness of separate identity and a permanent failure to set and impose goals for society as whole. In this disjunction lies the secret of the specific nature of the working-class movement in England. *The very intensity of its corporate class-consciousness, realized in and through a distinct, hermetic culture, has blocked the emergence of a universal ideology in the English working class.* It has not been lack of class-consciousness but – in one sense – excess of it which has been the obstacle to the commitment of the working class to socialism. It is this paradox which has been the foundation *both* of the immobile reformism of the Labour Party *and* of the failure to convert it to neo-liberalism, in imitation of the German Social-Democratic Party.

Historically, the reasons for this complex form of consciousness lie at the origins of English capitalism. The structural context has already been indicated: in the social world created by the hegemonic class, *all* classes had to appear and to see themselves as natural 'estates', defined by a fixed station and a fixed way of life – the working class no less than others. At the same time, the primary conjunctural influence was undoubtedly the savage repression and segregation which the working class suffered in its formative years, which drove it in on its own resources, to create its own culture in its own universe. This siege experience fixed an attitude to the outside world which has persisted to this day. However, the early years of the working class were also, of course, the one period in its history when it rose frontally, if confusedly, against capitalist society. In the absence of any structured socialist ideology, the crushing defeats it suffered were almost a pure loss. Armed with a coherent vision of the world, it would probably still have been defeated, but its experience and its aspirations would have entered an enduring tradition and have been saved for the future. The actual result was that the experience of fifty years was not cumulative, and played strikingly little role in the later development of the working class. Conversely, the increasing maturity and availability of socialism as an ideology, from 1850 onwards, was timed just at that moment in English history when the working-class movement was at its lowest and least receptive ebb.

A second conjunctural determinant of the evolution of working-class consciousness was the failure of any significant body of intellectuals to join the proletariat until the very end of the nineteenth century. The reasons for this fatal incomprehension, whose consequences bear heavily on the Labour Party today, lie partly in the peculiar sociological moorings of the English intellectuals of the Victorian period, and partly in the more general history of the time. The aristocracy had never allowed the formation of an independent intellectual enclave within the body politic of landed England. As early as the sixteenth century, it had prevented the emergence of a separate secular intelligentsia as a successor to the separate clerical intelligentsia (recruited from the poorer classes) of the medieval period, by flooding the hitherto predominantly closed educational institutions (Eton, Winchester, Oxford, Cambridge) with its sons. Thereafter it produced its own intellectuals, mainly from the lesser, professional reaches of the class. Thus a peculiarity of English history has been the tradition of a body of intellectuals which was *at once homogeneous and cohesive and yet not a distinct intelligentsia*. The reason for this was that the unity of the group was mediated not through ideas but through kinship. It therefore never became a more or less autonomous group integrated vertically by its relationship with its predecessors to form a continuous, internally unified intellectual

community, as in France; its unity was simply its external insertion into its class.

This is not to say that it showed consistent political conformity. The Victorian intellectuals did, in fact, collectively
produce a remarkably coherent and far-reaching critique of
Victorian capitalism – the tradition, mainly but not exclusively
of Romanticism, which forms the subject of *Culture and
Society*. But this critique, containing insights which closely
parallel some of the philosophical bases of Marxism, was nevertheless for good sociological reasons irremediably divorced from
the realities of economic structure and political conflict. At the
same time, the French Revolution chilled these intellectuals as
much as it did their class. Hence the tradition often foundered
in disastrous confusion and ultimately – in the twentieth century – was to become in political terms predominantly reactionary. Thus the one truly radical critique of capitalism
in the nineteenth century failed to encounter the one force
which could overthrow capitalism. The tradition of Romanticism and its sequels remained politically naïve and became reactionary. The working-class movement, after its repression
and its long retreat, was to fall prey to the progeny of the most
stunted bourgeois ideology of all – utilitarianism.

It is a general historical rule that a rising social class
acquires a significant part of its ideological equipment from
the armoury of the ruling class itself. Thus the universal axioms
of the French revolution were turned by the working class in
France against the bourgeoisie which first proclaimed them;
they founded a revolutionary ideology directed against the
initiators of the revolution. In England, a supine bourgeoisie
produced a subordinate proletariat. It handed on no impulse
of liberation, no revolutionary values, no universal language.
Instead it transmitted the deadly germs of utilitarianism, from
which the Labour Party has so manifestly sickened in the
twentieth century. For the first sizeable group of intellectuals
which finally joined the political struggle on the side of the
working class were the Fabians, in the 1880s.[1] The intellectual

[1] Tragically, Morris's thought was too isolated to become a major
influence on the movement.

lineage of the Webbs and their companions was brutally explicit and avowed: they were the direct successors of Jeremy Bentham and James Mill and the positivist ideologues of the mid-nineteenth century (Herbert Spencer, etc.). No more poisoned legacy could have been left the working-class movement. Complacent confusion of influence with power, bovine admiration for bureaucracy, ill-concealed contempt for equality, bottomless philistinism – all the characteristic narrowness of the Webbs and their associates became imprinted on the dominant ideology of the Labour Party thereafter. Even in its original form as an ideology of the bourgeoisie, the limitations of utilitarianism prevented it from ever becoming a hegemonic force. Shorn of its youth and fire, and diluted with paternalism, it was never, in its Fabian form, a serious challenge to the ideology of the dominant bloc.

Fabianism was not, of course, the only ingredient in the outlook of the Labour Party in its early years, although it was in the end the most politically important. The other component of classic 'Labourism' was, of course, the authentic working-class radicalism which stemmed from the I.L.P. (symbolized initially in Keir Hardie). It was this which gave the Labour Party its unshakeable social character and prevented it from ever becoming a simple party of middle-class reform. At the same time, the strictly ideological expressions of this powerful current never achieved anything like the coherence of Fabianism, remaining a heteroclite mixture of adulterated Marxism, transposed Methodism and inherited liberalism. In the early years of the Party's existence, the last element was of some importance, as it passed on the liberal tradition of internationalism and (partial) anti-imperialism to a section of the Labour leadership (MacDonald's refusal of the First World War, etc.). Its subsequent importance inevitably dwindled.

By and large, then, it can be said that the *one distinctive and coherent ideology which has taken root in the working-class movement in this century has been immediately tributary to the one distinctive, coherent and unsuccessful bourgeois ideology of the last century.* Yet this same movement has never been captured and turned into a purely adaptive political or industrial machine (as in Germany, U.S.A.).

It can be argued that the real historical content of the working-class movement has not in the main been articulated ideologically at all, but institutionally. In a famous passage, Williams has written: 'The culture which it (the working class) has produced, is the collective democratic institution whether in the Trade Unions, the co-operative movement or a political party. . . . When it is considered in context, it can be seen as a very remarkable creative achievement.' This idea represents a maximum statement of one of the two poles of socialist theories of the working class: in it, the constitutive nature of the working class prefigures the society which is its vocation to create. This is what has been called the concept of 'proletarian positivity', in contrast to its opposite: that of the proletariat as the negativity of history, total negation of the existent social order, a subjectivity flung towards absolute suppression of class society and therewith suppression of itself. Clearly, the reality in any historical situation involves a dialectic of both moments: pure positivity, the working class would be immobilized in its own fullness, incapable of launching any project of total social change. Pure negativity, it would be in permanent, suicidal insurrection. In England, there is no doubt which moment has dominated. The whole dense, object-invested universe described by Hoggart in the *Uses of Literacy* testifies to the monumental positivity of the oldest working class in the world.[1] Too much so: the weakness of Williams' argument is that it fails to make a distinction between corporate and hegemonic institutional forms. The very density and specificity of English working-class culture has limited its political range and checked the emergence of a hegemonic

[1] For the debate on negativity and positivity, See G. Lukacs, *Histoire et Conscience de Classe;* J-P Sartre, 'Les Communistes et La Paix' (*Temps Modernes*, nos 81, 84–85, 101); M. Merleau-Ponty, *Les Aventures de la Dialectique;* and L. Magri, *Problemi della teoria marxista del partito revoluzionario* (*Critica Marxista* nos. 5–6). In England, Hoggart's matchless phenomenology has been the major contribution, although not, of course, a theoretical one. Marx's work emphasizes both moments.

socialism in England. Williams's attempt to solve the difficulty by attributing an indefinite extendibility to working-class but not to bourgeois institutions, besides its factual weaknesses, rests on an evacuation of conflict concepts from his whole idiom. The truth seems to be that the nature of working-class culture is as he describes it, but that *the will to universalize it, to make it the general model of society,* which he tacitly assumes to be a concomitant, has only rarely existed.

Thus, at whichever level one chooses to look, the same fundamental paradox reappears. In Britain, the working class has generated over 150 years a massive, adamantine class-consciousness – but it has never developed into a hegemonic political force.[1] The very name of its traditional political party poignantly underlines this truth. Alone of major European working-class parties, it is called neither a Social-Democratic nor a Socialist nor a Communist Party; it is the *Labour* Party – the name designates, not an ideal society, as do all the others, but simply an existent interest.

In conclusion, it may be of use to recall – with maximum brevity – the historical moments at which the nocturnal structure of hegemony has been suddenly and vividly lit up by the lightning of a major political crisis.

1.   1926. The General Strike. This unique confrontation of class forces ended, of course, in disaster. But can the failure of the strike be attributed solely to 'betrayal'? Was a victorious outcome at all conceivable? The general judgement seems to be that it was not, for the simple reason that there never originally existed the political will to carry it through. Cole's description is classic: 'When the moment came, however, it was the workers who drew back. The inherent constitutionalism of the main body of the labour movement never asserted itself more plainly than in the great 'unconstitutional' movement known as the "General Strike". On the other hand, the readiness of the defenders of law and order to force the issue when the crisis came, rather than meet the Trade Union leaders'

[1] Parliamentarism, often held to be the root vice of the Labour Party, is thus only an expression of a deeper failure.

evident will to come to terms, showed a very different temper. The pacific General Council and the bellicose Mr. Winston Churchill, the mild *British Worker* and the furious *British Gazette*, presented a contrast no less instructive than ironic. . . . From the first the strikers' only real chance of success lay in frightening the government into surrender or persuading it into compromise. The temper of the government throughout the dispute excluded the latter solution, which the strike leaders would, of course, have welcomed. *The struggle therefore became one of morale – it was a question of waiting to see which side would crumple up first*. But with Winston Churchill in command and thoroughly enjoying the "scrap", the government was not likely to crumple up. . . . All things considered, the strikers from the first had little real chance of winning . . .' (my italics). There has never been a better description of a hegemonic class facing a corporate one.

2. 1931. The fall of the Labour Government. Provoked, inevitably, by a run on the pound, it ended in the worst catastrophe to overtake any government in British history, with the collective desertion of most of the top echelon of the party in power to the opposition, resulting in a near-annihilation of the party at the succeeding election. Tawney wrote of the Labour Party of 1931: 'It is the author, the unintending and pitiable author, of its own misfortunes. It made a government in its own image; and the collapse of that government was the result neither of accident – though that played its part – nor of unfavourable circumstances – though luck was against it – nor least of all, it must be repeated, of merely personal feelings. It was in the logic of history. . . . In spite of the dramatic episodes which heralded its collapse, the Government did not fall with a crash, in a tornado from the blue. It crawled slowly to its doom, deflated by inches . . .'

3. 1951. The Fall of the Third Labour Government. The Labour Party in 1945 won an absolute majority of seats in a constitutionally sovereign legislature – no working class in any other major West European country has ever won an electoral and political victory so complete. Within two years, the Attlee

government had lost the initiative, and the following years
were ones of steady retreat. The final collapse, a diminuendo
repetition of 1931, was precipitated by a balance of payments
crisis and splits inside the cabinet. Crossman has recently
pointed out that the débâcle was supremely unnecessary: 'Why
was Hugh Dalton able to reveal . . . that by 1947 – only two
years after the electoral triumph – the government was manifestly losing both its coherence and its sense of direction? . . .
What was it that so rapidly deflated the public demand for
social change that had swept the party into power in 1945? . . .
When the 1951 election came, there was no violent anti-
socialist swing of public opinion. On the contrary, the party
made headway in the country – polling the highest vote in its
history. . . . If only Mr. Attlee had held on, instead of appealing to the country in the trough of the crisis, he would have
reaped the benefit of the 1951 recovery, and Labour might
have stayed in power for a decade. . . . An independent critic
is . . . (likely) . . . to find that the electoral losses in 1950 were
quite unnecessary, and that the precipitate decision to resign a
year later was not an inevitable result of the crisis, but a consequence of physical exhaustion and loss of nerve. . . .'

The history of hegemony in twentieth-century Britain is tersely
suggested in these three comments.

III

It remains to evoke the way in which the hegemonic system
works as a total order, delimiting and defining the roles of antagonistic social classes within it. For this purpose, the crucial
moments are those at which the working-class party has won
overt political power and formed a government. The analytic
problem can be posed simply as follows: *what is the invisible
barrier between the formal control of unlimited state power
(enshrined in the sovereignty of parliament) and the actual
implementation of qualitative social change (enshrined in the
party's constitution)?*
Obviously, the first point to make is that power in advanced
capitalist societies is polycentric. The official mythology that it

is located uniquely in the site of political democracy, parliament, is so patently empty that nobody on the Left takes it seriously. Unfortunately, however, there has been an almost complete absence of attempts to replace it with a substantial, sophisticated theory of power in late capitalism – itself an example of the general atrophy in analysis of the *mediations* of capitalist society which has marked contemporary socialist theory. In the long run, to be sure, power coincides with control of the means of production. But at any given moment of history, this is not necessarily true. On the contrary, what is needed is not a reassertion of the banality that power ultimately derives from the pattern of ownership in a society; the urgent need is for a concrete typology of the different modalities of power today. A whole spectrum of possibilities exist, realized in more or less pure forms in different societies at different epochs. In the short run, power can be predominantly military, bureaucratic, economic, ideological, even – as a limiting case – purely political; it can be crystallized directly in the means of violence (Nazi Germany), the means of administration (Confucian China), the means of production (company-states like Honduras or Katanga), the means of communication (increasingly, Western societies), or the means of legislation (which would be socialism). The power structure of any society is never, of course, a pure monocentric system. However, this does not prevent it from being possible to make meaningful distinctions both in and between different patterns of power. In Britain, at any event, it is clear that there is a very specific configuration of power, the product of a particular historical and geographical situation.

There is no space here to discuss adequately the character of this configuration. But it can be suggested that there are three main idiosyncrasies of the structure of power in Britain: the relative insignificance of bureaucratic or military forms, the exceptionally immediate strike-capacity of economic forms, and the ultimate, crucial importance of ideological and cultural forms. Together this combination may be defined in terms used first by Hegel and then by Marx, as the supremacy of civil society over the State. Each element in the constellation corresponds to a fundamental moment in the history of the dominant bloc. Despite their manifest class character, neither army nor civil service are of such directly power-political importance in England as in most other advanced capitalist countries (France, until recently Germany and Japan). The insignificance of the army in England is the result of a long dialectical history: the late Middle Ages saw the worst over-militarization of the countryside in Europe (Wars of the Roses), leading to the radical demilitarizing policies of the Tudor Monarchy; then when the Monarchy itself attempted to build up a standing army (James II), the landowning class in return consistently prevented it as a threat to its independent power in the countryside; while the geographical isolation of England removed the need for permanent external defence. The absence of a major state bureaucracy is a correlate of the local, molecular character of agrarian power in the seventeenth and eighteenth centuries: the unpaid, sparetime J.P. maintained control of the countryside, uniquely combining economic, social and political power in his physical person; attempts to create a monarcho-bureaucratic machine (Charles I) foundered on this rock. The success of agrarian capitalism and then the spontaneous outbreak of the first industrial revolution produced the successive and cumulative anti-bureaucratic pressure of landlord politics and *laissez faire* economics (where industrialization was later, more deliberate and imitative, as in Germany, the State by contrast became one of the main engines of the industrial revolution). The modern civil service dates only from 1854. It is much more significant as a column of power than the army, and has undoubtedly had a braking influence on the Labour Governments of this century; but it has never been powerful enough to derail them.

In contrast, directly economic power in England is exceptionally great. Just as the relative insignificance of army and bureaucracy is a product of the original dominance of agrarian capitalism, so the immense, unmediated striking-power of capital stems from the specific situation of industrial capitalism in England. 'Economic power' is often invoked on the Left, but almost never analysed into its component forms: labour decisions (dismissals), investment decisions (dividend-levels), price decisions (tax transfers to the consumer), publicity decisions (subsidies to political parties) and so on. Here only one simple point need be made. It is that the aggregate political power of capital in England is both *exceptionally massive and structurally hysteric* because of the international position of the British economy. The ultimate sanction of economic power faced with a hostile government is flight of capital. In England, the historic organization of the Sterling Area has made this a permanent possibility rather than an emergency temptation, since the pound is so vulnerable to international speculation that the latter constantly threatens to trigger panic in the English capital market itself; thus a working-class government almost automatically faces the daily possibility that it will lose the 'confidence' of international capitalism, a loss which will in turn immediately provoke an outward flux of English capital of disastrous proportions, which the Sterling Area – closing the circle – makes it abnormally difficult to control. It is no accident that both major Labour Governments have fallen after a run on the pound. All this is on top of the normal discretionary power of capital to act in what it may choose to regard as an emergency.

Finally, the extreme importance of cultural institutions in the distinctive configuration of power in England has already been suggested. Control of the systems of education (public schools, universities) and communication (oligopoly of press) is decisive for the perpetuation of the hegemony of the 'upper class'. Both in turn derive from and conform to larger historical characteristics of the power pattern. The public-school/Oxford and Cambridge phenomenon forms precisely a *non-state* educational system (one which forms a striking contrast to the bureaucratized educational system in, say France). The unparalleled centralization and oligopolistic control of the Press faithfully reflects the degree of concentration and national integration which the oldest industrial capitalism in the world has achieved.

This triangular topography is the true sociological 'setting' of parliamentary democracy, whose concrete, operational character can only be understood in terms of it. In one sense, the remarkable formal aspect of parliamentarism in England is the absolute, unlimited sovereignty it gives the legislature. This – theoretically – should give a devastating weapon to any working-class Government: no other bourgeois state has ever taken the risk implicit in the non-existence of a written constitution in England (many have even had the sanctity of private property written into their constitutions, besides severe checks on the legislature). This peculiarity of the English political system must, again, be referred to the historical evolution of the ruling bloc. The House of Commons was for centuries a one-class institution: there was always a sociological guarantee of its predictability that made juridical safety-rails unnecessary. Subsequently, the upward pressure of the bourgeoisie and then the working class was accommodated within the same framework, simply by widening the franchise. The parliamentary democracy which eventually emerged, and for which Britain is famous, was from one point of view the most vital and enduring victory of the working class. At the same time, it was also the *necessary concomitant* of the adaptation of traditional forms of social domination to a new situation. In England, democracy was the ransom of hegemony. Faced with the rise of the bourgeoisie and then of the proletariat, the hegemonic class had either to break with its whole tradition and try to maintain itself in exclusive power by military or bureaucratic coercion; or it had to yield entry into the political system to these new social forces, and neutralize their efficacy within it by powerful extra-parliamentary means, *which were consonant with the whole strategic style of its past*. Faced with the rise of the middle class, it chose the latter, redoubling the specifically cultural and ideological dimension of hegemony (mystique of aristocracy, etc.) and progressively dissolving its immediate opponent by selective co-optation to its own ranks. The new unified bloc then turned to contain the proletariat. There was no possibility of dissolving this as a class, but the incorporation of the industrial bourgeoisie into the dominant bloc supplied a substitute second weapon: the sheer strength of massed capital.

Thus today, parliament, the formal site of political power,

is two quite different 'places' according to which Party is in power. Its role in the power system is analytically distinct in each case. When a Conservative Government is in power, it is an integral part of a continuous landscape which extends in a smooth, unbroken space around it. When a Labour Government is in power, it is an isolated, spot-lit enclave, surrounded on almost every side by hostile territory, unceasingly shelled by industry, Press and orchestrated 'public opinion'. Each time it has in the end been overrun.

Of course, the actual balance of forces is more complex than an image of this kind suggests: in particular, the power of the unions could be an immensely strong supporting force for a Labour Government, although it has never so far really been used as such. However, the customary assertion that the working-class movement has 'counter-vailing power' under democratic capitalism simply evades the real question, which is not – are there two sets of forces? – but – what is *the final balance of forces*? The countervailing power of Galbraith and Strachey scarcely amounts to more than the ability of the industrial working class to prevent the relative depression of its standards of living in an expanding economy.

In reality, two unequal forces are in perpetual shock against each other, pushing the point of collision between them now in one direction and now in another, but over a period of time establishing a *relatively stable equilibrium* at a point favourable to one and unfavourable to the other. This partially stabilized equilibrium, neither total victory nor drawn combat, but *permanent net superiority* of the hegemonic class is the reality of social peace and political democracy in England today. A reforming Labour Government, as after 1945, can push the equilibrium lastingly to the left (nationalizations, creation of health service, etc.), so that the whole zone of its future fluctuations is situated more favourably to the working class. This does not, of course, preclude successful roll-back pressure, which can – as in the period 1951–63 – push the point of equilibrium some way back along the distance it has come (reversal of income redistribution, exploitation of the public sector, etc.). The present equilibrium in England remains a

crushingly capitalist one, with inequalities which rival or out-
distance those anywhere in the capitalist world: 1 per cent of
the population owns 43 per cent of the fixed property, over
the last decade half the Cabinet and one third of the directors
of the major banks, insurance houses, etc., came from a school
of 1,000 out of a nation of 50,000,000. The narrow area in
which at any given period it moves back and forth can be
defined as the precise elasticity of the hegemonic order at that
conjuncture.

c. *Increasing Entropy*

In conclusion, both the character of the present crisis and
initial relation of the labour movement to it follow from the
preceding analyses:

The present crisis is a general malady of the whole society,
infrastructure and superstructure – not a sudden breakdown,
but a slow, sickening entropy. All the conditions which constituted the unique good fortune of the ruling bloc in the
nineteenth century have turned against it. The 'law' of uneven development has produced its customary dialectical reversal – with a vengeance. Today, Britain stands revealed as
a sclerosed, archaic society, trapped and burdened by its past
successes, now for the first time aware of its lassitude, but as
yet unable to overcome it. The symptoms of the decline have
been catalogued too frequently and copiously to need repetition here: a torpid economy, a pinched and regressive education, a listless urban environment, a demoralized governing
class, a wretched cultural provincialism. All these burdens of
the present have their origins in blessings of the past. *This past
is not merely that of the imperialist era,* as so many socialist –
and capitalist – critics now repeat. It extends both backwards
and forwards far beyond the late nineteenth century, which, as
has been indicated, in the main saw only a final consolidation
of the superstructure of modern British society. The major
single cause of the present crisis is, of course, the prolonged
international decline of the economy, which itself both derives

and dates from the completion of the world system of British imperialism in the period from 1880–1914. Export of capital, under-investment at home, lagging technological innovation, all mark the British economy from the last decades of the nineteenth century onwards. But the huge quantitative returns of the Empire and British overseas investment masked this qualitative deterioration for a long time, and ended, inevitably, by severely exacerbating it. The final incarnation of Empire, the post-war Sterling Area, has at length become the *bête noire* of all the most vocal bourgeois publicists of today, the *malum malorum* of the British economy in our time. Yet this last form of empire is dominated by the first historic nucleus of British Imperialism, the City, whose origins go back not to the nineteenth but to the seventeenth century. Colonized by aristocrats during its long history as no other sector has been, the City is now both the most sociologically revealing and the most sectionally decisive single determinant of the shape of the economy. It subsumes and symbolizes all the defects of the whole. For the living palimpsest which is the ruling bloc in Britain is now decaying from its immemorial accretions. The industrial bourgeoise which in its prime merged with the landed aristocracy has in their union become infected and cor-roded with the vices of the latter. Amateurism and nepotism spread from the councils of state to the inner sanctum of the bourgeoisie itself, the boards and directorates of industry. By the fifties, the most efficient firms in Britain were found by Barna to be predominantly enterprises which were either started by foreigners (refugees, etc.) since 1940, controlled by minorities (Quakers, Jews), or branches of international cor-porations (mainly American). . . . The world-conquering entre-preneurs of the mid-nineteenth century had become flaccid administrators in the mid-twentieth.

Simultaneously, the State co-ordinate of the capitalist sys-tem revealed a disastrous weakness. The Treasury became, after the City, the second great albatross round the neck of English economic growth. The historic achievement of the English governing class in all its metamorphoses, its long maintenance of the supremacy of civil society over the State, has here fatally undermined it. Today, capitalism throughout the world is becoming more and more streamlined, rationalized and oligopolist; the gigantic international corporation is increasingly emerging as its basic unit; and the State intervenes ever more decisively in the national economy, steering and controlling it in the interests of the capitalist system as a whole. Neo-capitalism everywhere demands indicative planning by the State. This planning must necessarily be executed by highly skilled technocrats working within a powerful State apparatus. *In England, the whole cumulative tradition of the governing class disables it from this role*: its virtues have been those of agrarian squirearchy and industrial *laissez faire*. Now that these are gone, only its vices are left: universal dilettantism and anachronistic economic liberalism. Inevitably, then, the Treasury has been what one critic has called the 'apotheosis of dilettantism' – with calamitous results for the prestige and success of the Conservative régime of the fifties.

Lastly, the final good fortune of British capitalism, its victory in two World Wars, was also an immediate cause of its decline. It was never forced by the mass physical destruction of its plant, radically to reconvert and renew itself. On the contrary, bloated and immobilized by its successive survivals, it fell dramatically behind the dynamic, modernized economies of Germany, France, Italy and Japan. Now at length, however, slogans of 'planning' and 'growth' and 'efficiency' are heard in every government speech, and the need to rationalize the whole composition and direction of the economy is pressed in every journal of the Right.

Socially, too, the triumphs of the past have become the bane of the present. The English bourgeoisie had never been outstanding for its devotion to technological and scientific education: the slow, epochal maturation and sudden 'natural' blossoming of the industrial revolution had rendered unnecessary the 'bureacratic' creation of a widespread, efficient system of technical education, like that which so greatly assisted industrialization in Germany. However, this fortuitous advantage was soon cast in a more extreme and deliberate mould. In the mid-nineteenth century, the burgeoning middle class sold its birth-right for the accent of a gentleman. The public schools which sealed the pact between industrial and agrarian capitalists reduced to a common denominator the abilities and aspirations of the two classes, and imprinted it on the following generations. The bourgeoisie contributed least to the new, 'humanist', public school personality: its repression and puritanism; the aristocracy most – its arrogance and amateurism. In either case, science and technique went by the board. The ruling bloc was trained to rule, and did so; but a century later its skills had become mere manners, and its manners, increasingly, affectation. In the fifties, the big, capital-intensive corporations belatedly began to endow the public schools (and universities) with science blocks and laboratories. Too late: the entire educational system was becoming unworkable, and would inevitably be challenged. The state system, under-financed and underprivileged as the English form of capitalist hegemony demanded that it should be, was not even fulfilling its menial role of providing intermediate and lower echelon personnel for the economy. Thus, today, private and public sector alike are put in question by the most reputable spokesman of capitalist England, and the 'unprecedented' expansion of education advocated by the recent Reports is everywhere greeted as an imperative necessity. But more important, the traditional social hierarchies perpetuated by the extreme stratification of the educational system are now for the first time widely questioned and rejected. This revulsion has reached a point where Macmillan, in the final days of his premiership, could call a Conservative Conference to battle in the following terms: 'This country has got to be prepared for change . . . We are all more or less planners today . . . we are still as a nation too set in our ways, too apt to cling to old privileges, too unwilling to abandon old practices that have outlived their usefulness . . . there are too many demarcation lines, social and industrial – one might almost say a sort of caste system. . . .' The Conservative Party as a whole has not, of course, been converted to the new creed of efficiency and 'equality'. One section sincerely believes it, another demagogically uses it, another rejects it altogether. In the panic after

Macmillan's resignation, despite the manifest necessities of the moment, the party obeyed its oldest and deepest instincts and chose as its leader a caricature of its past aristocratic eminences. But for all that, the important fact is that today, for the first time in British history, some kind of ostensible egalitarianism has at last become inscribed on the banner of the English bourgeoisie.

It is in the political field proper that the present crisis has, of course, produced its most spectacular – if also in a sense superficial – manifestations. The debilitating palpitations of economic policy, the continuing duet of speculation and slums in urban life, the ignominious fiascos in military policy, the colossal humiliation of rejection from the Common Market, the scandals which followed it: all these were the outward signs of the inner disarray – and then demoralization – of the governing class of England, confronted with a world which had passed it and all its monuments by. Its real moment of truth had come in 1958, and it had not seen it. When the Conservative Government refused to join the incipient European Economic Community, it threw away its one great chance in the fifties to renovate British capitalism without a major political and social crisis at home. With fatal hubris, it thought England was a nation apart; apex of a world-wide Commonwealth, Britain would be guaranteed its special position within the contradictory unity of international capitalism. Four years later it realized the truth, but the Fifth Republic was now firmly installed, and the gates clanged brutally shut on it as it turned to the Community for refuge.

In retrospect, the famous flavour of the Conservative decade takes on an eerie significance. Under Macmillan's aegis, a neo-Edwardianism reigned and politics in England became more aristocratic than they had been in the Conservative decade of twenty years before. The Edwardian era was, of course, the last period in which the unique international paramountcy of the British governing class was still intact. In the fifties, it was as if by an unconscious, instinctive mimetism, the same class was re-enacting its former role down to its most trivial details, in the hope of somehow recreating the confidence and

splendour of the last unchallenged epoch of the past in order
to face the perils and – soon – the disasters of the present. The
crisis, then, is a logical outcome of the long pilgrimage of
British capitalism from its origins to its present precarious
position within the world of the second half of the twentieth
century. As a result of it, the dominant bloc in Britain today
must, if it is to preserve its hegemony, undergo yet another
metamorphosis. Re-enacting the past has not restored it: the
class now, in the main, realizes that it must change itself once
again. The international pressures of contemporary capitalism
required a radical adaptation. The unfinished work of 1640
and 1832 must be taken up where it was left off.

The opportunity this crisis offers the labour movement is
very great. It is clear from the preceding (indeed any) analysis
of the history and ideology of the movement that for structural reasons it is not able to pose the challenge of an immediate socialist transformation of English society. It will have to
transform itself first: there can be no socialism without an
authentic socialist movement. But between this extreme and
the simple role of executor of bourgeois reform and stabilization, which some socialists are already predicting for it, there
lies a wide and explosive gamut of choices. What will these
choices be? What forces will fight to determine them? It is
these questions which will dominate the coming years.

THE DRIFT TOWARDS PLANNING[1]

Thomas Balogh

The concept of planning has provoked bitter acrimony and suffered startling changes in fortune in Britain since the end of the war, without the more influential protagonists understanding much of the implications either for or against.

1. *The Post-war Failure*

Planning was first hailed as the certain way to a new and better world in peace, as it had enabled the full mobilization of available resources in war.[2] No longer would the destiny of the nation be dominated by the uncontrolled sway of the market. Unemployment would be done away with and social priorities enforced. A new era of economic equality, stability and progress would dawn. In reality, war-time planning was rather rudimentary, crude, and negative. It was forced on a reluctant bureaucracy by the irresistible needs of defence. The Labour Government was eager to claim credit for deliberate planning, but did nothing to adapt direct controls to the new peace-time needs, and co-ordinate their work flexibly with financial incentives and penalties.

In consequence one unforeseen crisis followed another. Each

[1] This paper was originally written in 1963 for the occasion of Prof. Mahalunobis's seventieth birthday. It was adapted for republication in September 1964 prior to the Election and Mr. Balogh's joining the Cabinet Office as Economic Adviser. It in no way reflects official views.

[2] Sir Oliver Franks, *Central Planning and Control in War and Peace*, London. Also the bombastic claims of the least fortunate among the unfortunate British Chancellors of the Exchequer, Dr. (later Lord) Dalton (*The Fateful Years*, London 1957).

was unnecessary and easily preventable with some professional knowledge: coal and dollars in 1947, devaluation in 1949, re-armament in 1951.

The Labour Ministers took refuge in claiming that their failure was due to their reluctance to coerce, rather than their incapacity to discern the problems. Once they had entered on the path of liberalizing the economy instead of creating positive peace-time controls, they were irretrievably lost. They could not compete with the Tories in freedom, nor had they the support and confidence of the owning and managerial classes. Thus each step towards financial liberty brought nearer the point where private financial power could reimpose a veto on economic policy. Planning as a concept was completely discredited and disgraced. It became a dirty word.

Next, reliance on the price mechanism was saluted, especially by the Civil Service, as the one final solution to our problems. full convertibility of a floating pound would be supplemented by monetary policy controlling the volume of currency and ensuring by its subtle influence a perfect balance between global supply and demand. The commands of the sovereign consumer would then be implemented by being transformed into profit opportunities, while incentives to higher productivity, higher production and higher investment would be recreated by abolishing state interference. Provided monetary balance was enforced in this indirect and impersonal way, optimum progress would automatically be within our grasp. Planning would be done by individuals and firms, co-ordinated by market forces.

Alas for these illusions; Tory 'freedom' did not work better than Labour 'planning'. In the renewed crises, 1955, 1957, 1959, 1961; in the purposeless alternation between policies trying to stimulate and repress demand, enforced by the monotonously recurrent deficit in the balance of payments, and by fears of crises of confidence, stultification was complete. Investment was cut and economic competitive power and growth reduced below that of our great industrial rivals. Our growing impotence was due mainly to the successful election tactics of the Conservative Cabinet which necessitated the premature release for consumption of the vast resources, some £1,500m per annum, suddenly presented to Britain by the improvement of the terms of trade. Had they been reserved for investment we should now be well on the way to catching up with the growth of Germany, if not Japan. The fitful pattern of economic policy forced on us by foreign exchange crises has cost the country an appreciable loss of income through decreased investment, productivity and growth – by now certainly not less and possibly much more than 15 per cent of the national income, or say £3,000–£3,500m per annum. This shameful failure has resulted in British national income per head dipping below that of Germany and France for the first time in several hundreds of years. Even more ominous, Soviet output per head has now surpassed ours. Twenty years ago it was less than half. Forty years ago less than a quarter. Here is a portent which has been steadfastly ignored by the Tories.

The monotonous recurrence of crises seems at last to have made some impression. Having experimented with, and failed, both in beating the Trade Unions into acquiescence by deflation and laying down unilateral guiding lines for wage increases, and in increasing decisively the share of investment and innovation to strengthen our power of resistance, the Conservative Government seemed at the turn of 1960–61 to have realized that new tactics were needed. Confronted with the 1960 crisis Selwyn Lloyd, then Chancellor of the Exchequer, went somewhat beyond the conventional reaction. No doubt he followed his Labour and Conservative predecessors in adopting for the sixth time since the war an orthodox programme of restrictions. But advancing beyond them he announced that he was determined to get a new policy launched – forward looking and expansionist.

With the benefit of hindsight this all now looks ironical: Selwyn Lloyd was brusquely dismissed by Macmillan in 1962 precisely because he was, in fact, unable to initiate a new policy. Still, he left an awkward problem for his successor because, spurred by the F.B.I., he committed himself more and more to some sort of deliberate planning of our economic development. It was to be Tory planning, of course, with a difference. The Japanese and, conspicuously, French planning was invoked to show that informal, persuasive planning in an unchanged economic and social framework could work successfully its miracles of refreshed dynamism. For instance, it was asserted that it could overcome the comprehensible reluctance of single entrepreneurs to chance their luck and invest at a higher rate than customary for fear that they would be left in the lurch by their fellows.

In both France and Japan the majority of industrial leaders were made to believe that the high rate of expansion was both imperative and possible. This was achieved in both countries by preparing long-term – ten- to twenty-year – plans of accelerated development to prove that a logical and consistent basis can be found for an upward surge, and that the entrepreneur did not have to fear failure. In both cases almost complete success crowned these efforts. Why not imitate them?

The National Economic Development Council (N.E.D.C.) was the result of this belated doubt about the perfection of 'free' markets, and of untrammelled working of the price-mechanism. It was the beginning of that extraordinary internecine struggle in the Tory Party which culminated in the violent fluctuations of policy and opinion between extremes: the headlong, unthinking stampede towards the Common Market, the new drive against monopoly and the abolition of resale price maintenance, the attacks of Enoch Powell on N.E.D.C. and the Government, the soul-searching of the 'Tory' in *The Times*, the declaration of faith in planning for steady progress both nationally (the Robbins report) and regionally (North-East, Scotland and South-East) – mainly in the pre-election period, in an attempt to widen the appeal of the Tory Party.

2. *The Limitations of N.E.D.C.*

If one wishes to evaluate the appropriateness of a new organization from the viewpoint of its declared functions, if one wishes to differentiate between an honest attempt to deal with a genuine problem or a mere deceptive covering for unadmitted ulterior designs, one must ask oneself how precisely its duty is to be implemented. Here the contrast of the British scheme with French and Japanese plans could not be more blatant. Not merely were the general economic conditions far more auspicious for success in those countries, but the arrangements were far more aptly fitted for dealing with their problems.

In both cases the planning staff was organized outside the Treasury, but with access direct to the Cabinet – through a Finance Minister (who was also responsible for the National Economy) in France, and through the Prime Minister himself in Japan. They formed part of the Civil Service. Moreover, in both cases the strategic position of the Government had great advantages as compared with Britain. The high command of the Japanese industry is once more highly concentrated following the failure of the American Occupation Authorities to smash the Zaibatsu, the great family trusts. In France too, there is an informal control over the economy by the high bureaucracy who traditionally also provide a large part of the commanding personnel of the key institutions and firms, especially the great banks and the great insurance companies (all in national ownership). Thus a pervasive influence over industry is secured through the control over short and long-term credit, and by the close relations of these new and well-trained professional bureaucrats in and out of the Civil Service, whose technical economic competence facilitates the smooth implementation of any policy.

All this contrasted regrettably with the dilettantism of our own Civil Service and the wide diffusion of power over the economy. It was obvious that the nomination in Britain of five or six industrialists with no experience in planning and no particular weight in industry, could not be a substitute for the intense concentration of professional competence and close co-operation between industrial leaders and Government officials, which characterized both France and Japan.

This was the more significant as there were vital differences between our situation and that of these two other countries. In both these countries there was a powerful basic conjuncture of economic forces making for expansion. In Japan, devaluation aggressively cut real wages. This sharpened Japan's competitive power, and provided a positive stimulant to economic expansion. There was a huge reserve army of labour, in agriculture and in the primitive artisan sector, whose weight kept wages relatively low, despite spectacular increases in productivity. This enabled the reconquest of foreign markets, the key to Japanese expansion: with the expansion of national income, import requirements rose but could easily be met by the sharp rise in exports.

In France economic growth during the Fourth Republic, up to the take-over by De Gaulle in 1958, was the concomitant, if not the consequence of the sharp inflationary increase in demand due to colonial wars and uninterrupted internal investment. The possible external effects, the tendency for imports to rise when demand rises at home, were repressed by a tight tariff policy and an almost comprehensive quota system. The French economy is, in any case, rather self-sufficient; it depends far less on imports than that of England. This relative self-sufficiency was consciously fostered in the post-war period by a system of imperial preference prevailing in the French colonies, through duties, quotas, and exchange regulations. The Sterling Area, even at its most restrictive, was a free trade system in comparison with it.

When some of these buttresses were dismantled on joining the Common Market, a sharp devaluation of the franc reduced real international costs.[1] Wages did not rise parallel to the rise in prices. Thus the balance of payments abruptly improved. An excess of exports restarted domestic expansion which had been stifled at first by the orthodox deflationary policy of M. Rueff. Profits further increased, and with them investment. Finally consumption also rose. The second French economic 'miracle' has been the outcome of a sharp redistribution of the national income towards profits, combined with a return of 'confidence' in the entrepreneurial class as a result of the Gaullist régime. Eventually, *ex-post*, a rapid increase in wages

[1] The overseas franc zone still remains an almost exclusive French preserve.

became possible without inflationary effects, as a result of the combined effect on productivity of accelerated investment and expansion. Consequently the militancy of the Trade Unions did not revive, even after the charismatic glamour of the General had worn rather thin. Thus both French and Japanese planners could restrict themselves to controlling and dissuading over-optimistic firms, and encouraging certain basic industries whose huge needs for capital investment make them particularly sensitive to uncertainty. For both purposes the planners possessed ample power and influence.

In Britain in 1962, objective economic conditions were particularly difficult for planning expansion, and the failure of the Brussels talks early in 1963 did not relieve the position.[1] In view of the magnitude of the task, the new planning agency seemed ill-conceived. It consisted of representatives of the Government and of the great vested interests of the economy: of the industrialists and the heads of two nationalized industries; and, after some hesitation, and some qualifying conditions, of representatives of the Trade Unions. The non-Government members were to serve in their individual capacity. Two independent members, and, as the sole representative of the secretariat, its Director-General Sir Robert Shone, made up the list. None of these had any special experience in, and so far as one knows would not claim any special aptitude for, large-scale economic planning. The Council was fortunate, however, in obtaining Sir Donald Mac-Dougall's services as the Director of their Economic Research Division (though he did not become a member of the Council itself). A talented but very small staff was recruited with great difficulties. At first there were no consequential changes even in the Civil Service structure itself. Subsequently, at the end of July 1962, Sir Frank Lee's retirement presented an opportunity for some overdue reform. What eventually emerged left the British Administration still woefully short of the requirements for a serious effort at conscious domination of our economic destinies.

[1] The entry of Britain into the Common Market would certainly have demanded a sharp devaluation of the pound.

The British Civil Service structure evolved in the period of Britain's economic supremacy in a framework of *laissez faire*. Administration was strictly separated from technical knowledge. Its structure was based on the claim that expertise could always be secured, if needed, from outside, and that expert views needed to be examined by 'non-committed administrators' acting on the basis of common sense. Pure intelligence and detachment was therefore made the basic requirement for recruitment and for further successful promotion.

The only possible justification for this dilettante approach would be success. But, who, looking at the run of fiascos since the war, can permit the Treasury that claim? There was the premature convertibility of sterling, leading to the purposeless exhaustion of the American loan and thence to devaluation. There was, to take another example, the attempt to 'let the pound find its own level' in a 'free' market, which led to the crisis of 1955. There was 1957. And there was 1960–61. What the Treasury officials never seemed to grasp was the fact that the restrictions which seemed to them necessary to maintain 'freedom' (that is, freedom of the financial interests sponsored by the Bank of England) were bound to weaken the competitive position of the economy. Each time investment was cut, demand fell and imports dropped off; and productivity also suffered. The pound could be saved, but only at the price of weakening Britain against her competitors and setting the scene for yet another crisis once the immediate pressure was relieved. A great deal of energy, moreover, had to be spent on exhorting the Trade Unions to accept a wage-freeze at a time when real wages in other countries of Europe were rising faster than ever before. There was never a sensible policy for increasing investment, innovation and productivity; there was never a social policy which would have won the active co-operation of the unions.

There were changes in the government; Chancellors came and went. But nothing seemed to make any difference in the Treasury at George Street – either to the official hierarchy's habits of mind or to the internal organization of the Treasury. Indeed, even the modest progress made during the war years was progressively lost. During the war an impressive Economic Section of the Cabinet had been created, which had access to all ministers. It survived the exodus of the temporary war-time staff which had been drawn in from the universities to revolutionize British economic policy-making. If this Section had continued in existence it might, with luck, have counterbalanced the baneful influence of the Treasury and the Bank of England. But the chance was lost when Sir Stafford Cripps, who had been made economic co-ordinator after the 1947 convertibility crisis, had to replace Dalton as Chancellor. He organized a so-called 'planning staff' in the Treasury, distinct from the Economic Section – and the latter was further weakened when the Treasury absorbed it. Things were not improved by Macmillan's reorganization of the Treasury: the introduction of Sir Roger Makins from the Foreign Office scarcely raised the dust in George Street, though it was humiliating to the high officials, and even that breath of wind soon passed.

In 1962, for the first time, there was a change that seemed to be more than the routine shuffle caused by retirements and promotions. It was the most radical reform attempted since Lloyd George so unwisely gave the head of the Treasury supreme authority by making him also head of the whole Civil Service – and, later, secretary to the Cabinet. The job, at long last, was broken up and divided among three people. But that was not all. There was the sudden and imaginative elevation of relatively junior officials. (The most important post went to a man who had not even been knighted – an unprecedented shock to those with a sense of the settled decencies!) Their promotion brings to an end the epoch, beginning with Warren Fisher and ending with Lords Bridges and Normanbrook, in which progress in the hierarchy bore little relation to technical ability if not knowledge.

Under the new arrangements the head of the Civil Service concentrated on management and personnel problems. The secretary of the Cabinet was to be confined to that function. The successor to Sir Frank Lee at the Treasury was to control national expenditure (supply) as well as financial and economic policy – the former function having been performed by Sir Norman Brook in addition to his general duties for the Civil Service and the Cabinet. The Treasury was correspondingly reorganized into three departments; such economic experts as were available were integrated into the division dealing with economic policy in general (in contrast to financial and monetary policy and interdepartmental co-ordination). And a national expenditure and resources division was to plan expenditure on a more expert basis.

The division of labour at the Treasury as it emerged from this reform still remained illogical. Financial and monetary policy cannot be separated from general economic policy, or dealt with by men who are not economic experts, leaving co-ordination to the man at the top. The system is even less likely to work effectively if the same man also remains burdened with the supervision of financial control – the Treasury check on spending by other departments. For this is a task which requires technical knowledge of departmental expenditure and it ought, as in most other important countries, to be assigned to a special Ministry of the Budget. The Treasury should be able to consider the economic repercussions of the Budget and it should not be encumbered with the detailed scrutiny of all expenditure. The two tasks are distinct and require a different approach. As successive scandals about contracts showed, the Treasury had lost or abandoned all pretence of the old-fashioned candle-end type of financial control. But the new scientific efficiency accountancy, as exercised in the U.S.A. by the Bureau of the Budget, did not replace the outmoded type of supervision.

How far the Treasury, and especially its establishment side, remained from realizing the needs of an orderly economic management of a mixed system (which is far more difficult than that of a totally planned one) is shown by the extraordinary arrangements made to provide economic education for the young men (selected on the basis of what amounts to an intelligence test without necessarily professional economical knowledge) who are to serve in departments.

The 'integration' of the economists with the general administrators, moreover, could be successful only if the economists really had been integrated into the Service: that is, accepted into the establishment and given appropriate ranks and prospects of promotion. Otherwise 'integration' meant little more than a perpetuation of their previous low status in a new guise. For the need is to spread professional knowledge through the whole Civil Service, not to confine it to specialized groups that are isolated and ineffectual. This, in the long run, means a change in the patterns of power and in those who wield it – and that the reform did not achieve.

In addition there were no economists in the various departments who could draw up detailed suggestions for alternatives from which the central organ could make its choice to fit in with general conceptions. Moreover the N.E.D.C. as the new planning organ remained outside the normal Civil Service hierarchy. It could demand authoritative information or the elaboration of investment projections. Its functions in the process of framing budgetary, fiscal and other policies remained most obscure. In 1963 the Trade Union members felt that their representations and the papers of the Secretariat had an important influence on the Chancellor. This view was not shared by many insiders.

The drawbacks of this equivocal arrangement are obvious. Either the N.E.D.C. Secretariat duplicates the functions of the economic departments of the State in order to harmonize general policies with its own plans, in which case it must force the Government to adopt the latter – or it has to modify its own plans according to the policies of the Government. In the latter case long-term planning would go by the board; in the former an *ad hoc* body would usurp the most important economic function of Government. In either case violent conflicts might arise. Whatever this arrangement and conception might be, it cannot possibly be termed long-term planning. So long as a do-nothing Cabinet was combined with an ignorantly dilettante bureaucracy, progressives in this country might derive a sardonic satisfaction from the fact that poor Selwyn Lloyd (who was so cruelly and unjustly dismissed for carrying out his master's policies) should have left a thorn in the flesh of the Government and the bureaucracy in the shape of the new planning organization. But it is not a set-up which can plan in any real sense of the word. In point of fact such a conflict did arise when the Economic Adviser of the Government gave evidence to the National Incomes Commission which was in violent contradiction to the growth 'plan' of the N.E.D.C. Secretariat – which had received the blessing of the Chancellor (and, incidentally, made any approval of a rational incomes policy impossible through its thoughtless insistence on $2\frac{1}{2}$ per cent limit on wage increases).

In contrast to these conceptual and organizational weaknesses, the problems facing Britain are extremely complex and perplexing. The harmonization of an increase in demand with a balance in international payments is exceedingly difficult. The protective buttresses which enabled France to achieve a high investment level cannot be reproduced without far-reaching reforms in Britain. We now lack the control mechanisms internally and externally. General de Gaulle's brutal rupture of the negotiations for Britain's entry into the Common Market has given Britain an uncovenanted new chance of putting her house into order. But this new opportunity has yet to be exploited. Nor is it possible for Britain to create expansion by a tremendous fillip through devaluation, coupled with pressure on real wages, a situation which was reproduced, as we have seen, in the second French miracle. A mere exhortation to industrialists will not produce the investment, the technical leap forward, coupled with the squeezing of manpower from inefficient firms in order to enable the technically up-to-date to expand. In the last two years Britain has benefited from the existence of unused capacity built up in years of stagnation. This will become exhausted; meanwhile current investment is completely insufficient to sustain even the 4 per cent N.E.D.C. rate of expansion (not to speak of the short-lived 5–6 per cent spurt in 1963–4).

It is clear that much more is needed than an assembly of scattered investment projects to attain that end. A mechanism is necessary which could elaborate, and implement, a set of coherently chosen targets enforcing social priorities, in a plan which takes into account the effects of the totality of investment projects. Such a plan would have to make these projects consistent with one another, through general economic policy measures, and see to it that they did not conflict with the balance of payments, while achieving an acceleration of growth. A real development plan, moreover, must be based on a definite conception of economic advance, the projects so selected that they realize that basic conception – while at the same time forming a good basis for a general expansion in which each of the projects is economically justified.

3. *Electioneering and Economic Policy*

The contrast between the magnitude of the task and the weakness of the institutional arrangements was so striking as to suggest that the Conservative Government was not so much convinced that a new national agreement about a well-conceived plan could be used to energize the country and secure new harmony for greater effort – but rather that they hoped to use the plan as a vote-catching gimmick for the election, showing a rosy future for all.

There were other possible advantages too. The creation of the National Economic Development Council could serve – or so Selwyn Lloyd seemed to think – a hardly less important and favourable purpose. The Trade Unions, by their maladroitness, had relieved the Tory Government of much unpopularity since 1952. It was not the Government that got the blame for its helpless incompetence in matters economic, exemplified by our relative eclipse in the world economy, and the foolishness of the handling of our relations with the Continent. It was the Trade Unions who were blamed for restrictive practices, for strikes and high prices; it was they who provided the working-class votes, especially among womenfolk, necessary to put the Conservative Government twice back into power. The National Economic Development Council, it seems, was to be used to perpetuate this happy state of affairs.

The Trade Unions did not dare to state clearly their price for joining the Council. Nor have they ever seriously considered (let alone reached agreement on) the conditions under which they would consider acceptance of a coherent wages policy. Their tactical position therefore remained weak. Once they consented to participate in the work of the Council, they could be forced further onto the defensive. If they showed themselves reluctant to name a price for their acquiescence in creating the conditions for stability, in agreeing to what must appear to the 'man in the street' a nationally essential wage restraint, designed to harmonize the increase in wages with an increase in productivity, they might easily discredit themselves and the Labour Party. The average voter by now must be rather muddled about the rights and wrongs of the case. As a consumer, he has certainly benefited from the relative stability in prices. The N.E.D.C., it is clear, had powerful immediate attractions for the Tory Government in 1961.

If on top of everything else, the Conservatives had been able to get Britain into the Common Market by the end of 1963, the stage would have been set for a fourth electoral victory and the disintegration of the Labour Party and Trade Union resistance, in an economic 'miracle' on the French pattern of 1958. If the original tactical plan of the Conservatives had succeeded it would have been the Labour Party that would have had to defend its dissatisfaction with the entry into the Common Market, that is, with *an accomplished fact*. It would have had to propose a new change and could have been accused of a lack of internationalism, of failure to look forward. The possible unfavourable economic repercussions of joining the Common Market would not have been apparent at that stage. The tactical plan of the Conservative Government was, as always, ingenious. After Wilson's accession to the leadership of the Labour Party, however, everything seemed to go sour for the Conservatives. Macmillan's careful tactical plan was completely disrupted even before General de Gaulle vetoed our entry into the Common Market, Miss Keeler's entry on the world scene postponed the election and the Conservative Party became torn by internal personal fights over its leadership.

The negotiations with the Common Market countries were so drawn-out by the French diplomats at Brussels that Britain could not have joined the Common Market before a general election.

Thus the Labour Party was given a possibility to plead for the *status quo* and attack the Government's policy, which implied a change that seemed risky in the extreme. As the traditional conservatism of the British voter is normally his most important quality, this would in any case have put the Conservative Government at a definite disadvantage. It would have been the Government which proposed an uncertain change and the Labour Party which defended the *status quo*.

The French technocrats were extremely skilled. They faced the British with unanimous pressure by the Six on certain vital points, on which the Conservatives were at great disadvantage: British agriculture; imports of temperate zone food from the old Dominions; pledges to the Free Trade Area. On all these points the French were able to mobilize their partners. The British Government would have run the grave risk of not being able to carry its own party in the fight for ratification. If they had, they would almost certainly have been repudiated by the electorate. They were saved from this by de Gaulle.

The General's brutal interruption of the talks, to some extent, came to the rescue of the British Government. Having been forcibly excluded they could claim – even if with some violence to truth – that the negotiations had been on the point of success. They could also assert that they had not surrendered and prejudiced those pledges to British Agriculture, to the Commonwealth and to the E.F.T.A. partners which – as is clear from the Belgian Government's Memorandum which has since been published – had in fact been violated. The violation of these pledges, once it became obvious, would have caused even more extreme dissension in the Tory Party than Resale Price Maintenance.

In the meantime the Government's policy on the home-front had also run into trouble. Despite the reforms at the Treasury, speeches by the Chancellors in the latter half of 1962, and the testimony of Professor Cairncross, their economic adviser, made it clear that the Government's official experts expected a renewal of inflationary tendencies before the end of

1962 – hence the brake was kept on economic activity. They were sadly mistaken. Mass unemployment reappeared and with it political agitation for Government intervention. By the time that Professor Paish, Selwyn Lloyd's *eminence grise* at the Treasury, was beginning to feel comfortable, with unused productive capacity reaching the 20 per cent mark, the pressure to reflate the economy was mounting. Ministers were discovering that their attempt to ensure stability without planning – by deliberately causing unemployment – was politically unacceptable. Hence, even before the end of 1962, fumbling ministerial hands were beginning to relax the brake.

The retreat from deflation early in 1963 became a rout. Maudling suddenly favoured expansion, but at first could not get started. Even the National Institute for Economic Research supported a whopping reduction in indirect taxes – notably purchase tax on cars. This is the easiest and politically most profitable method of stimulating the economy. But its long-term consequences are serious: by throwing more cars on our congested roads, we shall be forced to devote more and more of our limited investment resources to such non-productive purposes as roads and town-planning, and at the same time shackle our economy more and more tightly to the uncertain fortunes of the car industry. At the same time strong incentives were given to private investment. When this seemed to fail and the unpopularity of the Government increased – for non-economic reasons – a vast array of public investment plans were brought forth in the last four or five months of 1963 and in 1964. Roads, hospitals, universities, schools, housing, regional planning, a large part of the Labour programme was suddenly taken over and a start was made on a great number of projects – without any of the safeguards which Labour sponsored.

The Treasury thinking behind this new policy seems to have been the reverse of the old assumption that the way to increase exports was to restrict the home market; the new theory was that a rise in home sales will boost exports too. This belief is as foolish as the first. There are only two ways to increase exports – by holding down relative costs (especially wage-costs) or by devaluation. And devaluation without an effective incomes policy is itself only a temporary remedy. But an incomes policy, as the unions have made clear, is impossible without overall planning to ensure a fair distribution of the burdens and an acceleration of economic growth.

The only way in which the new policy could succeed was if foreign countries' efficiency costs rose more rapidly than our own. In this the Conservative luck seems to have been rather steadier than in other respects. If the German inflation which gave rise to such hopes in 1963 receded and the export surplus reappeared with a vengeance, French and Italian relative costs deteriorated very rapidly in 1963–4 and the 'stabilization' measures have, up to the middle of 1964, proved ineffectual. Even if the British share in world manufactured exports did not rise, the crisis atmosphere elsewhere steadied the pound in the teeth of a deteriorating foreign current (and much worse overall) balance.

On the other hand, the concept of the National Economic Development Council, instead of serving to discredit the Unions, recoiled on the Government. The Secretariat had in 1962 presented a statistical picture of the possible development of the country in the next ten years, at that point still assuming that Britain would join the Common Market.

This picture was quite ambitious and favourable, although perhaps somewhat perplexing. Gross domestic production was assumed to increase by 4 per cent per annum. This was, of course, in accordance with the directive and must not be taken as a forecast and even less as a target. On this basis the Secretariat came to the conclusion that an overall increase in consumption of almost £3,000m. per annum over five years, or 3·2 per cent a year, could be contemplated – with Government expenditure increasing by about £1,000m per annum overall, or by 3·6 per cent a year. This partly revealed the immense gain which could be obtained if dynamism were restored to the country, and also disproved the Conservative argument (used at the previous Election) that it is impossible to finance social services on a 'lavish scale' by accelerating economic growth.

The overall increase in investment was set at £1,700m a year over five years, or 6·2 per cent a year. This implied that annual growth could be accelerated from 2 to 4 per cent of the national income by an increase of only from 18 per cent to 20 per cent in gross investment. Between 1957 and 1961 investment increased from 16 per cent to 18 per cent. The growth in national income did not accelerate. The incremental capital output ratio had been 7·5. It was now to be 4·8. This was rather optimistic and could only be explained by the fact that the Secretariat assumed that the substantial capacity unused at the moment would be brought quickly into production. While this represented a welcome break with the Paish doctrine, according to which any increase in the rate of capital utilization would produce severe inflationary disturbances, it was very difficult to square with the assumption that imports were only going to increase by 4.5 per cent – remember that it was also assumed that we were going to join the Common Market.

It is difficult to believe that on the basis of complete *laissez faire*, even the increase in the utilization of capital could yield the contemplated increase in production. In the past few years a very large portion of total capital investment has been used for less than immediately productive investment and it is difficult to imagine that this would suddenly and substantially change. Certainly there was no indication that the Government would will the drastic changes in instruments of policy which are needed if there is to be a substantial change in the composition of capital investment towards productive types. Yet without discriminating policies and direct measures, none can be expected.[1]

Even less plausible were N.E.D.C.'s subsequent publications – from this point of view. These assumed that imports and exports would rise faster than originally contemplated (this was a curious sidelight on the view taken about the impact of the entry into the Common Market on trade prospects). Once, moreover, policy measures came to be discussed it was obvious that the Government wanted to use the Council to help it establish a one-sided wage restraint. Neither the

[1] Cf. Harold Wilson's review of 'Planning in a Vacuum'. *New Statesman* 1962.

Government nor the employers were willing to contemplate an all-round policy of income-stabilization with adequate policy measures, though they accepted the targets.

The N.E.D.C. plan was weakest, however, on the attainment of balance in international payments. It rejected by implication both structural changes in import restrictions and devaluation, hoping that wage restraint by itself would sufficiently increase the buoyancy of British exports. This aim would be rather audacious even in extremely favourable economic circumstances. But are the circumstances going to be favourable? Bilateral planning of foreign trade, the most obvious solution, is still frowned upon. In any case it is difficult to believe that it will be possible to restrict the rise of imports to the level contemplated by N.E.D.C. without some drastic measure of wage restraint. Yet either devaluation or import restriction would raise difficult problems for incomes policy. There is continued agitation abroad for cuts in tariffs. These would further aggravate the British international position, as they have done in the past.

Thus both the target for investment and for the foreign balance obviously called for a very determined effort to keep consumption from rising less than parallel to the increase in productivity. This indeed was foreseen. Productivity was to rise 3·3 per cent per annum, and consumption only 3·2 per cent. The achievement of this aim is inconceivable without a progressive taxation policy so as to obtain most of the increase in investment capacity from the rich, and to obtain close co-operation from the Trade Unions. The Conservative Government could not contemplate such a complete change in attitude.

This contradiction was made apparent when the plan of implementation was published – after it had been leaked to the Press. The Council, however, did not endorse it and for obvious reasons: the Secretariat suggested a number of radical reforms, the establishment of a compulsory National Redundancy Fund, reorganization of training and education towards the attainment of higher productivity, a housing drive to encourage the mobility of workers, and a tax on wealth. As against this it demanded a restraint on incomes, which the unions in these conditions categorically rejected.

This frustration had one excellent consequence. As the result of the negative attitude of both employers, and of the Government, the establishment of N.E.D.C. could not be exploited by the latter to discredit the Unions as the sole threat to the continued and stable prosperity of the country.

Indeed the superior tactical ability of Wilson decisively turned the tables on the Government. In the first place it obtained support of the Trade Unions for a well-conceived plan for an incomes policy. This pointed clearly to the basic incapacity and selfishness of the Conservatives. In the second place it succeeded on a number of occasions in highlighting the Tory Government's clumsy attempts to embroil important Unions in labour disputes. This was the case especially in steel, electricity and the post office. The most vulnerable flank of Labour was thus protected: the ignorance of the public was a grave menace. Finally in a number of speeches and broadcasts Wilson went farther than any contemporary leader in explaining in detail how planning of the economy is to be evolved under Labour, what reforms of the Government machine would have to be undertaken and what far-reaching changes in taxation, investment, foreign trade, and education (to name only the most immediately pertinent) would have to be ruthlessly carried out if Britain were to succeed in transforming herself into a dynamic and social community, and so restore her influence internationally.

The contrast could not be greater. Writing more than two years ago I said:

'British economic policy is remarkable in a single respect: it is a crashing bore. Not a bore in the sense of a killjoy as many politicians regard it. For them, economic policy imposes what others might think is a salutary limit or discipline on their pet schemes. Nor is it a bore in the sense of being uninteresting as county people might regard it – something to be left to vulgar tradespeople or economists. It is boring in a straightforward sense like the endless repetition of infantile burbling is boring. It just goes on. It is just a repetition. And it has no meaning or purpose.

'The basic weakness of Britain after both World Wars has sprung from the same cause: policies leading to insufficient investment, weakening our competitive position abroad and our capacity to provide a good material standard (or a strong war effort) at home. This was aggravated by the misapplication of a large portion of what was invested. Paradoxically Keynes, who fought (at any rate until 1940) most bitterly against the Civil Service and Financial Establishment which was responsible for our weakness, unwillingly contributed to it. By attacking Montague Norman for the return to the pre-war gold parity in 1925 and by over-emphasizing the superficial monetary problem, he obscured the more fundamental structural causes of our debility.

'The years 1927, 1931 and 1937 mark the resultant external pre-war crises. Crisis milestones in the post-war period are 1947, 1949, 1951, 1955, 1957, 1959–61.

'Ten crises.

'All are of the same pattern.

'All, without exception, were responded to by the same old method of restriction, accompanied by a monotonous chorus of ministerial platitudes, echoed in the City, about the need to "stiffen our economy", "cut the cloth", and so on. Meanwhile, first the Soviet Union, then Germany, then Japan (soon it will be China) ejected Britain, the erstwhile leader in industrial development, from the second, third and even fourth position in production. The increasing bore of repetition proved to all except those in positions of influence that these slogan policies were inappropriate and deeply damaging. Britain was impelled by them towards frustration and weakness, year by year.'

Since this was written the only novel elements in the repetitive cycle have been, as we shall see, disturbing.

4. *The Strangled Economy*

Even though the post-war Labour Government failed to develop effective planning, its record was in some respects quite impressive. During the period 1945–51, despite the immense difficulties inherited from the war years and the additional economic setback created by the Korean War, exports expanded rapidly and a growth-rate of about 3·2 per cent a year was maintained. This was a firm foundation on which a Tory Government might have built; and in addition, they were presented when they took office with an unexpected bonus – the reversal of the terms of trade in Britain's favour, equivalent to about £1,500 million a year. Nevertheless, after 1951 British economic development was uneven and considerably inferior to that of most other industrial countries. Over the whole 13-year period, annual growth has averaged under 2·5 per cent. Sharp advances at the rate of 6 per cent and more in 1955 and 1959 were followed, in 1955–8 and 1959–63 by long and lengthening periods of stagnation. The periods of expansion occurred invariably before elections, the stagnation began soon after the Tory victories, induced by overloading of the economy, lagging exports and surging imports. In a period of vigorously expanding world trade, our exports consistently failed to prove competitive and our share in the world trade in manufactured goods fell from 22 per cent in 1951 to 13·8 per cent in 1964. This, in turn, was reflected in the slow growth of our national income. Between 1959 and 1962 (the last year for which comparable figures are available: but in 1963 and 1964 the economy lagged farther behind) it increased by a mere 12 per cent, compared with 15 per cent in the U.S., 15 per cent in Sweden and 31 per cent in Germany. If our output since 1951 had increased at the same rate as in western and southern Europe – socialist or capitalist – we should now be better off by some £10,000 million a year.

This is equivalent to an overall wage increase of 36 per cent – or £6 a week for every wage-earner in the country.

The slow growth of British exports since 1951 – a mere 42 per cent in 13 years – has meant, despite the massive improvement in the terms of trade, continuous trouble with our balance of payments. As a result, pressure on sterling and panic withdrawal of funds from London forced the Government in 1955, 1957 and 1960–61 to cut public expenditure, impose high interest rates to cut private investment, and raise taxes to cut demand. What is more, in each cycle, investment and employment fell more, and subsequently rose less, than in the preceding one. In the 1958 trough, for example, unemployment rose only to 2·1 per cent; in 1963 it rose to 3·1 per cent, even discounting the influence of excessively bad weather. Again, at the 1955 peak, unemployment was reduced to less than 1 per cent; in 1961 it was 1·2 per cent; and in the summer of 1964, despite all the efforts of the pre-election boom, it could not be reduced below 1·4 per cent. Not only does Tory economic policy produce a series of vicious cycles; the evidence shows they grow more vicious each time. In addition, the regional unbalance within these phases consistently worsened. Even in periods of pre-election boom, when the Midlands and South-East experienced labour-shortage and wage-inflation – forcing the Government to take deflationary steps – heavy unemployment persisted in the North. Tory policy, in fact, produces the complementary evils of urban decay in the North and overcrowding in the South. Indeed, we may already be on the threshold of the worst balance of payments crisis since the war. Certainly the situation is far worse than in 1951.

We now appear to face an entirely new conjunction of economic evils: for the balance of payments is in crushing deficit, while, at the same time, the economy is functioning more and more lethargically. Not only are our exports failing to compete overseas, but imported manufactured goods are successfully competing with British-made goods produced for the home market. This accounts both for the massive rise in imports and the stagnation of home production. Nor can the blame be laid on the trade unions: since 1960, labour costs of production here increased 50 per cent less than in Germany, but our export prices rose by 10 per cent more.

The conclusion relentlessly forced upon us is that our economic paralysis springs from a deep-rooted failure to acquire technical and scientific dynamism. We are thus forced into a series of logical steps, each of which accelerates our relative economic decline. The absence of competitive edge in our exports leads to trade imbalance, this then forces the Government to impose deflationary measures; deflation, in turn, discourages investment and the introduction of new techniques, and so our competitive edge is still further reduced.

This is borne out by our industrial investment record under the Tories. During 1956–62 productive investment here was about 12·7 per cent of national income, against 15·9 per cent in Sweden and 18 per cent in Germany. And the rate of expansion of the national income was, as we have seen, even worse. We could have achieved steady expansion through policies based on Tory economic philosophy only if exports rose faster than national income. It was their ability to export surplus production which allowed the Germans, French and, to some degree, the Italians to develop larger production units (with consequent economies of scale) despite the fact that relative abundance of manpower caused wages to lag behind the expansion of production and so limited domestic markets. Without this ability to export, the qualitative advantage of a highly dynamic economy disappears. And this in turn means that productivity and wage increases will be insufficient to keep labour content during a period of booming profits and investment.

Without this export advantage, therefore, we can create economic dynamism only by a consciously contrived expansion based on the selective encouragement of investment and technical innovation. And it is precisely this principle of selectivity which Tories find anathema – and for which the existing Government machine is unfit.

THE WITHERING AWAY OF CLASS

A Contemporary Myth

J. H. Westergaard

The years since the early 1950s have echoed with the claim
that the old class structure of capitalism is steadily dissolving.
The labels attached to that new order of society which is believed to be emerging from the ruins of the old – the 'welfare
state', the 'affluent society', the 'home-centred society', the
'mass society', 'post-capitalism', and so on – have become the
clichés of contemporary debate. Their variety and imprecision
indicate some of the uncertainties of diagnosis and prognosis.
Evaluations, too, have differed widely: reactions to the trends
discerned range from triumph to despondency. But the descriptions offered of current trends generally have much in common:
the assertion that the old sources of tension and class conflict
are being progressively eliminated or rendered irrelevant;
that the structure of contemporary Western societies is
being recast in a mould of middle class conditions and
styles of life; that these developments signal 'the end of
ideology'. Such notions in turn are infused with a sense of a
social fluidity which is felt to falsify past characterizations of
capitalism.

Yet arguments and evidence alike have often been taken for
granted, rather than stated precisely and scrutinized carefully.
Rhetoric has obscured both links and gaps in the chain of
reasoning. Hunches, impressions and assumptions have been
given parity with facts. Minor changes have been magnified
into major ones, uncertain indications into certain proof. Evidence consistent with several interpretations has been treated as
if only one were possible. The labelling of trends has been extended into a labelling of sceptics as 'fundamentalists', their
criticisms dismissed as the product of a psychological inability
or unwillingness to recognize a changing reality. These are

reasons enough for even a cursory review of the main themes and postulates of the fashionable interpretations of mid-twentieth century capitalism and its allegedly dissolving class structure, as they have been formulated especially in Britain and the United States.[1]

Whatever their variations, these interpretations hinge on two basic assumptions. The first is that the substantive inequalities of earlier capitalism are both diminishing and losing their former significance. The second is that, for these or other reasons, radical dissent is progressively weakened as new patterns of living and aspiration negate or cut across the older class-bound horizons and loyalties. Substantive inequalities are reduced, it is argued, by a continuous redistribution of wealth and the extension of economic security; by a growth in the numbers and importance of occupations in the middle ranges of skill and reward; by a progressive narrowing of the inequalities of opportunity for individual advancement; and by a widening diffusion of power or influence. In so far as power remains concentrated, it no longer derives from the accumulation of private property, but from control over bureaucratic organizations of diverse kinds – public at least as much as private – in which authority is divorced from wealth. Thus two crucial dimensions of inequality no longer coincide.

---

[1] The following are examples of recent literature, differing greatly in approach, emphasis and interpretation, in which the thesis is stated or implied that capitalism has been fundamentally transformed and that its class structure is being eroded or rendered innocuous: C. A. R. Crosland, *The future of socialism*, 1956; J. Strachey, *Contemporary capitalism*, 1956; T. H. Marshall, *Citizenship and social class*, 1950; D. Butler and R. Rose, *The British general election of 1959*, 1960; M. Abrams *et al.*, *Must Labour lose?* 1960; F. Zweig, *The worker in an affluent society*, 1961; R. Dahrendorf, *Class and class conflict in industrial society*, 1959; J. K. Galbraith, *American capitalism*, 1956; D. Bell, *The end of ideology*, 1961; K. Mayer, 'Diminishing class differentials in the United States', *Kyklos*, vol. 12, no. 4, 1959; R. A. Nisbet, 'The decline and fall of social class', *Pacific Sociolog. Rev.*, Spring 1959. This is only a small, and in some respects haphazard, selection; but it illustrates varying expressions of a thesis which has been postulated, or simply assumed as self-evident, in a great deal of recent socio-political commentary.

In so far as inequalities remain in the chances of wealth, health, security and individual advancement, these disparities lose their psychological (and, it is often implied, their moral) force as sources of conflict because, with steadily rising levels of living and a widening base of common rights of 'citizenship', their effects are confined to a continuously narrowing area of life. Analysis and speculation concerning the cultural, psychological and political repercussions of these changes have, of course, focused primarily on the manual working class, whose homogeneity and distinctive character, it is argued, are being eroded. Among manual workers, according to one interpretation, old loyalties of class are being replaced by new pre-occupations with status: a former unity of industrial and political interest is dispelled by a growing sensitivity to invidious distinctions of social prestige and subtle variations in the styles of life, by which everyday patterns of social acceptance and rejection are symbolized. Alternatively, workers' aspirations are seen to focus more and more narrowly upon the home and the immediate family, a concern with material achievement predominating that involves little or no concomitant preoccupation with the rituals of status or with the ideological orientations of class. In either version, loyalties of the world of work are replaced by loyalties of the hearth; the values and perspectives of the labour market are replaced by those of the consumers' market; a faith in collective action is replaced by a reliance on individual achievement or family security; in short, an ethos traditionally thought of as middle class is assumed to be spreading widely among manual workers. In addition, it is sometimes argued or implied, new dividing lines of cultural distinction or political tension are coming to the fore which bear no relation to the old divisions of economic class or social status: for instance, between adults and adolescents, the latter inhabiting a distinctive 'teen-age culture' of their own; between 'high-brows' or 'egg-heads' and the 'masses', irrespective of social position; between the old, the retired and those living on fixed incomes, on the one hand, and earners – employers and employees alike – on the other hand; between people in their role as producers and (somewhat schizophrenically, it would seem) in their role as consumers; between professionals and 'organization men' in both private and public administration; and so on.

The general tenor of these arguments is familiar; the balance within them between truth and falsehood, fact and speculation, plausibility and implausibility, much less so.

1. *Inequalities of Wealth*

In its simplest form, the 'post-capitalist' thesis postulates a continuous tendency towards the reduction of inequalities in the distribution of income and wealth.[1] In particular, it is pointed out, incomes as recorded in the reports of tax authorities and official surveys have shown a fairly marked convergence towards the middle ranges since the late 1930s. This argument can be challenged on two major scores. The first, as critics both in Britain and in the United States have emphasized, is that in part at least the reduction in measured income inequality merely reflects an increased use of devices to reduce the heavier tax liabilities of the wartime and post-war period. Such devices involve the conversion of real income into forms which

[1] The discussion in this section draws, *inter alia*, on the following analyses of trends in the distribution of income and wealth: for Britain, H. F. Lydall, 'The long-term trend in the size distribution of incomes', *J. Royal Statist. Soc.*, series A, vol. 122, no. 1, 1959; *idem, British incomes and savings*, 1955; *idem* and D. G. Tipping, 'The distribution of personal wealth in Britain', *Bull. Oxford Univ. Inst. Statistics*, Feb. 1961; J. A. Brittain, 'Some neglected features of Britain's income levelling', *Amer. Econ. Rev.*, May 1960; J. L. Nicholson, 'Redistribution of income in the United Kingdom', in C. Clark and D. Stuvel (eds.), *Income and wealth: series X*, 1964; R. M. Titmuss, 'The social division of welfare', in his *Essays on the welfare state*, 1958; T. Lynes, *National assistance and national prosperity*, 1962; for the United States, S. Kusnetz and E. Jenks, *Shares of upper income groups in income and savings*, 1953; R. J. Lampman, *The share of top wealth holders in national wealth, 1922–1956*; H. F. Lydall and J. B. Lansing, 'A comparison of the distribution of personal income and wealth in the United States and Great Britain', *Amer. Econ. Rev.*, March 1959; G. Kolko, *Wealth and power in America*, 1962; H. P. Miller, *Trends in the incomes of families and persons in the United States, 1947 to 1960*, 1963; *idem, Rich man, poor man*, 1964.

escape normal rates of income tax – and which do not appear as income in the usual sources of information. There are no means of assessing the full amount of income which thus goes unrecorded. But since such devices are more readily available to those with relatively high incomes in general, and to private business in particular, the net result is an understatement of income inequality in current data.[1] In fact, the few attempts made to adjust the data, in such a way as to make allowance for some of the distortions resulting from tax evasive devices, have indicated a much milder redistribution of effective income than usually assumed – and one confined largely or exclusively to the 1940s.

The second objection relates to this last point. Even when no allowance is made for the effects of tax evasion, such reduction in the inequality of incomes as can be traced in both British and American analyses is in the main a phenomenon of the Second World War and the years immediately around it. Signs of any consistent narrowing of income disparities in the recorded data during the decades before then are slight and uncertain; and if account is taken of the probability that means of tax evasion were further developed and more elaborately institutionalized in the 1950s, this last decade or so may well have witnessed a slight regression towards a distribution of effective income more unequal than in the 1940s. This may remain uncertain. But it is clear that such reductions of income inequality as have occurred are both limited in extent, and very largely the result of the special demands of the wartime economy and of policies introduced at or around the time of the war.

There are factors, it is true, which might be expected to make for a general, longer-term trend towards income equalization: the decreased proportion of unskilled and casual workers in the labour force, as well as other changes in occupational structure; diminished pay differentials of skill, sex and age; an increased progression in the rates of income tax. In the

[1] For a detailed examination of the variety of devices available for tax evasion in Britain, see R. M. Titmuss, *Income distribution and social change*, 1962.

latter case, however, the redistributive effects are limited – perhaps indeed neutralized – by the continued importance of non-progressive forms of taxation, by the regressive operation of income tax allowances, and by the adoption of tax evasive devices.[1] In general, moreover, except in the 1940s the redistributive effects of these and other factors seem not to have been sufficient substantially to outweigh other long-run factors working in the opposite direction: among these, the increased proportion of old and retired people in the population, coupled with the fact that – at least in Britain – the real incomes of retired people dependent on public support have not kept up with general increases in income. This might seem to suggest a shift in the nature of income inequality – from disparities between classes and occupations to disparities between age groups. Indeed, such an interpretation is frequently implied, and fits in with the general thesis of a dissolving class structure. But it is essentially misleading. Poverty in old age is not a general phenomenon of the retired – but of those who in retirement have neither property income nor the proceeds of private (though tax-supported) pension schemes to rely on. The burden of poverty – on a contemporary definition of the term – has been shifted progressively into the tail-end of working class and lower middle class life; but it remains a problem of those classes.

The inequality of incomes is thus maintained in part through differential access to fringe benefits and tax-free sources of income generally. Old disparities take on new forms appropriate to the corporate economy of the mid-twentieth century. But, despite a drop during the 1940s in the reported ratio of income from capital to earned income, property ownership remains a potent, direct source of income inequality; especially so, if regard is paid to effective rather than nominal in-

[1] Some remarkable recent calculations suggest that, both in Britain and the United States, there may be hardly any progression in the proportionate incidence of all forms of taxation combined as between different levels of income. See Clark and Peters, 'Income redistribution: some international comparisons', in Clark and Stuvel (eds.), *op. cit.* (footnote 1 on page 80 above).

come. And the distribution of private property remains strikingly unequal. In Britain in the mid-1950s, two-fifths of all private property were estimated to be in the hands of only 1 per cent of the adult population, four-fifths in the hands of only 10 per cent. Concentration was still more extreme forty years earlier; but such diffusion as has taken place – and the estimate may overstate its extent – has only marginally affected the bulk of the population. Legal ownership of private corporate business is especially highly concentrated, four-fifths of all share capital being held by only 1 per cent of the adult population, and nearly all the rest by another 9 or 10 per cent. The concentration of private property in the United States is not quite so extreme–the result in part, no doubt, of a wider diffusion of home ownership and a rather larger surviving element of small-scale enterprise, especially farming; but it is still very marked. In the middle 1950s, 1 per cent of the adult population owned a quarter of all private property. Moreover, the American figures show no substantial and consistent decline in the unequal distribution of property over time; and despite a slightly greater diffusion of shareholding, the concentration of legal ownership of private business corporations follows much the same general pattern as in Britain.[1]

Thus the argument that a continuous trend towards income equalization and a wide diffusion of property are dissolving the class structure of capitalist society can hardly be sustained. Nor, therefore, can any weakening of the 'radical consciousness' be attributed to such forces. This is not to say that the significance of the economic divisions characteristic of capitalism remains unchanged. It is obvious that the much milder character of the trade cycle since the 1930s has reduced the insecurities of working class life – even though the manual worker is still more exposed to the risk of short-time working and of redundancy, cyclical or technological, than others; and even though unemployment has increased in the last decade, especially in the United States. It is clear, too, that the extension of general social services – while their redistributive effects

[1] See also E. B. Cox, *Trends in the distribution of stock ownership*, 1963; and the references in footnote 1 on page 97 below.

are commonly exaggerated – has released personal income for expenditure in other fields, shifting the effect of income differentials from the 'more essential' towards the 'less essential' areas of consumption. Even so, such enlargement of the basic rights of 'citizenship' has been neither an automatic nor a continuous process. In the recent history of both Britain and the United States, it is essentially a phenomenon of the 1930s and the 1940s. The last decade and more have seen little or no extension of such policies: in Britain, indeed, regression in some respects; while in the United States measures introduced primarily during the New Deal have left vast areas of basic social security or insecurity – health and housing in particular – to the more or less unrestricted play of market forces, property interests and private charity, in a manner reminiscent of the late nineteenth century Britain.

The mitigation of the effects of inequality through an extension of citizenship rights and economic security has thus depended – as it does in the future – on the assertion of a 'radical consciousness'. Overall levels of living have, of course, also risen, as a consequence of forces of a more continuous and less directly policy-determined character: the long-run, though intermittent, upward trend in productivity; and (a factor often neglected) the spread of the small-family pattern, involving a curtailment of some of the traditional fluctuations in the economic cycle of the working class family, and the shift of relative poverty largely to a single phase of the cycle, that of old age.

In short, inequalities of income and property have been only marginally reduced. But they operate in areas of expenditure increasingly removed from those of bare subsistence living, and against a background of generally rising average levels of real income. It may well be, therefore, that the persistent inequalities of wealth are coming to assume a different significance in the eyes of those who remain 'more unequal than others'. The visibility of economic inequality may diminish, obscured by past and prospective rises in the overall levels of living. Persistent disparities may be veiled, too, if their effects are felt increasingly late in life rather than in the early stages of a worker's career. Resentment may diminish, or change in character, as inequality is relevant more to the 'frills' of life than to essentials of survival.

Arguments to this effect are, in fact, implicit or explicit in a number of the more sophisticated versions of the 'post-capitalist' thesis. They point, not so much to a transformation of the economic structure of class as such, as to a transformation of the conditions relevant to the formation and direction of class consciousness: it is not the inequalities of class that have been reduced, but their 'transparency'. But in this shift from an economic and institutional analysis of class structure to a psychological analysis of class perceptions, assumptions are involved which are neither self-evidently true nor yet often enough made explicit. Of these, the most central – and a very simple one – is the premise that what the observer regards as 'frills' will also generally be so regarded. It cannot be realistically denied–though it may be forgotten–that 'standards' of living, in the sense of notions about what constitutes a tolerable or reasonable level of living, are not fixed, but tend to rise *more or less* concomitantly with actual levels of living. The logic of the 'post-capitalist' thesis then requires that this should be 'less' rather than 'more'. It implies the assumption, either that the rise in actual levels of living generally keeps one step ahead of, or on a par with, the rise in the standards or expectations which people set themselves; or that any discrepancy in the other direction will be insufficient to generate the degree of tension which in the past was a major component of political radicalism and industrial militancy. Indeed, the argument that class consciousness among working class people is being progressively replaced by an increased concern with status, or by a 'home-centred' preoccupation with sheer material achievement, appears to postulate that any such excess of expectations over the level of living which can actually be achieved at any given time will provide, not a potential for social protest, but only an incentive for further individual effort within the limits of the existing economic and political order – a spur to efficient conformity.

Such postulates and assumptions, however, need much more

explicit statement and concrete evidence than they have hitherto been given. Political trends in the post-war Western world
are no proof of their accuracy; for those trends cannot be
described simply in terms of a progressive reduction of class
conflict; nor, in so far as they can, are they amenable to
plausible explanation only in terms of the kind of arguments
outlined above. Again, no proof is provided by the numerous
studies, impressionistic observations and inspired conjectures
which have pointed to heightened material aspirations and an
increased adoption of 'middle class' standards of living among
workers. Doubt arises, not about the general truth of such observations, but about their interpretation. The notion that
workers must somehow 'catch' middle class values and orientations when they adopt spending habits that earlier were possible
only for middle class people is, of course, naïve in the extreme.[1] It is hardly necessary to belabour the point that the
process by which the luxuries of yesterday become the necessities of today, and in turn are replaced by new luxuries, is a
long-standing one, and one whose end does not seem in sight.
What is important, however, is that the process may be changing its character – and not necessarily in the directions assumed
in fashionable commentary. For it is arguable, indeed plausible,
that the luxuries of today are increasingly widely seen as the
necessities – not of tomorrow or a remoter future, but of
today also; that the prerogatives of one class are increasingly
demanded as the rights of all; in short, that the rate of increase in standards or expectations of living is accelerating
faster than the rate of increase in actual levels of living. Ordinary standards of aspiration may to a growing extent be set by
the levels in fact achieved only by the prosperous minority –
through direct comparison, or under the impact of advertising
and the mass media generally. Indeed, the dynamics of the contemporary capitalist economy requires such a sustained

[1] For a cogent critique of this and a number of other assumptions
embedded in the postulate of working class 'embourgoisement', see
D. Lockwood, 'The "new working class"', *European J. Sociology*,
vol. 1, no. 2, 1960; *idem* and J. Goldthorpe, 'Affluence and the British
class structure', *Sociolog. Rev.*, vol. 11, 1963.

pressure for consumption, as the defenders of advertising are prone to stress.

If this is so, then the nature of the class structure is certainly changing. The character of individual classes as 'quasi-communities', as partially separate sub-cultures each with its own fairly distinctive set of norms, standards and aspirations, will be loosening. Parochial, tradition-bound ceilings on hopes and demands in the various strata and groups of the working class will be in process of replacement by a common, 'middle class' yardstick of material achievement. Though not a new phenomenon, the probable contemporary acceleration of the process is significant. This, in a sense, is precisely what the apologists for contemporary capitalism claim is happening; yet the conclusions they draw need by no means follow. Precisely opposite conclusions are equally, or even more, plausible. For while the common 'middle class' yardstick is continually being raised, the levels of material achievement which it prescribes are perpetually, and by very definition, beyond the reach of the bulk of the population. The persistent economic inequalities thus guarantee a built-in tension between goals and the objective possibilities of achieving them. Whether tension is translated into political radicalism, or finds other forms of expression, is a separate question, and will be briefly discussed later. Its answer will depend in part on non-economic factors. But if the analysis is correct, it is clear that in at least one respect the potential for class conflict in contemporary capitalist societies, far from decreasing, may instead be growing.

2. Inequalities of Opportunity

It is a major theme of much contemporary commentary that Western societies are becoming steadily more 'fluid'. Not only is it believed that economic and other distinctions between the social strata are getting blurred; but movement between the strata is assumed to be more frequent than before, the opportunity for such movement more equally distributed. The internal homogeneity, the external distinctiveness and the hereditary character of the working class are being weakened, so it is argued – as individuals increasingly acquire rather than inherit their class position; and as in any case the continuous growth in numbers of white collar jobs provides new openings for upward social mobility. Assertions along these lines are common – even in general socio-political commentaries by social scientists who, in their role as technical specialists, must recognize the flimsiness of the evidence.[1]

For in fact the evidence flatly contradicts some of the formulations of this thesis; and it leaves others open to serious doubt. First, so far as can be seen, overall inequalities of opportunity for social ascent and descent have not been reduced in either Britain or the United States during this century – or, for that matter, in most other Western countries for which information is available. In comparison, for instance, with the son of a professional or a business executive, the odds against a manual worker's son achieving professional status, or just a middle-class job in general, have remained very much as they were at the turn of the century. More adequate data might alter the detailed picture, but hardly the general conclusion. Most of the evidence relates, of course, to the experience of people fairly well advanced in their careers – not to today's younger generation. But data on the distribution of educational opportunity in contemporary Britain, and on post-war trends of social mobility in the United States, do not suggest any prospect of striking changes in the future.[2]

Secondly, however, it may be argued that *relative* inequalities of opportunity between those born in different classes

[1] Among the studies on which the following discussion is based are: D. V. Glass (ed.), *Social mobility in Britain*, 1956; N. Rogoff, *Recent trends in occupational mobility*, 1953; articles in *Amer. Sociolog. Rev.* by E. Chinoy (April 1955), G. Lenski (Oct. 1958) and E. Jackson and H. J. Crockett (Feb. 1964); G. Carlsson, *Social mobility and class structure*, 1955; K. Svalastoga, *Prestige, class and mobility*, 1959; S. M. Miller, *Comparative social mobility*, vol. IX, no. 1 of *Current Sociology*, 1960; S. M. Lipset and R. Bendix, *Social mobility in industrial society*, 1959.

[2] See E. Jackson and H. J. Crockett, 'Occupational mobility in the United States', *Amer. Sociolog. Rev.*, Feb. 1964; and the references in footnote 1 on page 90 below.

matter less than *absolute* chances of advancement: the absolute chance, say, which a working class boy has of climbing out of the class in which he starts life. If changes in the occupational structure (or other changes) substantially increase such absolute chances of upward mobility – even if the same changes improve the career prospects of those born higher up the social scale, and relative opportunity thus remains as unequal as before – this could be significant in reducing the degree to which working class status is, and appears to be, permanent and hereditary. In fact, shifts in occupational structure have occurred, and are still occurring, which could appear to justify some such expectations. The general consequences of these shifts need separate discussion. But their net effect on social mobility has been to increase upward movement no more than at most rather marginally. The evidence is patchy and not all of a piece. Nevertheless, there has been no sign of any marked expansion in the chances of climbing up the social scale.

This is not to say that the Western capitalist countries are 'closed' societies – Britain any more than the United States, despite the old stereotypes. There is a good deal of movement of individuals between the different strata, even though much of this movement covers fairly short distances in social space, involves shifts within either the manual or the non-manual group far more often than between them, and is characterized by sharp and persistent inequalities in the distribution of opportunities. The point is that, partially 'open' as they are, these industrial societies have not become *more* open during this century. Factors which might have been expected to alter rates of mobility over time seem either to have been insignificant in effect, or to have cancelled each other out. Educational opportunities, for example, have been extended. But their extension, in large measure, has benefited all classes. Inequalities of educational opportunity remain marked – at the higher levels of education generally provided today in comparison with the past. The educational qualifications normally required at any given point of the occupational scale have simply been raised. It is true that the overall expansion of education has been accompanied by some reduction in the inequalities of educational opportunity. But this – a slow trend, so far as Britain is concerned, and one not noticeably accelerated after 1944 – has occurred to a more limited degree than is usually assumed; so limited, that its consequences have evidently been roughly neutralized by concomitant restrictions on social mobility through channels other than the educational system.[1] These restrictions are often forgotten; but the increasing emphasis on the role of education in social recruitment is a direct reflection of them. In particular, with the professionalization, bureaucratization and automation of work, appointment to jobs in the middle and higher reaches of the occupational scale comes to depend more on school, college and university qualifications than on personal qualities and experience acquired at work. The frequency of social mobility has not been significantly increased; but its incidence is steadily more confined to a single phase of the life cycle. If the individual is to be socially mobile, he must be so during his years of formal education: the chances of promotion or demotion, once he has entered on his adult working career, are almost certainly narrowing. The position of the adult manual worker – and to a growing extent, that of the routine grade clerical worker – becomes a more, not a less, permanent one.[2]

[1] See A. Little and J. H. Westergaard, 'The trend of class differentials in educational opportunity in England and Wales'. *Brit. J. Sociology*, Dec. 1964. See also the various major special studies of the distribution of educational opportunity in post-war Britain: J. Floud *et. al.*, *Social class and educational opportunity*, 1956; R. K. Kelsall, *Report on an enquiry into applications for admission to universities*, 1957; Ministry of Education, Central Advisory Council, *Early leaving*, 1954; *idem*, *15 to 18*, 1959–60 (Crowther report); Committee on Higher Education, *Higher education: report* and *Appendices I and II*, 1963; and especially, J. W. B. Douglas, *The home and the school*, 1964. Cf. also D. V. Glass, 'Education and social change in modern England' in M. Ginsberg (ed.), *Law and opinion in England in the 20th Century*, 1959. For some United States data, see, e.g., D. Wolfle, *America's resources of specialized talent*, 1954.

[2] Evidence suggesting a decline over time in the proportion of industrial managers or directors who reached their positions by promotion from low-grade clerical or manual jobs can be found for Britain in: Acton Society Trust, *Management succession*, 1956; R. V. Clements, *Managers: a study of their careers in industry*, 1958; C.

Nevertheless, it might be argued, this very change in the character of social mobility may alter people's perceptions of the chances of advancement. Mobility becomes more of an institutionalized process. The educational system is geared to it. Career opportunities become more predictable, as they come to depend more on a formalized kind of scholastic achievement. 'Elbows', 'string-pulling', connections and luck will matter less. In consequence, the chances of rising in the social scale may *seem* to be greater, even though they are not; and failure may be accepted with more resignation, if it is the result of a 'fair' process of selection. The argument, however, is double-edged. Failure may be the more unacceptable, if accepting it means to recognize one's intellectual 'inferiority'. Moreover, the very institutionalization of education as the royal road to success is likely to increase expectations to the point where they will come into conflict with the harsh reality of existing limitations on opportunity. There again, the question turns on psychological imponderables, about which very little is known. But there is good reason to believe that the demand for education is spreading well down the social scale. In part, indeed, this is a logical reaction to the growing importance of formal education as the main channel of social mobility: as the adult worker's hopes of promotion for himself become still more evidently unreal, aspirations focus instead upon the children's prospects. Be that as it may, such heightened recognition of the importance of education is another example of a weakening of the old cultural distinctions between the classes. But precisely as workers increasingly share 'middle class' aspirations for the education and future careers of their children, so the existing limitations and persistent inequalities of educational opportunity must result in the frustration of those aspirations as the

Erickson, *British industrialists: steel and hosiery, 1850–1950*, 1959. The Civil Service has shown increased recruitment of administrative class officials by promotion from the lower ranks (R. K. Kelsall, *Higher civil servants in Britain*, 1955), but is probably a special case. R. Bendix, *Work and authority in industry*, 1963, *inter alia* summarizes some American data on trends in the recruitment of industrial management.

common experience. Such frustration may be the harder to bear, because the condemnation of both parents and children to permanently inferior status is more final and irreversible than before.

The strength of the various factors involved is still unknown. The balance of probabilities, and the forms in which frustrated aspirations might find expression, are thus uncertain. Yet the conclusion stands that in this field, too, the potential for social protest is at least as likely to be growing as to be declining. Contemporary capitalism generates a tension between aspirations increasingly widely shared and opportunities which, by the very nature of the class structure, remain restricted and unequally distributed.

3. *Changes in Occupational Structure*

The share of white collar jobs in total employment has been growing throughout this century. Commentators have often exaggerated the implications of this trend hitherto. They have tended to underplay the facts, for instance, that the very marked 'white collar trend' in the United States in large measure has reflected a general shift from agricultural to urban employment; that the occupational composition of the male labour force has been very much less affected than that of the female labour force, within which 'white blouse' work has replaced domestic service as the dominant form of employment; and that the expansion of the 'tertiary sector' of the economy has increased the relative number, not only of white collar jobs, but also to a small extent of non-domestic service jobs, many of them low-paid and demanding little skill. It is true, nevertheless, that shifts in occupational structure overall have involved a fall in the share of unskilled and casual work, and a rise in the share of both semi-skilled manual and various kinds of black-coated work.[1] Moreover, much of the com-

[1] Shifts in occupational structure can be more accurately traced for the United States than for Britain; see, e.g. U.S. Bureau of Census, *Occupational trends in the United States, 1900–1950*, 1958. Official British classifications of occupations have changed a good deal over

mentary has been directed to the future rather than the past. Not only will the 'white collar trend' continue for some time; but automation in industry is likely to produce a sizeable growth in the numbers of skilled workers and technicians, in place of that growth in the numbers of semi-skilled workers which in the past has been associated with the mechanization of industry and its conversion to conveyor-belt production. These prospects have been widely hailed as yet another source of capitalist social stability: a strengthening of the centre in place of 'polarization'.

There is, however, considerable room for doubt about such complacently enthusiastic interpretations.[1] The balance between the two trends – of automation, with its increased demand for skill and technical expertise, and of continuing mechanization of the older kind, with its increased employment of semi-skilled workers – is still uncertain, and may remain so for some time to come. The adoption of automation is likely to be a slow and uneven business. The relevant criteria, of course, will be profitability, not work satisfaction through 'job enlargement' for its own sake. Since capitalist economic organization provides no mechanisms for the sharing of gains and losses, resistance to automation from small business may be, and from trade unions will be, considerable. Labour resistance, indeed, is certain to grow if the American pattern of recent years spreads – the paradox of high unemployment rates persisting during a boom. There is a danger here for the working class movement: of a division between those – the unskilled and workers in the declining industries – most affected

[1] The work of G. Friedmann includes admirably balanced and careful assessments of the implications of technological change for labour; see his *Industrial society : the emergence of the human problems of automation*, 1955, and *The anatomy of work*, 1962.

time. But it is fairly clear that the approximate two-to-one ratio of manual to non-manual workers in the male population of 1951 represented only a rather limited relative decline of the manual element during this century. When the relevant 1961 Census figures are available they may show some acceleration of the rate of decline. For one estimate of the growth of 'middle class' occupations, see A. L. Bowley, *Wages and income of the United Kingdom since 1860*, 1937.

by technological unemployment, and those whose labour is at a high premium in the changing market. But the unpredictability, and the potentially sweeping character, of the incidence and effects of automation may reduce that danger, if not eliminate it. Technological innovation thus generates tension of the very kind that, allegedly, is a matter of he past. And since the source of such tension is inherent in capitalist economic organization, it can only be overcome through extensive public intervention of the kind that, allegedly again, is a contemporary irrelevancy. If both the fruits and the sacrifices involved in automation are to be shared, they must be socialized: the case against private property and private economic control is underlined. Technological innovation may be inhibited, too, as it is at present, by shortages of skilled labour and technical expertise. But in so far as these shortages are overcome through extension of education and training, the premiums which the new skills can command in the labour market will diminish. Whether 'job enlargement' through automation will decrease political radicalism by increasing work satisfaction is unpredictable; for the relationship between work satisfaction and class consciousness remains as yet virtually unexplored. But in economic terms, any 'middle class' potential of the new 'aristocracy of labour' rests on conditions in the labour market which happen now to be favourable, but which may well not continue to be so.

In general, the 'optimistic' evaluations of current and prospective shifts in occupational structure are based on a static view of the relative rewards, prestige and conditions associated with different occupations. Premiums for scarce skills are implicitly assumed to persist, even if the scarcity itself is unlikely to do so. White collar work is implicitly assumed to retain its traditional status and characteristics, even though the expansion of such work is almost certainly also changing its traditional features. The rationalization, mechanization and perhaps even the partial automation of clerical work will accentuate the division between controllers and supervisors, on the one hand, and routine black-coated operatives, on the other. If so, the latter increasingly are reduced to the status of bureaucratic counterparts of the semi-skilled manual workers of industry.

There has, no doubt, already been a long-standing trend in that direction, but a slow one. It is likely to be accelerated, and to gain greater significance, as the traditional compensation of routine clerical work disappears: that of a reasonable chance of promotion. The forces which now tend to block previous channels of upward mobility for those who start their careers in low-grade white collar jobs have already been discussed. Whether these and related changes will – at last – result in a social and political identification of routine clerical workers with the manual working class is a moot point. Their long history of middle-class associations allows room for doubt.[1] The changes in their status, conditions and prospects could produce other reactions – in particular circumstances, as recent historical precedents suggest, considerably less pleasant ones. The point remains that to interpret the continuing expansion of white collar work as a uniform strengthening of the 'stable' middle strata of society is to apply a yardstick of decreasing contemporary relevance.

4. The Distribution of Power

The controversy concerning the power structure of contemporary capitalism has revolved around two related conservative theories. The first is that of the 'managerial revolution' – although the interpretations of this current in the post-war era have carried few, if any, of the pessimistic overtones which earlier were expressed in Burnham's book of that title.[2]

[1] D. Lockwood's The black-coated worker: a study in class consciousness, 1958, is an acute and elegant analysis of the roots of white collar workers' longstanding social and political separation from the manual working class. See also C. W. Mills, White collar, 1956.

[2] J. Burnham, in The managerial revolution, 1941, drew in part on earlier work suggesting a drift of business control into the hands of salaried 'controllers': notably A. A. Berle and G. C. Means, The modern corporation and private property, 1932. Evidence that the formal divorce between ownership and control had been greatly exaggerated was produced by the U.S. Temporary National Economic Committee, especially in its Monographs no. 29, 1940, and no. 30, 1941. (See also, for Britain, P. S. Florence, The logic of British and American industry, rev. ed., 1961.) The most sophisticated, and at the

The second can be crudely categorized as the theory of 'countervailing power' or 'pluralism'. Each needs examination here, even though brevity demands some simplification of the arguments.

The theory of the managerial revolution in its post-war versions postulates that, with an increasing diffusion of stock ownership on many hands, effective control of corporate business is exercised by non-owning executives. Since the power of these 'managers' derives from their positions in the bureaucratic hierarchies of business, not from wealth, their interests and motives differ from those of the older owner-entrepreneurs. Their control will be directed less to profit maximization as such than to other purposes, which may conflict with profit maximization: the maintenance and growth of the corporations, as an end in itself; the interests of employees, customers, the public at large, as well as of shareholders. If there are dangers, these arise from the concentration of power common to all bureaucratic organization: they are unrelated to the distribution of private wealth. In any case, the controlling 'managers' form – not so much a new ruling class, as Burnham feared – but a profession whose ethic is one of service. So private enterprise has been tamed from within. Nationalization has become an irrelevancy, it is concluded – though this conclusion seems hard to square with the implication of the theory that private ownership, in the form of shareholding, no longer has any obvious function: profits distributed as dividends can be no incentive to managerial efficiency.

So much for the theory. In fact, however, this analysis glosses over the real nature of the distribution of legal ownership. For shareholders – themselves only a very small fraction of the total population – are sharply divided into the many with little and the few with much. It is true that diffusion has increased. The many own a somewhat higher, and the few a somewhat lower, proportion of total voting stock than in the

---

same time 'optimistic', post-war British version of the thesis of managerial control is C. A. R. Crosland, *The future of socialism*, 1956 (reproduced in cruder form in the Labour Party's policy pamphlet, *Industry and society*, 1957).

past. But the distinction remains. Stock ownership is still very highly concentrated. And precisely because of diffusion, large stockholders – companies or individuals – need a diminishing share of the total to exercise effective influence on policy. Such influence need not be – and evidently often is not – exercised through direct participation in formal control. Instead, it may operate through a natural identity of interest between controllers and large stockholders. To assume such an identity of interest is not to resort to semi-metaphysical speculation. For the controllers – directors and top executives, in whose hands the major, strategic policy decisions lie – are, in fact, owners of large stockholdings themselves: the wealthiest shareholders of any identifiable groups in society. Their holdings may be distributed over a number of companies; their share of the voting stock in those corporations where they hold office is usually relatively small – though considerable in absolute terms. But it is hard to believe that, as wealthy stockholders, they voluntarily allow their policies to be dictated by considerations conflicting with those of long-run profit maximization. The contemporary formulations of management ideology certainly refer to the social responsibilities of corporate business – and no doubt do so without conscious hypocrisy. But there seems to be no evidence to suggest that the ultimate yardstick by which policies are determined, and 'social responsibilities' defined, is other than one of profit maximization. Policies are likely to be more efficiently and 'professionally' directed towards that end than was the case with the smaller-scale enterprise of classical nineteenth-century capitalism. Profitability may also be assessed over a longer time-span – as it doubtless is, too, by large shareholders and corporation executives alike, in comparison with small shareholders. But for an inherent conflict of interest between large shareholders and controllers there is no plausible case on the evidence. In societal perspective, the two overlap to the point of near-identity: private wealth is not divorced from private corporate power.[1]

[1] Evidence on these various points will be found, *inter alia*, in: P. S. Florence, *The ownership, control and success of large companies,*

But if capitalist enterprise has not been tamed from within, it may still have been tamed from without. Such a postulate is the crux of the theory of 'countervailing power' in its different versions. Power, it is argued, is distributed among a variety of groups. The alignment of these groups with each other will shift from issue to issue. The result is a general, if not necessarily a static, balance of diffused power, in which no single set of interests is dominant. Bureaucratic rigidity, the 'iron law of oligarchy', may tend to separate leadership from rank and file within the individual groups and organizations; but such inequalities of power would cut across the traditional inequalities of class, property and wealth.[1]

[1]'Pluralist' interpretations of the distribution of power, often in recent formulations accompanied by an idealization of the 'politics of consensus' (a concept which is virtually a contradiction in terms), have been most explicit in American socio-political analysis. See, e.g. J. K. Galbraith, *American capitalism: the concept of countervailing power*, 1956; D. Bell, *The end of ideology*, (new ed.) 1961; S. M. Lipset, *Political man*, (new ed.) 1963; and several 'pluralist' interpretations of, or commentaries on, the power structure of local communities, e.g. N. W. Polsby, *Community power and political theory*, 1963; R. A. Dahl, *Who governs?* 1961; E. C. Banfield, *Political influence*, 1961; *idem* and J. Q. Wilson, *City politics*, 1963. In Britain, somewhat similar assumptions and preoccupations have been expressed or implied, e.g. in C. A. R. Crosland, *The future of socialism*, 1956; S. E. Finer, 'The political power of private capital', *Sociolog. Rev.*, Dec. 1955, July 1956; *idem*, *Anonymous empire*, 1958; R. T. McKenzie, *British political parties*, (new ed.) 1964. Among general critiques, see, e.g. C. W. Mills, *The power elite*, 1957; T. Bottomore, *Elites and society*, 1964; R. Presthus, *Men at the top*, 1964; S. W.

1961; H. Parkinson, *Ownership of industry*, 1951; L. R. Klein *et al.*, 'Savings and finances of the upper income classes', *Bull. Oxford Univ. Inst. Statistics*, Nov. 1956; M. Barratt-Brown, 'The controllers', *Universities and Left Rev.*, Autumn 1958; D. Villarejo, 'Stock ownership and the control of corporations', *New University Thought*, Autumn 1961, Winter 1962; F. X. Sutton *et al.*, *The American business creed*, 1956; as well as in the references to property distribution given in the footnotes on pp. 80 and 83. For general criticisms of the thesis of managerial control, see also, e.g. P. M. Sweezy, 'The illusion of the managerial revolution', in his *The present as history*, 1953; C. W. Mills, *The power elite*, 1957; R. Bellamy, 'Mr. Strachey's guide to contemporary capitalism', *Marxist Qtly.*, Jan. 1957.

It is clear that there is an element of truth in such a description. It should also be clear that the element is no more than the obvious: there is no *total* concentration of power in the hands of any single group. The 'theory' may provide something of a 'conceptual framework' for analysis of the distribution of power; it is no substitute for such analysis. For it leaves two crucial questions unanswered. First, how far do the various formally separate groups among which power is distributed represent in fact, not distinct and competing interests, but broadly similar interests in different institutional dress? Closer analysis may reveal, not a scattered diversity of influences, but a broad clustering of major sources of pressure. Secondly, once such major clusters of interests have been identified, at what point between them has the balance of power been struck? To answer these questions requires examination of the composition of the various *élites* and pressure groups in the main institutional fields of power, to establish the degree of identity between them in terms of social recruitment, everyday associations and politico-economic orientations. But it also requires direct examination of decisions made and policies executed. This in turn cannot – as is often assumed – be confined merely to establishing the outcome of conflicts between expressly formulated alternative policies and views: to seeing whether the ultimate decision in particular cases is closer to the explicit proposals of this or that party to the conflict. For those proposals themselves have been formulated within the limits of a 'realistic', tactical appraisal of the likely outcome, and within the limits of that institutionalization of conflict which is the essence of contemporary politics. Such institutionalization means that conflict is regulated through a series of compromises which define, not only the means and procedures of conflict, but also the area of conflict at any given time. Compromise thus enters into the initial determination of the limits of controversy: only a small band of the full range of alternative

Rousseas and J. Farganis, 'American politics and the end of ideology', *Brit. J. Sociology*, Dec. 1963. See also the commentary by A. W. Kornhauser, ' "Power elite" or "veto groups",' in S. M. Lipset and L. Lowenthal (eds.), *Culture and social character*, 1961.

policies is effectively ventilated and disputed. Indeed, on some issues the band may be so narrow that decisions seem not to be 'made' at all – they just flow automatically from the 'climate of opinion' formed by the initial compromise. To determine the locus of power, therefore, one must examine the nature of that compromise itself: the location, within the full range of alternatives which represent the long-term, objective interests of the contending groups, of that narrower span of policy alternatives to which controversy is effectively, if perhaps temporarily, confined.

If these criteria are applied to contemporary Britain, it is clear that power is not in important respects diffused among a multitude of diverse interest groups, each with a distinct and separate identity. There is instead a clustering of power. The dominant grouping is that of a small, homogeneous *élite* of wealth and private corporate property – politically entrenched in the leadership of the Conservative Party; strongly represented in, or linked with, a variety of influential public and private bodies; assured of the general support of the press, if not at the overt political level of the publicly controlled mass media; its members sharing for a large part a common, exclusive educational background, and united by fairly close ties of kinship and everyday association. The broad contours of this *élite* are familiar from a good deal of recent research, the general similarity of which with pre-war evidence points to a strong degree of continuity. It is an *élite* which, while its economic base is that of financial and industrial capital, yet has its own uniquely British features, in part inherited from the agrarian-mercantile nobility and gentry of the pre-industrial era. It is neither a tightly closed group – indeed, much of its viability may derive from its absorptive capacity – nor a monolithically united one. But internal divisions remain generally confined to particular issues, and do not develop into major fissures of a durable kind. The challenge to its power comes, not from within its own ranks, but from outside. This is the challenge presented by the labour movement: other possible sources of challenge are either minor and impermanent, or tend to be absorbed into the labour movement as the only effective channel of opposition in the long run.[1]

The rise of labour – which, in distinct contrast to the dominant conservative group, has a socially heterogeneous political leadership, but a pretty homogeneously working class mass support – has clearly imposed restraints upon the exercise of power by the primary *élite*. Since the war, especially, rights of property have been curtailed in certain fields, concepts of the public interest and of social welfare widened, areas of effective political conflict shifted leftwards, by comparison with the past. In very general terms these influences continue to operate whether or not the labour movement is in formal control of the government. The rightward swing in social and economic policy during most of the past thirteen years of Conservative government has certainly not been negligible. But the fact that the larger part of the measures introduced by Labour after the war remain more or less intact – and that some of them would have been at least partly matched by Conservative measures, had Labour not won a majority in 1945 – illustrates the limits imposed on the power of the main *élite* by the existence of a permanent opposition. Yet there is no 'equal' division of influence between the two groups. Labour remains in opposition even when, in constitutional terms, it forms the government. During the six years of its post-war Parliamentary majority to 1951, it continued to operate the existing machinery of government with few, if any, of such changes as radical policies would have required. Economic controls were exercised – as during the war – to a large extent through the agency of private business. Nationalization was confined to a limited, specialized and in part unprofitable field; it was implemented with little coherent conception of the use of nationalized enterprise as an instrument of public policy; the membership of the boards was drawn in large measure from private business; and their responsibility to the government,

---

[1] A great deal of the relevant evidence can be found in W. Guttsman, *The British political elite*, 1963. See also, e.g. C. S. Wilson and T. Lupton, 'The social background and connections of "top decision makers",' *Manchester School*, Jan. 1959.

Parliament and the public was left limited and ambiguous.[1] This is not to deny the very real achievements of the post-war Labour Government, or the genuine leftward shift which resulted. The point remains that the challenge presented by the labour movement has modified, but not radically curtailed, the power of the dominant *élite*, or the rights of private corporate property which are the economic source of that power. That this is largely the choice of the labour movement itself, the result of long-standing uncertainties of purpose on its part, does not alter the fact. The institutionalized compromise which characterizes the scene of political conflict has been drawn up at a point which still predominantly favours the interests of capital.

Those interests, however, are still more strongly favoured by the 'balance of power' in the United States. This is so evident that it might seem unnecessary to belabour the point. Yet it is a curious fact that support for the theory of countervailing power has been most strongly voiced by American commentators; and that a number of these in recent years have contrasted an allegedly 'pluralistic' pattern of diversified power in the United States with an *'elitist'* pattern in Britain where, it is argued, a concentration of power remains supported by widespread attitudes of deference to 'legitimate authority'.[2] That British social and political values include an element of such deference cannot be denied. But to use this element as the basis for a comprehensive characterization of the British scene,

[1] On the exercise of economic controls by the post-war Labour Government, and on nationalization, see: A. A. Rogow, *The Labour Government and British industry, 1945–50*, 1955; Acton Society Trust, *Studies in nationalized industry*, 1950–53; J. H. Smith and T. E. Chester, 'The distribution of power in nationalized industries'. *Brit. J. Sociology*, Dec. 1951; C. Jenkins, *Power at the top*, 1959; A. H. Hanson, *Parliament and public ownership*, 1961.

[2] See, e.g. S. M. Lipset, 'The value patterns of democracy', *Amer. Sociolog. Rev.*, Aug. 1963; H. H. Hyman, 'England and America: climates of tolerance and intolerance', in D. Bell (ed.), *The radical right*, 1963; E. A. Shils, *The torment of secrecy*, 1956; R. R. Alford, *Party and society*, 1963. The 'bible' of this school of interpretation of British politics appears to be W. Bagehot, *The English constitution*, 1872.

and a contrast with the American, involves the most flagrant absurdities. For to do so is to ignore the outstanding fact that in Britain the predominant power of private capital has been challenged by the labour movement, whose opposition finds institutionalized expression in the political as well as the industrial field. It is true that the effectiveness and radicalism of this challenge are weakened through a partial persistence of deference, in leadership and rank and file, to the forms and symbols of traditional authority. It is also true that the process by which the clash of interests has been institutionally limited involves a continual risk – as is evident today – of the reduction of the conflict between the parties to little more than a symbolic ritual. Even so, the challenge is there, as an actuality or as a potentiality which continues to colour British politics and condition the prospects of policy. This is so at least by comparison with the United States, where any such challenge is virtually absent from the political scene. The failure of the American labour movement to develop a permanent and coherent political arm is a well-known exception to the general pattern in the industrialized societies. Its causes have been long and widely debated.[1] Its effects are that the power of private property has been subjected to far fewer restrictions than generally elsewhere. This is evident, for instance, in such fields of everyday social welfare as housing, land use planning and medical care, where any measures proposed or adopted are conditioned by the initial assumption that entrenched rights of private ownership and private profit are sacrosanct to an extent inconceivable even to the conservative parties of most other advanced industrial capitalist societies. In so far as various interests and pressure groups participate in, or make their voices heard in, the making of decisions and the formulation of policies, they do so only within the context of that initial assumption. Such is the extent of 'pluralism'. The compromise has been struck at a point as yet a good deal to the right of the 'balance of power' in Britain; and in such a way that, outside the field of 'civil rights' at least, effective political

[1] See, e.g. D. D. Egbert and S. Persons (eds.), *Socialism and American life*, 1952.

controversy and social criticism have been reduced to a still narrower span than in Britain. Indeed, it is a feature of the currently fashionable idealization of the 'politics of consensus' – American in origin – to elevate the restriction of effective political debate to a virtue. The presence in Britain of a political labour movement, and also within that of a semi-institutionalized left wing minority, has, for all the inhibiting factors, kept the area of practical conflict, genuine debate and tolerated nonconformity still a good deal more open than in the United States.

5. *Class Culture and Class Solidarity*

Point for point the evidence underlines the same broad conclusion: the structural inequalities of capitalist society remain marked. Disparities of economic condition, opportunity and power persist – modified, if at all, only within fairly narrow limits. There is no built-in automatic trend towards diminishing class differentials. But it does not necessarily follow that the persistent, objective lines of class division will also be, or continue to be, the lines within which consciousness of class takes shape or across which conflict occurs. That there need be no such neat correspondence is very clear from the example of the United States. It is the claim of many contemporary commentators that Britain, and Western Europe generally, are now going the way of North America in this respect. Among arguments in support of this claim are those which stress a lessened significance or visibility of inequality – as the old insecurities of working class life are reduced or eliminated; as overall levels of living increase; as opportunities for individual social mobility, while not increased, become institutionalized through the system of formal education. The conclusion, as I have tried to show, in no obvious way follows from the facts. But other arguments have emphasized rather a general erosion of the cultural distinctiveness of working class life, and of those features of the local environment from which, it is assumed, class consciousness among workers has traditionally derived its strength. Old loyalties to kin, locality and traditional patterns of life are on the wane; and so, it has been implied (especially in contributions to the debate from the 'new left'), the basis for class cohesion and political radicalism is dissipated. A 'sense of classlessness' or of middle-class identification replaces former values of solidarity.[1]

Though the evidence is far from adequate, there is no reason to doubt that in a number of respects working class 'patterns of culture' are changing, and becoming less distinctive in the process. It seems reasonable to assume that those features of working class life will be weakening which, in the past, were conditioned primarily by low absolute levels of living, extreme insecurity and marked local or social isolation. There are indications in that direction.[2] Class differentials in mortality, for example, seem to have been diminishing at certain points, or assuming a more complex pattern than

[1] These assumptions have often been made in an implicit, rather than an explicit, fashion. See, however, S. Hall, 'A sense of classlessness', *Universities and Left Review*, Autumn 1958 (also the criticism by R. Samuel, 'Class and classlessness', *ibid.*, Spring 1959); F. Zweig, *The worker in an affluent society*, 1961; D. Butler and R. Rose, *The British general election of 1959*, 1960; R. Williams, *The long revolution*, 1961. In the background to this debate there have been such studies of, or commentaries upon, traditional working class 'community' life as M. Young and P. Willmott, *Family and kinship in East London*, 1957, and R. Hoggart, *The uses of literacy*, 1957. F. Pappenheim, *The alienation of modern man: an interpretation based on Marx and Tönnies*, 1959, is relevant to this debate at a much more abstract, general and theoretical level. See also footnote 1 on page 86.

[2] Evidence for some of the following points will be found in: General Register Office, *Registrar General's decennial supplement for England and Wales, 1951: occupational mortality*, 1954, 1958; J. N. Morris and J. A. Heady, 'Social and biological factors in infant mortality,' *Lancet*, 12th Feb.–12th March, 1955; A. J. Mayer and P. Hauser, 'Class differentials in expectation of life at birth', in R. Bendix and S. M. Lipset, *Class, status and power*, 1953; D. V. Glass and E. Grebenik, *The trend and pattern of fertility in Great Britain*, Royal Commission on Population Papers, vol. 6, 1954; Census of England and Wales, 1951, *Fertility report*, 1959; National Bureau Committee for Economic Research, *Demographic and economic change in developed countries*, 1958; R. Freedman *et al.*, *Family planning, sterility and population growth*, 1959; C. F. Westoff *et al.*, *Family growth in metropolitan America*, 1961.

before, although the relative disparities in infant mortality in Britain have hitherto remained remarkably constant. Class differentials in fertility have recently narrowed substantially in the United States and some other countries. British data have so far shown only the most uncertain of hints of a similar change; but it seems plausible that it may occur here, too. Indeed, it is not inconceivable that the familiar gradient of fertility may be reversed. If working class people increasingly adopt the same kind of material and educational aspirations as middle class people, while persistent inequalities prevent them from realizing those aspirations, they may reduce the size of their families below the middle class norm. There are signs of some such reversal in Norway, for example. Whatever the trends in fertility differentials, the absolute size of family has, of course, been considerably reduced in the working class, as it has in the middle class. This by itself has undoubtedly played a major part in transforming the general character of working class family life. A traditional urban British pattern of fairly strong extended ties of kinship, coupled with a rather marginal domestic role for the man within the nuclear family, may well have been the result of material poverty and economic insecurity, the sharp fluctuations in the economic cycle of the family associated with high fertility, and local isolation of working class communities. Though this pattern persists, it is giving way to one closer to contemporary middle class family norms. This process seems more likely to be a long-standing secular trend, resulting from the reduced significance of the underlying causes, than the product primarily of post-war suburbanization, as has been suggested. But suburbanization has also been pointed to as part of a more general change in working class residential distribution and conditions of life, to which wide significance has been attached. The closed, homogeneous, one-industry, one-class, one-occupation community, familiar from earlier industrialism, is no longer typical. Suburbs and new towns are taking the place of the old mining villages, textile districts and dockside areas. And, through these and other changes, the street, the pub, the working-men's club are losing their importance as centres of local social contact, in a world where working class families lead increasingly 'home-centred' lives.

There is as yet no certainty about the extent and pace of all such changes in working class culture and environment. The main dispute, however, is not about the facts, but about their implications. Sweeping social and political deductions have been drawn, with gay abandon but little documentation. Not only has it become almost fashionable to deplore the dilution of traditional working class culture *per se* – a reaction which reflects an odd, conservative nostalgia for a way of life moulded by insecurity, local seclusion and crude deprivation, both material and mental. But this 'cultural dilution' has also, not infrequently, come to be equated with an alleged decline of class consciousness, and its replacement by narrow preoccupations of status and 'respectability' or by sheer apathy. No substantial evidence has been offered for this equation: it has been assumed, not proven. Underlying it, there is commonly a premise which deserves explicit examination. This is an assumption that the kind of working class unity which finds expression in industrial, or more especially in political, action draws its nourishment from the simpler and more intimate loyalties of neighbourhood and kin. Consequently, it is postulated, as the latter are weakened so the former declines. The assumption is highly questionable. For it implies that the solidarity of class – which is societal in its sweep, and draws no nice distinctions between men of this place and that, this name and that, this dialect and that – is rooted in the kind of parochial solidarity which is its very antithesis. To doubt the implied identity between the two antitheses is not to deny that sectional loyalties of region and occupation have contributed in the past to the formation of wider loyalties of class; but the permanence of that contribution has depended upon a transcendence of the original narrow basis of solidarity. Thus the developing labour movement has in many cases drawn special strength from the workers of such locally cohesive, homogeneous communities as the mining valleys of Britain and the timber districts of Scandinavia (though not in this century, for instance, from the mill towns of Lancashire to any marked extent); and the industries located in communities of this kind are still characterized by a comparatively high incidence of strike action.[1] Yet, at the political level especially, the collective force of the labour movement grew precisely as the local isolation of these and other working class communities declined. The two trends are not just fortuitously coincidental, but logically related. For the growth of a nation-wide movement – uniting, say, miners of South Wales with shipyard workers of Clydeside and others throughout the country – entailed of necessity a widening of horizons, and the displacement (if not a total suppression) of local and sectional loyalties by commitment to a common aim, however uncertainly defined. In sociological jargon, the 'particularistic' ties of neighbourhood, kin and regional culture provide no adequate basis for the maintenance of the 'universalistic' loyalties involved in class political action.

This historical widening of once parochial horizons also entailed the progressive abandonment of aims and aspirations restricted by static, traditional definitions. Past experience and purely local criteria no longer set the limits to individual or collective ambition. The standards of comparison by which workers judged their own condition and their children's future increasingly were raised, increasingly were shared, and increasingly reflected the conditions and prospects which industrial capitalism offered the more prosperous minority. Working class adoption of 'middle class' aspirations is thus no new phenomenon. Nor therefore can the process in its contemporary dress, or the general attenuation of traditional working class culture of which it is part, be regarded as one which must necessarily induce social complacency and political paralysis. On the contrary, precisely because it involves an inbuilt discrepancy between common demands and the unequal distribution of means for their fulfilment, it provides a continuing potential for social protest; the more so, the more 'middle class' demands become the norm.

[1] See, e.g. C. Kerr and A. Siegel, 'The inter-industry propensity to strike,' in A. W. Kornhauser *et al.*, *Industrial conflict*, 1954.

6. *Prospects for the Future*

To say that there is such a potential for social protest is not to say that it will necessarily be converted into active political radicalism. The absence of any significant socialist working class movement in the United States, and the long-standing nature of the social perspectives with which this fact is associated, make any marked leftward trend there unlikely, at least for the present.[1] The prospects in Britain, and in Europe generally, are quite different, because labour and left-wing parties there provide an established channel for the political expression of social protest. Indeed, the debate of the last decade or so has been obscured, rather than illuminated, by the slapdash application of American analogies to the British political scene. It is of course possible here, too, that the sense of tension inherent in the contradiction between aspiration and opportunity may be dulled by overall 'affluence', by a general conviction that next year will bring what this year will not, or by such apparent complexity in the organization of society that the sources and mutual inter-connections of persistent inequalities become increasingly difficult to identify. But though this is possible, it is very far from certain. For one thing, our knowledge of the nature and interplay of the socio-psychological attitudes involved is virtually nil. What has passed for knowledge in the debate of recent years has been little more than a series of disguised guesses and assumptions. Secondly, overall affluence cannot be taken for granted. On the contrary, the insecurities and the haphazard distribution of gains and sacrifices associated with the very processes of economic expansion, industrial change and technological innovation seem likely to bring the structural inequities of the existing social organization into sharper relief in the future. Thirdly, recent political trends offer no proof one way or another, although they are often assumed to do so. For Labour's defeats at the polls in the 1950s reflect, not a decline in manual working class support, but a falling-off in that minority support which the

[1] E. Chinoy's *Automobile workers and the American dream*, 1955, is interesting in this context.

party draws from the non-manual strata of the population – these strata, in turn, forming a gradually increasing proportion of the electorate. According to the one published series of opinion surveys covering the entire period from the early 1940s on, manual working class support for Labour, if anything, grew slightly in the 1950s by comparison with the previous decade.[1]

This, clearly, provides no confirmation of 'embourgoisement' and a faltering of political loyalties in the working class – though it is true that we need to know far more than we do about the underlying factors, and about any shifts of political orientation which may have taken place within particular sub-groups of the two broad categories, manual and non-manual. There is room for varying deductions about immediate, short-term tactics. But it is indisputable that the Labour leadership's policy of 'softening' the image of the party to attract a larger middle class vote has, so far at least, produced no firm, positive results. It can, of course, be argued that the image has still not been sufficiently 'softened'. It can also – and with greater plausibility – be argued that to pursue such a policy in conventional terms is to chase a will of the wisp. A competition with the Conservative Party is almost always likely to work in the latter's favour, if the terms of reference are those of 'legitimacy' of authority, 'respectability' and 'efficiency' within the general framework of the existing socio-economic structure; and the long-run effect may well be a political alienation of the established – so far stable, though not significantly increasing – basis of Labour support in the working class. Labour's effective survival depends upon its capacity both to maintain its present support, and to extend its strength into those sections of the population – whether manual or non-manual – who share much the same socio-economic situation as the bulk of Labour supporters, but have hitherto abstained or voted against the party. Neither aim can be achieved on a durable basis through promises of moderate reform, economic efficiency and 'dynamic' administration, however worthwhile each of these may be in itself. For the Con-

[1] R. R. Alford, *Party and society*, 1963.

servative Party can generally – thought not at all times – compete successfully in these fields; and it has the added advantage – in the eyes of at least some of those critical marginal sections of the electorate whose permanent support Labour needs for its survival – of its aura of status and experience. In the long run the Conservatives are sufficiently flexible to adopt a number of moderate reform proposals for their own; to redefine criteria of economic efficiency; and even to discard some of the ritual mumbo-jumbo and gentlemanly amateurism inherited by British government and industry from the mid-nineteenth century cultural compromise between nobility and bourgeoisie, in favour of practices more in tune with the demands of a late-twentieth century capitalist economy. None of these involves any serious challenge to the established structure of power and property. By the same token, none will fundamentally affect the major, persistent inequalities which are inherent in that structure. It is those inequalities which offer the potential for a radical political programme; and which, because increasingly they characterize the condition of the lower 'middle' strata as well, provide the only durable basis for the maintenance and extension of Labour support. A successful extension of that support cannot be guaranteed. But there is no other way, if the criteria are those of long-term political strategy; and every justification for a genuinely socialist policy, if the criteria are those of a morality which rejects the validity of the structural inequalities of the present social order.

It may be said that the past ten or fifteen years have demonstrated an absence of sufficient popular support for a substantial leftward swing in policy. To attribute political moderation or apathy in this way to the Labour electorate rather than to the party leadership is to put the cart before the horse, or at least to argue from the unknown to the known. The end of the Labour Government of 1950 was the result, after all, of internal hesitations within the Cabinet and party officialdom. Since then – and the last few years are no exception – no sustained attempt has been made to present a policy of direct attack upon the established structure of power and property; to demonstrate the relevance of such a policy to the aim of substantially reducing the inequalities of condition, opportunity and human fulfilment which are inherent in that structure; to underline the pervasiveness and interconnections of those inequalities; or to relate them, their sources and the measures needed to tackle them to those issues of international relations, defence, economic aid and domestic cultural policy with which they are enmeshed. Even proposals by themselves of a radical character, or with at least a radical overtone, have been put forward piecemeal and *ad hoc*. In short, there has been no coherent attempt to exploit the potential for effective social criticism. This failure must be seen as, at least in the first instance, the result of what has been called the institutionalization of class conflict. Labour's rise to an influence which falls a good way short of power, here as elsewhere, has of necessity involved large-scale organization, the bureaucratization of party and union structures and, more importantly, the establishment of a regularized *modus vivendi* with the opposing side.[1] These trends are neither avoidable nor deplorable in themselves. But they carry with them the risk that the *modus vivendi* becomes permanent rather than temporary, accepted by those who operate it as a virtue in its own right rather than a tactical step on the way. In consequence, the area as well as the means of political conflict is narrowed; and the responsiveness of the organizational machinery to the potentialities for change latent in the wider society is reduced. There has, as yet, in Britain been no total freezing of the *status quo*, no final and irreversible hardening of the bureaucratic arteries of the Labour movement. To that, the continued presence of the left-wing minority as a focus of dissent has contributed. But the danger grows that, unless channels of communication are kept reasonably free, and the leadership sensitive to interpretations of current and future needs other than those which

[1] R. Miliband's *Parliamentary socialism*, 1961, is an excellent account of the process by which the British labour movement's protest became 'institutionalized', and of Labour's early and generally willing acceptance of the limitations inherent in the process. See also *idem*, 'Socialism and the myth of the golden past', in *The Socialist Register*, 1964.

derive directly from the day-to-day maintenance of the *modus vivendi*, the potential for radical social protest inherent in the persistent structural inequalities of the society may find no rational political expression. It may then instead, for example, produce a predominant pattern of resigned political indifference, coupled in unpredictable proportions with irrational surges of hostility towards large-scale organization as such; with epidemics of unofficial strike action, parochially oriented and uncoordinated; with a continuing element of juvenile gang crime and xenophobia; or with other manifestations of social tension – each unrelated to the others save through their common source, lacking the focus and direction of a common perspective and political purpose. This is possible; it must not be accepted as inevitable.

THE NEW CAPITALISM

Robin Blackburn

The traditional aim of socialist thought has been to become nothing less than the self-awareness of capitalist society. In a society profoundly ignorant of itself, it was the task of socialists to comprehend the principles on which the society worked. By discovering the real nature of capitalism, they were attempting to recapture for man a social and economic system that had escaped his control.

Today this intellectual task remains as formidable as ever, because capitalist society is by the law of its own nature in a continual state of restless transformation. The true character of capitalism has to be rediscovered by each new generation of socialists. And at this point it is necessary for the socialist to ask whether capitalism has not changed so much since the classic period that we are now really confronted with an altogether different type of society. It is this possibility that I wish to examine. My conclusion will be that today we confront a radically new *form* of capitalism, but that the most novel features of neo-capitalism, far from mitigating or abolishing the fundamental contradiction of capitalism, rather pose this contradiction *in a purer and more dramatic manner*.

What defines capitalist society is its property system. Though private property has not been abolished in any legal sense, it is frequently argued that the private ownership of the 'means of production' has somehow been drained of real social significance. It is said that modern companies are controlled by professional managers with little reference to the interests of the 'capitalists' who formally own them. It is also claimed that the growth of Government intervention – through the creation of a public sector, welfare services and the introduction of economic planning – reduces still further the traditional importance of private wealth. The first transformation infuses industry with a new sense of social responsibility, the second ensures the supremacy of social justice. The two complementary theories provide an account of the economic structure of society which is comprehensive enough to provide an alternative to the traditional socialist account. The true political economy of the new capitalism may be less comforting than these theories suggest; at least a confrontation of them can enrich socialist theory itself.

THE MANAGERS' REVOLUTION

1. *The General Model*

In Britain, the view that capitalism has been overtaken by a managerial revolution is most systematically expounded in two books by C. A. R. Crosland, *The Future of Socialism* and *The Conservative Enemy*. It also appeared in the Labour Party document *Industry and Society* and in John Strachey's *Contemporary Capitalism*.[1] The major point of reference for the prophets of the managerial revolution is the classic capitalism of the nineteenth-century – and it is usually Marx's account of this classic model which they invoke and contrast to their own analysis of the contemporary reality. In this classic epoch, the entrepreneur united in his person the functions of manager and owner. What has occurred since that date is what is called a 'decomposition of capital' with a consequent separation of ownership and control. Nowadays most large companies have a great many nominal owners – 12,000 in the typical large British company. The theorists of the managerial revolution

[1] In most respects Strachey's book is more interesting than either of Crosland's works, but it does not provide such a good account of the managerial revolution. The most celebrated presentation of the theory is, of course, James Burnham's *Managerial Revolution*. Ralph Dahrendorf has restated the argument competently in his *Class and Class Conflict in Industrial Society*, relieving it of the wilder prognostications of Burnham. One can search in vain for any mention of the managerial revolution in most textbooks on management. Cf., for example, M. E. Stern: *Mathematics for Management*, 1963, but also E. S. Mason 'The Apologetics of Managerialism' *Journal of Business* Jan. '58.

argue that it is impossible for all these owners to exercise any real control over the company they own. They are, in fact, forced to delegate this power to the paid managers of the company. These managers may have only a minimal shareholding in the company, or at any rate, a shareholding which only represents a tiny fraction of the total. These changes are re-inforced by the increasing technical complexity of manage-ment which delivers still further power into the hands of the managers. Naturally, these changes in control lead, so the argument runs, to changes in company policy. There is an in-creasing emphasis upon the welfare of the company employees and a growing indifference to high dividends. The interest of the manager lies in harmonious work relations and in the long-term growth of the company, not in dividend maximization. Crosland summarizes his own version of the argument thus:

> Because . . . the new managers do not have the same re-lation to private property as the old owners (though also for other reasons), there are significant differences in the nature of the profit goal and the degree of responsibility with which economic power is exercised. These differences constitute one feature of present-day, as opposed to capitalist, society. *(The Conservative Enemy)*

The reasoning which produces this bizarre addition to social typology (present-day society), can be shown to be funda-mentally deficient in describing the character of *any* modern capitalist society, and even a corrected schema cannot be applied without further modification to the specifically British variant of modern capitalism. These deficiencies can be con-sidered under the following three headings.

A. *The Social Unity of Managers and Owners.* The sociological critique of the managerial revolution thesis is now fairly well established. In *The Power Elite*, for example, Wright Mills showed that in the U.S.A. top managers could be closely identified with large shareholders. In Britain a survey of share-owning by the Oxford Institute of Statistics found that directors of companies held shares to an average value of £28,000.[1] This was the *largest average holding* of all the groups about which information was available; the next largest group was that of titled persons with an average holding worth nearly £14,000. Those few directors and managers who have no important shareholding are still likely to be tied to the owners by their aspirations and values, by a respect for the institution of property and by a common social background.[2]

B. *Economic Logic of the Market.* Marx himself never considered that the capitalist entrepreneur, in any real sense, *controlled* the economy as a whole, nor that any individual capitalist controlled, except in a very secondary sense, even his own enterprise. 'Capitalism subjects every individual capitalist to the immanent laws of capitalist production as external coercive laws. Competition forces him continually to extend his capital for the sake of maintaining it . . .' In their daily actions men in a capitalist society produce and reproduce a certain type of economy; but this economy, which conditions the actions of the capitalist as well as of the worker, has *escaped their command.* In this sense, according to Marx, 'The possessing class and the proletarian class express the same human alienation. But the former is satisfied with its situation, feels itself well established in it, recognizes this self-alienation as its own power and thus has the *appearance* of a human existence' (1844 Manuscripts). The essential alienation of capitalist society is that it is presided over not by man, but by the market. The domination of the market has to be mediated

[1] *Bulletin of the Oxford Institute of Statistics,* November 1955. Other relevant references will be found in the essay by J. H. Westergaard.

[2] A recent Young Fabian pamphlet reported that 64 per cent of the executives of the one hundred largest British companies went to Public Schools, and that 'at the growing points of power, in the large industrial firms, the influence of the Public Schools has been growing'. H. Glennerster and R. Pryke: *The Public Schools.* This conclusion is supported by a study in *The Director*, January 1965, where it is revealed that over 75 per cent of directors in the age group 25–35 were at Public Schools compared with an overall average of 60 per cent.

by men, but in following its dictates, they do not assume full responsibility for their actions.

The most notorious example of market domination of social priorities today is, of course, juxtaposition of private affluence and public squalor noted by Galbraith. Some left-wing writers have created a new demonology of advertising agents and sales managers to account for this. The truth is more disquieting:

How many businessmen resolutely decide that they must leave schools and hospitals to rot, and press on with doubling their TV commercials and lacquering their reception rooms with the money saved? Do any at all? On the contrary, how many mightn't even feel a stealthy susurrus of dismay if they learnt that this was the end outcome of their harmless, familiar routines? . . . What finally defines the whole system is that it utterly expunges men from the place of its essential working. These decisions are not taken in the board room or the bank manager's suite or even the exclusive club or the pleasure yacht. They are taken *nowhere*. They are *not taken*, they are not decisions: fatalities. Nobody calculates them and enacts them, they happen unmeant. Our callous and malformed priorities are the prodigious obverse of a thousand discrete, blameless gestures.[1]

Marx emphasised the *anarchy* of capitalist production. 'Anarchy' was used in a double sense. Firstly, it referred to the fact that the ultimate goal of capitalism as a system was the accumulation of capital and the making of profit, whereas the only goal of the socialist economy would be the satisfaction of human needs. Secondly, it referred to the fact that the actual mechanisms of the capitalist economy – the market system – were not subordinated to human control. This compounded anarchy afflicted the traditional capitalist economy with endemic imbalance – in particular, with the wild cycle of boom and slump. At the level of the enterprise the autonomy left to the entrepreneur was the ability to interpret, more or

[1] Perry Anderson, 'Sweden: a study in Social Democracy' *New Left Review* No. 8.

less successfully, the dictates of the market. Thus, the workings of the law of value ensured that his enterprise could only survive if it corresponded to some demand effective within the market.[1] Moreover, he was constrained to supply that demand in a manner which yielded him a return on his capital that did not fall too far below the average. If he made a loss, he might find himself in the bankrupt's court or, at best, his capital would begin to dwindle and he would gradually cease to be a capitalist.

If this analysis was correct, then the 'control' of modern capitalist economies will only be different to the extent that the market mechanism has been modified. The market has been and is being modified considerably (some of the implications of this will be explored later), but the 'managerial revolution' is not an important modification of the market mechanism, if indeed it modifies it at all. Even at the enterprise level the initiative in the hands of the manager is to subordinate, with greater or less efficiency, his company to the changed market situation. That the modern manager 'controls' any more than the traditional entrepreneur is in this sense very unlikely. It is interesting that two recent studies of 'managerial' capitalism both emphasize the crucial importance of the market. Robin Marris in *The Economics of 'Managerial' Capitalism* sees a determinate 'economic framework' as disciplining the manager; the sanction of the take-over raid becomes under the new conditions a powerful deterrent to company policy not directed towards market demands. Sargent Florence writes:

> For a grasp of its movement and working as well as its structure, the capitalist free enterprise system may be pictured as a number of unit firms, great and small, floating or tossing in a 'sea of troubles'. Outside these firms there is the anarchy of the market. Though firms and industries are linked and inter-dependent – the input of one, the output of another – yet there is no authority set over them. Instead, there is competition (however imperfect), trade fluctuations, uncertain supplies and uncertain

[1] This *effective* demand reflects the existing distribution of wealth and income.

demands for which firms must produce in advance, investing in specialized capital still more in advance. . . .
Apart from some peripheral control by the State and some auxiliary institutions and services, the main coordinating factor in this anarchy is through the price-mechanism.[1]

Improved methods of interpreting the market only make the manager's subordination to it more complete.

Crosland claims, however, that the ultimate goals of profit-making and capital accumulation had been modified by increased social responsibility in those companies where ownership and control are most clearly separated. The only admissible evidence on this point would be observed differences in managerial behaviour. Too often the champions of the managerial revolution indulge in arbitrary speculation about the *personal* motives of managers. The motives behind the decision of a manager may well be very complex and seemingly removed from economic calculations: he may desire to impress his wife or secretary, to further a personal vendetta, etc. But finally all these aims, by a sort of reduction of quality to quantity, will have to be mediated by the market; managerial decisions will have to be vindicated in market terms, as failure within the market will frustrate almost every kind of personal ambition and, indeed, threaten to deprive the manager of his managerial functions.

Moreover, it is by no means clear that the motives of the modern manager are so different from those of his predecessor. It is frequently claimed that the modern manager is growth-orientated: but was the idea of growth for its own sake, of capital accumulation instead of profit consumption, really so foreign to the nineteenth-century captain of industry? Marx himself certainly did not think so: 'Accumulate! Accumulate! That is Moses and all the prophets,' he wrote, explaining this capitalist commandment as follows:

Fanatically bent upon the expansion of value, he (the capitalist) relentlessly drives human beings to production

[1] Sargent Florence *Economics and Sociology of Industry*, p. 119–20.

for production's sake, thus bringing about a development of social productivity and the creation of those material conditions of production which can alone form the real basis of a higher type of society, whose fundamental principle is the full and free development of every individual. . . . that which in the miser assumes the aspect of mania, is in the capitalist the effect of the social mechanism in which he is only a driving-wheel.

Indeed, it is likely that in many cases the modern manager can *less* afford to ignore the need for profit distribution than the capitalist who manages his own firm. All studies agree that the manager of the modern company must allow for a certain minimum dividend even during the most inappropriate periods. By contrast such companies as Beaverbrook Limited, which was owner-managed, went for decades without any increase in dividends despite booming profits.

Turning to observable differences in behaviour between professionally managed and owner-managed firms, the two criteria most often cited by advocates of the managerial revolution are the extent of dividend distribution and the degree of concern shown for the welfare of the worker and the community. Where company paternalism is concerned, however, this can certainly not be claimed as an invention of those companies where ownership is divorced from management. To this day, the most striking examples of company concern for employee 'welfare' occur in the owner-managed concerns (in Britain, the chocolate companies; in Italy, Olivetti; in Japan, Matsushita). It is true that company paternalism is now more generally prevalent than before, but this is due to factors other than the simple rise of professionally-managed industry: for example, to the pressure of the trade unions and the greatly increased productivity of modern industry. Above all, the manager of both types of company today faces a shortage of skilled workers at a time when they are increasingly vital to the productive process. A multiplicity of fringe benefits and welfare schemes can become a market necessity, a device for tying the skilled worker to a particular factory. If, as is sometimes the case, company paternalism is too prodigal for its market situation, then the company will be weakened as a result. The recent takeover of an Olivetti division is a case in point.

As for dividend policy, the significance of the differences between owner-managed and professionally managed firms are equally often misinterpreted. It is argued, for instance, that the tendency for manager-run companies to plough back profits and give smaller dividends is a visible mark of concern for growth. But the long-run operation of the market will ensure that if the manager does not distribute much of the profit to the shareholders then the rise in the value of the company brought about by re-investment of profits in the company will result in a rise of share values. These capital gains can be converted for the individual into (untaxed) current income. During certain periods this has been an attractive option given the prevailing tax structure. Some idea of how attractive this can be, is suggested by the fact that the average Directors' shareholding, worth £28,000 when the Oxford Institute survey was carried out nearly ten years ago, *would now be worth about £60,000 even if he has purchased no additional shares*.[1] The owner-managed company is less in a position to take advantage of escalation in share values – if share gains are realized to any extent (by selling company shares) then the owner-managers will graually cease to be the dominant owners.[2] In other words, in a capitalist economy, growth can never be opposed as a goal to capital accumulation and profit-making. On the one hand, growth will produce profits and more capital; on the other the resources for expansion will tend to come from private or institutional capital which demands certain returns (the 'minimum' mentioned above, and, in the long run, more than this minimum).

If there is a difference between the logic of professionally-

---

[1] In *Contemporary Capitalism*, John Strachey says of the director that his 'motive is the acquisition of prestige and power rather than wealth', as if such goals were exclusive. The truth is that the achievement of a wide range of goals, including those of an altruistic nature, has to be mediated through success in capital accumulation.

[2] To circumvent this, non-voting shares are sometimes issued, but they will only be bought if there is some prospect of good dividends.

managed and owner-managed companies, it is that the former more exactly reflects the rationality of the market. The manager has less freedom to make decisions which answer to a purely personal whim or obsession. As professionally-managed companies come to dominate industry and commerce, artificial rigidities, preventing the free flow of capital in response to market pressures, disappear. Even where the new managers re-invest a very high proportion of the companies' profits, they must always estimate the 'opportunity cost' of such investments: that is, they must ensure that their return on capital compares satisfactorily with the return typical of the rest of the economy. Growing expertise in management has thus had one consequence that might disconcert the proponents of the managerial revolution:

> The spread of budgeting in the business world has helped to re-establish and clarify the importance of the profit objective. A recent survey of more than four hundred companies established that more than 95 per cent of these engage in comprehensive planning for defined short-run profit objectives, and that of these about nine-tenths specify the objective concretely, in writing.[1]

The responsible modern manager will probably aim at a 'fair' profit rather than a short-term maximization, but in doing this he will neither be ignoring the pressures of the market nor be acting so differently from his nineteenth-century predecessors. Dividends cannot be too low or it will be difficult to attract share-buyers in future, and the 'responsible' manager will, presumably, wish to see a wide safety margin between his company and the take-over raid or the bankruptcy court. If he judges wrongly then these two regulators will ensure that resources are not deployed inefficiently in market terms. Of course, in some societies rather low profit levels can come to be tolerated in the name of caution, comfort and safety – this may often be the case in Britain today. But again the position of the manager is not necessarily relevant to this phenomenon – indeed one rather suspects that it would be precisely the

[1] Neil W. Chamberlain. *The Firm: Micro-economic Planning and Action.* 1962.

ambience of the owner-managed family business that encourages such attitudes.

But within the international economy it is impossible to evade the operation of the market. Relative decline is the price of too much caution, tradition or comfort. In the decade of the fifties, the rate of profit in British industry fell by about one quarter; J. R. Sargent[1] has persuasively argued that this fact is directly related to technical stagnation and the decline of Britain's international industrial and trading position.

To deny that a managerial revolution has occurred is not to refuse all significance to the facts on which the theory was based. One of the truly momentous changes which have occurred in the train of the so-called managerial revolution is a change in the forms of property income. What appears in one perspective as a 'decomposition' of capital appears in another as a more effective means for its accumulation. The retention and re-investment of profits by the modern company continually increase the value of its shares – and as capital gains they are untaxed or only lightly taxed. For this reason, as Professor Meade has pointed out:

> In the United Kingdom, there is a special reason why the figures of personal incomes derived from the Income Tax returns will seriously underestimate personal incomes from property. They exclude capital gains. But the increase in the value of companies' shares which is due to the accumulation of undistributed profits represents in effect a personal income of the shareholders which has been saved for them by the companies themselves.[2]

c. *The Decomposition of Management*. Finally, the technical dimension of contemporary management must be considered. One of the claims of the managerial revolution is that the

[1] *Out of Stagnation*. A fall in the rate of profit on capital does not mean that the *volume* of profits has declined – in fact it has increased.

[2] J. E. Meade: *Efficiency, Equality and the Ownership of Property*. The disguised distribution of profits occurs not only as a consequence of capital gains but also through the distributing of extra shares in lieu of dividends (bonus issues, etc.). Cf. R. M. Titmuss *Income Distribution & Social Change*. D. Jay *Socialism in the New Society*.

technical complexity of modern management is a major factor conferring autonomy on the managers who are professionally trained in skills that lay owners cannot hope to acquire. The truth today is that the whole trend of modern technology is tending to undermine the omnicompetence of the top manager. The 'decomposition of capital' is being followed by a 'decomposition' of the managerial function. Hardly had the manager been hailed as the executor of a successful revolution than, as a pure type, he began to disappear. For in modern industry, whole departments of specialists are entrusted with one or other managerial function (marketing, operations research, investment allocation, process control, etc.). The decomposition of management accelerates as computers prove able to interpret the market situation more successfully than men. As this occurs it becomes clearer than ever that managerial 'decisions' are imposed by the total market situation which only admits of a very few optimal solutions. Some writers have even advanced the startling thesis that the development of capitalism itself is making the boss redundant. David Foster, author of a standard text on *Modern Automation*, recently wrote the following:

Automated Management: perhaps the most intriguing impact of automation related to employment is in the management sector. Having myself been in the past a director of a number of British companies it may be considered unfair of me to give away what is the stock-in-trade of management. But truth will out and the fact is that what passes for top-management ability is really a question of a certain special type of Pandora's Box possessed by top managers and hidden away from the sight of hoi-polloi, usually locked up inside one of the more secure type of filing cabinet. It consists of three things, namely, vital statistics, trend graphs, and simplified business formulae. Thus the chairman of a large company who may have acquired a reputation of quite extraordinary sagacity and business sense is really able to do all these marvels by cunningly referring in secret to his Pandora's Box which has enabled him over perhaps 30 years to distil the essence of his business into a number of numerical tables, graphs, and ready-reckoning formulae. If only the workmen in his factory realized how easy it has now become for the chairman to control a business of 10,000 people they would not only be very surprised but they would entirely agree that he was entitled to go off and play golf every Tuesday and Thursday afternoon.

Computer automation threatens the very existence of top management in all specialities because their Pandora's Boxes are about to become a millisecond routine on a magnetic tape.[1] (My emphasis.)

Though it may never be realized, this vision of the future manifests the secret of the system. The computer presiding over the destinies of men and resources expresses the impersonal nature of the market which it interprets. Instead of being the servant of man, the machine reflects man's failure to assume a full dominion over his own collective powers.

2. *Britain*

The theory of the managerial revolution has so far been discussed as a general model. Crosland apparently believes that his general model can be imposed, swiftly and without modifica-

---

[1] *New Society* Sept. '63. Cf. also, for a more moderate view H. A. Simon 'The Automation of Management' in *Management* Edited by H. Koontz and C. O'Donnell.

(This is particularly interesting at a time when the question of workers' control is being debated in the labour movement. The opponents of workers' control have always claimed that workers were incapable of running complex industry. These claims ludicrously overestimate the ability of directors and managers under capitalism, and they characteristically underestimate the potentialities of workers – as the experiments even in relatively underdeveloped Yugoslavia and Algeria have shown. Moreover they ignore that in an economy, where the anarchy of market laws had been replaced by democratic planning, the artificial 'complexity' of capitalist economics would no longer exist. Nevertheless, the trend revealed by Foster suggests that modern technology makes workers' control even more feasible.)

tion, on the particular instance of Britain. It is perhaps no coincidence that in the book in which Crosland first applied the
thesis of the managerial revolution to Britain, he also displayed
a complacency 'about the future performance of the British
economy which now appears astonishing. That the economy
would achieve an adequate rate of growth was simply assumed
and an impressive weight of argument was placed on this un-
sure foundation; at this time no 'conservative enemy' seems to
have troubled his vision of socialism's future. In a similar
vein the Labour document, *Industry and Society*, which welcomed the managerial revolution, contained the ill-fated statement that 'on the whole, British industry is serving the nation
well'. The history of the past few years has dramatically
revealed how different British capitalism is from the abstract
and anonymous schemas of managerial society. As I have suggested earlier, late capitalism does introduce some genuinely
novel features – it is these elements of truth which the
ideologies of the managerial revolution inflate to such extrava-
gant proportions. Among the two most important features of
late capitalism has been the professionalization of management,
and a tendency for the big oligopolistic companies to rely more
and more on self-financing for their investment. The industrial and commercial sectors of the economy have mush-
roomed to such size with the expansion of a mass consumer
market that the financial sector is no longer in a position to
dominate them and impose its own economic criteria upon
them. The goals of capital do not change but industrial and
commercial capital win the prize of successful accumulation.

These tendencies, which gestated slowly throughout the
capitalist world for a number of decades, have been given a
decisive momentum in the period of sustained economic
growth that began with the outbreak of the Second World
War. In Britain they appear to have been going forward only
lethargically even since the nineteen-forties. The historical
reasons for the distinctly archaic cast of British social and
economic institutions are examined elsewhere in this book.
What is clear is that in Britain large sectors of industry remain under the tutelage of finance capital. Indeed there is some

evidence that the City, having lost some of its interests overseas, has turned inwards and extended its influence over
domestic industry: merchant banks have, for the first time,
opened branches in the Midlands. One of the most important,
studies of the social relations of British industry revealed that
the directors of the leading merchant banks and commercial
banks held some 560 other major directorships mainly in the
150 largest British industrial enterprises.[1] The same study
documented the ways in which certain large owners of capital
(most of them connected with the City) contrived to perpetuate their influence over companies where otherwise the top
managers might have assumed sole responsibility. In fact most
large British industrial companies are linked to the City by two
or three outside directors. Even if these directors are only part-
time, their presence seems to be a sort of symbolic tribute paid
to the totems of financial orthodoxy. And of course the City is
not only a unique emblem of financial respectability, it is also
the source of much development capital and, no doubt, a great
deal of inappropriate financial advice. In Britain bank advances are twice as important as a capital reservoir as they are
in the United States. But at the same time the City is also an
inadequate source of capital, because it is still orientated as
much to overseas investment as to investment in domestic industry. Between 1952 and 1962 – when levels of investment in
the home economy were generally low – no less than £2,780m
was invested abroad.

Associated with the pervasive presence of the City within
British industry is the notorious absence of professionalism in
British management. Britain, with some half a million managers, has only *six hundred* who have graduated in management
studies. As Bonnard has shown, British managers do not even
compensate for their lack of training in management by technical qualification in any other field. It is thus not surprising
that the critical defect of British industry has been, precisely
the productivity of management. Dunning has shown that
American companies investing in Britain and using British

[1] M. Barratt Brown: 'The Controllers', *Universities and Left
Review*, No. 5.

labour are able to achieve an output as much as a third higher than their British competitors for each unit of capital.[1] Such facts are now widely acknowledged even if they are usually accompanied by tendentious rhetoric about faults on 'both sides' of industry (workers will only become accountable for the efficiency of the enterprises where they work when they are also allowed to manage them). A further point is, however, worth making. One of the most important tasks of management is to decide the timing and nature of new investment. The traditional criteria of finance capital are likely to be profoundly inappropriate in an era of rapid technological change. The financial world, ignorant of the technical factors influencing obsolescence, is prone to impose a rigid and purely financial formula of amortization on the industry it can control.[2]

Of course, there are both stagnant and dynamic sectors in British industry. The growth of the consumer durable market and of the industries associated with it (cars, synthetic fibres, chemicals, etc.) has transformed the balance between the different sectors of British capitalism. But this change has so far not been reflected in national economic policy. The City, occupying as it does the true 'commanding heights' of the economy, has been able to ensure that economic policy served its own sectional interests rather than the interests of British capitalism as a whole. Under successive Conservative Governments high interest rates and severe deflations were employed to defend sterling at a time when the Sterling Area generated a significant income only for the City not for the national economy as a whole. Conflicts of economic interest in this period produced some curious anomalies. Thus in an economy where consumer durable industries are predominant, deflationary policies do not in fact succeed in halting a rise in prices. Less spending power leads to shorter runs, which in turn lead to higher unit costs and thus inevitably higher prices. Or, again, the short burst of growth in the economy in 1963 was

[1] J. H. Dunning *American Investment in British Manufacturing Industry*.

[2] Cf. *National Institute Economic Review*, November 1964.

accompanied by very low profit levels for the banks, who seem to prosper only during stagnation. The last decade has witnessed a number of dramatic battles beween the old and the new in British capitalism. Most take-over bids have, at least in part, expressed this conflict – although it has only rarely erupted into an open confrontation such as the British Aluminium episode.

Very few sectors of the economy are as yet fully modernized. Perhaps one of the most successful has been the motor-car industry. It is probably no coincidence that it was Ford, a foreign-owned company, which was the first large consumer durable company to free itself from the financial establishment, by setting up its own hire purchase company. Despite the great importance of car manufacture for any modern economy, it is still clear that even major enclaves of dynamism can easily be swamped in an environment of overall economic archaism. Thus 1964 was both a record year for car exports, which rose 12 per cent over the previous year, and a disastrous year for Britain's balance of payments as a whole. In other industries there has been considerable growth but not enough to match that of Britain's competitors. The British chemical industry has, for example, expanded only half as rapidly since 1955 as its French counterpart. In an article about I.C.I., Michael Shanks wrote:

> One of the major points of controversy in the 50s between the old Guard and the Young Turks concerned the length of life over which capital should be amortized. 'They wanted to work the plant till it fell to pieces' one of the representatives of the newer divisions told me. 'We worked on the basis that technological and commercial change was so fast that the plant would be obsolete in ten years or less.' This approach is fundamental in an industry as capital intensive as chemicals, and the current thinking of I.C.I.'s top people is emphatically on the side of the 'quick write-off' men. But there are still parts of the company where this new thinking has yet to penetrate.[1]

The dividing line between the advanced and the archaic in

[1] *Sunday Times*, September 27, 1964.

the British economy is very blurred and ambiguous. Nicolas Davenport has written:

> In my investment work I have always tried to avoid the shares of companies which have a public school banker in the Chair because I know that the money influence will be predominant and that the scientist-technician on whom our industrial future depends, will be conspicuous by his absence from the Board. But I have found this simple investment rule almost impossible to follow.[1]

According to Davenport such companies are so few 'they would not fill a page of an investment folio'. The more we learn about British industry the less it seems to belong to the world of advanced capitalism. Nevertheless even the staidest merchant bankers are now aware of the new field for exploitation that the mass consumption market offers. The British financial world will certainly try to adapt itself, though it may be less than adept to begin with, as the Bloom episode showed.

NEO-CAPITALISM

The very backwardness of the British economy is forcing British governments to adopt the techniques and stratagems of neo-capitalism at the level of national policy – for this reason they are worth discussing at this point. The essential feature of neo-capitalism is not so much a modification of the internal structure of companies as a modification of the national economic framework as a whole and even an attempt to regulate international market forces. In Britain the first really important intervention by the State in the national economy was produced by the exigencies of war production during the First World War. But State intervention only became truly effective with the use of Keynsian techniques of regulating aggregate demand. This in itself was worth any number of managerial revolutions in its transformation of the workings of a capitalist economy. This is hardly the place to explore the historical reasons for the introduction of Keynesian techniques into

[1] N. Davenport *The Split Society*.

modern capitalism. This would require a separate study in it-self. But it should be noted that the conventional view, that it was democratic pressure from a reformist labour movement which primarily induced the change, is far too simple. In effect, the explanation of why any given capitalist country adopted Keynsian techniques only acquires a true perspective when the *general history* of capitalism is considered. Such a general history is a necessary and much neglected dimension of analysis which should complement those so far discussed (the pure model and the particular instance). Thus it is possible to consider Fascism as a particular type of capitalist society – an 'ideal' model of this sort would be defined in terms of a particular political order and a given relation between classes, etc. On the other hand, an explanation of, say, German Fascism would have to provide a conjunctural sociology and history of Germany of the period before 1933. But in addition to this, although Fascism should certainly not be examined as if it were a stage through which all capitalist societies pass, it is useful to consider, for example, Nazism as an episode in the general history of capitalism. For one key consequence of this episode was the introduction of Keynsian techniques into the capitalist economies. Hitler, himself, was the first politician to employ successfully public expenditure as a means of generat-ing full employment in the wake of the great depression. Later it was the war against Hitler which brought full employ-ment to the other capitalist countries. In 1938 there was more unemployment in the United States than there had been in 1933. The war succeeded where Roosevelt had failed in making Keynesian methods acceptable to American capitalism. Ever since, permanent preparations for war have played something like the same role. Even the placid social democratic experi-ment in neutral Sweden was under-pinned economically by Hitler's rearmament and war purchases. It is a comment on the fundamental irrationalism of capitalism that the successful introduction of techniques for avoiding slumps owe more to the demented ambitions of Hitler than to the conscious efforts of Roosevelt. In our own day new advances in the structure of capitalism, in particular the introduction of indicative planning, have been achieved under the mystical and national-ist banner of de Gaulle and not by the well-intentioned, 'reasonable' régimes of Kennedy or Johnson. The significance of these advances, which are being introduced to Britain, must now be explored.

In the typical neo-capitalist economy, the ultimate goals of capitalism are not changed, but increasingly rational methods are employed to attain these goals – the accumulation of capital and the making of profits. Of course, the ultimate irrationality of these goals continually and endemically contaminates the 'rational' means being used to pursue them. The cycle of boom and slump is checked but other imbalances continually manifest themselves. In the last American recession, unem-ployment increased to over seven million; the loss of produc-tion even in boom years runs to many millions of dollars with some four million workers remaining permanently unemployed. Meanwhile, within the capitalist world as a whole, vast popula-tions in the underdeveloped countries are pauperized by the anarchic movements of world commodity prices. Within nearly every advanced capitalist country itself, heavily populated regions are mysteriously condemned to stagnation and decay (N.E. England, Northern Ireland, Scotland, Massif Central, Southern Italy, Wallonia, Kentucky, etc.). Whole industrial sectors in each country are neglected or retarded and a per-sistent imbalance between public and private goods manifests itself. The relation of the capitalist economy to the natural environment is predominantly one of wasteful plunder in the pursuit of private profit: rivers are polluted, dust bowls are created, the air is contaminated and precious resources are squandered. The cluttered sprawl of most capitalist cities is a vivid testimony to the absence of any ultimate human control over the workings of the system. But, despite all this, rationality of a kind is being, and has been, introduced. When all the forms of this rationality are taken together they constitute a qualitative development in the history of capitalism. The national co-ordination of production, Keynesian techniques, monopoly agreements, the existence of nationalized industries and incomes policies, all contribute to this change and most of them enhance the control of the State over the national economy.

It is sometimes thought that the increased importance of the State means that the State is increasingly independent. It is argued that increase in the effectiveness of government economic policy and of the size of public sector is a counter-vailing power which offsets that of private capital. It is indeed true that a modern government could, for a short time at least, ruthlessly subordinate the interests of private capital to those of the community as a whole – but in practice this has simply not happened. Naturally, the 'interests of capital' are never, as we have seen, completely homogeneous and so all sorts of marginal interventions by the State are possible, with old interests giving way to new. But examination of the actual role of the State in modern capitalist economies fails to reveal any genuine independence *vis-à-vis* capital.

1. *Images*

In Britain the State, at first sight, appears to occupy a com-manding economic position: quantitatively it accounts for about a third of the economy (the public sector), while quali-tatively it can dominate the domestic market (through its armoury of monetary, fiscal and other controls). Taking the quantitative aspect first, we find that no less than 42 per cent of all property is owned by some public authority. But this figure, by itself, is misleading because it takes no account of the extent to which the State is indebted to the private sector. In fact the size of the national debt exceeds considerably the value of public property so that the State is mortgaged up to the hilt to private capital. Professor Meade has estimated that so far as the ownership of real property is concerned the pub-licly owned sector of the economy is actually a negative quan-tity – minus 14 per cent. He concludes 'as far as the net owner-ship of property is concerned we live, not in a semi-Socialist State, but in an anti-Socialist State.'[1] The importance of this is not that private capitalists command the state because in one

[1] Meade, Op. cit. p. 69.

sense they own it, for this is clearly not the case.[1] The real 'anti-socialist' consequence of a huge national debt (£28,000m) is that it creates a large class of purely parasitic rentier capitalists and thus accentuates inequalities of wealth and income. At the present time some £1,000m a year is paid out in interest on the public debt with the great bulk of this income going to large owners of capital. In other words expansion of the public sector could only have a genuine effect on the distribution of real wealth if it involved expropriation without compensation.

However, those who are impressed by the countervailing power of the modern State are usually thinking more of the qualitative than the quantitative aspects of this power. Again, it is probably true that a determined government could conceivably lend a truly anti-capitalist significance to the management of the public sector as well as of the economy as a whole. It could only do this if the activities of the public sector were planned as a whole, with no restraints placed on public enterprise where it threatened to undermine the position of private industry. Needless to say the history of the public sector in Britain contains no episodes of this sort. Instead the public sector has function as a sort of beneficent milch cow for private capital. Techniques whereby successive governments have allowed the public sector to be exploited include the following:

(1) Straight subsidies and grants from the public exchequer – over the last decade £3,500m has been paid out in subsidies of one kind or another to private industry and agriculture. The public contribution of £20m towards the Cunard liner is a recent example.

(2) Public contracts farmed out to private industry, especially those industries concerned with construction, transport and

[1] Though where the debt is owed to foreign interests the situation is different. Wilson rightly commented on this in his speech to the Trade Union Congress in 1964: 'You can get into pawn but then don't talk about independent foreign policy or an independent defence policy ... if you borrow from some of the world's bankers you will swiftly find that you lose another kind of independence because of the deflationary policies and cuts in social services that will be imposed on a government that has got itself into that position.'

armaments. In most cases a guaranteed profit is offered and genuinely competitive tenders are rare. The sums involved annually in public contracts of this sort run into many thousands of millions of pounds. The Ferranti scandal gave a glimpse of the super-profits made on these contracts.

(3) Cheap prices for public services. The much publicized losses of some nationalized industries are merely a concealed subsidy which private industry receives through less-than-cost charges for the services it uses.

In his Fabian Pamphlet[1], John Hughes has given an exhaustive account of this multiple exploitation of the public sector. Here is just one example:

> Many steel companies used to own collieries . . . They were compensated for these pits (about £35m). However, subsequently they received coal at prices *lower* than the cost of production (if allowance for replacement cost depreciation is made); at the same time they were relieved of the need to provide additional capital to maintain and expand the capacity of 'their' pits. They are thus, economically, considerably better off than when they owned the pits. Nevertheless they were *compensated* for the loss of these pits.

This subordination of the public sector to the interests of the private sector has been, in Britain, systematic but not necessarily efficient. In the aftermath of their victory in 1951 the Conservatives may have had an interest in showing the nationalized industries to be failures. The investment policies of public services were frequently sacrificed to short-term deflationary considerations – perhaps because this was the easiest way to cut overall investment. At all events it is important to note that the internal management of public corporations has hardly differed at all from the management of the large buraeaucratic private firms. This is less surprising when one considers that half the directors of the public companies are also on the boards of private firms, while most ex-Ministers, retired Civil Servants and senior army officers, etc., can expect to receive lucrative directorship in private industry. Of the

[1] *Nationalized Industries in a Mixed Economy.*

180 members of boards and publicly-owned companies, no less than 93 are simultaneously the directors of companies in the private sector and these share between them 467 director-ships. In most cases both the chairman and vice-chairman of the public corporations come from private industry.[1]

So much for the character of the present public sector. The really critical power of the modern State lies rather in its ability to control the national economy. There are, of course, limits in this field – not least the position of a national economy within the anarchic international economy. But though any government has a certain latitude in its conduct of economic policy, it is not really free to ignore the interests of the private sector. Indeed, so long as the preponderant section of the economy is privately owned, it will be difficult to im-prove the position of the economy as a whole without also improving the position of private capital. The earnest en-deavours of governments to foster economic growth invariably produce an undeserved windfall for capital. In Britain, the post-war Labour Government was concerned with recon-struction and economic growth – it was largely successful in these aims. As a result, while wages were frozen, gross in-dustrial profits rose to record heights. The succeeding years of Conservative rule primarily benefited property speculators, rentier and finance capitalists, take-over bidders and capital gains merchants. Rents rose 144 per cent to an annual £579m in 1962 and as a proportion of national income they rose by one-third. Nicolas Davenport says of this period:

All this time the workers must have felt they could not relax in their struggle to keep their wages ahead of the rise in prices. A gain in their real standard of living of only 50 per cent in about thirteen years does not stand up against the rise of 183 per cent (in real terms) in the value of equity shares (225 per cent with net dividends added) which the owners of capital enjoyed.[2]

Under Labour, it had been primarily the parasitic class of

---

[1] *List of Members of Public Boards of a Commercial Character*, November 1963.

[2] *The Split Society*, p. 68.

industrial capitalists who had prospered: under the Conservatives it was rather the parasites on these parasites.

Despite these aspects of economic growth the modern State is often thought to play a major redistributive role in society. The creation of a 'welfare state', it is thought, ensures that the wealthy are heavily taxed to pay for the provision of social services to the poorer sections of the community. It is true that some redistribution from the very rich to the poor does occur in our society. Two recent studies gives us some idea of the exact limits of redistribution through taxation and welfare.

Research by J. L. Nicolson reveals[1] that in 1959 the lowest 25 per cent of all British household incomes, paid 29·9 per cent of their income in taxation, whereas the top 1 to 5 per cent of households paid only 28·0 per cent. Income tax in Britain is a 'progressive' tax (that is, it takes a greater proportion from high incomes than low incomes), but it is to some extent offset by national insurance contributions and sales taxes which are largely 'regressive'. The combined result is that:

In the United Kingdom, families within a wide range of income, from nearly the lowest to nearly the highest, constituting in fact the great bulk of the population, pay taxes at an almost uniform rate. It will also be seen that there has been a marked reduction of progression between 1953 and 1959 towards the upper end of the income scale. (*Income and Wealth*, Series X).

This tendency certainly continued after 1959 with the reduction in surtax rates and the abolition of Schedule 'A'. Turning to the benefits side, the ability of the middle class to use the high cost sectors of the welfare services reduces their redistributive effect. The Government magazine *Economic Trends*[2] has estimated the net effect of taxation and the various social services on different income levels for 1962. It is clear from this survey that the great mass of the working class and of the population as a whole receive back in services no more than they pay in taxes. A man with two children earn-

[1] In *Income and Wealth* Series X, edited by Colin Clark and Greer Stuvel.
[2] February 1964

ing a wage in the region of £16 per week in 1962 (about the average for Britain as a whole) suffered a small net loss as a consequence of the Welfare State. A single man earning in the region of £8–9 per week suffers a net loss of 12 per cent of his initial incomes once taxes are set against benefits. The survey suggests that the most important kind of redistribution produced by the Welfare State is not so much redistribution between classes as redistribution *within* classes. In particular, there is noticeable redistribution from single men and childless couples towards larger families, and also from those who are working to old people.

The small scale of income redistribution revealed by these studies helps to explain the persistence of poverty amid the general rise in living standards:

> ... in 1953–4 about 8 per cent of the population – nearly four million people – were living at a standard no higher than the average family on National Assistance. *Preliminary results for 1960 showed that the number had nearly doubled.* Seven and a half million people were in households with incomes at or below the average amount allowed to similar families on National Assistance. As many as two million had less than the *basic* National Assistance scale on which, it has been officially stated, nobody is expected to live ... [my emphasis][1]

Even the most well-intentioned attempts to secure a full and effective social citizenship for all, have foundered on the stubborn facts of class division. The work of a generation of sociologists shows that contemporary capitalist society produces a blind partiality even, indeed especially, in the areas of social life affected by universal welfare provision. Here are just three of the more remarkable recent findings.

(1) The Robbins committee on higher education discovered that the proportion of male university students who were of working-class background was no higher in the early 1960s than it had been in the pre-war period before university entrance had been widened and student grants provided.

(2) Peri-natal mortality (death at or near birth) is twice as

[1] Tony Lynes, 'Poverty in the Welfare State', *Aspect*, August 1963.

high in the lower working class as it is in the upper middle class.[1]

(3) A recent large-scale survey examined, among other things, entry into 'selective schools', that is grammar schools and efficient independent schools: one conclusion was that: 'Comparing children of equal measured ability at eleven, those from the upper middle class get three times as many selective school places as those from the lower manual, more than twice as many as those from the upper manual and one and a half times as many as those from the lower middle class.'[2]

The provision of welfare mirrors the differentials of wealth and income. Public provision (of health, pensions, education, housing) is in every case supplemented by a superior private provision for the rich – *and in each case these privileged private services are indirectly subsidized by public money through tax rebates and allowances.*

The working of capitalism has certainly been modified by the features discussed above, but it has not been modified in quite the direction that its apologists claim. But the most ambitious innovations of contemporary capitalism have yet to be discussed – namely the national coordination of production and the introduction of incomes policies.

2. *Realities*

It has been a main contention of socialist writing that a socialist society would be distinctive above all in its *transparency*. We live in a society which is essentially opaque; the origin and sense of events in it systematically escapes us. The movements of the economy remain obscure and unsuspected by even the most expert. In a socialist society men would restore to themselves that control over the society they live in which the market has confiscated from them. A certain premonition of the transparency of socialist society seems to haunt

---

[1] *Peri-natal Mortality*, Neville R. Butler and Denis G. Bonham 1963.

[2] J. B. W. Douglas *The Home and the School*, 1964, p. 122.

neo-capitalism. It does this by giving added lucidity to the workings of the economy. Above all, it increases *the visibility of exploitation* produced by capitalist social relations.

Keynesian theory offers no solutions to the problems of growth and inflation; indicative planning and incomes policies are the new devices intended to meet these problems. In practice, neo-capitalist planning has mainly consisted in the exchange of information between the State and the big private companies and the harmonization of their plans.[1] The general effect is to enhance the instrumental 'rationality' of the process of capital accumulation. But however 'indicative' neo-capitalist planning remains it does marginally increase our awareness of our own society; Joan Robinson has commented:

> Without some aim how are planners to know what to plan? The new cry for growth (apart from the urgent need to get the balance of payments into shape) is not an aim in itself. What is to grow? How long can we accept the tale that we 'cannot afford' an adequate supply of teachers and doctors when we can 'afford' the profits made by selling motor-cars? Even the mild degree of planning represented by Government intervention to assist the great firms to co-ordinate their activities brings economic questions into the arena of democratic politics, from which the doctrine of *laissez faire* was designed precisely to fence them off.[2]

However, the most critical field of State intervention in the advanced capitalist economy is that of incomes policies. The attempt to regulate the overall levels of profits and wages is potentially the most explosive development of all those which constitute the new form of capitalism. Socialists have often suggested that the real relations of production were in many ways much less visible in capitalist society than they had been in pre-capitalist societies. The serf could not fail to know that he actually gave a part of his labour time or his crop to his

---

[1] Cf. E. Mandel 'Economics of Neo-Capitalism', *Socialist Register*, 1964 and Barbara Castle 'The Lessons of French Planning' *New Left Review*, 24.

[2] 'The Final End of Laissez-faire', *New Left Review*, 26.

feudal lord, whatever notions he might have held to justify this. By contrast, in the classic capitalist society the very anarchy and alienation of the productive process obscured the worker's vision of his relation to the capitalist – he knew that he was *bossed* but not necessarily that he was *exploited*. Joan Robinson has called the equations that express Marx's labour theory of value the most demagogic in all economic theory. But demagogic though they may be to the economist, to the layman they were abstract and complex. Rises in the *absolute* level of wages have obscured the remarkable fact that the relative shares of profits and wages have displayed a 'historical constancy' since the end of the nineteenth century (periods of was provide the only significant exception)[1] The factor income of capital has not given ground to the assaults of organized labour.[1] It is this which suggests that the effective-

---

[1] N. Kaldor *The Theory of Capital* edited by F. Lutz and D. Hague (1961). In 1938, the ratio of gross profits to all employment incomes (including directors' salaries) was 1 to 4.5, in 1952 it was again 1 to 4.5, in 1962 it was 1 to 4.8 (Cf. *Annual Abstract of Statistics*, 1956 and 1963). Of course there are other important forms of property income in addition to gross profits – namely rent and interest. The proportion of wages in the national income has fluctuated around 42 per cent. In 1948–51, it reached 43.4 per cent while by 1960–62 it was 42.0 per cent. However this decrease more or less corresponds to the decline of the working class as a proportion of the total population.

[2] The work of P. Sraffa suggests that in some ways wages may be no more than a fixed and predetermined variable in a capitalist economy (*Production of Commodities by Means of Commodities*, 1960; cf. also C. Napoleoni and F. Rodano in *Revista Trimestriale* Nos. 1–4). If this is the case why is there a need for an incomes policy? In guaranteeing a certain proportion of the national income to profit the capitalist system does not guarantee either the optimum amount of profit or the most satisfactory composition of that profit. Traditional trade union action may be unable to secure a relative increase in the return to labour; but its defensive struggles for money wages trigger off counter-tendencies (inflation, etc.) which disturb the balance between different types of capital and also adversely place a given capitalist nation *vis-à-vis* its competitors.

The 'circularity' of the capitalist economy thwarts even the most resolute attempts to change it. For example, it is very difficult to prevent a 'corporation tax' being to some extent passed on to the

ness of the labour movement as a 'countervailing power' is severely limited. Comparing different countries it can be seen that wage increases and the provision of welfare services are not uniquely correlated with the strength of the labour movement. Some notable forms of welfare provision have been created under the political influence of the labour movement (the health service in Britain, insurance and holidays in France, pensions in Sweden). But on the other hand certain spectacular recent increases in wages have occurred in countries where organized labour is comparatively weak (West Germany). The overall position of the working class is determined more by the general increase in productivity than by any other factor: the main consequence of most trade union activity of the traditional type is to ensure that the relative position of the working class does not deteriorate.

In its classic phase the contrast between the income of labour and capital at a national level was much less tangible than the absolute increases in wages. Indeed, to this day, many union leaders appear to be under the impression that the relative position of wages and profits has somehow been fundamentally transformed. Classic capitalist society did, it is true, replace the particular and purely local confrontation of each feudal lord and his serfs by a social conflict involving a working class that was conscious of its national and even international identity. But although profits also had a universal existence, they did not have this in any way which was immediately perceivable by the popular consciousness. Instead of profits being apprehended as a global entity opposed to wages, there was a tendency only to denounce the fairly isolated cases of flagrant 'profiteering'. *The introduction of attempts to coordinate incomes unintentionally makes possible a return to something like the pre-capitalist visibility of exploitation but in a more universal context.* The first beginnings of an awareness of the opposition of aggregate wages to aggregate profits

---

consumer in higher prices. Similarly an increase in the so-called 'employers' contribution' to national insurance is rapidly absorbed as part of labour costs: the process is documented in G. L. Reid and D. J. Robertson *Fringe Benefits, Labour Costs and Social Security*, 1965.

can be detected during the post-war labour government wage-freeze. But the establishment of N.E.D.C. and N.I.C. by a Conservative Government led to a full-scale debate on the question of wages and profits. It could be that this will become merely the beginning of a political consciousness that would pierce to the very roots of class formation in the relations of production. Marx's theory of class consciousness depended upon the class becoming more and more aware of its objective class interests as it engaged in struggle. Under neo-capitalism the struggles which are likely to occur over the share of labour in the national income are exactly calculated to foster a more far-reaching class consciousness than any we have witnessed hitherto. Of course, this argument assumes that the labour movement will be ready to learn the lessons of this experience. It is equally possible that the new configuration of capitalism will create new mystifications. The rationality of the new capitalism with regard to means may well be mistaken for a rationality with regard to ends. But in Britain where the labour movement is comparatively strong and united, there is no reason why it should not resist this error. Marxists have formulated the basic contradiction of capitalist society as a contradiction between a *social* process of production and a private form of appropriation. The new capitalism which reveals the increasingly social nature of production more clearly than ever before can only accentuate this contradiction.

The socialist critique of capitalism in all areas of society must have both a qualitative and a quantitative aspect. For example, the content and organization of education are as important as the amount of money spent on it. The context of the market continually encourages a reduction of qualitative considerations to quantitative considerations – this is the logic of capitalism and it must be resisted. But a socialist strategy which engages bourgeois society at all points may nevertheless confer a crucial significance on the confrontation between wages and profits.

In the *Conservative Enemy*, Crosland complains that the complete 'collectivization' of the economy would only make available some 5 per cent of the national income for alternative uses; re-invested profits would have to continue to be re-invested. Even 5 per cent of national income, or some £1,250m, would have considerable importance in its own right: such a sum would enable expenditure on health, pensions, overseas aid, education and *all* the other social services to be simultaneously raised by 25 per cent. But Crosland underestimates the purely economic consequences of social ownership. Crosland's figure completely ignores the transformation of social priorities which social ownership would make possible. The expenditure of huge sums on armaments, prestige construction, built-in obsolescence, etc., would all be called in question by such a transformation. The relevant figure for socialists is that of gross property incomes[1] – this is the economic surplus, the investment of which decides the nature of the society as a whole. Social ownership would both subordinate the economy to democratic control and abolish the great inequalities of income and wealth that exist today. The confrontation of wages and gross property income, which is endemic in the new capitalism, unites the qualitative and the quantitative aspects of the struggle for socialism, and does so at the most effective political level.

[1] This figure would include both profits (after allowing for depreciation these come to 18 per cent of factor incomes) and rent and interest (which comprise together some 10 per cent of national income). Taking all types of property income into account and also allowing for the changed methods of distributing property incomes, *consumed* property incomes must be at least 8 per cent of the national income.

THE LESSONS OF 1945

Richard Crossman

The first essential for the election of a Left-Wing government in Britain is the creation of a favourable climate of opinion among non-political voters. And, although the practical politicians hate to admit it, the truth is that this favourable climate can never be created by the Labour Party itself, but only by the 'disloyal intelligentsia' – the journalists, writers, playwrights and critics who are able to discredit the Establishment and to air Left-Wing ideas when they are still too novel for the practical politicians to adopt.

The most obvious example of this process was the transformation of public opinion which took place during the thirties and which continued throughout the party truce of the Second World War. It was not the speeches of Mr. Attlee, Mr. Morrison or even Sir Stafford Cripps, nor yet the propaganda of Transport House, which, before the 1945 election, transformed a distrust of the Tories and a reluctance to go back to pre-war conditions into a positive decision to face the future under a Labour Government. The psychological landslide to the Left was set in motion not by party organization or party propaganda, but by those who contributed to the *New Statesman*, joined the Left Book Club, taught evening classes for the W.E.A. and, during the war, lectured for the Army Bureau of Current Affairs.

There is one other function – the task of self-criticism – which can never be adequately carried out inside a democratic socialist party. In a Communist state, this task is the perilous responsibility of the voluntary *élite* constituted by the party members. It is for them to assess successes, to raise the awkward issues and to expose faults of administration. In our British democratic system, however, where two big parties are competing against each other, self-criticism of this kind is too electorally damaging to be permissible. Since the introduction of universal suffrage, party loyalty has come to be the prime virtue expected of the M.P. and of the active party worker; and the test by which his loyalty is measured is whether he supports his leaders when he disapproves of what they are doing, and whether he defends the party line when he feels in his bones that it is wrong. That is why the task of self-criticism is usually left to those socialist journalists and academics who are professionally free to undertake the kind of cool analysis or outraged exposure that are likely to get a career politician into trouble.

George Bernard Shaw was the first and most famous of these socratic gadflies. In his Fabian days, his incursions into practical Labour politics exasperated the leaders almost as much as they stimulated the rank and file. Since then, a long line of intellectuals has carried on the Shavian tradition, forcing the Labour Party to face awkward facts and even on occasion to accept new ideas. Some of them, Kingsley Martin and H. N. Brailsford, for example, have been pre-eminently journalists. More often they have been academics who, in addition to their independent writings, have worked for the party behind the scenes, sitting patiently on its working parties and helping on occasion to draft its manifestoes.

But in order to fulfil their function – the provision of an intellectual dynamic to a party that instinctively distrusts intellectuals – they have been forced jealously to guard their independence and so have laid themselves open to the accusation of irresponsibility. Whenever he wanted to wither them with his contempt, Earl Attlee used to call them 'the Newstatesmen'.

The phrase was coined in irony, but it contains a very large grain of truth. After the collapse of the 1931 Labour Government, the party faced catastrophe with a magnificent display of instinctive solidarity. But its political self-confidence had been shattered by the MacDonaldite betrayal, and the job of creating a programme of action and a structure of doctrine on which their self-confidence could grow again was quite beyond the Trade Union leaders and the professional politicians. The Newstatesmen took it over. It was Tawney, Laski, Cole – and later Durbin – who analysed frankly and candidly the defects of the 1929 Labour Government and worked out the changes that the party must accept in its doctrine and in its procedures, if the MacDonaldite betrayal was not to be repeated in the future.

This new thinking first appeared in books and pamphlets that only a minority of practical politicians bothered to read. But by the time the war broke out, the writings of the Newstatesmen had been vulgarized into a popular version that could be heard in speeches at Labour conferences and in Parliament. That popular version found its final and most famous expression in the 1945 Labour Party election pamphlet *Let us Face the Future*.

Neither Lord Morrison nor Earl Attlee has ever shown much anxiety to acknowledge the extent to which the achievements of their administration were made possible by the critique to which the Newstatesmen had subjected the MacDonald Government, and by the researches which they and their pupils had undertaken in order to work out a realistic programme of socialization. If in addition to borrowing their ideas, the politicians had heeded their warnings, those achievements could have been far greater.

When one compares the fifties with the thirties, one is struck at once by the contrast between the role of the independent intellectual in those two long periods of political defeat and frustration. This time, the first years in the wilderness were dominated by the Bevanite split. This time, the post-mortem was conducted not by Newstatesmen outside the party machine but by the professional politicians. As a result there was much more verbal fisticuffs than serious self-criticism; and, when exhaustion came, the new socialist policy emerged not from a creative public controversy conducted in books and pamphlets, but from a long string of working parties established by Labour's National Executive – each of them responsible for a long and sometimes not very inspiring policy document. No wonder that when the 1959 election was fought many Labour voters were quite unable to name any differences between the Conservative and Labour policies.

The third successive electoral defeat caused a renewed bout of questioning. How could the party achieve victory, the Right Wing asked, unless it could be dissociated from its working-class tradition and given a new public image? Is it possible to have the kind of controversy required to produce new ideas, the Left Wing wondered, without precipitating another disastrous split? Hugh Gaitskell set himself to grapple with this problem. By a supreme effort of personal leadership he attempted to provide a substitute for the dynamic controversy which had restored the party's morale and stimulated the new thinking in the thirties. With a series of hammer blows, first left then right, he began to beat out a New Socialism in terms of his own personality. But he had worn himself out; and with Harold Wilson's election as his successor, the Labour Party has whipped back into its traditional posture. It has become once again a party where leaders are expected not to give the marching orders to the rank and file but to express the inner momentum of a mass movement. For the first time for many years, the Labour Party now suddenly feels the need for the stimulus of controversy which will help to create the political climate in which a Labour Government can maintain its sense of direction and do a real job of work.

Alas! The time is short. After 1951, as contrasted with 1931, no attempt was made to assess the achievements of the Labour Government, and to analyse the reasons for its defeat. To publish criticism of the foreign policy of Ernest Bevin, the economics of Dalton, Cripps and Hugh Gaitskell, or the sagacity of Clem Attlee in timing his appeals to the country, was treated as an act of disloyalty. Indeed, it has taken twelve years to purge the Labour Party of the disease of 'ex-minister-itis' which first crippled our parliamentary leadership in the early fifties and then blighted the self-criticism which should have made the political wilderness blossom with socialist ideas. A few books – by John Strachey and Anthony Crosland, for example – and a handful of Fabian tracts were devoted to socialist theory. But the authors were careful to avoid the one essential requirement for a creative controversy – a determined attempt to hack away the jungle of complacent myth and self-congratulatory legend which obscured the real record of the Attlee Government from the eyes of the faithful.

Now this mood of jellied self-deception has been swept away. The inexperience of the present Labour leaders may well be used against them. But it brings with it one enormous advantage – the release of the Labour Party from pious servitude to its own past.

The force on which Conservative electoral strategy depends is lethargy. The voter who is permitted to feel himself non-political between elections can be persuaded when the campaign starts that he has never had it so good. But it is controversy that provides the dynamic of a Labour opposition fighting for power. It is the voter whose mind is opened by argument to the need for radical change who can be persuaded to prefer Harold Wilson at Downing Street. In creating this atmosphere of controversy, the Newstatesmen have a vital part to play. While the professional politicians concentrate on future planning, I hope that some of them will undertake that analysis of the Attlee Government which should have been completed years ago. This exposure of the harsh truth behind the comfortable façade of party legend, will, I hope, uncover definitive answers to some of those awkward questions that first began to worry me as I sat on the back benches and watched the Attlee Government in operation.

What shook me then and what has perplexed me since was the rapidity with which the Cabinet lost its initial *élan*. Mr. Attlee had arrived at Downing Street with the clearest mandate for radical change ever given to a premier since 1906. Despite the wrecking activities of the Irish Nationalists and of the House of the Lords, the Liberals were able to achieve re-election in 1910 and to sustain the momentum of social change until 1914 – a period of eight years. Why did the Labour Government lose its inner dynamic so much more quickly? Why was Hugh Dalton able to reveal in the third volume of his memoirs that by 1947 – only two years after the electoral triumph – the Government was manifestly losing both its coherence and its sense of direction? Why was it that, once the proposals of *Let us Face the Future* had been rushed through the Commons, the leadership was so obviously at a loss for what to do next – so that in 1950 there was no programme for a second stage of socialism on which the appeal to the country could be made? Finally, what was it that so rapidly deflated the public demand for social change that had swept the party into power in 1945? What transformed the militant activism of the rank and file into a heroic but unhappy loyalty to a remote leadership?

In their memoirs, ex-ministers such as Lord Morrison have taken the view that if the Labour Government was at fault, it erred on the side of doing too much rather than doing too little – passing too much social legislation, pushing too many reforms down the throat of the electorate, and sacrificing personal consumption too recklessly to expenditure on public services and capital investment. Herbert Morrison was rightly proud of the skill with which he steered the legislative programme through Parliament and maintained both the morale and the discipline of his backbenchers without resort to standing orders. His record as leader of the House of Commons is indeed beyond reproach. But was he as wise and successful outside the Chamber? Was he right to coin the slogan of 'consolidation', and to argue privately that a public reaction exploited by the Tories against controls, rationing and austerity made it impossible to campaign for a second stage of socialism?

With the hindsight of history, we can now see how flimsy the case for consolidation really was. For when the 1951 election came, there was no violent anti-socialist swing of public opinion. On the contrary, the party made headway in the country, polling the highest vote in its history and losing its parliamentary majority exclusively owing to an altruistic redrawing of constituency boundaries. Although the Labour Party had no programme of action, and although its public image had been damaged by the Bevanite split, it still enjoyed more public confidence than the Tories. If only Mr. Attlee had held on, instead of appealing to the country in the trough of the crisis, he would have reaped the benefit of the 1951 recovery, and Labour might have stayed in power for a decade.

If this analysis is substantiated by an independent investigation, it would have an immense importance for the present Labour leadership. For it can hardly be denied that the orthodox socialist legend makes gloomy reading for a Labour prime minister. After all, the political conditions under which Mr. Attlee took office in 1945 were considerably more favourable than any that are likely to confront Mr. Wilson. As members of the war-time coalition, Attlee and his colleagues had during the war achieved entrenched positions in Westminster and Whitehall. Moreover, they took over an elaborate system of war-time planning and controls which enabled them to tackle any incipient financial crisis and suppress any economic sabotage – provided only they had equipped themselves with a staff capable of assessing the situation well in advance, so enabling the Cabinet to base its decisions on a correct appreciation.

In 1945 both the conditions in Westminster and Whitehall and the whole political climate of the country outside were extremely well suited for a big and sustained advance towards a socialist planned economy. If the fate of the Attlee Government was really inevitable, if it was beyond its powers to avoid losing most of its majority in the 1950 election, or to control the economic crisis that swept it from power a year later, then we had better admit straight away that any Labour Government will be faced with the choice of either spinning out its term of office by 'doing nothing and doing it very well', or, alternatively, of cramming all its socialist measures into its first months of office – before the inevitable public reaction sets in. To put it mildly, both prospects are depressing.

Fortunately, however, these are not the conclusions likely to be drawn from a candid study of the record of the Attlee Government. An independent critic is much more likely to find that the electoral losses in 1950 were quite unnecessary, and that the precipitate decision to resign a year later was not an inevitable result of the crisis, but a consequence of physical exhaustion and loss of nerve. In all the circumstances, Mr. Attlee's decision to go to the country, with more than three years of his term of office to run, was understandable; and his motives for doing so, as explained in a recent book, were unimpeachable. Nevertheless, the results of his mistaken calculation were almost as disastrous to the cause of socialism as the events of 1931. But whereas the MacDonaldite collapse was frankly admitted by the labour movement and the correct lessons were drawn from it, the failure of 1951 has been treated as a wicked Tory invention.

Once the mistakes of 1951 are freely admitted, it becomes possible to look back objectively on the record of the 1945 Government, and in particular to submit its loss of direction and its rapid decline in momentum to frank investigation. Every Labour M.P. who won his seat in the 1945 election will have his personal impression of the causes of that decline. It is my opinion that the Attlee Government revealed three grave defects, of which the first and most culpable was its failure to do its homework in the years before it achieved power. Of course, the Cabinet had its socialist successes – nationalized electricity and civil aviation among them – and one socialist triumph. Despite more than a decade of Tory erosion, the National Health Service still stands out as the only example of a radical, socialist solution, imposed by a minister who knew how to split the powers that be and call the bluff of the professional pressure groups. But there were ministers charged with huge plans for nationalization who took office without any adequate blueprint for the job.

Labour's plans for the Welfare State were equally vague, and the Minister of National Insurance found himself almost automatically committed to the Beveridge system of flat-rate contributions and benefits, which was obsolescent years before it was introduced. Even more serious was the little advance thinking that had been done about the way of achieving the transition from a war-time siege economy to peace-time socialist planning. This intellectual vacuum was only too easily filled by a continuance of war-time controls and rationing. Socialism as a result became disastrously identified in the consumer's mind with shortages and austerity; and industrially with bureaucratic interference from Whitehall.

When the fuel crisis hit us in 1947, it blew this gaff. So far from imposing a full-scale national plan on the economy, the Attlee Government had not furnished itself with the information on which any plan must be based – far less with the instruments for carrying it into effect. In the convertibility crisis a few months later, the socialist Chancellor of the Exchequer at the Treasury was far less well informed about the flight from the pound than his opposite number in Washington.

The final exposure of this failure to forestall trouble, by advanced planning based on the best available information, and so designed to meet predictable difficulties, came with the outbreak of the Korean War. The Government's attempt to spatchcock a huge rearmament programme into a fully-employed economy, without either import controls or an incomes policy, only aggravated the inevitable inflation and indicated clearly enough the inadequacy of the planning staff on which ministers were relying. It was because he had lost control of the situation that Mr. Attlee decided to resign.

My second main criticism of the Attlee administration relates to personnel. As members of the war-time coalition, its senior ministers had already been accepted into the Whitehall Establishment; and it did not occur to Mr. Attlee that the election of a Labour Government pledged to radical social reform required any radical changes in the civil service. The claim that top people in Whitehall could serve a post-war Labour Government pledged to socialization just as faithfully as they had served a pre-war National Government pledged to prevent socialism, was accepted with complete sincerity. In a nervous attempt to avoid the charge of 'jobs for the boys', ministers fell over backwards in appointing administrators who could show an unblemished record of anti-socialism to run the new nationalized boards, in collaboration with a few retired generals and ageing Trade Union leaders. Railway nationalizaton was the extreme example of this uncritical reliance on Whitehall. A huge price was paid for a private enterprise on the verge of bankruptcy, which was then allowed to run down under an ineffectual minister at the beck and call of his civil servants.

How much more humane and imaginative our post-war reconstruction would have proved if government departments had been invigorated by an influx of experts with special knowledge, new ideas and a sympathy for the Government's domestic and foreign policies. But the Premier dismissed such suggestions as Left-Wing claptrap. Once again, as after 1918, the best of the temporary civil servants returned to their peacetime occupations, and the old Establishment ruled unchallenged over a bureaucratic empire which had been both enormously enlarged and dangerously centralized during the war.

At the Foreign Office, Ernest Bevin soon got rid of Philip Noel Baker, his only minister with any knowledge of foreign affairs. As a result, while the Prime Minister and Sir Stafford Cripps – confident in their personal knowledge of India – were pushing independence through in defiance of the civil servants, Mr. Bevin was building his reputation as a great Foreign Secretary by giving a Trade Union gloss to Sir Winston Churchill's Fulton speech. The economic ministries – above all the Treasury – were nearly as successful in excluding unorthodox outsiders. If in 1931 the MacDonald Government was killed by the aristocratic embrace, in 1951 the Attlee Government quietly expired in the arms of the Whitehall Establishment.

In describing these first two defects of the Attlee Government, I write without inside knowledge and must base my judgement on the impressions of a backbencher who had only one opportunity to observe for himself how Mr. Attlee and Mr. Bevin put their socialist principles into practice. In 1945, I was appointed to the Anglo-American Commission on Palestine, and from then until the loss of Abadan I saw at close quarters each stage of Mr. Bevin's disastrous Middle East policy – in particular his self-inflicted defeat by the Palestine Jews. Seldom can a socialist Foreign Secretary have accepted more conscientiously the advice of the Foreign Office and the Chiefs of Staff, or spurned more roughly all those who suggested that he would best serve the cause of expediency, as well as of honour, by keeping his promises and sticking to his principles.

The record of the Attlee Government in the Middle East is a classic example of what happens to a powerful trade union leader who takes over the Foreign Office, full of good intentions and bursting with self-confidence, but without either prepared plans or selected personnel to carry them out.

So we come to the third defect – the breakdown of the Government's relations with the rank and file of the labour movement. When the story of the Bevanite revolt comes to be written, it will be seen that the Cabinet quarrel about teeth and spectacles was not the cause of the trouble. It was merely the occasion of an explosion of rank-and-file disillusionment which blew Morrison and Dalton off the Executive and created the rift between 'loyalist' M.P.s and the party outside that is still not completely healed today. For years before the three ministers resigned, a crisis of confidence had been brewing between the Labour Establishment – politicians and Trade Union leaders alike – and their active supporters throughout the country. In this oligarchic country of ours, the people traditionally think in terms of 'We' and 'They'. 'They', of course, are the rulers and 'We' the ruled. When Mr. Attlee was summoned to Buckingham Palace in 1945, he was felt to be forming a government on behalf of 'Us' as distinct from 'Them'. And Lord Shawcross sensed the mood in his notorious remark 'We are the rulers now'.

But that dawn was soon over. Long before the election of 1950 had made us a party in office but without power, and therefore at the mercy of the enemies of socialism, it was clear that the Attlee Government dismissed the vision of a government that would make 'Them' responsible to 'Us' as silly syndicalism. In the history of the British Left, there can seldom have been an administration so conservative in its solicitude for the stuffier constitutional conventions, so instinctively suspicious of all suggestions for popular participation in decision-taking and workers' control, and so determined to damp down the fiery demands for a new social order that had won them the election.

Already in 1913 Robert Michels had written the classic description of how a democratic labour movement, dedicated to the cause of social revolution, becomes enslaved to its own leadership. I read *Political Parties* in the twenties as a deadly account of what was wrong with Weimar socialism and I gaily assumed that it had no relevance to Britain. Reading it again in 1947, I began to have doubts. Today I recommend it unhesitatingly as a textbook analysis of how the labour movement's complex structure of internal democracy was being almost unnoticeably changed into a system for maintaining in power a self-perpetuating industrial and political oligarchy – until the Bevanite revolt upset the process.

If Michels' picture is regarded as a perverse caricature and I am asked for a realistic study composed by a fairminded academic, I need only turn to Robert Mackenzie's *British Political Parties*. The facts described by both observers are exactly the same. Michels, however, believed that the job of a Labour Party was not to manage parliamentary democracy as well as the Tories, but to transform it into a social democracy, in which the ordinary people for the first time lost their sense of helplessness and shared in the task of taking decisions. And in this transformation, he saw that a Labour Party's internal democracy had an essential role to play. Hence his horror at its destruction. Mr. Mackenzie sees things differently. His book is inspired by the warmest admiration for the way in which the Labour Party under Mr. Attlee's leadership was becoming an oligarchy almost indistinguishable from the Tory oligarchy. His analysis completely confirms Michels' famous 'Law of Increasing Oligarchy'. But unlike Michels he seems to regard this process as praiseworthy.

Was Michels or Mackenzie right in his conclusions? I myself have no doubt of the answer. Surely when it was faced with a tacitly hostile Establishment in Whitehall and an actively hostile press in Fleet Street, the Labour Government should have felt the need for a politically conscious and politically educated rank and file, such as was beginning to emerge in the Thirties with the help of the W.E.A. and the N.C.L.C. Surely after 1945 the party machine should have been instructed to organize a nation-wide crusade of workers' education so as to give the rank and file the feeling that they were needed by the leadership, not merely to man the electoral machine, but to create that pressure of active Left-Wing opinion required to combat Tory propaganda. If a Labour Government is to survive the attacks of its enemies and to make some advance towards socialism, it cannot do so by treating the party that puts it into power merely as a useful vote-getting machine. It was because the Attlee Government trusted the Whitehall Establishment and distrusted its own movement that its dynamic was halted within two years of its election victory. After that, disintegration was inevitable. The Bevanite split finished off a dying administration. But as a result the labour movement was saved as it had been saved in 1931.

Of course there is another side of this picture which the historian of the Labour party will have to take into account. Within its limits, the Attlee Government was competent and successful. It not merely prevented a relapse into pre-war conditions, but consolidated the social revolution that the war itself had brought about, and so prepared the way for the development of the new managed capitalism and the Affluent Society of the fifties. In this respect, its historical role is of the greatest importance. But in this essay my concern has been not so much with the past as with the future. It is only by forcing ourselves to see the errors of the forties that we shall prevent a repetition of them in the sixties.

THE NATURE OF THE LABOUR PARTY

Tom Nairn

The British Labour Party is obviously one of the greatest political forces of the capitalist world. With its six million and more members, it is by far the largest of social-democratic parties. The twelve million votes cast in its favour at the last General Election were the votes of the majority of the working class – of a working class undivided on religious or ideological grounds, and sociologically the dominant class in an overwhelmingly proletarian nation. It is used to power, although the modalities of that power may seem limited. There have been three Labour Governments, and there is now a fourth – a major event in the political evolution of Europe, and indeed of the world as a whole.

But inseparably associated with the Labour Party's strength there are less evident weaknesses, and both strength and weakness are aspects of a unique historical and political evolution full of its own characteristic contradictions, too little analysed until now. As a part of its well-known general antipathy to theory, the British Left has been notably averse to thinking critically about itself. The Labour Party did not come into being in response to any theory about what a socialist party should be; it arose empirically, in a quite piecemeal fashion, like so much in British bourgeois society before it. And it rapidly became accepted as a permanent, inevitable feature of that society – a kind of monument about which it was pointless, if not impious, to ask too searching questions. Something of the mindless complacency of British bourgeois society was in this way transmitted to British socialism. And besides this, the Labour Party dominates the scene so totally in Britain, it embraces so much and has sunk such deep roots that any radical change in it seems unthinkable – what criticism could affect a leviathan like this?

Any adequate account of the Labour movement must, naturally, be historical. Like other mass socialist parties, it is essentially a novelty – nothing else than the embryo of a new society – but this element is concealed and qualified in its case by a singularly dense integument tying it to the past. This integument is at once the ideology and customs of Labourism and beyond them the reflexes of the labour movement and of the working class as a whole. It is linked to, and in part dependent upon a, specific kind of organization and bureaucratic control. It was the natural, effective instrument of adaptation of a working-class movement to a society which itself – during the whole existence of Labourism – leaned instinctively and whole-heartedly towards the past. The Labour movement's empirical, undoctrinaire origins, the indigenous nature of all its roots, signify a particularly intimate bond with the society that gave birth to it. But we must also try to see to what extent the situation of the Labour Party under Harold Wilson is a new one. British society as a whole has begun to change more rapidly and consciously, after a long era of stagnation, generating a multitude of tensions and new contradictions. Labour has returned to power at a critical moment in this process, which is also a process of rupture, of awakening consciousness and the collapse of traditional modes of hegemony. What new possibilities and dangers confront the Labour Party under these conditions? What new problems are being added to the old ones?

British Trade Unionism

After the defeat of Chartism began the greatest era of prosperity for British capitalism, the twenty-five years from 1850 until about 1875. Cyclical crises practically disappeared. "Shortly before the middle of the century there began everywhere a substantial advance in the standard of living. At first this was due not to rising wages but to falling prices; but later, when prices again rose, wages . . . rose more than enough to meet them . . . Revolts and mass movements gave place to the well-organized but moderate Trade Unions and Co-operative Societies of the new order."[1] The epoch of integration had begun. This moderate trade-unionism, whose basic structures and outlook endure to this day, was to become the nucleus of Labourism. Not until 1918 did it turn aside, even nominally, from a general acceptance of capitalist society.

To retrace the origins of Labourism in Victorian trade-unionism is to see the inevitability of the moderation afflicting this, the nucleus of all later developments. In Britain, from 1850 until around 1890, Trade Unions were the working-class movement. There was nothing else. There were no socialist ideas or movements with any influence; until the 1880s there was not even a significant radical movement to which the workers could look for support. The voices of intellectual protest were few, and remote from politics and the working class: distorted by the immense pressures of Victorian conformity, they tended towards an impossible and Utopian rejection of capitalism and industrialism (as with Ruskin and William Morris) or retreated into obscurity and eccentricity (like the novelists Meredith and Samuel Butler). In such a void – following earlier defeat – profound subordination was unavoidable. The bourgeoisie disposed of more and more ample means of corruption, both material and spiritual. Its world economic dominance enabled it to concede something to the upper strata of skilled workers, those involved in the first Trade Unions, while to the inherent mystifications of British bourgeois society was added the sense of belonging to a superior race, which owned a large part of the world and supplied the wants of the rest. Belonging to it was a kind of privilege, even in misery. From the 1880s onwards, when British capitalism was for the first time challenged in world markets, this feeling of superiority was enormously increased – instead of disappearing – by the new climate and mystique of imperialism.

For forty decisive years, class conflict was reduced to relatively mild and tolerable proportions. By the end of the period,

[1] G. D. H. Cole, *A Short History of the British Working Class Movement*, p. 126.

habits and traditions had been formed, founded on the strength and prestige of the Trade Unions, enduring reflexes which impressed themselves on all that happened later.

The politics of the British working class was conditioned by this trade-unionism. Trade-unionism was to dominate politics absolutely – the contrary of what happened in, for example, the evolution of the German working class. When the workers began to think politically for themselves, slowly and still hesitantly, in the last decade of the century, they could only start from the accomplished fact of trade-unionism. How could any working-class political movement have any success, if it did not somehow lean upon the Trade Unions and make use of their strength, their funds, their prestige? All the more so, because of the great expansion of the Unions in the last ten years of Victoria's reign, after the famous London dock strike of 1889. This strike led to the entry into trade-unionism of masses of unskilled workers. Large 'general' Unions of unskilled workers supplemented the old 'craft' unions. Total Trade Union membership rose in a few years from around 750,000 to 1,500,000, and by 1900 there were 2,000,000 trade-unionists.

This growth and partial change in the character of trade-unionism had been produced by the severe cyclical crises and generally more difficult conditions imposed on British capitalism since the ending of its world-monopoly. It coincided with the beginning of serious socialist agitation in Britain by the first Marxist group, the Social-Democratic Federation (founded in 1883), the Fabian Society (founded in 1884), and the most important socialist party – and forerunner of the Labour Party – the Independent Labour Party (founded in 1893). And it gave rise to something of a counter-offensive by the employers, culminating in the Taff Vale court case (1901) when a legal decision in effect abolished the right to strike. Both factors moved the Trade Unions towards political action. But of the two, the second was alone really decisive – the Trade Union leaders were only convinced of the necessity for working-class politics when such action became necessary to safeguard trade-unionism itself.

The historical function of trade-unionism was the protection of the workers' material standards of life and work, through a constant struggle against the mechanisms of the capitalist system. In itself, this did not require a consciousness of the working class as being more than one section of society, with particular problems arising out of its particular situation. Its ideal does not have to be any more than that of obtaining a 'square deal' for the workers, in the general terms permitted by that situation. The last decades of the century saw the British working class, through its Trade Unions, first of all acquire a more comprehensive consciousness of its essential unity (in contrast to the fragmentation of the craft unions), and then attempt to pursue its collective interests through forms of political action. But without stepping beyond the limits of its corporativism.

A Non-Marxist Universe

Who were the socialists that tried, without success, to convert the Trade Unions to more ambitious ideas? Plainly the arrival of Marxist ideas in Britain should have been of the great importance. Was not Marxism the evident, only answer to the intellectual and political voids of British historical development? At once the natural doctrine of the working class, and the summing-up of the Enlightenment and all the highest stages of bourgeois thought into a new synthesis? Its superiority to British bourgeois conservatism was such, surely, that by appropriating it the working class could attain its own *hegemonic* ideology? A few years after the foundation of the Social-Democratic Federation, however, Engels frankly admitted the problems confronting it: 'One can see that it is by no means easy to drill ideas into a big nation in a doctrinaire and dogmatic way, even if one has the best of theories, developed out of its own conditions of life . . .'[1] In fact, the task was to prove impossible. The reason is, in part, that Marxism – in the elementary form embraced and propagated by the Federation – was *not* really developed out of the 'conditions of life' of Britain and the British proletariat. It was based upon an

[1] Engels, letter to Sorge, 7th December 1889.

extensive analysis of the *economic foundations* of that life, certainly – but the dominating characteristic of social life in general was, precisely, the variety of ways in which those foundations were masked for the average consciousness, the web of false relations and ideas woven around them. Marx and Engels had devoted little time to examination of these super-structures. This cannot be considered a reproach to them, but it plainly imposed special problems on their disciples in Britain. A theory can only become practically effective and a cultural and political force when it is felt to echo experience; but experience, actual consciousness, is mediated through the complex of superstructures and apprehends what underlies them only partially and indirectly. Hence, in Britain it was vitally necessary to decipher social reality as a whole. This required a creative development of Marxist ideas – Marxism can never be 'applied', every genuine use of it implies a development of the theory itself – on a very considerable scale. At this time, unfortunately, the British intelligentsia had other preoccupations. It was engaged on discovering Hegelian idealism and re-expressing it in the appropriate imperialistic terms (as in Bosanquet's *Philosophical Theory of the State*, for instance, published in 1901); one sector had undertaken a timorous revolt against Victorian puritanism, inspired by G. E. Moore's *Principia Ethica*, but this was confined strictly to 'personal' and 'aesthetic' terms.

The nullity of native intellectual traditions proved to be the most serious of obstacles to socialism. The Marxists of the Social-Democratic Federation – and their later successors – were destined to remain a small and sectarian group. The leaders of Labourism thought that, however appropriate Marxism might be in foreign countries, it just had no reference to Britain. Nevertheless, some kind of theory was necessary to the working-class movement. The trade-unionists had adhered originally to *laissez faire* liberalism; when this was no longer possible and they had committed themselves to autonomous political action, they tried for as long as possible to avoid any doctrine justifying such action. Pure empiricism reigned during the first decades of Labourist politics. When the movement had become a great mass force, however, threatening to depose liberalism politically (after the First World War), empiricism had to be at least adulterated with something else capable of furnishing a minimum of cohesion. The void left by the failure of the Marxists had to be filled by the other socialist currents active from the 1880s onwards.

British Socialism

These indigenous theories were uninteresting and, in any wider perspective, quite unimportant. Essentially, they reflected nothing but the intellectual parochialism of the bourgeoisie, its complacent self-absorption and optimism. They adapted and transformed third-rate bourgeois traditions into fourth-rate socialist traditions, imposing upon the working class all the righteous mediocrity and worthless philistinism of the pious Victorian petty bourgeois. Fabian socialism derived from Utilitarianism, the timid and dreary species of bourgeois rationalism embraced by the British middle-class during the Industrial Revolution. In it, bourgeois rationalism became socialist rationalism chiefly through the substitution of the State for the magic forces of the *laissez faire* capitalist market: the former was seen as bringing about the 'greatest happiness of the greatest number' almost as automatically as the latter had been. According to this ideology of minor functionaries, although the working class made socialism *possible* (with their votes), the new society would actually be created by an eternal '*élite* of unassuming experts . . . exercising the power inherent in superior knowledge and longer administrative experience'.[1]

The Independent Labour Party's socialism, on the other hand, was derived from the religion of the Protestant sects. Since the seventeenth century sectarian Protestantism had always been to a certain extent a movement of popular protest against 'established' religion. Militant Protestantism died hard in a nation whose great revolution had after all been carried out under the aegis of Puritanism. But long before the foundation of the Labour Party, this tradition had decayed into a

[1] Beatrice Webb, *Our Partnership*, p. 97.

relatively subordinate, impotent – and therefore acceptable – force, a kind of domesticated national conscience, for ever indignant at the 'excesses' of capitalism and at the iniquitous conduct of the very rich and the very poor alike (the vices of the latter being essentially identified with alcohol). Such was the cadaver passed on to the labour movement. If the ideas of Fabianism were few and tedious, this post-Christian socialism had no ideas at all. The dissenting sects had viewed intellect with the gravest suspicion, as being probably associated with the Devil. Socialism, hence, was apprehended only as a moral crusade propelled by emotions of outrage at injustice and suffering. Speaking of the greatest propagandist of Independent Labour Party socialism, G. D. H. Cole points out how in spite of Robert Blatchford's immense influence as a journalist, 'his contribution to socialist *thought* . . . was next to nothing. He was neither a theorist nor a planner, and to socialist doctrine he neither contributed nor sought to contribute any original idea'.[1]

It is of the utmost importance to grasp the relationship between these two currents. In the first place, they had enough in common to come together in one body and act in alliance. They both accepted – the Fabians by conviction, the I.L.P. socialists for want of an alternative – the *evolutionary* character of socialism. Socialism had to be constructed piece by piece, over a long period of time. This evolutionism, in effect, denied entirely that a decisive struggle for *power* played any necessary role in the process – the conditions of British bourgeois society had clothed the fact of power so well, and reduced the conflict of classes so much, that this mystification was entirely natural. The Fabians actually thought of the whole capitalist epoch as being, not the domination of one class over others, but a mere 'period of anarchy' in social affairs, a period of 'administrative nihilism' in between feudal administration on the one hand and the new collective, socialist administration on the other.[2] Society was recovering spontaneously from this

---

[1] G. D. H. Cole, *A History of Socialist Thought*, vol. III, part I, p. 167.
[2] See Sidney Webb, 'The Basis of Socialism: Historic' in *Fabian Essays* (1889).

anarchy, as State intervention and control were extended, and socialists had simply to assist this natural, healthy tendency by the appropriate propaganda and action in support of national-ization and municipalization. Since present society was not really a power-structure but a sort of historical mistake, socialism could not be a struggle to replace one hegemony with another.

The logical consequence of evolutionism was, in concrete terms, *parliamentarism*. Parliamentary action should suffice to build socialism up piece by piece. Again, although the I.L.P. was much less enthusiastic about Parliament than the Fabians, it accepted it in practice. Instinctively, the workers and advanced Trade Union militants in the I.L.P. distrusted these things – but they saw no alternative.

The common subjection to these ideas, and to this fatal context of political action signified the permanent hegemony of Fabianism, ideologically. The Fabians were the technicians of reform – perhaps the most able reformers of this kind pro-duced by socialism in any country. Their effort was always con-centrated upon what was immediately practical; their acute sense of the possible, their great respect for the facts that con-cerned them, their armoury of information and argument, all these things made them *effective* reformers. And their perspec-tives were, naturally, the perspectives proper to 'evolutionary' socialism and parliamentarism. The socialists of the I.L.P., by contrast, were predominantly working class (the party was strong above all in the great northern industrial towns, while the Fabians were Londoners) and lacked the formation and outlook of the technocrats. Their revolt against society was, in a sense, far more *real* than that of the Fabians: they reacted against capitalism with passion, they took the ultimate aim of the socialist movement seriously and wanted to see the be-ginnings of a real change in their own lifetime. Instinctively, they rejected the perspectives of evolutionism and parlia-mentarism; but because they accepted the latter intellectually, they were constrained to accept the leadership of Fabians with-in the wider ambit of the working-class movement.

The I.L.P. tradition was destined to become, so to speak,

the *subjectivity* of the political wing of Labour – the emotions of the movement in contrast to its Fabian 'mind' or 'intellect'. When the two traditions were united inside the Labour Party, other factors also contributed to the hegemony of Fabianism. But one can see how the Fabians were bound to be naturally in command – how I.L.P. socialism, in spite of its working-class base, in spite of a certain authenticity of reflex and feeling rendering it infinitely more humanly admirable than Fabianism, could only become a 'left' opposition fixed in more or less impotent attitudes of protest. It was destined to become a Left Wing permanently, necessarily in rebellion against Fabian mediocrity – but unable to formulate and develop coherently this revolt, intellectually empty, paralysed inside the larger body of Labourism, a permanent minority opposition lacking the resources to assume hegemony of the movement in its turn.

Second-best Socialism

These considerations may help us to identify the second fundamental problem of Labourism. Because of its size and power, trade-unionism was – as we saw above – bound to dominate the nascent political movement. The dilemma confronting all the socialist pioneers is described by Cole (speaking of the Independent Labour Party): 'They speedily realized that . . . they must either induce the Trade Unions to throw in their lot with them or be content to build up very slowly a party based on individual membership on the Continental socialist model. As they were not prepared to wait, most of them preferred the shorter cut of a Labour Party based mainly on Trade Union affiliations, even though they realized that they could get such a party only by a considerable dilution of their socialist objectives . . .'[1] The Labour Party was, indeed, a kind of historical 'short-cut' to socialism, but a short-cut that has proved very much more long and difficult than the early socialists believed, perhaps longer than the alternative would have been.

[1] G. D. H. Cole, *A History of the Labour Party from 1914*, p. 152.

When the Unions finally agreed to co-operate in setting up a working-class political movement at the time of the Taff Vale decision, the socialists were in fact only too happy to accept the Unions' conditions. The proposed political party would be, not socialist, but devoted to 'the direct interest of Labour' – that is, trade-unionism translated on to the political plane, a political party representing the interests of the working class in the way that an individual union treats the interests of its members. Although the Trade Unions were furnishing the finances and laying down the general orientation of the new party, the greater part of its active organizers and leaders were, naturally, socialists. The Fabian Society and the Independent Labour Party were affiliated to the new organization, in the same way as the Trade Unions, and furnished the cadres. Here was the matrix within which the character of British socialism was formed, the character which the Labour Party as a whole would assume when it became a socialist party, at last, in 1918.

It is the internal dynamic of this socialism which constitutes the second basic problem of the Labourist movement. In the Labour Party, Fabianism became the dominant, Right-Wing leadership tradition, the source of the ideas governing most of the action of the party. Its leaders were all to be either avowed Fabians (Attlee, Gaitskell) or implicit Fabians, whatever their apparent background (Macdonald, Henderson, Lansbury). The I.L.P. became the Labour Left Wing, in chronic instinctive protest against the leadership, but intellectually subordinated to it and incapable of effectively replacing it. Labourism, therefore, acquired from the beginning a *peculiarly weak left*.

This is, in a sense, the intimate tragedy of Labourism – for the left has always expressed the most vital working-class elements, the most active and genuine socialist forces *potentially* able to develop their own hegemony over party and State. But expressing them in the fashion and under the conditions indicated, the Labour Left has really completely frustrated these forces, putting them at the disposition of the Right-Wing reformists. It has been unable even seriously to influence the leadership, except under rare circumstances and momentarily.

Hence, the Fabian-inspired leadership tradition, permanently supported by the Trade Unions, could acquire a great stability and continuity – a kind of dynasty, in fact, with its own characteristic internal procedures of recruitment and co-ordination, almost independent of the party in general. And this permanent, organic power in its turn of course *obstructed* any further real evolution of the Left Wing – it is as if the Independent Labour Party tradition, which was apparently the beginning of a real British mass socialist party, was *paralysed* by entry into the matrix of Labourism. Hardie and the other I.L.P. leaders anticipated that they would be able rapidly to convert the Labour Party to socialism. Instead, the conditions of labourism, and their own weakness, transformed them into a more permanent opposition, always urging the Labour Party to move Left and always unable to make it move, only half conscious of their own position and its true meaning, unable to act within Labourism but unable to see any alternative to Labourism, oppressed by Fabian triviality and timidity but with no workable alternative to offer. It is clear that the Labour Party has only been able to become the one great political expression of the British working class and survive in the same form for so long, *because* it has had a Left Wing of this general type. Other socialist traditions and ideas would not have been able to tolerate the Labour Party, and it would not have been able to tolerate them – schisms of the kind familiar in other movements would inevitably have occurred, decisively altering the political evolution of the working class and the whole nation.

Hypocrites and Traitors

From 1906 onwards, the Labour Party functioned essentially as a kind of Trade Union 'pressure group' (or, more widely, as a 'pressure group' for the working class as a whole). It was not a very effective pressure group. Its supine acceptance of parliamentarism made of it for most of the time a subordinate wing of the Liberal Party. Something of the evolution of the early Labour Party can be seen in the contrast between two statements by Ben Tillett, one of the Trade Union militants who had played a prominent role in founding both the Independent Labour Party and the Labour Party. Speaking in 1893, he asserted that socialists should aim first of all 'to capture the Trades Unionists of this country, a body of men well organized, who paid their money, and were socialists at their work every day, and not merely on the platform, who did not shout for blood-red revolution, and when it came to revolution sneaked under the nearest bed . . . With his experience of Unions, he was glad to say that if there were fifty such red revolutionary parties as there were in Germany, he would sooner have the solid, progressive, matter-of-fact, fighting trades unionism of England than all the hare-brained chatterers and magpies of continental revolutionists'.[1] Here was the authentic spirit of Labourism: proudly anti-theoretical, vulgarly chauvinist, totally deluded by the false social-democratic contrast between 'revolution' (conceived as twenty-four hours of 'blood-red' violence) and 'evolution' (conceived as a sort of arithmetic adding-up of socialism by little, regular instalments). Yet the same Ben Tillett, fifteen years later denounced the Labour deputies as 'sheer hypocrites' who 'repaid with gross betrayal the class that willingly supported them'.[2] But the 'Parliamentary Party' was only the logical consequence of the outlook and policy Tillett himself had preached in 1893. 'Hypocrisy' and 'betrayal' were the natural result of the 'solid, progressive, matter-of-fact' economism and philistinism he had defended so complacently; ordinary trade unionists were *not* 'socialists at their work every day', and the Labourist assumption that they were and that a great political movement could be founded on them just as they were, led to the creation of politicians who were not 'socialists at *their* work every day', either.

The missing dimension characteristic of Labourism emerges clearly from Tillett's remark: socialist education, the complex, difficult task of changing consciousness to express (and, by expressing, develop) the instincts of the masses at their work

[1] G. D. Cole, *British Working Class Politics, 1832–1914*, p. 141.
[2] See R. Miliband, *Parliamentary Socialism*, p. 28.

every day. Labourism's relation to the class it represents is in essence a *passive* one. Historically, it accepts the working class and the organizations the latter evolved in its long development, the Trade Unions, as given, decisive facts. Arriving late upon the scene, the organ of a class already profoundly adapted to the conditions of bourgeois society and imbued with its conservatism, it sees its function as no more than a continuation, a further step in this evolution. But the evolutionary models at the root of Labourist thought and action are false. Their falseness is the crucial falseness of labourism as a whole. The advance on to the political plane embodied in the Labour Party is not really another step on the same evolutionary road, a 'natural' process of growth on the same basis. There is a factor of novelty involved in it, requiring a more radical and complete change than the analogy allows – a qualitative change, as it were. The political plane is the plane of power: a political party lays claim to a specific form of hegemony over society as a whole, and a socialist party intends using such hegemony to remodel society. The problems of hegemony are of an order different from those confronting Trade Unions – at least, Trade Unions as they existed in Britain up to 1906. They impose upon a hitherto subordinate social class and its organizations a vast, energetic development, a new tension and perspective, violent and positive adjustments in the field of culture – if the hegemony is to be really new, in fact, a sort of metamorphosis. The drive towards this change does not arise mechanically from the working class – least of all from the British working class as it was in the imperialist era – and is not transmitted to political leaders by a passive link between the latter and the former.

An apparent paradox is the key to this typical, central defect of Labourist socialism. The political potential of the working class is not realized when the political movement founded on it accepts as determinant the structures and outlook already created by the workers in their struggle as a subordinate class. These structures cannot *really* determine the form and content of a political movement – hence, as the entire story of Labourism so clearly demonstrates, when political parties embrace this basis they finish by being determined by quite different factors. That is, by the pressures of bourgeois society outside the proletariat, by paralysing conventions and myths. The miserable 'respectability' of the new-born Labour Party, its abject political manœuvrings, its lead-heavy 'moderation' – its whole apparatus of 'betrayal' – arose paradoxically from its purely proletarian basis. The latter apparently determined the nature of the political, socialist movement; but because in reality – for the reasons indicated – it could not do so, the effective political culture of the socialist movement was bound to be not proletarian but bourgeois. The way was left open for what may be more accurately defined as a sub-bourgeois political culture, for the sweepings of the great Anglo-Saxon ethos, a servile imitation of the ruling class's corpus of ideas and customs quite dissociated from the latter's historical *raison d'être*. The paradox functions even on the plane of personalities: to the solidly working-class character of the Labour Party's militants – immediately visible at any Labour Party Conference – there corresponded *necessarily* ruling cadres derived directly from the ruling class, imbued with its outlook and traditions, such as Attlee, Gaitskell, Dalton and many others.

Does this mean that the working class can only evolve a true socialist movement under the tutelage of revolutionary intellectuals, of an intelligentsia whose own origins are not proletarian? This, in turn, is surely only one aspect of the truth. The conception of the intellectuals mechanically 'manipulating' the working class is a mere antithesis to that of the political movement arising spontaneously out of the working class. In reality, only a dialectical relationship between leaders and masses can create a geninely proletarian and socialist political movement (a relationship which makes, as Gramsci pointed out, for the abolition of the distinction between 'intellectual' and 'executant'). And it was the absence of this dialectic which crippled Labourism. The historical failure of the intellectuals – the particular *trahison des clercs* incarnated in labourism – signifies therefore, not the lack of an *élite* mandarin class benevolently bestowing its wisdom upon the workers from above, but the lack of the catalyst element a socialist movement requires in order to be itself.

Socialism, declared Macdonald in 1912, 'must begin with the facts of social unity, not with those of class conflict, because the former is the predominant fact in society'.[1] So it was not surprising that, two years later, after its ignominious and subordinate parliamentary career, the new Labour Party plunged into active participation in the First World War. 'By 1914,' it has been pointed out, 'the more enlightened members of Britain's ruling orders had come to see the leaders of Labour *both* as opponents and as allies.'[2] After 1914, they ceased for years to be opponents. The Labour Party took part in government for the first time when it entered the war-time coalition of 1915, and later played a more important role (with three Ministerial posts) in the Lloyd George coalition. The war led to a general weakening of socialist influence within the labour movement, and to hostility between the trade-unionists and the socialists of the I.L.P. – chiefly because of pacifist protest among certain I.L.P. leaders.

But if the First World War brought about a further assimilation of the labour movement, and a further weakening of the already feeble socialist influence, in other respects its effects were quite different. It *made* the Labour Party, in the form we know today. War conditions forced the Government to evolve a very extensive system of State control of the economy – including prices and rents – in a country previously devoted to *laissez faire*. This was seen by the labour movement as a proof of the inadequacy of capitalism, and as a sort of 'war-time socialism' that could be preserved and extended after the war. A part of the Fabian vision was being realized in practice, and this was far more persuasive than any rhetoric to the 'practical' Trade Union leaders. More generally, the shock of the war created a sense of new possibilities, and a vague demand for a new world, propitious to the advance of socialist ideas. Even the Liberal Prime Minister, Lloyd George, felt in 1917

[1] James Ramsay Macdonald, *Syndicalism: a Critical Examination*, p. 50.

[2] R. Miliband, *Parliamentary Socialism*, p. 38.

that he had to advise a Labour delegation that 'The whole state of society is more or less molten . . . you can stamp upon that molten mass almost anything, so long as you do so with firmness and determination . . . Think out new ways; think out new methods . . . Don't always be thinking of getting back to where you were before the war: get a really new world'.[1]

In the same year, the Russian Revolution added another stimulus. How strong this stimulus was, was demonstrated in one of the most extraordinary episodes of Labour Party history, the famous Leeds Convention of 1917. At this meeting, organized for the purpose of welcoming the Russian Revolution, British workers were astonished by the spectacle of MacDonald and other equally improbable personages supporting a resolution that demanded 'the establishment in every town, urban and rural district, of Councils of Workmen and Soldiers' Delegates (Soviets) for initiating and coordinating working-class activity . . . and for the complete political and economic emancipation of international labour'.[2] This euphoric cry for a repetition of the Russian Revolution in Britain soon vanished, but the fact that it happened at all showed how the labour movement had become temporarily open to change and new ideas.

The Modern Labour Party

Hence the First World War accomplished what the small British socialist groups had not been able to accomplish. Under its influence the labour movement moved towards the acceptance of a form of socialism: at last, the Labour Party could become a socialist party and not a mere Trade Union party. But, because this happened at a time when the socialists themselves were particularly weak, it took the shape of an absolutely *minimal* conversion to the new ideas. The socialists were in a poor position to foster and push further the process of conversion. If the majority of Trade Union leaders liked the abstract notion of socialism more than previously, they disliked

[1] Labour Party Annual Conference Report, 1917, p. 163.
[2] S. Graubard, *British Labour and the Russian Revolution*, p. 38.

and distrusted most actual socialists more than previously and were not prepared to envisage a radical transformation of the Labour Party. The key figure in the transition was Arthur Henderson, the old trade-unionist and war-time leader of the Labour Party. He saw that the possibility existed for the Labour Party to become a real, national political party, and that a real political party must have an ideology. In the case of the Labour Party the new ideological appeal *could* only be socialist in orientation. One more prudent, empirical step forward, one more cautious phase of British 'evolution', one more insanely complex compromise, and the instrument of British socialism was there at last, occupying its proper place in the British firmament midway between the House of Lords and the Boy Scouts. The product of endless, grudging, political manœuvrings and an infinity of compromises, a half-hearted mixture of socialism, trade-unionism, Protestant moralism and all-engulfing respectability, the Labour Party arrived haltingly and late upon the historical scene; yet its arrival also co-incided with, and partly expressed, new and wider stirrings in the consciousness of the masses, and in spite of its short-comings it powerfully developed this consciousness. The new horizons it offered were part mirage, part real. Time would disentangle the two. But to present new, partly autonomous perspectives to the working class, even with so many qualifications and defects, and so late, was a great, permanent achievement in this country of the past.

A new constitution was drafted for the Party, principally by Henderson and Sidney Webb, and approved at a special Conference in February 1918. It remains in force today, with only minor changes. The new constitution was designed to give the Party a new organization corresponding to its new ideology and ambitions. Hitherto, it had been simply a collection of affiliated organizations, mostly Trade Unions and socialist groups, and had had no individual members of its own; now it was to recruit members like other social-democratic parties. Hitherto, it had led an uncertain existence in an undefined limbo somewhere between politics and trade-unionism; now the political embryo was to develop into a full political being, with real political aims, drawing its force from a nation-wide network of political militants instead of from other organizations, at second hand.

The speeches and discussions about the new constitution show a consciousness of how important the change was. This was something like a rebirth of the Labour Party. Consciousness, however, again fell far short of the objective implications of the development, as had happened at the birth of the Party. We saw already how new and great the problems of a socialist political movement are, in comparison with those of trade-unionism, how exacting are the new dimensions of power; in 1917 and 1918, Henderson and the other leaders still only partially recognized these dimensions. To the original 'short-cut' of Labourism they could only add another empirical, improvised 'short-cut' in the general direction of socialism.

The social changes envisaged by socialism are vast. They can only be realized by generations of men, through difficult struggles we are only beginning to understand. And if any one thing is certain about socialism, it is that such changes – if they are to be conscious and controlled – require the dedication and active participation of vast numbers of people. They cannot be brought about by a few dozen party leaders, or a few hundred men in a Parliament, whatever the laws they make. But what is a party's way to such mass energy, to a harnessing of the popular will which alone can really bring a new social order into being? Its way is the people in it, its socialist militants, those now commonly referred to even on the left by the odious label of 'the rank and file'. From a socialist point of view, they *are* the party and the movement, it is they who can turn ideas into a material force and become the guiding nucleus of otherwise indeterminate energies. Because of what socialism will be, and because a socialist party must as far as it can prefigure this future in its own existence, it follows that socialists must be conscious of being the movement, must feel that it is theirs and entirely governed by them – because an all-embracing democracy will be part of socialism, it cannot fail to be a constitutive element of any real socialist movement. Hence, one may say that certain principles of organization follow from the very meaning of socialism, and impose themselves upon any socialist party. Whatever problems lie in the way of such democracy – problems indicated by many critics in the past – the effort to realize and maintain it is nevertheless a fundamental obligation of any socialist party, and one of the vital indices of its real nature.

In the events of 1918 and the new Labour Party constitution we see crystallizing *organizational* deficiencies that precisely parallel Labour's cultural weakness, and render it permanent by embodying it in a great new national structure. Within the Labour Party itself, one finds great confusion about simple organizational questions, and the most total ignorance about how the party works and ought to work. The Labour Right has customarily ignored these problems for the good and sufficient reason that the present organization of the party keeps them permanently in power; they study the niceties of its manipulation, not the principles of its structure. The Left has ignored them, because it has always felt – with characteristic moralism – that men's souls can be converted to the cause by preaching, however they happen to be organized. And if socialists themselves are not concerned to understand their organization – that is, their own society, their way of life – why should those outside the Labour Party understand it better?

In fact, the Labour Party's organizational structure is a perfect embodiment of the whole historical experience of the labour movement in Britain, and incarnates both its achievements and its failings. Arrived at 'empirically', that is by a blind series of piecemeal compromises among various historical forces, it naturally expresses on the practical plane the dominant balance of such forces. But we saw how in Britain the dominant pattern of working-class life and institutions had, inevitably, become a conservative one capable of generating at most a kind of class-sectional or corporative outlook. The Trade Unions were the guardians of this outlook, as well as of the standard of living of the workers. Hence, the continuation of their hegemony over the Labour Party after 1918 meant the continued hegemony of this outlook within Labourism. Whereas the objective task posed to socialism in Britain was the reform of this world-view, this fruit of subordination and defeat, it remained fixed in the heart of socialism itself, the rock-like basis upon which the Labour Party was built. The rebirth of 1918, the step into the future of socialism, was also a step back into the past, a decision to remain anchored in the history whose outlines we considered previously. There is no better illustration of the true meaning of British 'empiricism' or 'evolutionism' than the story of the Labour Party's formation. This philosophy of cautious, practical realism and profound respect for the past, a perfect ruling-class intellectual organ tried and tested through centuries of experience, was inherited by the working class for lack of anything better or more fitting; deprived of its original purpose and *raison d'être*, it immediately turns into something else altogether, and all its principal characteristics assume a different sense. Realism turns, in Labour leaders, into mere cowardice, a kind of timid hypnosis in the face of events; practicality turns into wilful short-sightedness, a ritual pragmatism wielded to exorcise the sort of theoretical thinking socialism requires; dignified reverence for the past becomes a depraved fetish-worship of idols which seem to change into dust at the very touch of such falsity – the symbols of a nationalism whose significance should, after all, be transformed utterly by the social revolution labourism nominally stands for. Born out of an iron ring of conceptions like these, the modern Labour Party could only be a compromise. Not a crafty, innocent compromise of the kind the British are for ever boasting about, but one in which all the forces pressing towards the future are mortgaged absolutely to the past and have the life drained from them in useless, secondary struggles.

The Dead Souls of Labourism

Transforming itself into a socialist party, the Labour Party remained an organ of trade-unionism, a Trade Union 'pressure group'. The one was simply grafted on to the other. In theory, as with other political parties, the controlling body of the party is the Annual Conference. Over 80 per cent of the votes which can be cast at this Conference come from the Trade Unions. In recent years they have represented about five million members, as against the one million members from the Constituency Parties – that is, the individual members or militants of the Party. Through the block vote system this vast mass of inactive members are counted, like Gogol's dead souls, as so many votes at the Labour Party Conference, far outweighing those of the active members.

It may be objected that a high proportion of active tradeunionists must be Labour Party activists as well. Does not this redress the balance to some extent? In reality, it serves only to accentuate the paradox of the dead souls of labourism, for in most cases, of course, the trade-unionist actively supporting the party is *also* an 'individual' member enrolled in one of the Constituency Parties. A high proportion of the individual militants are, naturally, trade-unionists. The great double political effort of the latter, in the Trade Unions and the Labour Party directly, cannot however come near equalling the crushing weight of the dead souls, the purely nominal voices which theoretically govern the destiny of the Labour Party, and sometimes of Britain as a whole.

Because they are dead souls, and not an active political force, these voices cannot of course really have this power. They are wielded by the men who do have the power, the delegates to the Labour Party Conference. These delegates are in fact representatives of the different Trade Union *leaderships*, of the great variety of bureaucratic organs which control British trade-unionism. A few large unions, in turn, have a preponderant share of the Trade Unions' majority.

In what sense, then, is this great power employed by the Trade Union leaders? British trade unionism is not a centralized or coherent force – like everything else, it grew up on an empirical, piecemeal basis and no later attempts at rationalization have succeeded. Hence, no one line is represented by the Trade Union delegations at the Labour Party Conference. However, although a small minority of Unions are traditionally Left Wing, the substantial majority has consistently, throughout the party's history, supported characteristic Fabian policies of extreme caution. The corporative and conservative attitudes of the working class are commonly found in their most aggressive form among Trade Union bureaucrats, who rise to power entirely within the ambit of this narrow, tradition-bound type of trade-unionism and identify its categories with their own success and position.

It is possible to see how this dynamic takes its place within the larger dynamic of the Labour Party. Fabianism was intrinsically superior to Labour Leftism, and in the British context was bound to dominate it unless it could evolve greatly and find a superior intellectual expression. But the Labour Party's distinctive organization also gave a permanent bureaucratic form to such dominance, and imposed a permanent bureaucratic barrier to the further evolution of the Left. With a few exceptions, notably Ernest Bevin, the Trade Unions did not use their power in the Labour Party to elect trade-unionists to the party leadership in Parliament. Their hegemony did not bring about the active hegemony of trade-unionism over all the other elements in the movement – for the simple reason that British trade-unionism did not contain within itself the capacity needed for political and cultural hegemony, even the minimal hegemony of a Right-Wing social-democratic party. It could only result in the active hegemony of the intellectual group most congenial to the majority of Trade Union leaders, the moderate Labour Right. The permanent alliance between these forces – sometimes called simply the 'labour alliance' – has been the heart of Labourism. The British Trade Union leaders made clear their distrust of 'intellectuals', their innate reverence for the 'practical' and for moderate, unintellectual 'reasonableness'. Nevertheless, in the Labour Party they always in fact maintained in power a clique of intellectuals; through their agency one particular stratum of the intelligentsia has been able to achieve an extraordinary unity and continuity of domination over the British working-class movement. The clue to this paradox lies, naturally, in the characteristics of the stratum in question. It is composed of a type of intellectual who does not, in a sense, appear *as* an intellectual because of his profound acceptance of the prevailing categories of social existence. Contemptuous of rebels, the British Trade Union bureaucrats could only bestow power upon the unrebellious, traditional intelligentsia – upon intellectuals reared within the old conformity of British intellectual life, educated in the customary fashion at the ancient universities, and wishing to change society not against, but in accordance with its essential taboos. If, therefore, the corporative tendencies of trade-unionism represented a sort of instinctive, primitive conservatism, by means of the 'Labour alliance' this is joined to a much more refined and intellectually elaborated conservatism, to the deeply-rooted, solid, but very un-radical traditions of the British liberal intelligentsia. In this coalition of forces, the ideological dead-weight of the past upon the working class assumes a precise organizational form. The British form of socialism, the force of the future, remains deeply and paradoxically tied to the past, not only in its ideas and sentiments but in its practical structures.

One might say that the design of Labourism systematically alienates the socialist militant, the individual member who is in the movement primarily out of political conviction and who naturally feels that socialism is something to be realized within the horizons of the living. Labourism inevitably canalizes such revolutionary energy, since it is the unique representative of the working class and of indigenous socialist tradition; it exploits its socialists, who have always played the most important of roles in the everyday functioning of the party; and ultimately it frustrates them in virtue of its very character, alienating all the forces which will not yield to built-in mediocrity. The painful and shameful impotence of the socialist militants at the base of the party has never been more neatly and cruelly depicted than by Richard Crossman: '. . . the Labour Party required militants,' he pointed out, 'politically conscious socialists to do the work of organizing the constituencies. But since these militants tended to be "extremists", a constitution was needed which maintained their enthusiasm by apparently creating a full party democracy while excluding them from effective power. Hence the concession in principle

[1] Labour Party Annual Conference Report, 1947, pp. 212–14.

of sovereign powers to the delegates at the Annual Conferences, and the removal in practice of most of this sovereignty through the Trade Union block vote on the one hand, and the complete independence of the Parliamentary Labour Party on the other.'[1]

Nonentities, Fanatics, Cranks and Extremists

Such was the improbable political machine built up from 1918 onwards. It was built up around a word: socialism. Looked at critically, in relation to the actual functioning of the Labour Party, this word seems in turn dream and utter delusion, justification and mask, essence and mere appearance. The essential meanings attached to it were as clearly expressed at the 1918 Annual Conference as at any later occasion; they are little changed today. The new constitution of the party contained Clause 4, committing the movement 'To secure for the producers by hand or brain the full fruits of their industry, and the most equitable distribution thereof that may be possible, upon the basis of the common ownership of the means of production and the best obtainable system of popular administration and control of each industry and service.'[2] Even then, at its moment of most daring advance, the language of Labourism was bureaucratic in expression. But the spirit behind the words inspired even less faith in their supposed meaning. In the very first debate on the very first resolution proposed by the N.E.C. to the first Conference after the adoption of the new constitution, the issues were made sufficiently clear. This resolution was about 'Social Reconstruction' after the First World War, and envisaged '. . . the gradual building up of a new social order based . . . on the deliberately planned co-operation in production and distribution, the sympathetic approach to a healthy equality, the widest possible participation in power, both economic and political, and the general consciousness of

[1] R. H. S. Crossman, introduction to *The English Constitution*, by Walter Bagehot, 1963.
[2] G. D. H. Cole, *History of the Labour Party from 1914*, p. 72.

consent which characterizes a true democracy'.[1] It was not easy to pierce this miasma of well-turned clichés. But the more clairvoyant of the Left Wingers noticed the absence of any definite reference to the *ownership* of the means of production and distribution, and a Mr. Fairchild of the British Socialist Party[2] rose to protest. This resolution was hardly in accordance with the fine new constitution, he pointed out, and might even be interpreted as advocating 'co-operation' between workers and employers. 'The resolution entails the creation of an army of bureaucrats and experts,' he insisted, 'and there is no recognition of the claims of *Labour* to direct the means of production in the interests of the class represented at this Conference . . .'[3] No less a person than Sidney Webb replied to Fairchild (a typical example of the Left-Wing group Webb characterized elsewhere as 'nonentities . . . fanatics, cranks, and extremists').[4] It was true, he admitted, that the constitution said what Mr. Fairchild claimed. But really, they all had a great deal of work to do, including no fewer than twenty-six more resolutions, and '. . . they did not want repeatedly, over and over again, to ring the changes on the old shibboleths'.[5] It is a little hard to see how the *first* discussion of the party's new objective could be a monotonous repetition of anything . . . but of course this is precisely the point. Once was, indeed, far too often for Webb and the leadership majority – for them, the great new principle and hope, the new socialist image assumed by the party was already a 'shibboleth' to be evaded in all the concrete work of the party. Socialism, in short, belonged in its proper place, the constitution, where it could be admired occasionally and referred to in moments of emotion. The nonentities, fanatics, cranks and extremists who wished to relate it to the actual work of the Labour Party had to be suppressed.

[1] Labour Party Annual Conference Report, 1918, p. 43.
[2] Op. cit., p. 44.
[3] Op. cit., p. 44.
[4] Beatrice Webb, *Diaries*, 19th May 1930.
[5] Labour Party Annual Conference Report, 1918, pp. 44 and following section.

Another lesson was administered to them in the discussion of resolution Number VII. This dealt with unemployment, and accomplished the not inconsiderable feat of omitting all reference to the cause of unemployment, the capitalist system. Would it not be better to attack the capitalist system openly, someone objected, and so demonstrate to the ruling class their outlook and intentions? Again Webb rose to answer the objection. It was quite unnecessary to 'bring in once again an old shibboleth. They had heard the same speech over and over again . . . and it got a bit monotonous'.[1] Capitalism, as the cause of social evil, and socialism, as its cure; both were 'shibboleths' to the Labour Right, at the very foundation of the modern Labour Party. It is quite wrong to think that the leadership has 'betrayed' socialist principles, at any of the later dramatic turnings in the Party's history. 'Betrayal' was always an integral part of it, inseparable from it. Nor was this betrayal the result of individual hypocrisy or moral degeneration, as the Left has too often said; it followed logically from the whole orientation of Fabianism. Evolutionism, or 'gradualism', divorces the end-state of socialism from the actual steps taken to achieve it: the former exists at an intangible distance from the latter, hence they cannot be judged solely by their efficacy in promoting it. They are seen as good 'in themselves', justifiable by more immediate criteria deriving from society as it is here and now. The Left, on the other hand, wants each step to be related to the end – an insistence which *is* fanatical and extremist in evolutionary perspectives.

This tension, or something close to it, has existed in all socialist and communist parties. The peculiarity of the Labourist version lies in the relative strength and character of the two poles creating the tension. As we saw, for many different reasons the Right-Wing, moderate tendency was exceptionally powerful in Britain – it was, and still is, rooted in the profound and diffused conservatism of British society. And the Left-Wing pole of force provided by Nonconformity, traditional radicalism, and the I.L.P. and Labour-Left tendencies was exceptionally weak. Objectively, the task set to the Left is

[1] Op. cit., p. 64.

the overcoming of this tension *dialectically*, through an ideological and practical synthesis uniting the immediacy of reforms with the remoter ideal of a socialist society. Incapable of
rising to these difficult heights, the Labour Left is forced into
crude and repetitious formulations of its positions, into a
mindless passion which is only the obverse of its ideological
subjection. We saw how the Labour Left Wing was, as it were,
the 'subjectivity' of the movement, and how the distinction of
Right from Left in labourism is like a distinction between a
barren – and therefore petty and cramped – intellect, and an
impotent source of feeling, a passion with no voice. The
analogy can be carried further. The profundity and apparent
permanence of the determining conditions have made of the
Labour Left a *neurotic* subjectivity – that is, a contradictory
complex of ideas and attitudes unable to comprehend its own
nature but also *unwilling* to do so, detesting the terrible weight
lying upon it and yet completely loyal to Labourism, gripped
in an oppressive dream which it *chooses* and clings to rather
than face a reality still more painful. The 'short-cut' to
socialism embraced so eagerly at the beginning of the century
has turned into a permanent, intolerable labour of Sisyphus –
but would not the Labour Party's socialists be even more
impotent if they renounced the party, abandoning it as hopeless? The failure of the Communist Party, and a desert of
futile Left-Wing sects, stand as a warning against this.

Hence, the extreme and constant inner tension generated by
labourism has never exploded. Its own inherited inadequacies,
and the evident lack of any practical alternative to the Labour
Party, have tied the socialists of the Left Wing remorselessly
into the pathological internal dialectic of Labourism. We saw
how two basic conditions of Labourism as a system were, firstly,
the very defective ideological matrix behind British socialism,
and secondly – and intimately related – the weakness of the
entire Left-Wing political tradition incorporated into Labourism. Now, considering the organizational dimension of Labourism, we have seen another of its fundamental characteristics:
Labourism is in part an organised *contradiction* between the
two really vital sectors of the working-class movement, a sys-

tem according to which they mutually inhibit one another instead of engaging in a genuine dialectic of growth towards socialism.

United We Fall

What is the main justification of Labourism, put forward by socialists at its birth and still advanced by its apologists? What is the cry that rings out at every Labour Party Conference, to repress all serious dissent and maintain the incredible system intact? That Labourism attains the *unity* of the working-class movement, in a definitive and final form from which any departure would be treason and defeat. This call touches the deepest chord in the entire historical experience of the working class – the dispossessed, fragmented into atoms by the alienating pressures of capitalist society, who found and asserted themselves wholly through uniting in collective action. It echoes everything most sacred in the secular struggle of trade-unionism, everything that renders it more than merely another facet of the bourgeois order, everything which connects it potentially to socialism and to the future beyond the bourgeois order. It suggests that an organization embracing trade-unionism and socialism together, and summing up all the latent might of the working class, *must* be right in principle.

The truth inherent in this call cannot be denied. It deserves to be called the truth of Labourism, its characteristically positive element. Yet we have seen in how many ways, and how profoundly, the Labour Party betrays its own truth – the historical falsehood with which it is organically linked, the antagonistic and regressive form which it gives to 'unity' in the concrete. At a moment when the question of uniting working-class forces has appeared again as a living possibility in more than one country, it is important to grasp fully the lesson of Labourism. In any given period, the working-class movement as a whole – like the working class itself – contains many contradictory tendencies. In part it is tied to the past, in part it looks hesitatingly towards the future: it is both the product of capitalism and the social force which can overthrow capitalism. Any unified movement must reflect these contradictions to some extent. Hence, its ultimate significance depends entirely upon which elements hold the initiative within it, upon how it actually expresses the contradictions in reality and in turn modifies their conflict. We have seen why, in Britain, the conservative burden borne by the workers was so heavy, so embedded in organization and popular psychology, why their type of class-consciousness contained subordination in its own texture.[1] This meant that it was absolutely necessary for a revolutionary left to dominate any unitary organization such as Labourism, assuming as its first task the reform of this massive nexus of traditional consciousness – that is, the nexus which in fact constituted the heart of Labourism. The conflicts inside Labourism could not have been avoided; but they might have been rendered conflicts of growth. Labourism's unity has paralysed the vital contradiction of tendencies inside it, imprisoning British socialism instead of liberating it, and deforming its whole development.

The instrument of Labourist involution has been the Trade Union majority, the permanent hegemony of trade-unionism over socialism. But by and large, the Trade Unions could not help being what they were; nor could they act other than they did inside the framework provided by the Labour Party. This is the whole tragedy of Labourism. British trade-unionism could not avoid stifling British socialism within one unified body, given the immense strength of the former and the weakness and incoherence of the latter. The price paid by the British Left for 'unity', therefore, was high – half a century of frustration for the most vital and militant forces in the working class, the formation of the permanent Fabian dynasty as their leadership.[2]

The Labour Party encountered many vicissitudes in the twenty years after 1918, most of them unfavourable to it. It gradually increased its parliamentary representation, displacing the Liberal Party as the official Opposition, and formed the

[1] Cf. P. Anderson, *Origins of the Present Crisis*.
[2] See M. Duverger, *Political Parties*, p. 166.

first Labour Government in 1924. This short-lived, minority Government accomplished nothing, but was less of a disaster than the second Labour Government of 1929–31. The latter suffered the full impact of the Great Depression totally unprepared, and had the task of trying to restore British capitalism to health 'without the shadow of a constructive, or even a defensive, policy'.[1] Inevitably, MacDonald and the other Labour leaders were forced to attack working-class interests in order to save the pound, by reducing wages and payments to the unemployed, and this was too much. The Trade Unions rebelled, as well as the Left Wing. Disappointed by the reluctance of the working class to follow the logic of Labour's class compromise to its rational conclusion, MacDonald abandoned class and party to form the infamous 'National' Government in coalition with Liberals and Conservatives. The 'National' Government easily won the elections of 1931 and 1935, and by the beginning of the war in 1939 the Labour Party had scarcely recovered its position and strength of ten years previously. In between its two periods of government, the Labour Party had stood apart from the crucial test of the working class, the General Strike in defence of the miners in 1926, as if it did not exist.

Significant as they were in many ways, from our point of view these traumatic experiences are not of the first importance. The Labour Party survived MacDonald and humiliating defeat by the 'National' régime without a major schism – it threw off individual leaders, but not the basic ideological traditions of leadership they represented. There were small Left-Wing rebellions, but the greater part of the Left remained loyal. We have already explored some of the reasons for this extraordinary cohesion, in the face of events that would surely have shattered most socialist parties. Another can be seen in the excuse so constantly offered by the Labour Right for the miserable showing of both Labour Governments: that is, that since both were minority Governments dependent upon Liberal support, the principles of Fabianism had not really been tried,

[1] G. D. H. Cole, *Short History of the British Working Class Movement*, p. 432.

Labourism had not had a genuine chance to prove itself. In spite of their acute discontent, this argument appealed to the pragmatic instincts of the Left and to the universal sense of 'fair-play'. It held the Left Wing in its accustomed role of trying to push the leadership 'further to the Left', and left untouched the assumption underlying this role: that socialists and the Labour leadership were in fact travelling along the same road, towards the same destination. Fundamentally, in spite of many superficial symptoms of torture and crisis, Labourism drifted along intact through the inter-war years. It was waiting for power, for the chance to prove itself.

The chance was given it in 1945. The third Labour Government of 1945–50 is the decisive happening in the history of Labourism, after 1918. In retrospect, the Labour Party seems always to have been tensed for this moment. A great electoral triumph, massive popular support, an overwhelming majority in Parliament – Labourism's moment of self-realization had arrived at last, it entered upon its inheritance. But, as we have seen, the contradictions and confusions it was made of were such that its period of affirmation was bound also to be a period of crisis and disintegration; being a bundle of disparate forces united in a delusion, Labourism could not rise to express its true character without at once threatening this unity, without disentangling dream from reality in a way fatal to its own continued existence. Its political victory necessarily presaged its own division and defeat. This fact is the key to most of what has happened to the Labour Party, between 1945 and the present day.

The Zenith of Labourism

The First World War had made the Labour Party. The Second World War provided it with its great historical opportunity – by far the most favourable opportunity that ever confronted any socialist party.

Up until 1939, the Labour Party had existed in the midst of an inert, backward-looking society full of taboos and rigidities, a society whose metabolism was essentially the using-up of old accumulated stocks of economic and political capital. It had experienced a relative decline in wealth and power for over fifty years, faced with competition from the younger, more modernized and energetic capitalist systems of other countries, especially Germany and the United States. Yet this decline and stagnation had not produced any dramatic repercussions within society, no violent mass movements had arisen on either Right or Left to demand radical changes. The conservative torpor following the Industrial Revolution was stiffened further by imperialism, into an impenetrable blanket of complacency – while change accelerated everywhere else, it was as if time stood still for the British, fixed in a pattern that could never need more than minor modifications. Economically, the empire was an indispensable cushion against the effects of the Great Depression. Germany, Britain's main competitor, was twice ruined by war and suffered more from the Depression. Thus, external circumstances protected this fossilized régime and permitted British capitalism to adapt to modern times '. . . slowly and in the most inefficient manner, with the maximum wastage of unemployed human potential and amidst the desolation of whole regions of the land'.[1]

Then, from 1939 until 1945, circumstances altered completely and administered a violent shock to British society. The war shook the crumbling edifice of British conservatism to its foundations. Violent collective effort replaced the old myopic sloth of the 'National' régime as the keynote of the national ethos. Abruptly, the ruling class discovered that it needed the working class in order to escape annihilation; the masses of unemployed vanished, there was soon an acute labour shortage, and the status of the workers rose miraculously. The pseudo-feudal class structure and all the social impedimenta associated with it were thrust into abeyance, and 'war-time socialism' introduced an egalitarianism – even a sort of semi-heroic proletarian ideology – in complete contrast to anything known before 1939. An extensive system of State economic planning and control replaced *laissez faire*. After 1941, with the Soviet alliance, Communism became fashion-

[1] M. Barratt Brown, *After Imperialism*, p. 144.

able. It is true that this awakening was neutralized to some extent by the extreme nationalist colour it assumed, as in Churchill's famous war-time speeches. Yet even this was not entirely negative, seen from a socialist point of view. Britain was an extraordinarily fragmented nation, culturally. The British 'nation' had never been integrally re-made in a bourgeois revolution, as had France in the years after 1789. Instead, the British bourgeoisie had clung to and utilized anachronistic forms in its own affirmation – retaining, on the collective cultural level, a semi-aristocratic idiom quite unrelated to its own experience. The world-renowned 'frigidity' and lack of ready communication of the British is in part a product of this cultural history – in effect, of the absence of a valid, universal vehicle of expression within the hegemonic class. The universal cultural 'language' was the dialect of a ruling *élite* assimilated to the aristocracy, and bred chronic inarticulacy everywhere else in society because of its inherent limitations. At the same time, success in inhibiting the class-struggle had permitted the formation of a powerful sentiment of national unity – a unity which, because of such extreme cultural fragmentation and mass inarticulacy, could only exist *on the lowest possible level*, with the minimum of ideal content. The war re-created this unity on a higher level, in spite of the imperialist and racialist rhetoric that was so common, giving it a new democratic content, a meaningful popular voice. It brought about 'the emergence in Britain of a new popular radicalism, more widespread than at any time in the previous hundred years'.[1]

This was the situation inherited by Labourism in 1945. Half a revolution had already been accomplished by the war. Capitalism was a discredited memory, associated with unemployment and the slump. Public opinion was malleable and open. The vague image of a new world of social relationships, half dream, half reality in the peculiar context of the war, hung over society, a more significant vision of the future than socialist propaganda had ever fashioned. Britain was not ruined by the war; economically, she remained a major nation,

[1] R. Miliband, op. cit., p. 272.

politically she was free from any threat of intervention. Not one of the obstacles that have blocked or distorted the rise of socialism everywhere else was present. The chance was unique.

The Labour Party did not exploit this chance. The reasons for this failure must be obvious, after what has been said of the Party's character. The parliamentarism and moderation of the Labour leaders had been greatly reinforced by service under Churchill in the war-time Coalition Government. A conscious, political revolution was needed to realize the potentialities of the situation; but the ideas implicit in any revolutionary action, the idea of hegemony and the struggle for hegemony, the idea of the class-struggle as the basis of the political or party battle – all were farther away than ever. The Labour Party advanced a few cautious steps on the evolutionary road long marked out. However, it did accomplish these steps fully, under the new favourable circumstances, as the previous Labour Governments had not been able to. Fabianism was put into practice. This was sufficient to open the critical drama of Labourism: since then, it has been beset by an inevitable, chronic malady, at times debated openly, at times wilfully ignored, almost always misrepresented and misunderstood. The English Ideology makes practice the touchstone of all reality and value, and no one had held to this faith more keenly than the Fabians. Now Fabianism was to be tested and found wanting, disconcertingly, in its own sacred terms. Practicality had been its essence, its virtue, as against the fanaticism and idealism of the Left; now practice itself was to demonstrate the delusion in this practicality, the ideological sleight-of-hand behind it.

The Success and Failure of Fabianism

The Labour programme of 1945, *Let us face the Future*, was directly descended from the original statement of 1918, Sidney Webb's *Labour and the New Social Order*. It proposed the nationalization of the coal-mines, the gas and electricity industries, all principal transport services, the Bank of England, and the iron and steel industry. These were the industries and services 'ripe for public ownership'. The economy as a whole was to be 'planned', in the public interest, but in reality the Government's powers over the private sector were very limited and were decreased with the passage of time: this was a form of planning without objectives or powers, affecting the economy only marginally. The Labour Government did not even have the information and statistics required for the most minimal planning.[1] A new range of social services was also in the programme, many of them agreed on by all parties; the most important was the National Health Service, making all forms of medical care free. In foreign policy, the Labour Party's main aspiration was to function as a mediating and uniting influence between the U.S.A. and the U.S.S.R.; but doubt of its capacity to do this arose at the first international conference attended by Attlee and Bevin, the new Foreign Minister. Both Roosevelt and the American Secretary of State, Byrnes, were disconcerted by Bevin's aggressiveness towards the Russians.[2] Shortly afterwards, Bevin disclosed his views on colonialism: 'I am not prepared to sacrifice the British Empire,' he told a critic, 'because I know that if the British Empire fell . . . it would mean the standard of life of our constituents would fall considerably.'[3]

By 1948, most of the programme had been achieved. The details of its execution, the particular effects it had on society, do not concern us here. In general, Labour's reforms ended by being accepted as necessary even by Conservatives. The major exception was the plan to nationalize the steel industry; while nationalization was a convenient fate for bankrupt and deficitary industries like coal-mining and the railways, capitalists were determined to retain a profitable key industry like steel in private control. The Labour Government left this part of the programme until the last moment, and carried out the nationalization in a weak manner which made it simple for the Conservatives to restore the industry to private ownership after

[1] A. A. Rogow and P. Shore, *The Labour Government and British Industry, 1945–51*, pp. 45–7.

[2] J. Byrnes, *Speaking Frankly*, p. 79.

[3] Speech in House of Commons, 21st February 1946.

1951. It is more important for us to grasp the general sense of the evolution of British society from 1948 onwards, and the relationship between this evolution and the traditional evolutionary perspectives at the centre of Fabianism.

Fabian gradualism had seen the goal, socialist society, as produced by successive instalments of reform which would one day 'add up' to socialism. As we noticed, they did not think there was any real barrier of force capable of reacting against this long-term trend: Sidney Webb described it as the 'inevitable outcome' of the universal franchise, a 'stream of tendencies' against which all opponents were 'ultimately powerless'.[1] In Britain at least – where everyone was reasonable – socialism would be a march of events, guaranteed by the ordinary machinery of democracy: once started, nothing would halt it. The Labour Government of 1945–50 was the start. And yet, from 1948 onwards, its progress resembled anything except an irresistible march of events. Apparently its first programme should have launched it forward in a momentum carrying it across all obstacles. But in reality the Labour Party's loss of confidence was the dominating fact, after these first achievements. Instead of finding itself, labourism had obviously lost its way; success engendered inertia, not automatic advance. Then the inertia turned into retreat. The Labour Party lost the elections of 1951, then (by a much larger majority) those of 1955 and those of 1959. During most of this period, there seemed no good reason why Conservatism should not retain power for ever. Labourism's loss of heart became bitter internal conflict and paralysis, year after year; the mass hope of 1945 became indifference, apathy, even hostility – all remote from the mild, reasonable optimism the Fabians had counted on. British socialism had encountered a barrier invisible to its eyes, its old world-view. Like the barrier of sound an aircraft meets at a certain speed, this force had flung it back into confusion and impotence.

What had happened? The electorate had not behaved as expected: the first experience of socialism ought to have impressed all rational beings and made certain further progress.

[1] Sidney Webb, *Fabian Essays* (1889), pp. 65–7.

Why not? Clearly, because the Labour reforms had not been in reality exactly what Labour leaders had believed they would be – self-explanatory 'instalments' of the socialist future, 'islands of socialist virtue in a sea of capitalist greed'.[1] And what had prevented them from being this? Partly, no doubt, the limited and bureaucratic form given to nationalization – from the origins of the movement, Labour leaders had been inflexibly opposed to the conception of workers' control. Partly the fact that the purpose of the deficitary public sector was to 'serve the public', and the public consisted mostly of the industries in the capitalist sector; caught between a weak Government policy and the pressures of the private sector, the State industries could not help becoming subordinate to the latter – and so, an instrument assisting the rebirth of capitalism, of the new wave of capitalist prosperity and ideology destined to drown labourism in the fifties. The complex of forces which had turned their work into something other than what was intended was the critical factor ignored or minimized by Fabianism: the general dynamic of the system as a whole, the hegemonic pattern rooted in a certain organization of the economy and certain institutions, and incarnated in a ruling class. Here was the vast power which had turned against Labour's arithmetical dose of 'socialism' and transformed its meaning so utterly – making of it, finally, an integral structure reinforcing the conservative renaissance.

Perhaps – a defender of Labourism might object – there is too much retrospective wisdom in this analysis. Could the party itself possibly have understood what was happening, fifteen years ago? Given its indifference to theoretical questions, was not labourism bound to grope blindly forward at that point, slowly absorbing the hard lesson of practical experience? But it is difficult to see any real excuse for what followed, in such reflections. Whether the party's theorists were able to analyse the situation or not, it was at least evident from 1951 onwards that British socialism had met a major obstacle and was in a

[1] R. Miliband, op. cit., p. 288. Perhaps the best analysis of the question is in John Hughes, *Nationalized Industries in the Mixed Economy* (Fabian Society Pamphlet, 1962).

crisis *needing* the most intensive debate. The acid test of practice had exposed essential defects in the movement's whole historical programme and outlook; the very meaning of its existence was no longer clear. A searching revision of its theoretical basis was the prelude to any future. The incredible slowness of response to this crisis, the protracted confusion and uncertainty which actually followed, are the final condemnation of Labour's so-called empiricism. In the awful decade following the Attlee Government, Labourism demonstrated its inability to learn from the hard experience it had always cherished ideologically. In a sense, of course, it is true that practice is the real test of theory. But, paradoxically, practice only bears such truth in it when it exists in the light of ideas – when, in spite of its primacy, it remains part of a dialectical relationship to theory, a relationship in which the theoretical element has real autonomy and worth. In other words, acute ideal consciousness is a necessary condition of *real* empiricism, of the vital capacity to respond directly to and learn swiftly from practical experiences. The British ruling class had avoided this necessity: it had been able to adopt a kind of fetishic pseudo-empiricism as its ideological banner *because* it had never been forced to undertake any great, conscious practical reformation of society. What is British 'empiricism' and British faith in practical 'instinct' except systemized indifference to ideas? And how did this anti-ideology come to exist? Because hard facts, the demands of practical experience, had never coerced the bourgeoisie into looking for something better – its good fortune had preserved that basic stupor of outlook which a popular expression calls 'muddling through'. Piously accepting this stupor as the last word in realism, British socialists had shrunk socialism to fit it – pretending, so to speak, that socialism was not a colossal, intractable, practical problem but a mere question of 'evolution', not a revolution but a piece of Sunday-afternoon tinkering. From 1951 onwards, this superstitious trance stood exposed in the cold wind of disproof. Yet for years the only result was a further numbing of sensibility, a sterile involution only half-related to circumstances.

Nobody would deny that in certain respects the 1945–51 Labour Government was successful. In others, nobody can deny the failure of its work. This paradox contains, precisely, the lesson of the experience, the lesson for which Labourism was unprepared and which if assimilated, would be fatal to Labourism. In themselves, and for their immediate, short-term effects, the Labour reforms were necessary from any point of view, and some of them were popular. But in society nothing exists and has meaning 'in itself'. Its true meaning emerges from its relationship to the whole social complex at a given moment— that is, to a complex organism having a definite character and central dynamic, *the* general meaning of society. Hence a phenomenon can have one face at the particular, isolated level, and another face when seen in relationship to its context. The nationalization of the mines vastly improved the standard of living and conditions of work of the miners, and abolished one of the most ugly phases of the class-struggle in Britain. But the rationalization of the mining industry and its whole structure of costs, effected after nationalization, has made it the prey of private sector monopolies and reinforced their position in a way the old coal industry could never have done. And so with the other reforms, in their different ways. In other words, from a socialist point of view reforms have a socialist sense only when carried out as parts of a strategy aiming at the heart of society, at the pattern of social hegemony which bends everything into its own design – they are socialist reforms only when really placed within a revolutionary perspective, seen and executed as such. Society, its pre-existing 'natural' tendency, its 'evolutionary' force – these are enemies, on the whole, not allies. Unless socialism is tensed against them in every fibre, in every moment, in an arc of action as wide and varied as the forces of hegemony themselves, it will be imprisoned and petrified by these forces, the liberating potential of its work annulled for ever. This recognition was fatal to Fabianism and the assorted ideological baggage associated with it. It struck the foundations away from Labourism, as it had existed up to 1950.

The Labour Party had failed to grasp the revolutionary

opportunity furnished by the conditions of 1945. It had failed, in the sense indicated, even according to the much more modest traditional criteria it had always respected. The shadow of this failure is the dominating fact in the evolution of the party since 1950, and an essential part of the explanation of Wilson and Wilsonism. For about ten years after the defeat of 1951, Labourism seemed to drift at the mercy of events, feebly trying to discover a new formula. Then, at the same time as external conditions had changed radically – and in a way favourable to the Labour Party – the rise of Wilson appeared magically to fill the void, heal the chronic dissensions of the party and re-knit a unity and purpose comparable to those known previously. A large part of Wilson's power derives from his role as the restorer, whether real or illusory, of the innocence existing before the Fall.

Labour in Limbo

During the 1950s, the Labour Party was haunted by its failure. But, characteristically, the compulsions agitating it were expressed only partially and fitfully in the actual debates of the era. The traditional Left-Right battle became more acrimonious and bitter – but it remained in substantially the same terms as before, in an objective situation which had changed profoundly. The society which emerged out of the first Labour régime was significantly different from the old one, and presented different problems. Labourism, like the Left-Wing parties in other European countries, had to confront the new difficulties of a more and more prosperous capitalist society relatively free from recessions. The growing revolt against colonialism, the great new interrogatives in ideology and international relations created by the disintegration of Stalinism after 1955 – these familiar questions too were bound to exercise its mind. If it did not deal with them very effectively, perhaps this was due in part to the fundamental doubt in its heart. Naturally, since nothing can really stand still in an explosive era, stagnation and vacillation was also retreat, and brought about what Raymond Williams calls 'the visible moral decline of the labour movement.' In the fifties, he claims, 'Both politically and industrially, some sections of the movement have gone over, almost completely, to ways of thinking which they still formally oppose. The main challenge to capitalism was socialism, but this has almost wholly lost any contemporary meaning.' Under the pressures of capitalism, renascent, equipped with new methods and new appeals, more confident than ever and reinforced by Labour's own legislation, the Labour Party seemed to be sliding backwards into more and more hopeless positions.

The decisive experience of 1945–51 had in reality placed Labourism squarely at a parting of the ways. A tormenting crossroads lay in the facts themselves and compelled some response. The old straight way to socialism, to which all the party's essential mechanisms were geared, was lost. No route now connected the day-to-day life of the party to its goal, the rainbow-light it had called 'socialism'. Therefore, the party had either to abandon the goal – or reinvent and rediscover everything, from the beginning, find a new way to a new, better-understood goal. These alternatives were inevitable, whatever was to be the fate of the *word* 'socialism'. Obviously, social-democratic revisionists can cling to the word and re-define it to mean a particular species of capitalist society; a novel revolutionary conception, too, can be attached to the same word. But it did not seem that even the magic of this word could go on confusing the issue for Labourism, after 1951.

What were the full implications of this choice? We saw how tenuous and imaginary the links between concrete action and the ultimate ideal were, in Fabianism – how, instead of a significant unity, the entire bias of thought and activity were thrown into the former. Obviously, in it the goal and conception of socialism, as a global state-of-affairs somehow qualitatively different from bourgeois society, were inherently liable to atrophy. The adverse shock of the 1945–51 government was bound to produce just this disintegration, and make the Fabian tradition tend to identify its being and purpose more *openly* with the particular reforms, the concrete 'practical', 'empirical' projects which had always been in the centre of its attention. The logic of the Labour Right response to fundamental setback was abandonment of the ideal, an overt embracing of *technicism* as the party's universe. The British ruling class, too, was essentially pragmatic; but its disposition to empirical change was wrapped up in a hard cortex of sentimental conservatism and ritual, so that its reform always appeared as reluctant. The way forward for Fabianism was simply to strip pragmatism of this pious traditionalism, and replace it with a more aggressive, pseudo-scientific rationale: their new man was to be the zealous, hard-headed social engineer, even more deeply immersed in a practical present, equally indifferent to romances of the past and the future. Hence, the logical reaction of Fabian socialism to its defeat was to cease being socialist, in the old sense, and define a new pole of opposition in the characteristically British political world – a kind of pure, unideological reformism. The strengths of this approach are evident: its basic continuity with the past, with British socialist 'empiricism' (now in fact given a more intense and mystifying form than ever) – and at the same time a break with the past, with piety and 'evolutionism' and the inconvenient old dogma of 'socialism', sufficient to give an appearance of hard novelty and boldness. Associated with this, perhaps necessarily, was a more unashamed *populism* than the Party had been able to allow itself in the past. Socialism had been linked, however minimally and ineffectively, with the notion of *forming* public opinion in a new, better mould, with an educative function deriving from the socialist ideal itself. Post-socialist technicism could only think in terms of giving people what they want, here and now – that is, in terms of a mere consumers' ideology. Technicism entails the dominance of 'experts'; but it exonerates itself from the accusation of being a technocrats' dictatorship by claiming to do only what people want, in general.

The other direction at Labour's crossroads led not to abandonment but into the heart of socialism's problems. What went wrong after 1945 was, in essence, what had always been wrong with Labourist socialism itself. Hence, any authentic socialist response to it entailed a critical task of great dimensions. It was necessary to try and understand what had been wrong with the notion of socialism employed by the party, and with the party's relationship to that notion in its ordinary activity; this implied a drastic revision of Fabian orthodoxy, ideologically, and beyond ideology the criticism was bound to invest the whole movement, its structure and functioning – all connected to and expressive of the party's philosophy, as we saw. Logic is fatal to Labourism, in its traditional forms. No adequate reaction could possibly have stopped at the programmatic level – it could not have stopped anywhere short of the attempt to redefine British socialism integrally, as ideology, as organization, as immediate policy.

But this was just the difficulty. The first line of response to Labourism's crisis mentioned was, by and large, that of the Labour leadership in the decade after 1950 – though it adopted it only slowly and in hesitant stages, holding on to old myths and confusing the issues at the same time. The second, surely, should have been that of the Labour Party's Left Wing? Was not the crisis of Fabianism its long-awaited opportunity to come forward as the valid alternative? Was not the end of 'British Socialism' the possible beginning of socialism in Britain? But such a decisive break with Labourist tradition – and with *itself*, its own past function in the movement – was altogether beyond the powers of the Left. The Right took its logical course away from the checkmate of 1951, but the Left could not. We saw how the weakness of the Left Wing had always been one of the fundamental traits of Labourism, how it had fallen into the role of a permanent, neurotic opposition. This was to prevent it from grasping the opportunity – and so condemn it, as has become more and more clear in the last few years, to final sterility and exhaustion.

Consequently, if the Labour Party's great experience of 'British Socialism' in practice had withered away the latter, this development in its turn exposed and destroyed the pretentions of the Labour Left no less completely. In the last decade, the left-wing scene in Britain has changed greatly. The Labour leadership tradition has been transforming itself; new movements, new ideas and new modes of action, some with world-wide influence, have arisen outside Labourism, and have also – as we shall see below – reacted upon Labourism. But in this era of change, the Left Wing of Labourism has remained on the whole stationary, as if cut off from all the vital currents and tensions.

Some of the sources of this weakness were discussed above. In the long travail of the fifties they appeared as a kind of umbilical cord which tied the Left to everything dead, and compelled it to look permanently backwards into a mythical past. As a Left-Wing speaker put it, succinctly, at the 1955 Annual Conference: 'To a Socialist there is no necessity in 1955 to re-state a Socialist policy.'[1] In other words, the traditional vision of the party had been all right in substance, so that further progress signified loyalty to that vision. The Right had *betrayed* Socialism after 1948 – here was the cause of the movement's malady! It was necessary only to return to 1945, and another victory like that of 1945, another period of advance like that of 1945–8, would cure the movement. Another Left Winger said at the same Conference: 'If we are to impress the workers of this country . . . we must quite definitely get back to the old-fashioned socialism we knew . . . Our Party must get back to Socialist principles, the principles on which the Party was founded, as quickly as possible.' How can one deny the hopelessness of such typical Left-Wing attitudes? How can one fail to observe that Labourism's mortal crisis stemmed, precisely, from the sacred 'Socialist principles . . . on which the party was founded', that the condition and outlook of 1945 were the very things which had led to the failure oppressing the party, and that in 1955 there was an urgent necessity to re-state not simply a 'socialist policy' – for to think in terms of 'policy' was already a concession to the Right – but a policy, an ideology, a critical account of the period of government, in short a coherent global position worthy of the adjective 'socialist'?

The result, the general situation out of which Wilsonism and the present inner state of the party have emerged, has been

[1] Labour Party Annual Conference Report, 1955, p. 114.

described by Williams as one where 'Old Left and New Right in the Labour Party are unconscious allies in delaying any relevant analysis and challenge. The invocation of old habits . . . combines with the rejection of socialism as a radically different human order, to leave the ruling interpretations and directions essentially unchallenged.'[1]

A Permanent Question-Mark

Such was the party inherited by Harold Wilson in 1963. We have seen how it was modelled out of the distinctive historical experience of the British working class, how it bears the stamp of the relation evolved between that class and British bourgeois society. British society, with its permanent, massive congeal-ment of classes along clearly visible lines, had petrified the class conflict in a form tolerable to itself. Labourism was the issue of this petrification, the half-socialism which the working class could not transcend in its chronically inhibited cold war against society. Enmeshed in the dense web of archaic super-structures grafted on to British capitalism, in spite of – and even *because* of – its solidly corporative class-consciousness, the working class could not distance itself aggressively from society and constitute its own autonomous movement towards social hegemony. The cutting instrument needed for this task was lacking. That is, an intellectual stratum torn adrift from the social consensus with sufficient force and capable of func-tioning as catalyst to the new force striving for expression against the consensus. Hence the working class could only find its affirmation on the basis of its traditional corporate institu-tions, the Trade Unions, in a political movement emanating from and tied to them – 'The Labour Party reflects Trade Unionism and cannot surpass it', G. D. H. Cole observed in 1913. But, as we saw, it was forced to surpass it by the in-herent necessities of political action; and could only acquire as its new politico-intellectual dimension an organizing group derived from the old conformist intelligentsia. This stratum, functioning as a connective tissue between the working class

[1] Raymond Williams, *The Long Revolution*, p. 333.

and tradition, established an easy ascendancy over Labourism and permanently repressed all more revolutionary developments within it – the very organization of the movement systematized and made definitive the modalities of the 'short-cut to socialism', the compromise supposed to last a few years. Having found expression in Labourism, the working class was also imprisoned in it: the socialist Left that ought to have in turn transformed Labourism into socialism in fact sank into hopeless subordination to the system. 'British Socialism' did not break the ossification of British society, but became another layer of it.

Obviously, all these basic characteristics are still present in Harold Wilson's Labour Party. The experience which ought to have demonstrated to socialists that Labourism was no more than an unacceptable half-way house – the government of 1945–50 – did not in fact disrupt the Labourist compromise. Objectively, it confronted the movement with the bankruptcy of Fabian 'socialism'; but subjectively, only the Fabian Right was capable of responding to the challenge in its own fashion, while the Left lost the chance to take up again the drive of the pioneer socialists and push the party further towards socialism. The questions all remained in suspense. The vast interrogation mark surrounding the continued existence of Labourism is still there. If the Labour Party carries on upon the lines whose significance finally emerged from 1945–50, then how can it still be a socialist movement? If it ceases to be one, then how can socialists still participate in it – and, in the absence of the minimal goal holding the movement together, what will keep the Trade Unions participating in it in the long run? Is not the Labour Party bound to become either more, or less, than it has been in the past: either a genuine socialist movement, or a mere reformist party continuing the old liberal tradition?

However, the Wilson era is by no means simply a continuation of the past. Although the Labour Party cannot escape permanently the critical dilemma forced on it, all its problems at present appear in a vastly different light from a few years ago. The reason is, not that Labourism has changed internally, but that the external conditions it faces are in rapid flux. Born in an epoch of glacial immobility, built in time with the sluggish pulse of declining imperialism, the Labour Party is now living through the disappearance of the bone-deep conservatism which formerly shrouded it. Suddenly, British society has slid into an era of change. This is, at once, the new opportunity offered to Labourism, and the emergence of new problems for it in addition to the chronic ones described above – the profile of the new Labour Government's dilemmas.

Labour's New Façade

With Wilson, Labourism emerged definitely as the party of the new, rationalized future (at least on the plane of rhetoric). We saw how the Labour Right's evolution had tended towards the adoption of a neutral, 'technocratic' ideology whose ultimate ideal was the efficient and humane management of a permanent 'mixed economy'. Now, abruptly, at the turn of the decade the great crisis of British Capitalism exalted just these values. The Conservatives had tried, very unsuccessfully, to convert themselves from a genteel, patriarchal, traditionalistic *élite* into a juvenile, dynamic, 'managerial' *élite* exploding with long-forgotten capitalist fervour. Was not Labourism better prepared to furnish the new saviours? In its traditional forms, certainly not: Labourism's dominant ethos of timorous curmudgeonry and funereal moralism was as far from the needs of an expanding consumer capitalism as it could be. Gaitskell and the younger group in the party associated with him, notably Anthony Crosland, tried hard to give the movement more consumer appeal in the electoral campaign of 1959, but the change was scarcely convincing. Advanced publicity techniques could do little to project the one-dimensional personality of the Labour leader and his meagre ideas. The impression produced – and reflected in the electoral results – was that of an insincere striving to sell Labourism, as if it was a kind of political insurance policy one could buy, or invest in, with one's vote. This was hopeless. The secret Gaitskell was searching for, but had not the political intuition to uncover, was how to insert the movement into the new fabric of capitalist relations *without* appearing to do so. Wilson was the man the occasion demanded, and he invented the formula, with something approaching genius. His accession to the leadership was the fruit of pure accident, yet in retrospect no event could seem more providential and timely.

Under Gaitskell the Left had been defeated, but nevertheless it had risen to support him in a paroxysm of renewed faith at the time of the Common Market debate. In this situation, party unity had been re-established and the Left severely (perhaps permanently) weakened. Paradoxically, this was the pre-condition of the election of a relatively Left-Wing leader. There is no doubt that *relatively*, with regard to the past annals of the Labour leadership, Wilson represents a kind of progress. Wilson constantly professes the habitual Labour contempt for theory – 'theology', as he calls it – but has far more theoretical grasp than any previous leader. Unlike so many former Left-Wing figures who have moved towards power, he has never actually renounced or broken with his past; he is likely to be much more open to Left-Wing ideas and pressures than his predecessors. In contrast to Attlee and Gaitskell, Wilson seems singularly free from the bigoted anti-Communism which has been a surrogate for thought and action in many social-democratic movements. More important than these personal traits, perhaps, is the fundamental fact that he is part instrument and part agent in an era of general change. That is, he appears as a *potentially* more Left-Wing leader in a time of *potential* progress where great advances might be possible if socialists could seize the chance given by the fall of the older modes of hegemony. This is the secret of the hope he has inspired. But, obviously, in a typical contradiction, he has only been able to emerge and raise such confidence by incarnating *in fact* all the tendencies opposed to a socialist exploitation of the crisis. Capitalism and its newer agents and agencies strive to fill the void left where conservative stupor once reigned, with an ideology and customs correlated to the rejuvenation and strengthening of capitalism – rational, egalitarian, materialistic, modish, wrapped in a consumers' hallucination, eager for movement where the old society resisted

it. Wilsonism is, more than anything else, the bid of Labourism to meet this challenge in its own terms, the pose of an alert
technocracy capable of giving birth to such a new order. Yet
it bears with it the wider possibility of being more than this –
of meeting the challenge in other, more socialist terms, of
beating out of the present chaos a fabric that does more than
echo the exigencies of monopoly capital. What is the truth, if
any, in this halo of potency the Labour Party still contrives to
carry above it, even after the history described above?

A new Left?

For an open situation of transition to be exploited in a socialist
direction, there has to be a Left. But what Left could possibly
exert any influence on the Labour leadership? We have seen
how feeble is the position of the traditional left wing of the
Party. Always unable to act effectively, it has been eroded
and bemused still further by Gaitskell's victory and the
messianic atmosphere surrounding Wilson. Is it the case, then,
that a new Left has to come into existence to give reality to
socialist perspectives? Inside or outside the Labour Party?

In some sense, this is surely so – the history of Labourism
has demonstrated the inadequate character of indigenous
socialist traditions only too well. But, if they have to be sup-
planted by something better, one must ask on what basis new
socialist ideas and a new socialist movement could grow up.
Where are the growing-points, in the working class or the
labour movement, among intellectuals or young people, that
could generate new directions and pressures?

Unquestionably, the key area in any such development must
be trade-unionism. We have seen how trade-unionism, the
great historic contribution of the British working class to the
rise of the labour movement, constitutes the real basis of
Labourism; and how, at the same time, the sclerotic conservatism afflicting it paralyses Labourism and makes it permanently
the prey of a palsied moderatism. No socialist initiative has
ever unlocked this paralysis; neither could the General Strike
or the Great Depression. Only the Campaign for Nuclear

Disarmament accomplished the feat – ephemerally – in 1960. If this glacier were to melt or move, Labourism would be transformed and British socialism would have a different world before it. Any consideration of the possibility carries us to the innermost conflicts of British society.

In part – obviously – working-class and trade-union conservatism were intimately tied to the prevailing conservatism of society at large. The dissolution of the latter is therefore bound to untie the former, to some extent, and generate a consciousness of novelty, a possibility of reform. Far more important is the crucial fact that the whole evolution of British capitalism and its society – and above all the great, confused campaign of 'modernization' and 'rationalization' now gripping it – has profoundly altered the conditions of trade-unionism, in an irreversible way. Tearing itself painfully out of the anachronistic shell it grew about itself in the long solstice of imperialism, capitalism is bound to carry trade-unionism with it, willy-nilly. 'Rationalization' means a prolonged effort to match the severe competition of foreign producers, through determined selling, steady and competitive prices, and massive investment to increase productivity in the more profitable sectors of the economy. The most helpful single factor in such a programme would be a freezing or depression of wages for a considerable time. How can this be achieved in Britain? In spite of all their limitations, the Trade Unions remain immensely strong on this, their basic terrain of wage-bargaining; political apathy may have affected them, but they have suffered no real demoralization. A 'liberal' period of boom and reconstruction like that seen in Germany – and associated with prolonged quiescence of the Unions – is unthinkable. So is any active restraint on the Unions by government, like that of the Gaullist regime in France after 1958. The only possible way is that of *associating* the Trade Unions with economic development – which has therefore to be at least minimally planned – so that Union demands become predictable, tolerable factors in the growth process. According to this technique of subordination by concession, the Unions are persuaded to limit demands here and now, or in the near future, in exchange for a measure of participation in planning the economy – 'equally with employers and the State', as the now classic formula puts it – and for promises of regular future increments. A trend towards 'integration' of this kind is observable in several countries; it acquires a special urgency in the case of Britain from the very backwardness of its system, from its need to catch up rapidly by using every available means. Even the Conservatives – traditionally hostile to every sort of State intervention in the economy – were compelled to set up a primitive form of planning mechanism and made it clear from the beginning that the vital purpose of the exercise was to get the Unions to agree to an 'incomes policy'.

This trend imposes conditions of action radically different from those recognized by traditional trade-unionism. It makes of the Trade Unions once again – after a long epoch where the political party occupied the centre of the stage – the *avant-garde* in the struggle of the working class, the standard-bearers whose position dominates everything else. At one blow, it renders futile and anachronistic the old fragmentation of the British trade union movement, with its multitude of competing petty bureaucracies and its ineffectual central authority: faced with an overwhelming common problem that cannot be evaded, the Unions will be forced to try and think and act as one, to have a coherent common policy and an organ capable of expressing such a policy. Above all – and in the case of Britain, it is hard to exaggerate the importance of this fact – the traditional economic, sectorial, corporate questions of trade-unionism *become political questions* in an evident, immediately recognizable fashion. Trade Union leaders can no longer hide within their corporative shell, pretending to be 'only trade-unionists' and turning a deaf ear to demands for more involvement in political affairs. Furthermore, the political complexion given to problems in this way is an *authentic* one, light-years removed from the façades and mirrors where official Labourism has turned in circles. Trade-unionists are left in no doubt that the whole dilemma arises from the awkward, brute fact of their *power* over society and its development: the whole point is to get them to limit and sacrifice this power 'in the national interest'. Hence, the question of power – the real essence of politics, carefully obscured and disguised in the old evolutionary and Fabian ideology of the labour movement – emerges in something like a true light for the first time, at the heart of current discussion.

The new situation has already changed trade-unionism. The most important development has been the emergence of George Woodcock, devoted to reforming the structure of the movement and strengthening its central authority. Woodcock's own ultimate purpose is clearly that of *accepting* the new neo-capitalist programme of co-operation between Unions and State, in some form, with the trade union movement 'acknowledging its responsibilities' in relation to economic growth and obtaining a voice in economic planning. That is, he represents a frankly 'Right-Wing' trend as regards the ultimate political directions possible. The 'political' sense of events appears to be for him the abandonment by the Trade Unions of 'party' and 'class' orientations within an organic association controlled by the State.

Beyond the Managers

In a sense, clearly, Wilson's and Woodcock's policies are a threat to the working class and any socialist future, and to some extent fit in with and assist one another. But it was perhaps inevitable that the labour movement be jerked out of its somnolence by forces of this character; under the British conditions we have observed, no full-equipped socialist orientation towards the problems of neo-capitalism could possibly have been born first and taken the initiative. Wilson's Labour Party and George Woodcock's ideal trade union movement are the beginning of a new era for the British working class and British socialism. They will not necessarily be its end. The contradictions gripping British society and the working class make equally possible the growth of counter-tendencies, and a quite different exploitation of the situation. The fundamental reason for an optimistic attitude towards a new Labour Government is not to be sought in the party's particular programmes, or in the particular personality of Harold Wilson, but in the relation between whatever it achieves and this wider context. Its work will not be woodenly accepted as another instalment of 'socialist' good works carrying humanity two and a half inches closer to the Fabian millennium, another remarkable demonstration of how well behaved British socialists are, creeping patiently along with the snail-shell of 'evolutionary' baggage on their backs. The ancient protective criteria and customs are lost, scattered in a tidal wave that leaves only defaced ruins behind it. Navigating in an ocean of uncertainty, Labourism will be unable to avoid debate and criticism of what it does, it will be exposed to conflicting currents of opinion and vital struggles which could be profoundly educative. In 1945, Labour came to power borne on a surge of optimism and faith, unanimous popular enthusiasm was the motor driving it along long-predicted channels towards a goal felt as familiar and secure. In 1964, nothing corresponds to these things. Labour must step, experimentally and uncertainly, into the void left by the perishing of the older order. Its positive assets are few: the opportunistic political genius of one man, the present disarray of its main opponent, a precarious rhetoric earning no more than a mild, indulgent curiosity from the masses. Yet, paradoxically, this difficult and chaotic situation is far more promising than was the earnest hope of 1945, the pious illusions from whose failure nothing was learnt, nothing derived but confusion and a long stalemate. Up to a point, the position of the British Left is like that of other classes, of society as a whole: after the centuries of stale constipation and sedimentary ancestor-worship, it needs anarchy as a plant needs water, it can benefit from uncertainty and an absence of totems.

Almost certainly, the Labour Government will give rise to a search for new ideas. What forces are there to respond to such needs, what can be offered to this uncertainty to prevent a new social-democratic ethos establishing itself as firmly as the old one? In raising this question, we touch again on what has been a central theme of these pages: the intellectuals, and what appears in retrospect as their great failure to assault the citadel of bourgeois hegemony in Britain and furnish the socialist movement with a more revolutionary ideology. The problem of any 'new' socialist Left in Britain assumes a more precise form, in the light of this past experience. What likelihood is there of the constitution of a stratum of intellectuals more effectively divorced from tradition? And more capable of mapping out an alternative power that has meaning from the point of view of the Trade Unions and the workers?

In this respect, too, the situation is perhaps more promising than at any time since the formation of the Labour Party sixty years ago. Obviously, the collapse of traditionalism is something intimately affecting the intellectuals – indeed, largely the work of the intellectuals. In a strikingly unanimous fashion, great sections of the traditional intelligentsia once buried entirely in the tribal rites of Oxford or literary London have responded to the critical plight of British society. The sense of a necessary 'renewal' of society – at bottom the urgent need of British capitalism for new conditions of operation – rapidly produced its apologists. Defenders of the old conservatism formulated by Edmund Burke were astonishingly few, champions of technocracy and rationalization were many; the main body of liberal opinion leaned towards the latter rather than the former. A majority of intellectuals were in favour of entry into the Common Market. The negligible, rather rear-guard nature of the opposition both to the Common Market and the rhetoric of modernization made it plain how dead the old order really was. It is scarcely too much to say that a new conformism has arisen to replace the old, in a very short period (though in the novel and the theatre the 'angry' school had been a kind of instinctive precursor of the trend). The intensified conservatism of the early fifties – caused among other things by the disappointments of the Labour régime–gave way to an equally generalized progressivism consciously or unconsciously promoting the new values and categories of neo-capitalism. It was as if the body of British intellectuals intended to become as strong a pillar of this new society as it had always been of the old.

However, the new orthodoxy is not comparable to the old. It will not become a parochial blanket of prejudice, stifling all contrary tendencies like its ancestor. The older English ideology was a complex, resistant structure with many faces: a most flexible, tolerant 'liberalism' deriving its mildness – paradoxically – from the very 'conservatism' to which it seemed opposed, from the very stability and somnolent complacency it disowned. It embraced a dilettantesque literary culture descended from the aristocracy and the crudest of lumpen-bourgeois utilitarian philosophies, and held them together in a bizarre Jekyll-and-Hyde union of attraction and repulsion. By contrast, the newer bourgeois ideology still in emergence is a brittle structure. It has no mystifying dimensions able to absorb or deflect challenges, it appears as propaganda, not as an entire mental universe from which escape is difficult or impossible. Along with its empire, the British bourgeoisie has lost its power of incantation over the intellectuals and (through them) over subordinate classes.

It is difficult to classify or predict the future evolution or the value of the Left-Wing intellectual trends seeking affirmation in this new and freer climate. The intellectuals no longer have to raise the dead-weight of the dead generations in their protest. But they cannot escape the general crisis of socialist thought, common to all countries at the same stage of development, and due essentially to the multiple regressions and paralysis of the Stalinist era. Britain had a very weak and limited indigenous Marxist tradition, quite unable to resist or modify the pressures of Stalinism; hence the identification of Marxism with Stalinism is especially pervasive. Confusion, hectic changes of orientation, successive phases of expansion and contraction in following, bitter internal dissensions: these are the symptoms – familiar at other times and in other countries – of the emancipation of the intellectual Left from its former claustrophobia. However chaotic and dismembered, a recognizable Left-Wing 'intelligentsia' distinct from the guardians of liberalism and neo-capitalism is emerging. And it no longer seems to have special, peculiarly British, barriers to surmount in its development. Except, possibly, the barrier presented by the economic organization of culture and information, which in Britain has reached a degree of more intensive and stultifying monopoly than elsewhere, and renders the voicing of minority opinion more and more difficult.

How the 'subjective' factor represented by the intellectual stratum develops will depend, in the long run, upon the development of the 'objective' situation mentioned above – that is, upon how the class-struggle changes in the new situation, how the Trade Unions (and so the Labour Party) react, upon the new needs created in this process. What is new is, precisely, the fact that one *can* envisage such a dialectic of development. On the one hand, fundamental economic and social conditions are compelling a change in the relationships and tensions of class; on the other hand, in the field of consciousness and theoretical response, there is at least the embryo of a subjective force capable of meeting the change more positively, of making it more than a dumbly suffered transformation. We saw how class-consciousness, however intense and ineradicable, was in a sense *passive* in Britain, and so not mobilized in the activity of the class-struggle. But the social and cultural conditions of such passivity are vanishing, and at the same time the conflict is becoming objectively more acute. Hence, there may soon exist conditions under which this legacy of class-awareness *can* be mobilized, converted into an active agency, as the motor of economic and political struggle. The way to a qualitative transformation of the class-struggle is difficult and painful, and extremely uncertain – how could it be otherwise? That it appears possible at all, that the old mountainous obstacles have crumbled – this is the striking fact, the new horizon of socialism in Britain which casts a fresh light upon Labourism and everything else.

A Certain Hope

Labourism was the product, the incarnation, of class stasis and intellectual stasis; it was the negation of any moving dynamic between theory and practice, the heavy domination of practice – in certain precise historically established forms – over theory and consciousness. It goes without saying that Labourism would be different in an historical situation where such stasis no longer endured. This is why one must approach with caution the familiar dilemma of whether any new left-wing movement must be 'inside' or 'outside' the Labour Party, whether it should try to take over Labourism or replace it with something else. The fact is, that the existence of any forceful Left-Wing tendency, with a mind of its own and some basis in the Trade Unions – a Left capable of hegemony and not only protest – would transform Labourism. Nobody can say how Labourism would react under a new strain of this sort. Would it be possible to preserve the positive side of Labourism – the unity it asserts among working-class organizations – on a higher, socialist level? Would a disintegration of the system be inevitable, as part of the ensuing battle? Only one thing is certain: Labourism, which has survived every internal and external vicissitude since its foundation, which has drifted on immutably through defeat and the disintegration of its ideals, would no longer be able to function in the same way. Hegel first stated the paradox that a party only becomes real when it is divided against itself, when contradictions battle within it. Labourism was what it was because *not* divided against itself in this vital sense – it centred upon a pathological battle of appearances with no possibility of resolution. What it would become when lifted out of such unreality by an authentic challenge, when lacerated by contradictions which it could not stifle or ignore – nobody can say.

It is very unlikely that revolutionary changes will occur with dramatic rapidity under the Labour régime. Nevertheless, change is under way, and it could eventually have a revolutionary meaning. After the long catalepsy in which the working class and the working-class movement were locked, new stirrings and a new climate will bring a different world. It could be a world more propitious to a real British socialism. The British working class could still realize a part of the great future Marx foresaw, over a century ago, when he predicted that it would lead the way to the emancipation of labour everywhere. Because the Labour Government may play a posi-

tive part in this process – whatever its limits, however contradictory its role – socialists everywhere should see its advent
with a certain hope, a certain critical confidence, and not merely
as the futile repetition of an old illusion.

PART TWO

PROBLEMS OF SOCIALIST STRATEGY

Perry Anderson

The Left in Britain has always been open to the damaging
accusation that it lacks any strategic perspective. It is difficult
to deny the charge. The Left has never, historically, been able
to offer a convincing or coherent answer to the question: how
is socialism to be achieved? It is striking that in all the
debates and conflicts of the fifties, strategic arguments proper
played almost no role at all. All sections of the Left were alike
in this: the basis of their politics was a *moral* critique of
society, dissociated from the complex historical process in
which values can alone ultimately find incarnation. This attitude, with all its characteristic strengths and weaknesses, has
been a hall-mark of the British Left since the foundation of the
I.L.P. Its best thinkers – Morris, Tawney, Cole – have never
departed from this tradition. Today, however, it has become
urgent to surpass it. The lack of any strategic perspective has
been one of the key reasons for the eclipse of the Left since
1961 – its swift and sudden effacement before the rise of Wilson. For Wilson above all has offered a strategy to the Labour
Party – it is this that has enabled him to temporarily cancel
the divisions within it and dominate the party. A strategy for
the Labour Party as it exists today, however, is one thing; a
strategy for socialism is another. It is precisely in this that so
much of the difficulty lies.

In effect, since the war, the failure of the Left to formulate
any viable strategy for socialism has been not simply a British
but a European phenomenon. At the present time, socialist
thought in Europe is undergoing a profound and creative renovation. The work of men as different in background and
preoccupations as Sartre, Williams, Mandel, Gorz, Lukacs,
Magri, Marcuse, Goldmann – a Frenchman, an Englishman,

a Belgian, an Austrian, a Hungarian, an Italian, a German and a Rumanian – reveals a range and depth that can stand comparison with any period in this century. The patrimony of contemporary socialism has been enriched in many fields: its theory of culture, its theory of history, its theory of man. Its comprehension, and its critique, of capitalist civilization have made significant advances. In striking contrast, however, its strategic thought remains almost as weak as ever. The problem of how – after so many years, and so many struggles, and so many defeats – to inaugurate socialism seems as far from an answer today as it did ten or twenty years ago. The historical reason for this blockage is not hard to see. During the long night of theory, in the worst years of the Cold War from 1947–57, the only free and vital socialist thought was that of isolated intellectuals. The great working-class parties of Western Europe, whether Social-Democrat or Communist, had no time for research or dissent. With few exceptions, their ambience paralysed it. A gulf opened up between theory and practice. The political practice of the period – whether the party in question was Communist or anti-Communist – tended to become a leaden immobilism, punctuated with occasional bouts of erratic and unavailing opportunism. The theory became increasingly recondite and remote from immediate political struggles. In particular, it was unable to broach the problem which constitutes the nexus between theory and practice – the most 'practical' of all theoretical problems: how is socialism to be achieved? An authentic socialist strategy can only be born *within* the internal dialectic of a mass socialist movement: it has no meaning or possibility outside it. Since 1957, the relaxation of the Cold War has seen a flowering of socialist thought and discussion. Many of the barriers between intellectuals and the working-class movement in Europe have begun to fall. But this evolution has not gone far enough to produce any major debate on strategy.

In England, the problem has taken a special form. The Labour Party has traditionally been more tolerant than its continental opposites: but then it could afford to be, since indifference to theory runs throughout the whole movement.

The theoretical weakness of the Labour Left is, in fact the condition of the greater permissiveness of the Party. The same basic situation remains. The Labour Party is unquestionably not a socialist party; yet it is the sole mass party of the working-class in England. It is thus equally impossible to formulate a strategy from 'inside' or 'outside' it. In these conditions, any attempt to consider some of the problems involved in a successful march towards socialism must necessarily be *abstract* and *inorganic*. For in the absence of a mass socialist party, there is no concrete, coherent perspective from which to embark on such an attempt. Reflection becomes, literally, dislocated. However, in spite of this fundamental difficulty, a survey of possible alternatives may still be better than the void around which socialist discussion at present endlessly circles. The suggestions which follow are inevitably elliptical and utopian. They are not intended to do more than offer very abbreviated and partial hypotheses for discussion.

A. STRATEGIC MODELS

1. *The Two Roads to Socialism*

Two strategic models have dominated our history, and divided the socialist movement in Europe from the turn of the century to our own time. The momentous schism between Social-Democracy and Communism derives directly from them. They can be called the parliamentary and the insurrectionary roads to socialism. Any discussion of socialist strategy in Western Europe today must begin with some consideration of these great traditional models, which have for so long haunted and fixed men's imagination. The difference between them can be summed up in two quotations, one from Lenin in 1917, the other from Sidney Webb in 1923. On the eve of the October Revolution, Lenin wrote: 'The substitution of the proletarian state for the bourgeois state is impossible without a violent revolution . . . The doctrine of the class struggle . . . leads inevitably to a recognition of the *political rule* of the proletariat, of its dictatorship, i.e. of power shared with none and relying directly upon the armed force of the masses. . . . The liberation of the oppressed class is impossible not only without a violent revolution, *but also without the destruction* of the apparatus of state power which was created by the ruling class . . .' Six years later, in his Presidential Address to the Labour Party Conference, Webb declared: 'Let me insist on what our opponents habitually ignore, and, indeed, what they seem intellectually incapable of understanding, namely the *inevitable gradualness* of our scheme of change . . . For the Labour Party, it must be plain, Socialism is rooted in Democracy; which necessarily compels us to recognize that every step towards our goal is dependent on gaining the assent and support of at least a numerical majority of the whole people. Thus, even if we aimed at revolutionizing everything at once, we should necessarily be compelled to make each particular change only at the time, and to the extent, and in the manner which ten or fifteen million electors, in all sorts of conditions, of all sorts of temperaments, from Land's End to the Orkneys, could be brought to consent to it. . . . But the Labour Party, when in due course it comes to be entrusted with power, will naturally not want to do everything at once. . . . Once we face the necessity of putting our principles first into bills, to be fought through Committee clause by clause; and then into the appropriate machinery for carrying them into execution from one end of the Kingdom to the other – that is what the Labour Party has done with its socialism – the *inevitability of gradualness* cannot fail to be appreciated.'

For Lenin, the road to socialism was short but sheer: it required the armed insurrection of the proletariat against the established State, its capture and destruction. Out of this conflagration the working-class would fashion a new State, the dictatorship of the proletariat. For Webb, on the other hand, the road to socialism was long, flat and winding: its terminus was always over the horizon. The working class could only create a new social order by slow, imperceptible stages. It must respect the constitutional framework into which it had been admitted. There was only one way in which to change society in these conditions: to win an election, a majority in Parliament, and then, gradually and peaceably, begin to legislate towards the distant pole-star of socialism.

These two conceptions became ruling visions on different sides of the great geo-political divide which runs between Western and Eastern Europe; they correspond to two worlds and two histories. In Russia, and in Yugoslavia, Lenin's vision came true: in the other Eastern European countries, it was realized artificially, and deformed. But all over a vast area, covering well over half the continent of Europe, socialism in the most preliminary sense was realized: the expropriators were expropriated, and social ownership of the economy achieved. To this day, these conquests – with all their blinding accompaniment of force and terror – remain the only indisputable monuments of the socialist movement which set out to transform Europe at the end of the nineteenth century. Ever since, the Social-Democratic movements of the West have rejected them *en bloc*. Their reason has always been the same. The Leninist revolutions of the East were not democratic, the societies they created were totalitarian – therefore they were not socialist, they were the antithesis of socialism. This belief, which remains deep throughout the labour movement in Britain, rests on a partial truth. Socialism in its full critical and philosophical sense – as the realm of freedom, the final triumph of man over necessity and alienation – has, of course, not remotely been realized in Russia or any other Eastern country. In this sense, it is right and necessary to repudiate the Communist states' designation of themselves as the 'socialist countries'. At the same time, it is pedantic, and parochial, to refuse a certain historical truth to the description: in a minimal-ideal sense, these countries are socialist – their economies are socially and not privately appropriated, and the ideology which regulates their operation is a socialist one. It is, of course, true that they are not democratic, and that democracy is integral to an authentic socialism. However, merely to denounce them as undemocratic and therefore as historically illegitimate is a form of blindness. The categories of this criticism are simply not fundamental enough.

Why did the October Revolution succeed? Why was the

inchoate new society of Russia not democratic? The answer to these questions underlines the truth that socialism – contrary to an easy belief widely held today – is not just democracy plus social ownership. For the real historical ground of Soviet Communism was neither despotism, nor collectivism, it was *scarcity*. This was the immitigable core of its agony and inhumanity. In the empire of scarcity, man ineluctably becomes the enemy of man. His relationship with his fellows is mediated through a world of matter, that is a priori *lack* for one and *luxury* for another. The struggle for its distribution has no humanly liveable outcome: it constitutes an interminable, implacable negation of man. In the twenties, it was as if Russia had become an immense compression chamber in which men, institutions, values, were slowly and mercilessly reduced to nothing by the pressure of this relentless absence. Everything was lacking. Scarcity of things: in 1921, the economy of this huge, ramshackle, backward country could not produce enough bread to feed its population, enough shoes to supply even one out of three of its inhabitants. Anything produced over and above the barest essentials went to a smaller and smaller minority, as the goods became more and more complex and expensive. Scarcity of men: only one out of four of the population could read or write, only one out of five hundred had received higher education; only one out of two hundred had any technical training, only one in forty had any experience of industrial work. Scarcity of values: there were no durable political institutions, no democratic cultural traditions, no widely-diffused social ideals, no full sense of national identity. Scarcity of time: ringed by hostile powers and under constant threat of an invasion which ultimately did not fail to materialize, industrialization had to be launched in half the time it had taken in the West. In this kingdom of necessity, neither liberty nor equality nor fraternity were possible. There can be no equality where goods are so scarce that only a minority can possess them; there can be no fraternity where rapid industrialization imposes iron hierarchy and work-discipline; there can be no democracy where lack of education creates an *élite*, lack of material possessions creates privilege, and lack of external security creates a permanent national mobilization. In these circumstances, terror is rooted in the structure of human co-existence itself.

This is not to say that everything which happened in Stalinist Russia was unavoidable. Far from it. Collectivization, purges, deportations, were all contingent political choices: crimes. No ulterior evolution will ever recoup or redeem them. They remain, irremediably, part of man's attempt to reach socialism in the twentieth century. For they were socialist, not liberal crimes – a violence consciously decided and willed, a deliberate reproduction and magnification of the violence inherent in an environment of scarcity. Liberal violence, by contrast, is a diffuse, nameless fatality. Its worst holocaust was more deadly than any crime of Stalinism: the First World War left ten million dead and twenty million wounded, for no purpose whatever. No one was responsible for the Great War – except a civilization everywhere defined by its alienation of human action and responsibility.

It is necessary to say this, because it is still customary in the West to proscribe the whole experience of Russian Communism as beyond the limits of respectable socialist discussion. In fact, the Russian Revolution and all that followed from it, forms part – an immense part – of the common heritage of the whole socialist movement. It cannot be renounced or evaded by any working-class party in Europe. It is thus essential to examine, honestly and lucidly, the lessons of the grandeur and servitude of Leninism.[1] This is not the place for such an attempt. But some reflections are a precondition of any discussion of socialist strategy in the West today. Leninism has been, as Social-Democracy has nowhere been, a success in its own terms and in its own context. It won power in Russia, carried out the expropriation of capitalism, and totally transformed the economy and society of the largest country in Europe. It later spread by force of arms and absence of serious opposition, to the whole of Eastern Europe. Finally it produced an authentic revolution in China. What was the secret of this success? The answer is surely this: Leninism was almost perfectly adapted

[1] See Isaac Deutscher's masterly writings on the subject.

to the specific conditions of its time and place. Its central strategy consists in the seizure and destruction of existing State power. *It is precisely in backward, inchoate societies, dominated by scarcity and integrated only by the State, that such a strategy has its meaning.* When misery and inequality are the destiny of an entire nation; when there is no technical infrastructure; when there is no literacy or common culture; when there is no civic political tradition; when there is no real national identity – the *State* tends to become the sole repository and reality of the society as a society. 'Civil society' is so protoplasmic, disarticulated, amorphous, impalpable that its only tangible existence is its crystallisation in the State. It is only there that this inchoate magma coagulates into a *form.* In underdeveloped societies – today even more than in Lenin's time – the State is the univocal meaning of the nation. It is, by definition, Hegelian. The sovereign source of all public action and creation, it enjoys, in the words of a recent writer, referring not to any Communist country but to neutralist state, Indonesia, 'a power and freedom of manœuvre *vis-à-vis* the rest of the population which . . . can rarely have been ex-

The osmosis between Party and State, to form the one-party state, was an exception and scandal to the West in the early days of Russian Communism. Now that Asia and Africa have re-entered history, it has become the most common type of régime in the world. The reason is clear. Where resources – human or material – are radically scarce, as soon as there is a real effort to climb out of the closed circle of 'underdevelopment', all existing resources must be rigorously pooled to make any impact on the colossal task of industrialization and acculturation. Thus scarcity – once it is lived as a task and not as a destiny – is *limitlessly centripetal.*[2] In this sense too, it acts as

[1] Robert Curtis, 'Malaysia and Indonesia', *New Left Review,* November–December, 1964.

[2] Even where underdevelopment is not seriously confronted by the political régime, an irresistible sociological drainage towards the centre tends to occur, in the form of an immense, parasitic growth of the capital city – 'macrocephaly', the scourge of almost every major Third World country today. Leopoldville, Karachi, Caracas offer some of the most spectacular examples.

a kind of compression chamber. The monolithic character of the State, its imbrication with the Single Party, is thus the necessary obverse of the weakness and atomization of society as a whole. In extreme cases, as in many African countries today – which are more backward even than Russia in 1917 or China in 1949 – penury of men and skills is such that the binary institution Party-State, although formally embodied in the constitution, is itself too complex: there are only enough cadres to make one of these a reality – the literal State.

Leninism has thus in a precise and limited sense been validated by history. That is to say, its single determination to attack and replace the State machine in Russia proved successful: it won power and launched industrialization. In those specific conditions there was no other way of changing society: *it could only be attained and transformed in its localization in the State*. To the extent that this is true, the conventional moral excommunication in the West of the whole experience of Leninism is parochial. Sociologically, values can never overshoot the historical and structural context which provides their sole field of substantiation. (Individually, of course, they can and often do.) This is not to say that there is a linear historical determinism, which prescribes the norms and options of every society or régime. It is rather that there is a certain negative determinism, which never *produces* any one possibility, but always *eliminates* several. History, in this sense, operates a permanent selectivity, which rigorously delimits the field of possibilities at any given moment, without ever finally structuring it. Variations of Leninism – what are benignly called 'development dictatorships' by Western spokesmen today – or a prolongation of the hopeless inferno of underdevelopment, were the alternatives to Communism in Russia: not liberal democracy.[1]

[1] It is striking that the creative and potentially liberating role of single-party régimes is explicitly recognized by many Western analysts today, as long as these are not Communist. Thus the American sociologist Morroe Berger writes of Nasser's Egypt and other Arab military régimes: 'Though perhaps not directly intending to promote democracy as a purely political arrangement, the military régime is, by its colossal effort to introduce social change, willy-nilly creating

Leninism, then, with all its inhuman costs, represented an immense, promethean progress for Russia, as it does today for China. But its very adaptation to its Eastern environment, which has been the secret of its success, radically *disadapts* it from the Western milieu where capitalism remains supreme today. For the societies of Western Europe constitute a wholly different universe from those of Eastern Europe, let alone Asia. Their highly advanced economies and their complex, dense, tessellated histories have created a social and cultural world entirely of its own. The great political achievement of this world has been democracy. Whatever its lacunae or limitations, this democracy represents a permanent acquisition of mankind – an experience so important that it will eventually itself become democratized, and cease to be the privilege of a region. For the moment, it is important to emphasize that a Leninist strategy in the West is fundamentally *regressive*: it threatens to destroy a vital historical creation, when the task is to surpass it. And, in fact, Leninism as such has not had any success in Western Europe; it has never come near to doing so. Neither as norm nor as strategy is it an acceptable option. It is refused by the whole cultural texture of the advanced capitalist societies of the West.

What is the alternative? Historically, it has been Social-

---

some of the socio-economic conditions, attitudes, and expectations that may one day be expressed in a greater demand for political democracy ... Under the 'populist' régime political freedom is suppressed but at least the possibility of its growth remains.' (*The Arab World Today*, pp. 407–408). Maurice Duverger, the orthodox theorist of Western political parties, is still more direct in assessing Ataturk's Turkey: 'The pluralist system of parties applied to countries of archaic social structure, in which the mass of the people is uneducated, maintains and consolidates the power of the traditional aristocracy, that is to say that it prevents the establishment of true democracy. The example of Turkey, on the contrary, seems to demonstrate that the technique of the single-party, applied with discernment, makes it possible gradually to build up a new ruling class and the independent political *élite* which alone make it possible to establish at some date an authentic democracy.' (*Political Parties*, p. 280). Neither Egypt nor – still more – Turkey, of course, have achieved economic growth commensurate with their needs.

Democracy – in England, Fabianism. The starting point of social-democracy has always been the ascription of decisive reality and value to parliamentary democracy – and the decision to work exclusively within its limits. This seemed the reasonable and natural thing to do, even to men trained all their lives in a Marxist tradition, in for example the German Social-Democratic Party: such was the evidence and power of the environment.[1] In the West, there has appeared to be no other solution. Even the mass Communist parties have almost always tacitly conformed to it.

The initial success of social-democracy was impressive: so much that it seemed, in the early years of the century, as if this was indeed the Western road to socialism. All over Western Europe, mass social-democratic parties came into being. In nearly every country they were for decades the largest working-class party. Their electoral strength steadily increased. The goal of participating in a democratically-elected government was reached almost everywhere, in most countries in the first years after the First World War. There have by now been governments with social-democratic participation in Denmark, Germany, Austria, Belgium, Sweden, Holland, England, Norway, France, Italy. However, in three countries only – England, Sweden and Norway – have there ever been majority social-democratic governments. Such is the electoral record of social-democracy, on its own terrain. More important, however, is obviously its political record – its degree of success in transforming the capitalist societies of Western Europe in the direction of socialism. This is the crux of social-democracy's historical role.

It is clear, to begin with, that there is not one socialist society in Western Europe, in any sense of the term, after sixty years of social-democracy's existence. There is not a social-democrat, even in Sweden, to claim the contrary. It may

---

[1] 'Social-democracy' is often – wrongly – used as a purely pejorative term on the Left today. It is well to remember that the Bolshevik Party itself was originally the Russian Social-Democratic Party, and that Engels was the political mentor of the German Social-Democratic Party. A sense of the wider historical unity of the European socialist movement is lost in the pejorative use of the term.

still, however, be argued that some countries of Western Europe are appreciably nearer socialism than they were forty or fifty years ago, and that this is precisely social-democracy's achievement. What yardsticks could be used to measure this? Within the framework of social-democracy itself, two suggest themselves: the size of the public sector, and the distribution of the national income. It is unnecessary to point out the limitations of these criteria; they can, nevertheless, serve as a base of reference. To take the first, every country in Europe today has a two-sector economy. What is the balance between the two sectors? The public sector accounts for the following percentage of the national gross fixed investment: Britain 32 per cent, Italy 27 per cent, Austria 27 per cent, France 25 per cent, West Germany 15–20 per cent, Sweden 15 per cent, Norway 14 per cent, Netherlands 13 per cent, Belgium 10 per cent.'[1] Thus in no case has the nationalized sector become anything more than a minority enclave, whose main function is to provide a cheap technical infrastructure for private enterprise at public cost. The primary role of public industries in a capitalist economy is, in fact, 'socialization of losses'. It is now common, of course, to argue that socialized industries as such are not intrinsic to the social-democratic programme, which is essentially one of income redistribution and welfare provision. Here again, comparisons are illuminating. In England, Kaldor has calculated that the 'historical constancy' of the returns to capital and labour has remained virtually unaltered since the nineteenth century – and he speaks of the similarity of these shares in different capitalist economies.[2] Taking a different basis for comparison, Needleman has reckoned that the most redistributive tax system in Western Europe (more than Sweden or any Scandinavian country) is that of West Germany – a purely capitalist régime which has never had a year of social-democratic government in its history.[3] In Britain, Tit-

[1] P. Lowell, 'Lessons from Abroad', in Shanks (ed.), *Lessons of Public Enterprise*, pp. 284–5.

[2] *Essays in Value and Distribution*, p. 210.

[3] 'A Note on the Burden of Taxation', *National Institute Economic and Social Review*, March, 1961.

muss's work has shown how doubtful any redistribution through the tax system has been since the war and immediate post-war years.

The Welfare State – in Britain the proudest boast of the labour movement – is usually thought of as a creation of social-democracy. But even here the reality is significantly different from conventional pieties. It is certainly true that Sweden, after thirty years of unbroken social-democratic rule, has the most munificent welfare services in Europe (it is also important that Sweden is the richest country in Europe). However, West Germany, France and even Spain also offer welfare benefits, which are in some fields more generous than those in Britain, as Morgan Phillips's official document *Labour in the Sixties* recognized. Thus, while social-democracy has played an important role in several countries in the advent of the Welfare State, there is no necessary linkage between the two: an enlightened – or even an authoritarian – capitalism can just as well create its own Welfare State.[1] The balance-sheet of sixty years of social-democracy is thus arrestingly poor. Not merely has it not brought about socialism anywhere: it has not in itself affected any major structural change in the societies in which it has acted. It is profoundly significant that the only great reformist thinker of this century, whose thought changed the whole course of Western societies, was a liberal capitalist, not a social-democrat – Keynes. It has been Keynesianism, not Social-democracy, which has effected the decisive changes in the West.

Everything initially happened, in fact, as if social-democracy

[1] As Titmuss points out: 'Welfare may be used to serve military and racial ends – as in Hitler's Germany. More medical care was provided by voluntary and State agencies not because of a belief in every man's uniqueness because of a hatred of men. Welfare may be used to narrow allegiances and not diffuse them – as in employers' fringe benefit systems. Individual gain and political quietism, fostered by the new feudalism of the corporation, may substitute for the sense of common humanity nourished by systems of non-discriminatory mutual aid.' 'The Limits of the Welfare State', *New Left Review*, September–October, 1964.

was destined to be in the West what Leninism was in the East –
the indigenous road to socialism. But it failed to become so.
Leninism represented a sombre but genuine adaptation to its
world; social-democracy represented a false adaptation. It
appeared to be appropriate for its time and place, but this was
not a genuine adaptation, it was in fact an *absorption*. Hence
the permanent discrepancy, peculiar to social-democratic
parties, between their regulative goals and their actual programmes. It is commonplace, of course, for there to be a conflict between a political party's ideals and its practice. But the
contradiction in contemporary social-democracy goes far
deeper than this. Ideals, values, principles are by definition
imprecise and intangible. There is invariably latitude to argue
their interpretation and application; they can always finally be
presented as embodied in action. Concrete, articulated goals –
'the common ownership of the means of production, distribution and exchange', etc. – are another matter. When these are
ignored or denied by the platform of a party, an enormous
functional strain sets in. The party, in effect, has *two* programmes, one of which perpetually tries to exorcise the other.
The result is a paralyzing tension which saps the whole morale
and confidence of the party. The reason for this dualism is
clear. The social-democratic parties of the West have been
forced to abandon or dilute their original goal under the en-
circling pressure of capitalist society. Contrary to their expectations, democracy has not been the chosen instrument for the
realization of their aims: on the contrary, it has been turned
against them, and has confiscated their projects. As a sociologist
has recently commented, 'What seems to have taken place in
the democratic countries up to the present time is not so much
a reduction in the power of the upper class as a decline in the
radicalism of the working class.'[1] The absorption and neutral-
ization of social-democracy has in no country been complete,
least of all in Britain. Since the realities of a class society remain, social-democracy almost never becomes a *pure* mechanism of integration. Its working-class character and the inertia

[1] T. B. Bottomore, *Elites and Society*, p. 35.

of its tradition prevent this. But absorption has gone far enough to produce a great gulf between its historic aims and its contemporary horizons. The distance between the two is the measure of its subordination. When this happens the whole intentionality of social-democracy is shattered. It becomes a paradigm of the 'unhappy consciousness', its will and motivation disintegrating in the strain of conflicting roles. The end of this road is in sight: it is not socialism, but the suicide of social-democracy.

What went wrong? The key error of social-democracy was a *strategic* error – a basic, ineradicable misconception of the nature of power in advanced capitalist societies and the means of attaining it.

The whole *modus operandi* of social-democratic politics is geared to an illusion: it is predicated on the existence of a monocentric democracy in which power is co-extensive with the means of legislation. In this vision, society becomes a translucent, formal design, in which power is distributed symmetrically to every adult citizen at regular intervals (elections), and is then immediately reconstituted into a new, unitary pattern (government). Power exists simply as this instantaneous prestation between electorate and Parliament. The entire energies of the social-democratic party are thus polarized towards this one supreme moment; everything else is secondary. Elections become autotelic contests which apparently govern the whole fate of the nation.

The naïveté of this vision of the power structure of advanced capitalism is obvious; but it has never been renounced by social-democracy. The reason is clear. This vision is itself one of the maintaining mechanisms of the true power structure. It acts as a gyroscope which keeps social-democracy unswervingly on course towards failure and subordination. For the reality is, of course, that power in advanced capitalist societies is not an object sited exclusively – or even primarily – in Parliament, to be passed to and fro as majorities change. It is not an object at all: *it is the totality of differential relationships that constitute a society.* These relationships are, of course, mediated and objectified in a range of crucial institutions. These institutions are infinitely more numerous and various than Parliament. They include a myriad microsocial formations: families, schools, universities, factories, offices, newspapers, cinemas, banks, laboratories, squadrons, secretariats, etc. These formations in turn make up larger agglomerations – the great institutional orders of the society: education, economy, communications, army, bureaucracy. Parliament is among these. Each has its own specific degree of autonomy. The legislature is thus *one* of a series of sectors of power, not their synthesis. The dynamic configuration of these different ensembles is the real constellation of power in the society. In Britain, the structure of power amounts to the *permanent hegemony* of one social bloc over another. This is a trans-electoral phenomenon. I have tried to outline the specific contours of this hegemony earlier. What is important here is social-democracy's blindness to the realities of the system which imprisons it. Mesmerized by the juridical sovereignty of Parliament, it utterly fails to see its sociological heteronomy. In effect, the attempt to win power by staking everything on the electoral contest is doomed from the outset. A social-democratic government is, of course, possible: but it is always unable to realize the radical social transformation which it is ostensibly committed to achieve. The reason is twofold. Objectively, it is circumscribed and neutralized by the immense aggregate power preserved by the hegemonic class in all the other sectors of the power structure. Subjectively – and this is far more important – it has already been contained at the level of its own announced intentions. As Westergaard points out: 'Conflict is regulated through a series of compromises which define, not only the means and procedures of conflict, but also the area of conflict at any given time. Compromises thus enter into the initial determination of the limits of controversy: only a small band of the full range of alternative policies is effectively ventilated and disputed. Indeed, on some issues the band may be so narrow that decisions seem not to be "made" at all – they just flow automatically from the "climate of opinion" formed by the initial compromise. To determine the locus of power, therefore, one must examine the nature of that compromise itself . . ."[1]

The traditional criticism of the Left has been that social-democratic parties like the Labour Party sacrifice principle in order to gain power. The real criticism to be made of them is rather that they *cannot* gain power as long as they sacrifice principle for the sake of winning elections. They may well win, but under these conditions. 'power' is simply permission to operate the status quo. It has no purchase whatever on the statute of the society. There is no 'mandate' for changing this. Social-democracy is thus trapped in the closed circle of electoralism. It restricts its own freedom to win a partial power which is then further curtailed by its initial restriction. The result is a profound impotence and demoralization.

What is the lesson of this long impasse, which over the years has altered European capitalism so little and European social-democracy so much? The answer lies within the terms of the comparison made at the beginning of this analysis. Leninism and social-democracy are apparently in every way poles apart: violence against legality, vanguardism against passivity, discipline against democracy. *Yet in one respect there is a fundamental similarity between the two. They both polarize their whole strategies on the State: civil society remains outside the main orbit of their action.* Here lies the clue to the real adaptation of the one and the false adaptation of the other. For in the East, the State was the sole vector of social action and transformation: civil society had no structured existence independent of it. To change society, Leninism in one form or another, was a necessity. *But in the West, just the opposite is true.* There, in conditions of diminishing scarcity, civil society predominates politically over the State, and determines it in its image. *The heteronomy of the State is the root cause of the failure of social-democracy.*

The differences between a parliamentary and an insurrectionary strategy are, of course, immense. One involves a seizure of arbitrary power by a disciplined minority; the other an electoral victory by a numerical majority. The democratic

[1] 'Capitalism without Classes'.

character of the latter has, in the eyes of social-democratic parties, been a self-sufficient value: it defines this strategy exhaustively for them. There is no question that this difference is a real and important one: but it has obscured a crucial convergence. Both parliamentary and insurrectionary strategies are aimed squarely at the State, to the exclusion of the whole terrain of civil society. The success, and tragedy, of Leninism have already been discussed. The failure of social-democracy can now be related to it. It has been seen how the whole structure of power in advanced capitalist countries is polycentric. In effect, beyond a certain point, diminishing scarcity tends to diversify and dilate the whole fabric of society. A multiplication of focal points, groups, institutions, takes place against the background of a continuous accumulation of capital and valorization of resources. Where goods, skills, values are relatively more abundant, civil society becomes more solid and structured. In Western Europe, this development in general coincided with the rise of the industrial bourgeoisie of the nineteenth century. The effects of this were decisive for the evolution of these societies. The nature of the property régime, and the *laissez faire* ideology of the time, ensured that the power of the dominant bloc in almost every country was equally incarnated in civil society and the State. As Gramsci remarked at the time of the Great Slump, in a crucial passage: 'Civil Society has become an extremely complex and resistant structure, immune to catastrophic "eruptions" of an immediate economic kind (crises, depressions, etc.); the superstructures of civil society are comparable to the trench systems of modern warfare. As in contemporary war, a blazing artillery attack can seem to destroy the enemy's whole defensive position, but in reality it has only destroyed its outer surface.'[1] There were important variations in this pattern in each country, usually depending above all on the role of the army. The phenomenon went much the farthest among the major countries in Britain, where it had already in the nineteenth century taken the form of the decisive supremacy of civil society over the State. The general tendency is, however, clear. It contrasts

[1] *Note sul Machiavelli*, pp. 66–7.

strikingly with the evolution of the 'administrative' bourgeoisies of the Third World today – as it does with the semi-feudal despotisms of Eastern Europe at the turn of the century. It was this balance between civil society and the State which *both allowed the growth of democracy – and its confiscation by the hegemonic class, in the successful defence of capitalism*. The autonomy of civil society prevented the permanent erection of an arbitrary State, *but it also made it unnecessary*. Power was not exclusively lodged in a top-heavy, massive State machine, whose democratization would de facto threaten to revolutionize the whole existing social order. It was diffused through the whole variegated, supple, intricate texture of civil society. It was the invisible colour of daily life itself. In these conditions, there was little risk of revolutionary consequences from parliamentary democracy. The history of social-democracy has offered an endless demonstration of this truth.

2. *The Hegemonic Party*

The impasse of social-democracy poses the key contemporary problem for socialists in the West. What alternative strategy for socialism is possible? A measure of the despair felt by many socialists before this problem is the current tendency to accord a primordial importance to the Trade Unions, and to substitute these for the political party, as the main vehicle of socialist advance.[1]

This substitution in effect puts the clock back fifty years. It amounts to an implicit attempt to make a clean sweep of the whole intervening experience. As a lucid judgement of the mediocrity and immobility of working-class parties almost everywhere today, this attitude is readily understandable. But history cannot be undone: a sophisticated version of

[1] The major theoretician of this view is the Italian socialist Vittorio Foa. See, for example, his essay 'I socialisti e il sindicato', *Problemi del Socialismo*, June, 1963. It should be recognized that this tendency has produced a creative and enduring revaluation of the role of Trade Unions in contemporary capitalism, a major achievement in its own right.

syndicalism, however attractive it may seem in the present conjuncture, is still ultimately retrograde. The overwhelming emphasis placed on the Trade Unions in recent socialist writings
reflects a real situation, in which Trade Unions do often offer
the best immediate chance of an advance. But no long-term
strategy can be built only or even primarily on them. The problem is not to replace the political party as the architect of
socialism, but to transform it.

What would an authentic mass socialist party be like today?
An a priori model is all that is possible to set out here. This
is not the place for an extended discussion of the problem, but
some brief remarks – of a necessarily abstract kind – may
serve for orientation. *In Western Europe today, any true
socialist party must present itself unambiguously as a hegemonic force. That is to say, it must propose a coherent, global
alternative to the existing social order, and represent a permanent drive towards it.* This universality of ideal and action
is the indispensable precondition of a hegemonic party.

A consideration of the composition of such a party must
start from a recognition of the way in which the social structures of the main West European countries have evolved since
1900. It is clear that the tendency towards an ever-increasing
polarization between a small capitalist *élite* and a vast, destitute
proletarian mass – predicted by Marx and postulated by
Lenin – has not occurred. The Leninist conception of a
party was founded on this premise. The reality has, in Western
Europe, been quite different and demands a different kind of
party. Technological and economic evolution has not operated
a dramatic simplification of the social structure, reducing it to
a single, unbridgeable confrontation between exploiters and
exploited. On the contrary, it has diversified and articulated
the social structure into an ever more complex and imbricated
ensemble. Exploitation and oppression are as real as ever, but
they are masked and mediated in a thousand ways.

In these conditions, a party based exclusively on the working-class is no longer viable or desirable – although it must, of
course, always be based *first and foremost*, in every sense, on

the working-class. In most European countries, however, the industrial working class only constitutes about 35 per cent of the population. This is not in itself the main reason why a single-class party must be rejected. The crucial reason is that a purely working-class party tends, by its very nature, towards either corporatism or outright subordination. The mechanisms by which this occurs have been so well analysed that there is no need to discuss them here.[1] It is enough to say that the relationship between the working class and culture, decisive for its consciousness and ideology, is *inevitably* mediated through intellectuals, the only full tenants of culture in a capitalist society. The absence of a progressive intellectual stratum within a socialist party merely means that a conservative intelligentsia inside or outside the party determines the working class's relationship to culture, deforming its vocation to autonomy and creativity. In the highly integrated capitalist societies of today, moreover, the importance of the superstructure has tended to increase rapidly. The technology of modern communications allows the ideas and values of the dominant class to irradiate the whole society as never before. The counter-attacking role of socialist culture, articulated by intellectuals, thus becomes more and more crucial.

However, the simple addition of a stratum of radical intellectuals to the industrial working class is still not sufficient to constitute a hegemonic political party. For in contemporary West European societies, there are large intermediate classes and groups which are also victims of the alienation and oppression of neo-capitalism. They include, in most countries, the peasantry, the white-collar salariat, and the technical intelligentsia. Characteristically, these groups reveal an oscillating, limited consciousness, strongly marked by sectional prejudice and filtered mystification. In some cases – peasants, technicians – the nature of their work gives rise to tenacious values which can potentially qualify their political outlook. At all events, these groups must find some representation in the contemporary socialist movement. Their inclusion is, in fact, built into the notion of a hegemonic party. For a socialist party

[1] By Tom Nairn, in *The Nature of the Labour Party*.

can only successfully pose its candidature to the direction of a society, when it is the bearer of *universal values*, which are recognized and experienced as such by a majority of all those whose humanity is denied and dislocated by the social order.

These, then, are the social forces which must find their truth in a socialist party for it to be capable of victory over the universe of capitalism. The task of the party is to unite them in *a new historical bloc*. The concept of a bloc is radically different from that of a coalition, which remains the normal type of political combination on the Left today. Such widely disparate parties as the Democratic Party in the U.S.A. and the Communist Party in France embody, in effect, heterogeneous social coalitions within the ambience of a promiscuous populism. In America, Negroes, Jews, Italians, Irish, Northern working class and Southern racialists are all grouped in the Democratic Party, and ensure its normal dominance. In France the industrial working class, the anti-clerical smallholders and sections of the malthusian petit-bourgeoisie support the Communist Party: its most durable electoral strength in recent years has come from the retarded peasantry of the South. In each case, a process of dilution occurs, in which the political programme of the party – catering as it does for every different group in the coalition – reduces the aspirations and demands of each *downwards* to the lowest common denominator on which they can all agree, in a kind of *descending integration*. This is what makes both parties, despite appearances, inert and conservative organizations, incapable of changing their societies in any significant way.

The structure of a historical bloc, as Gramsci conceived it, is diametrically opposed to this system of alliances. The unity of the bloc rests on an *ascending integration*, which fuses together different hopes and demands on a higher level. Partial and sectional demands are inserted into a coherent and articulated vision of the world, which confers on them a common meaning and goal. The bloc is thus a synthesis of the aspirations and identities of different groups in a global project which exceeds them all. Its critique of capitalism is the truth

of each particular claim; its programme for socialism constitutes them into a single hierarchy of aims. The vocation of
the hegemonic party is thus manifestly universal: it is the
dynamic unity of all the forces and ideals in the society which
are premonitions of a new human order.

In these conditions, the relationship of the party to culture
is a precise and specific one. It has already been pointed out
that an intellectual stratum is an indispensable component of
a socialist party. This, in itself, however, says little about the
content of a socialist culture. To have a decisive power of
attraction over the whole society, socialist culture must be the
heir of all the most advanced and critical traditions of the
nation. Every national culture in Western Europe today contains important traditions which in their time were radical and
creative, but were never able to express their deepest truth
because of the distorting impact of triumphant capitalism.
Jacobinism in France, social Catholicism in Italy, Romanticism
in England are very different examples. These traditions were
for the most part annexed and stunted by the vast weight of
victorious bourgeois ideology; they were never able to develop
their inner logic and so never became universal. Today they
remain as active sediments in contemporary culture, often in
a mystified and even regressive form: but incapsulating an
immense, imprisoned charge of unsatisfied needs and aspirations. It is these confiscated traditions, with their particular
values and resonances, which a hegemonic party must liberate.
It can only do so by including and *transmuting* them in a vision
of man which is a unitary totality. Such a vision preserves each
creative tradition of the past as one of its 'moments', but links
and validates them in a new consciousness. The ideology of the
party then, must be on a scale commensurate with the tasks
it confronts: the transformation of society and man. This involves a tremendous tension and effort in every cultural field, a
constant enrichment of ideas and language to capture the
moving current of history.

At the same time, the activity of the party must weld together the historical bloc which it leads. For this, its internal
constitution must be a living demonstration of its programme –

a prototype of the social organization of the future. Democracy, in fact, is indivisible from socialism within a hegemonic party of this kind. For the party is a prefiguration of the society it sets out to create; it must, therefore, be visibly superior, in its own practice, to the practice of the society around it. Democracy in the advanced capitalist countries is pre-eminently *partial* and *occasional*: exercised only within terms of the State, and operative only once every four or five years. In contrast, democracy in a socialist party must be *comprehensive* and *continuous* – affecting not only the election of leaders, but the whole work and orientation of the movement, at every level. This kind of democracy would be a new form of social action, involving the full participation of thousands of persons in a relationship of equality and reciprocity. A socialist party must be, within the limits of the possible, intersubjectivity in a society which everywhere suppresses it.

Finally, its *arc of action* must embrace not only the bare institutions of the State, but the whole complex landscape of civil society as well. This is the most fundamental of all the traits of a hegemonic party, the one which divides it most absolutely from social-democracy. It has been seen how, from one point of view, the defining characteristic of social-democracy is its confinement within the narrow limits of the parliamentary game, its ageing and hopeless electoralism. A hegemonic socialism in Western Europe today must resolutely and deliberately reverse the whole terms of this strategy. Its aim must be, not to win a numerical majority in elections, but to create a historical bloc capable of changing society. Power in advanced capitalism is not the prerogative of parliament: it is coterminous with the structure of society. In Western Europe, this means that capitalist hegemony is first and foremost entrenched in civil society, and must be beaten there. An important consequence follows. There can be no serious talk of 'smashing' the power structure in the West in the same sense that Lenin spoke of 'smashing' the State machine in the East. In Western Europe, this would mean shattering civil society itself, whereas the real task is to *free* civil society from the dominion of capital. This requires the liberating activity of the party in the *quick of social existence* – rather than in its formalized representation in Parliament. It must be present at every contradiction and conflict in the society, and at every effort at invention and creation. This is the only way in which the consciousness of men, rather than the opinions of voters, can finally be changed. And this is the crux of the whole problem. Millions of people are now dumbly enduring the pain of living in an inhuman society, unaware even of the possibility of an alternative existence; it is only by changing their consciousness that socialism – the integral socialism envisaged by Marx – can be achieved. It is often assumed that this consciousness is formed today primarily by the means of communication – press, radio, television, cinema, etc. – and that therefore the struggle against capitalist hegemony must be directed above all against the present organization of these. For all the increased importance of the media of communication, this is a facile and narrow conception of consciousness, an intellectual's error that must be rejected. The truth is that a man's consciousness is formed by his *total life-situation*, the complete continuum of his whole experience. Watching television or reading a newspaper is one moment in this, but not necessarily the most important. Consciousness in its typical forms – assumptions, expectations, hopes, habits, views – is usually moulded far more deeply by the impress of other moments, in particular the intimate realities of family, school, sexuality, work. The task of freeing it cannot be reduced to a struggle against capitalist control of the media, vital though this is. It has to be fought right across the width of a man's life-experience, in every milieu in which it is formed. The concentric rings which determine consciousness in our society – schools, factories, towns, regions, distribution circuits – must be the ordinary arena of political action. The fate of socialism is decided in them all.

The purpose of this poised, immediate presence must be to create out of the confusion and attrition of present conditions a social bloc united in its will to transform capitalism. Once this is created, the formal attributes of power will follow. Elections are always epiphenomena: by the time they occur, the die is already cast. They are simply imperfect registers, after the event, of the balance of forces at any given time. Their real significance lies, not in the distribution of votes cast, but in the range of issues debated. This is what reveals the basic configuration of power; after that, the outcome of the election merely decides its tonality. A new historical bloc would by definition transform power where it originates – in civil society. This in turn would transform the parameters of 'practical politics' – what is contested at elections. Finally, electoral success would formalize these fundamental victories. But it would be electoral success of a new kind.

The normal model of Western democracy is based on an 'alternation' of governments. This model only has meaning if there is a permanent political and social structure which the opposing parties are equally willing and able to 'administer'. The very notion of a new 'administration' embodies this implicit acceptance of the status quo. It is, of course, only this political continuity which makes the whole model of 'alternation' viable. Social-democracy has always accepted this vision of democracy; it has never seen how radically contradictory it is to the very idea of socialism – the *transformation* of politics and society. A hegemonic socialist party, however, aims precisely at this: its raison d'être is a rupture with the status quo. The model of electoral 'alternation' has no sense for it. It can settle for nothing less than a *permanent sociological majority*. This alone constitutes a new hegemony, not merely a new 'administration'. It is the only goal consonant with a true intention of creating socialism. Of course, this socialism requires the full preservation of civic liberties and a plurality of political parties: all the living heritage of liberal democracy. But the party system itself would be changed – not by political fiat, but as a sociological fact, which is necessarily altered by changes in the social structure. These changes would follow from the ordinary implementation of a socialist programme. The new framework of 'practical politics', within which elections would be fought, would be qualitatively different; and the party system would reflect this. Such a new framework would be the precise political meaning of a new hegemony. A permanent sociological majority is the precondition of its achievement. It is towards this single horizon that an authentic socialist party must work.

B. THE LABOUR PARTY

One has only to enumerate the characteristics of a hegemonic party to see how far the Labour Party is from being one. The gap seems so huge as to make discussions of the two in the same context almost impossible. Nevertheless, this is the only exercise which at present has much meaning in a discussion of socialist strategy. The actual modalities of the Labour Party's failure to be a hegemonic force in British society must, above all, be considered. In the light of the model outlined above, these modalities will themselves suggest the multiple, concrete transformations which the Labour Party would have to undergo to be capable of bidding for real historical and political leadership today.

The scale and profundity of the Labour Party's failure can only be measured by its unique opportunities. These can be stated quite simply. It is the only working-class party in a country in which the manual working class constitute an overwhelming majority of the nation, no less than 70 per cent of the population. *No other left-wing party in Europe has ever been vouchsafed a chance of the kind that is permanently lodged in the social structure of Britain.* The Labour Party's constitutional inability to seize this chance represents a monumental impotence, in any comparative perspective. In fifty years of existence, it has only won a parliamentary majority three times – and a normal working majority precisely once. The precondition of a serious socialist strategy is to solve the enigma of this failure.

1. *Party and Class*

The first step towards doing this is to see exactly what the relationship is between party strength and social structure in contemporary Britain. The class composition of British society has no parallel in any major industrial nation.[1] Perhaps its only equivalent occurs on a qualitatively smaller scale, in the small and divided nation of Belgium. English social structure can be summarized in occupational categories roughly as follows, on the basis of the 1951 census:

Manual Workers	69%	24,000,000
White-Collar Groups	11%	3,700,000
Entrepreneurial Groups	9%	2,900,000
Professional Groups	7%	2,400,000
Managerial Groups	4%	1,500,000
	100%	34,500,000

Of course, an occupational breakdown of this kind does not immediately reveal the actual class structure, since it is abstract in various crucial respects. Above all, it does not take into account the economic hierarchy within each 'middle-class' group. Thus, for instance, tobacconists and bankers are included together as 'entrepreneurs'. A more accurate picture of the class structure would be as follows[2] (see over):

[1] In France, for example, the working class is 36 per cent of the population. It is, of course, the absence of a peasantry which makes the decisive difference in Britain – a result of the unique achievement of British capitalism in agriculture which should, in a sense, have been its ultimate downfall.

[2] The figures are based on Bonham's calculation in *The Middle-Class Vote*. The figure for the upper class, reached on an income basis here, is confirmed by the figure for public school boys as a percentage of their age group. There is, of course, an important difference between the two, since an appreciable proportion of big businessmen, executives, etc., have not been educated at public schools, while an appreciable proportion of public schools are more middle than upper class in character. The aristocratic upper class is thus a good deal smaller than the percentage figure suggests – probably nearer 1 per cent. The characteristic term 'upper-middle class' suggests the wider group, numbering some 1,000,000.

All the figures used here are approximations; the whole point of this analysis is to suggest that small percentile differences, which form the staple of so much political and psephological discussion today, are not meaningful units for a socialist strategy. Debate over this must be posed in much larger terms.

Working Class		69%	24,000,000
Middle Class			
White-Collar Salariat	11%		3,700,000
Petit-Bourgeoisie	8%	}28%	2,700,000
Professional Strata	6%		2,000,000
Managerial Strata	3%		1,100,000
Upper Class		3%	1,000,000
			34,500,000

The 'upper class' consists of the most powerful business, executive and professional families of the nation. It is the hegemonic class in Britain today.

The main index of the sociological strength of each of the main parties is obviously provided by electoral support. This naturally fluctuates from election to election, but its fundamental pattern has remained constant since the war, and it is with this alone that we are concerned here. It can be generalized from the figures for the 1951 election for the purpose of this analysis. The distribution of party strength can be expressed in these terms (the upper class is not distinguished in the figures, since over 90 per cent of it votes Conservative): [1]

CONSERVATIVE PARTY	
Middle and Upper Class	6,500,000
Working Class	7,000,000
	13,500,000
LABOUR PARTY	
Middle and Upper Class	1,900,000
Working Class	12,000,000
	13,900,000

Breaking these figures down into occupational groups, the distribution looks like this:

[1] Bonham, op. cit.

CONSERVATIVE PARTY

Entrepreneurial Middle Class	2,440,000
Managerial Middle Class	650,000
Professional Middle Class	1,480,000
White-Collar Middle Class	1,920,000
Working Class	7,000,000
	13,500,000

LABOUR PARTY

Entrepreneurial Middle Class	370,000
Managerial Middle Class	190,000
Professional Middle Class	410,000
White-Collar Middle Class	900,000
Working Class	12,000,000
	13,900,000

The key fact which immediately emerges from these figures is that the Conservative Party commands the support of about 75 per cent of the middle class, and no less than 30 per cent of the working class. By contrast the Labour Party commands the support of only about 65 per cent of the working class and some 20 per cent of the middle class. *One in every two Conservative votes is working class.* The primary datum, from which an analysis of the Labour Party's efficacy – even as an electoral machine – must start, is simply this: the Labour Party's command of the loyalty of the class which it essentially represents is much lower than that of the Conservative Party. The haute-bourgeoisie votes 8 : 1 for the Conservative Party, and the middle class as a whole 3 : 1. The working class votes for the Labour Party only 2 : 1. Blondel comments: 'The middle class claims not to believe in classes, yet its vote seems to uphold the classical Marxian division of society into two classes. The manual working class is said to be class-conscious, and it has at its disposal a party which mainly caters for the working class, but not more than two-thirds of its vote go to that party.'[1] But the essential paradox stems not so much from

[1] *Voters, Parties and Leaders*, p.58.

a subjective belief or disbelief in classes, as from the objective unity and homogeneity of each class. *The working class, which is sociologically far more unified and homogeneous than the heteroclite, disparate gamut of middle-class strata, shows much less electoral solidarity.* In other words, *the relative political unity of each class is the reverse of their sociological unity.* The cohesion and consciousness of the middle class is decisively higher than that of the working class, despite a much less promising sociological base: a variegated mosaic of groups, including shopkeepers, doctors, businessmen, clerical workers, technicians, gentry – which contrasts strikingly with the massive uniformity of the working-class condition, based on the universal fact of manual work.

The Labour Party is thus *above all* defined by its failure to match the Conservative Party in the intimacy and strength of its bond with its class. This is the first, and most fundamental of the insignia of its subordination.

2. Party Vitality

To what extent does the internal structure of the Party confirm the implications of its external relationship to its class? Socialists have often been reluctant to spend any time considering the organization of the Labour Party, beyond calling for greater democracy within it. A careful look at the state of the parties, however, is illuminating.

To begin with, what are the realities of its membership? On paper, the Labour Party now has some 6,000,000 members. Clearly, however, the 5,000,000 or more who are included in this figure simply by virtue of Trade Union membership and a failure to contract out of the political levy, are not in any normal sense members of a party: they are merely tax-payers who contribute to its upkeep. The only real members of the party are those individuals who have performed at least the minimal act of signing a membership form. How many are there currently of these? About 800,000. The number of Conservative Party members, by contrast, is at present some 2,800,000 – or over three times as many. One out of every four or five Conservative voters is a member of the Conservative Party; only one out of every thirteen or fourteen Labour voters is a member of the Labour Party. Forty per cent of Conservative Party members – some 1,000,000 – are working class. *This means that the Conservative Party has more individual working-class members than the Labour Party – indeed than the Labour Party has in all.*

If one looks at the comparative number of *activists* in each party – the truly enthusiastic and energetic members, where one might expect the Labour Party to have an edge, the Conservative Party is still superior by a huge margin. There are over twice as many Conservative activists as Labour activists: perhaps 400,000 to 150,000.[1]

Further, this has not been a stationary relation of forces over the last decade. The Labour Party has actually lost membership steadily, while the Conservative Party has gained it spectacularly – more than trebling its membership in ten years. The table below shows the performance of the Labour Party:

Year	Individual Members
1953	1,005,000
1954	934,000
1955	843,000
1956	845,000
1957	913,000
1958	889,000
1959	848,000
1960	790,000
1961	751,000
1962	767,000
1963	830,000

The comparative figures, in effect, show more than a simple

[1] Blondel, op. cit., p.94. 'Activist' is here used to indicate members who are in a relatively full sense active in their party – Blondel reckons these to be perhaps half of the larger groups who are 'not completely foreign to the activities of their party'. A sample study by Dowse and Stanyer found that Conservative activists numbered as many as Labour and Liberal activists put together. See *New Society* October, 1964.

quantitative superiority of the Conservative Party. They admit of only one interpretation, scandalous as it may be to cherished Labour notions: the Conservative Party now has *a greater mass character* than the Labour Party.

3. *Penumbra*

The modern political party is normally characterized by a range of 'parallel' or ancillary' organizations and activities, which form a kind of penumbra around it. These are a revealing index of a party's vitality and catholicity in their own right. They testify directly to its degree of involvement and implantation in the society around it. The 'parallel' aspects of a political party's organization can cover a great number of different fields, from cultural activities to sport, from political education to co-operatives or orthodox business ventures. But there are usually at least two areas which claim special attention in most contemporary political parties. These are: youth and Press. It is normal, in effect, for a political party to have a distinct organization for youth, and to have one or more major newspapers which put the party's views to the nation. Taking these two indices, what is the Labour Party's record?

(i) *Youth*. The Labour Party's youth organization, the Young Socialists, is officially estimated to have a membership of 25,000. But it is openly admitted that this figure is a very approximate guess, and that the real number is almost certainly considerably lower. What is even more apparent is the nadir of demoralization and disintegration which the Young Socialists have reached. Within a mere four years of its foundation, the organization has all but collapsed. This miserable record contrasts with the flourishing vigour of the Conservative – and even the Liberal – youth organizations. The Young Conservatives number a crushing 100,000 – the Young Liberals, with a parent organization a fraction the size of the Labour Party, some 15,000. Moreover the dismal fiasco of the Young Socialists is not an isolated or fortuitous failure. On the contrary, it is a continuation of an unbroken sequence of débâcles stretching back over forty years. Each time the Labour Party has tried to create a youth organization, the attempt has ended in recrimination, demoralization and dissolution. The Labour League of Youth was founded to meet the challenge of the I.L.P.'s Guild of Youth in the twenties: it was closed down in 1939. The new Labour League of Youth formed in 1946 lasted nine years, before it was dissolved in 1955. The lifetime of the Young Socialists is likely to be even shorter than that of its predecessors.

The implications of this permanent failure are extremely grave for a party of the Left. A *constitutional* inability to use or integrate in any way the ardour and radicalism of the young speaks worlds of a party's capacity to respond to what is alive and moving in a society, let alone of its capacity to change the society. An explanation of this phenomenon is vital to an understanding of the Labour Party today.

(ii) *Press*. The indispensable adjunct of any mass political party is a Press which can give it a public voice commensurate with its real weight in national life. In every capitalist country, of course, the majority of newspapers are on the Right. Capitalist control of these media of communication inevitably means that most papers reflect the views of their millionaire owners: the main difference between them is simply the level at which they articulate these views. All socialist and social democratic parties have to face this basic situation. However, it is normally well within their powers to redress it to a considerable extent by creating their own Press, as a counterforce. In Britain, however, the Labour Party has never bought or created a newspaper. The T.U.C. has, of course. But the *Daily Herald*, the sole venture of the labour movement in this field, is now dead. It was a declining phenomenon in the last decade of its life, and was regretted by few. The Labour Party at present receives a fickle support from the *Daily Mirror* and the *Sun*: but the journalistic context in which this support is voiced renders it relatively nugatory. It is no sense whatever an educating force within the society, enlarging and liberating people's consciousness of themselves and their environment.

Increasing oligopolistic control of the Press, and the peculiar cost structure of British newspaper publishing, make it far more difficult today to enter the field than it was twenty or even ten years ago. To this extent, the Labour Party's crippling lack of a national means of expression is that much harder to overcome. But the financial problem is probably not, historically, the only reason for the Labour Party's failure to create its own newspaper. Even today, the money that could potentially be raised from the Trade Unions for one is considerable; T.U.C. reserves currently run into many millions. Anyone who has ever travelled in Scandinavia and spoken with Social-Democratic Party leaders there will recall the pungency of their comments on the British labour movement's inability to muster enough will or imagination to produce its own national newspaper. In Sweden, Norway and Denmark, of course, the social-democratic press – financed by the movement – is large and flourishing. In the opinion of Haakon Lie, Secretary-General of the Norwegian Labour Party, it contributes more than any other immediate factor to the differing fortunes of social-democracy in Scandinavia and Britain. In fact, as will be seen, there are profound reasons for the Labour Party's impotence in this critical field. For the moment, however, it is enough to register the cruel handicap which the absence of any national newspaper imposes on the Labour Party. Public opinion is constantly formed against it without it having any adequate means of reply or even intervention. Under these conditions, the long-term education and persuasion of public opinion towards socialism remains a hopeless dream.

4. *The Insignia of Subordination*

The Labour Party, faced with a social structure which favours it *naturally*, as a hospitable topography can favour an army, remains to this day an inferior and subordinate political organization. The marks of this subordination can be seen in almost every level and every aspect of its activity. It has been unable to unite its class, as the Conservative Party has done – an apparently much more difficult task. It has been unable to recruit even half as many ordinary members as the Conservative Party. It has been unable to match the Conservative Party in the 'numbers and enthusiasm' of its party workers – to quote Harold Wilson's report on party organization in 1955. It has never succeeded in building any viable youth organization. It has never founded any durable or significant press. With all this, it is small wonder that *even as an electoral machine* – let alone as a socialist party – it should have had such a poor record. At the limit, the Labour Party exists only as the inert, serialized unity of the British working class – a unity that is *inevitably* partial, because it is purely serial. Sartre defines the series as a group united only by negative reciprocities, in which each member sees himself as other than the others, so that the unity of the group is always *elsewhere*, a circulating absence. By contrast, a true political unity is only realized in a concrete action which defines each member as responsible to each other, for each other, in a common task. Every five years, twelve million or so individuals cast their ballots for the Labour Party in strict isolation from each other, each one ignorant of the identity and interests of all the others performing the same act at the same moment. This atomized, evanescent unity is the result of the monomania of electoralism. Voting is, of course, quite rightly a private affair. But if it becomes the *sole bond* which institutes a group, the group is simply a sum of solitudes – an impermanent, impalpable diaspora. In a word, the Labour Party will never be able to unify the working class – or indeed any social group – behind it, as long as it tries to do so through the essentially serializing and isolating electoral mechanism. The consequence of the attempt is ironic. By devoting all its energies to the single moment of the vote, the Labour Party necessarily suffers precisely at the vote – since it has neglected to build a more durable community which alone could create the basis for solid and habitual victory at the polls. Electoral success can only come *into the bargain*, as a consequence of a much more fundamental work of education and communication between party and society.

The failure to create a mass basis to the Labour Party of a kind which could act as a counterweight to the strength of the

Conservative Party is a direct consequence of this narrow electoralism. Its inability to arouse popular drive and enthusiasm reveals how far the party is from an hegemonic role.

Its limitations indeed, take on a specific and recognizable cast. It is noticeable that no other social-democratic party in Europe, whatever its size or defects, has failed to produce a *viable* youth movement. The usual explanation offered for the Labour Party's congenital incapacity to give birth to one that it is so stolidly right-wing, so dully reformist, that any spirited youth organization is incompatible with it: there is invariably a left-wing revolt against the adult party, swiftly followed by the closing down of the youth movement. In part, of course, this is true enough. The peculiar relationship between Right and Left in the British labour movement is reflected in its most extreme, and in many ways tragic, form in the fate of the Labour Party's youth movements. The passion and idealism of the young is caught between the oppressive nullity of Fabianism and the mindless virulence of various kinds of Left sectarianism – and is systematically destroyed, for want of a constructive ideological outlet. But the Labour Party, after all, is by no means the worst or most right-wing social-democratic party in Europe. It is not simply its politics, in the limited sense, which appear to render a youth movement impossible. It seems likely that it is at least partly its corporate working-class character that is responsible for its failure. Sheer dour repression of the young, gnarled puritan dislike of gaiety, fixated insistence on age and seniority – all these aspects of 'proletarian positivity' in England bear down on youth and tend to stifle it. A forthcoming study of the Labour Party's youth movements confirms this impression,[1] which is, besides, suggested by the many stories of constituency parties disapproving and disciplining Young Socialist branches for 'disreputable' activities such as twisting, etc.

Something of the same corporate working-class character of the Labour Party can be seen in its lack of a national press, too. What kind of a newspaper should the Labour Party ideally have? The question has only to be formulated, for the difficulty

[1] By Julian Atkinson.

of an answer to become apparent. In effect, there are two quite distinct types of British newspaper, with a gulf between them: the 'popular' and the 'serious'. The 'popular' newspaper is overwhelmingly commercial in purpose and trivial in content: it is openly designed to exploit the cultural inexperience of a mass readership. A newspaper produced mainly for a working-class audience will inevitably, under prevailing market conditions, tend to conform to this norm. However, 'populist' such a paper nominally is, its formal political commitment is simply swallowed up by the avalanche of sensation and prejudice it purveys: a whole affective universe which is not in the least apolitical, but is in the profoundest sense conservative – a stultifying and infantilizing force for the status quo. These distinctive products of British capitalism – despised throughout the rest of the world – could never become genuine vehicles of Labour politics, even as they are at present. What is the alternative? A 'quality' press produced exclusively for a middle-class audience, which overwhelmingly votes Conservative or Liberal at every election. This kind of newspaper offers a medium in which serious political ideas and information can be meaningfully articulated. Yet a Labour Party version of the *Guardian* or the *Times* is equally unthinkable. For it would be completely cut off from the predominant Labour public. Within the terms of the existing forms of journalism in Britain, the Labour Party is forked. It would have to settle either for an audience without a meaningful vehicle or a vehicle without a meaningful audience. This impossible choice is what makes the idea of a Labour newspaper in Britain so self-contradictory. This can be seen very clearly in the light of Scandinavian experience. In Sweden, for example, social-democratic newspapers, which are in most respects superior in coverage and discussion to the *Guardian* or the *Times*, are also among the largest circulation dailies in the country. The class structure does not create the huge cultural differences between social groups which it does in Britain – so that the same paper can be read by working class and middle class alike. Of course, this does not exonerate the Labour Party. The impossibility of existing forms of journalism in England should have forced it to invent new forms. But for this, one crucial component is lacking: an ideology. For only an articulated ideology could bridge the gulf between working-class habits and values and middle-class culture. It alone could mediate the two, by providing a horizon – socialism – where both would be reconciled, in which culture would cease to be middle class and solidarity purely working class. This would require a new idiom, a new journalism. The task would be immense. Meanwhile, the Labour Party continues to be, relative to its opponent, mute.

C. UNLOCKING THE SOCIAL STRUCTURE

This is the present condition of the Labour Party. In what direction should it be changed? There are two prevailing styles of discussion which must be avoided in considering this question. The first is that of the Labour Right, and of percentage psephology generally. In this perspective, the task of the Labour Party is to win over the necessary fraction of votes from the Conservative Party to win each election as it comes up: usually around 3 per cent or 4 per cent. Society becomes no more than a quantified aggregate of electors; politics becomes the struggle for a mathematical majority of them every five years. The consequence of this approach is invariably to emphasize the need for prudence and moderation, to win over a floating middle-class vote, which would take alarm at any radicalism. This was essentially the outlook of Gaitskell and his close friends. Counterposed to this is normally a Left-Wing approach, which denounces the Right for compromise and for its trivialization of politics. By contrast, it calls for a humanist view of people and society, and a radical appeal to their altruism and intelligence as well as their immediate self-interest. The two approaches are apparently extreme opposites. But in fact they share a fundamental *abstraction*. Whether society is seen as a quantum of electors, divided into four income brackets, or as a community of 'ordinary men and women', or 'common people', versus 'the interests' or 'the monopolies' – its concrete, determinate reality in either case vanishes. It is perfectly true that percentage psephology tends to reify and reduce human beings, as the Left has always claimed. But a vague populism which implies that all men of goodwill would rally to the cause of socialism if only it were presented eloquently and ethically enough, is no substitute. A *strategy* for socialism must be anchored in the objective structure of society, not merely in subjective sentiment. Above all, it must be based on a coherent class analysis, which articulates and differentiates the whole society into a totality of concrete, specific social groups.

What does this involve for the Labour Party? In the first place, an attempt to construct a global picture of the opposing forces which can at present be described as Labour and Conservative in Britain. This might run as follows. The Conservative Party welds together a vast range of heterogeneous social forces into a single, structured coalition under the leadership of a prepotent hegemonic class. Electorally, this coalition consists of a large proportion of the working class, the great bulk of the petit-bourgeois and white-collar lower-middle class, and the near solid phalanx of the professional, managerial, and entrepreneurial middle class – all integrated into a unified force by the power and prestige of the hegemonic class which dominates the Conservative Party, what Macleod has called 'the magic circle'. Arrayed against this coalition at each election is the Labour alliance: the majority of the working class, a minority of the – especially white-collar – lower-middle class, and a fraction of the professional and managerial middle class.

This is the position at present. What should the Labour Party's strategy to transform this equation be? The answer is provided by the sociology of British society itself. *The master aim of Labour Party strategy must be to unite the working class under its own leadership, and so win a permanent sociological majority of the nation.* No matter what other aims and considerations may also be important, it is this goal which must have strategic priority. The fundamental, long-term aim of the Labour Party must be *to unlock the social structure* – to convert the natural sociological shape of society into its *political* shape, in a new popular hegemony. This does not simply mean direct and crude bidding, at all costs, for the working-class vote. It involves very much more than this. How much more will become apparent in examining the different ways in which the present Conservative coalition can be weakened and diminished.

1. The Working Class

The primary aim of the Labour Party must be to win over the Conservative section of the working class. Yet for some years it has been often maintained that affluence has made the working class more 'middle class' and therefore less likely to vote Labour than before. The widespread belief in a creeping embourgeoisement of the working class has only very recently been examined critically and scientifically. The result of this critical analysis has been to demolish the idea that rising living standards necessarily and invariably erode working-class identity or support for the Labour Party and lead to an assimilation to the middle class and a swing towards the Conservative Party. The evidence bearing on this familiar problem has been thoroughly sifted by Lockwood and Goldthorpe, in a paper which marks a milestone in British social analysis.[1] Their conclusion is unequivocal: there is no factual basis for this belief, despite the innumerable claims made for it. In reality, the greatest monetary prosperity in the working class often coincides with the least tolerable and most dangerous work, with the fewest chances of any promotion – mining, fishing, building, heavy assembly work. It is not just income and consumption which determine social or political allegiance, even economically. Job security, fringe benefits, promotion prospects, are also important.

There is thus no inevitable, secular trend towards a more Conservative working class. The problem is not to stem an imaginary tide against the Labour Party, but to win over the traditional, stable proportion of the working class which is part of the Conservative electorate. This requires a careful study

[1] 'Affluence and the British Class Structure', *Sociological Review*, July, 1963.

of the reasons for its political allegiance. Who are the work-ing-class Conservatives? They cover a number of different groups. Old people and women clearly tend more than on average towards Conservatism, in the working class as in all social groups. Better off workers, especially in the Midlands, may also in recent elections have tended to be somewhat more Conservative, though this is least established. The influence of environment is more noticeable: workers living in a middle-class area are more likely to vote Conservative than those in a working-class area. Equally, workers employed in smaller and more traditional firms vote Conservative more frequently than those in large, modern enterprises. Each of these factors has a certain importance. But they are all overshadowed by one decisive phenomenon, which appears to determine a worker's political allegiance far more than anything else: Trade Union membership. To quote Blondel: 'Surveys have shown that manual workers who are members of Trade Unions are three to four times more likely to vote Labour than Conservative; manual workers who are not Trade Unionists are much more evenly divided.'[1] A British Institute of Public Opinion poll in 1959 found that 71 per cent of Union members voted Labour – and only 17 per cent Conservative. It is thus evident that *unionization* is the prime key to the consciousness of the British working class. It is this key, above all, which could potentially unlock the social structure and create a permanent Labour majority. At present, only some 40 per cent of the working class is unionized. The aggregate figure in recent years has dropped slightly. This static picture is somewhat mislead-ing, since it conceals a sharp drop in declining industries whose work-force is shrinking rapidly (cotton, railways, mining) and a marked increase in expanding industries (engineering). But the net stagnation remains only too clear. In fact, unionization of the manual working-class has actually regressed over the past five years, since the largest compensating increases in aggregate membership are in non-manual white-collar unions. It is thus evident that a massive drive to unionize the 60 per cent of the working class who are still outside the Trade Unions must be a

[1] Op. cit., p. 67.

first priority of the labour movement. At the legislative level, ratification of the I.L.O. Convention compelling employers to recognize Unions where any significant section of their employees are unionized, is crucial. Unionization offers the best single chance of effecting a radical change in the present balance of political forces. A tremendous effort should be put behind it.

Why does Union membership make so much difference to the political loyalty of industrial workers? Despite the lack of direct evidence on this point, it is possible to conjecture an answer. The Union introduces the worker into a new ideological and relational universe, however minimally. It creates its own loyalty (even if this may on occasion become very strained) and its own logic – a logic which leads to Labour allegiance. In a word, unionization changes the consciousness of workers, however imperfectly, and in doing so frees them from the elementary forms of mystification. The lesson of this is very important. It is that working-class political allegiance is mainly decided by what might be called 'proto-ideological' experience, not by immediate economic interest. The struggle to win the Conservative section of the working class can thus only be won, in the last analysis, on the *ideological plane*. This conclusion is amply confirmed by studies of the attitudes of working-class Conservatives. They are not the most prosperous of all sections of the working class. A recent paper by Runciman shows that the most loyal Conservatives of all tend to be those *lower-incomed* manual workers who rate themselves as middle class (41 per cent); comparable middle and higher-incomed workers are decreasingly Conservative (36 per cent and 18 per cent respectively).[1] Another study, by McKenzie and Silver, provides devastating complementary evidence of the ideological character of working-class Conservative loyalty and the extent to which it is a reflection of a general cultural hegemony over a much wider section of the working class. They found that working-class Conservatives were both better-informed and more committed to their party than were

[1] Runciman, 'Embourgeoisement, Self-Rated Class and Party Preference', *Sociological Review*, July, 1964.

working-class Labour supporters.[1] Moreover, they state: 'The evidence was stronger than we had expected of the extent to which Conservative *values* are spread throughout the whole working-class electorate, regardless of which party they vote for. There was, for example, overwhelming support for judicial flogging; for the barring of coloured immigration; and even Labour voters were opposed, by a clear margin, to any further extension of public ownership.'[2] McKenzie and Silver analysed Conservative support in terms of two basic types: 'deferential' and 'secular' – those who thought the Conservatives had an innate superiority and ability to rule, and those who merely thought they had ruled well recently. 30 per cent were deferential, 40 per cent were secular, 30 per cent were a mixture of both. It is clear that deferential Conservatism represents the hard core of working-class support for the Conservative Party: these are the workers who are least likely to change their allegiance. Their attitude in effect is almost purely ideological. It is striking that they, too, tend to be lower-income workers.

It is in the light of these facts that Lockwood and Goldthorpe's crucial thesis of 'instrumental collectivism' must be seen. In their view, probably the most real change in working-class consciousness has been a certain evolution towards a new kind of collectivism – no longer 'solidary', or based on instinctual social ties and shared traditional values, but 'instrumental', or based on rationalist calculation of interest. Now clearly, this development can involve a loss of class-consciousness and combativity, and its replacement by a narrower, sectional self-interest. But there is no reason why it must do so. On the contrary, 'solidary collectivism' is *itself* in many ways a

[1] The recurrent phenomenon of greater abstention by Labour supporters at elections confirms this point, and the whole general analysis of the Labour Party attempted earlier. In 1959, Butler and Rose remark, 'The turn-out rose most in Glasgow and Manchester, the places where the results were most favourable to Labour, the pro-Conservative swing was greatest in Leicester and Birmingham, where the turn-out hardly rose at all.' *The British General Election of 1959*, p. 239.

[2] 'The Working-Class Tories', *Observer*, 6 September 1964.

narrow form of social consciousness. It is, precisely, the entrenched, immobile, corporate, class-consciousness of the English working class – a world steeped in precedent and tradition and archaism, that mimics the traditionalism of the whole society. The advent of 'instrumental collectivism' means for the first time the penetration of *reason*, of rationality into this closed, affective universe. Of course, the form of this rationality may initially be that of the surrounding environment, the egoistic market rationality of neo-capitalism. It could hardly be otherwise, since there is none other at present available to the working class. An alternative reason would be, simply, a socialist ideology, and neither Labour Party nor Trade Unions offer this. The dangers of the present situation, then, are evident. But so are its opportunities.

The incursion of rationalism into the hermetic world of the English working class is a necessary stage in its emancipation – however limited or confusing its initial manifestations. It is the precondition of a genuinely ideological collectivism – founded on *ideas*, and not merely on instinct. Above all, this rationalism is likely to be directly destructive of the mystical values of deference, the paralysing complex which imprisons so many working-class Conservatives today. Capitalist hegemony in Britain is founded on an ideology of stupefied traditionalism and empiricism, an anti-ideology which is the enemy of all ideas and all calculation. 'Instrumental collectivism' threatens to weaken its hold radically. Already it is noticeable, that better-off manual workers, the most 'secular' Conservative supporters, are also those most likely to change allegiance – in the first instance, Runciman found, often to the Liberal Party.

The battle for the working class can, as we have seen, only be won on the plane of ideology. The new rationalism may be preparing the conditions for a real victory. It both allows the passage of traditional Labour loyalties in the working class to a higher, more freely assumed level; and threatens to subvert the whole mystique on which Conservative loyalties in the working-class mainly depend. A final consideration may complete this analysis. Assessments of the political allegiance of the working class are usually based solely on the post-war years, since this is the only period for which poll studies are available. Limited in this way, they give an almost static impression of the position of the two parties. But if one takes as a time-span the whole history of the Labour Party, a very different picture emerges. Assuming that the middle class proportion of the Labour vote has never been more than 20 per cent at most, the Labour Party's support among the working class has registered a long-term, but *discontinuous* rise from 1918 to the present day. Its growth is marked by three great qualitative jumps, in 1918, 1922 and 1945 – followed on each of the last two occasions by an undulating plateau lasting for a decade or more. This is the true perspective in which to see the phenomenon of working-class Conservatism. It can be formulated in a paradox. *The Conservative Party is the oldest major working-class party in Britain.* It proletarian support dates back far into the nineteenth century. The whole history of the Labour Party in this century can be seen as a progressive attempt to win over a class that had an *earlier* allegiance, whether Conservative or Liberal. Today, a large enough proportion of this allegiance still remains to deprive the Labour Party of political dominance in Britain. But the attempt to win it over now has the force and validity of history behind it. It will, in the final analysis, continue and complete the work of the last fifty years.

2. Lower Middle Class

The Labour Party at present enjoys the support of nearly two million members of the middle class. The group which contributes most to Labour strength is the white-collar salariat. About half its support comes from this stratum – some one million; and of these the overwhelming majority, some 80 per cent, come from lower-income white-collar workers. A further 400,000 or so supporters come from the lesser reaches of the professions – mainly teachers, nurses, minor officials, etc. Finally, some 200,000 in subordinate managerial positions also give their allegiance to the Labour Party.

It is clear from this distribution that the critical group for Labour strategy is the white-collar stratum. At present the

Labour Party commands the loyalty of perhaps 30 per cent of white-collar workers. The rapid expansion of the tertiary sector and the continuing influx of women into clerical jobs make this salariat the fastest growing group in the population (although the idea that it is swiftly undermining the numerical superiority of the working class is quite false: the industrial proletariat is likely to be an absolute majority of the population for another seventy-five years). There has been a tradition on the Left to try to minimize the differences between the industrial working–class and the white-collar salariat – and to maintain that both form a propertyless proletariat, selling their labour on the market, and suffering an identical exploitation by big capital. This tendency perhaps went farthest, implicitly, in Strachey's continual use of '10 per cent of property-owners' and '90 per cent of the propertyless' as virtually his only sociological categories in *Contemporary Capitalism*, an extreme example of the abstraction endemic in discussion of British society on the Left. In point of fact, the life-situations of manual workers and clerical workers have not hitherto been closely similar, and this has accounted for the difference in political outlook. As Lockwood remarks: 'The clerk has never been strictly "proletarian" in terms of income, job security and occupational mobility.'[1] The average white-collar worker has until now enjoyed a larger income, greater job security, better promotion prospects, less exacting work, longer holidays, and higher social status than the manual worker. Thus, the Labour Party's appeal to clerical workers should not be based on a fictitiously complete identity between them and industrial workers, which they anyway reject. They are, in fact, a necessary component of a new historical bloc – but will only become so if their specificity is respected and integrated into a socialist party. In many ways, the test of a socialist party's universal vocation today is its ability to win over a majority of this section of the population – so often gripped by pride and contempt, and so systematically denied and alienated in its work. The day that the labour movement succeeds in this, it will finally have triumphed over its corporatism.

[1] *The Black-Coated Worker*, p. 204.

The key to the consciousness of this stratum, too, lies in the Trade Unions. It is possible that unionization makes an even greater difference to the outlook of white-collar workers than to industrial workers, since unions are a much rarer and newer phenomenon in their world. In their case affiliation to the T.U.C. has a special importance, since this alone consecrates the 'militant' identity of the Union. White-collar Unions now provide the main growth point of British trade-unionism. Between 1957 and 1962, the Non-Manual Trade Group of the T.U.C. rose 31 per cent in membership, and Public Employees 24 per cent. White-collar Unions, with relatively higher contributions and more educated members and leaders, are now often pioneers in combative action, as a recent British Federation of Industry circular to employers admitted. Unions like D.A.T.A. (draughtsmen) and A.S.S.E.T. (technicians) have shown themselves much more imaginative and aggressive than the majority of traditional Unions. It is thus crucial that the drive for unionization be pressed unremittingly into the white-collar field. Both Unions and Labour Party stand to gain enormously, not only in numbers but in vitality, from the accession to their ranks of the millions of skilled and educated white-collar workers who are potential recruits to the labour alliance. The recent decision of N.A.L.G.O., the largest white-collar union in the world, to join the T.U.C. – after over twenty years of hesitation – is a welcome sign. It should be the signal for a concerted campaign to come.

The terrain for such a campaign is likely to be increasingly favourable in the years ahead, because of the evolution of white-collar work itself. The spread of bureaucratized, and to a lesser extent, mechanized clerical work tends to create a work-situation much more strictly comparable to that of manual work on an assembly line or in a rigidly, visibly hierarchical plant (although still in important respects distinct). The effect of this development on the consciousness of white-collar workers is likely to be marked. Already in 1958, Lockwood commented: 'It is not too much to argue that in fostering black-coated solidarity, bureaucratization has played a role analogous to that of the factory and labour market in the case of manual workers.'[1] Five years later, he and Goldthorpe went much farther and concluded, after studies on the evolution of the working class, that there may be, 'an *independent convergence* between the "new" working class and the "new" middle class',[2] as both move towards an instrumental collectivism. For the white-collar stratum, this move involves an abandonment, not of a solidary collectivism, but of a tradition of radical individualism. The levelling and unifying force of bureaucratization is, in fact, gradually transforming the statute of the white-collar workers, and assimilating it increasingly to that of the manual worker. The Labour Party has a great chance before it – to create from this slow sociological convergence a durable, political union.

3. *Intelligentsia*

So far, this discussion has been concerned with the quantitative problem posed by the quest for a permanent majority. But at each turn, it has emerged that there is a decisive *qualitative* dimension to the task – the need for a hegemonic socialist ideology, without which not one of the key strategic goals can be achieved. The problem of ideology leads directly to the problem of the British intelligentsia, in the widest and most catholic meaning of the term. Strictly speaking, of course, there is no intelligentsia in Britain comparable to that of other European countries – that is, a compact, cohesive enclave of intellectuals, clearly demarcated from the rest of society, with their own traditions and their own idiom. But there is a broad spectrum of groups which in very different ways and different contexts are the vectors of the society's explicit ideas and values. These groups include teachers, scientists, technologists, artists, lawyers, doctors, writers, students, and university lecturers. They are critically important for a socialist strategy, not because of their numbers – they amount in all to perhaps 2 per cent of the population – but because of their role as *sources of consciousness* in society. They are, in fact, the artisans of the

[1] Op. cit., p. 142.
[2] 'Affluence and the British Class Structure.'

formal culture of the society. No socialist ideology which does not enlist the support and participation of significant sections of these groups has any hope of making a serious impact on society at large. These intellectuals will be the inevitable mediators of any major intellectual change in Britain. The full conversion of the Conservative working class, for instance, can only be achieved by a *detour* through the sociological groups that generate the consciousness which mystifies it. In other words, the necessarily ideological contest for a permanent majority must also be fought and won where ideology originates – in the intelligentsia.

What does this involve, in Britain? To begin with, the magnitude of the task must be recognized. The majority of British intellectuals today, of whatever type, have a fundamentally conservative outlook. This is as true of the majority of those who nominally support the Labour Party as of those who support the Conservative or Liberal Parties. This deep inertia and resistance to intellectual change is a consequence of the whole history of British society in the nineteenth and twentieth centuries; it cannot be overcome in a day. But the crisis of British capitalism in the early sixties – in particular, the fact that it has been an internationally-determined crisis – has to some extent eroded the invincible insularity which has been the bedrock of English intellectual stasis. Although this erosion has not yet gone very far, it does offer a certain breach in a hitherto immovable status quo.

There are now three distinct sectors in the British intelligentsia – a traditional literary intelligentsia, a newer technical intelligentsia, and a much newer social science intelligentsia. The circulation of the three periodicals which command a majority audience of each probably indicates something like the relative size of each group; *New Statesman* – 90,000, *New Scientist* – 50,000, *New Society* – 30,000. The *New Statesman* readership is, of course, not wholly representative, since it is an avowedly Labour publication. But the type of its audience is such that this political commitment is relatively unimportant. Only one in seven *New Statesman* readers is a member of the Labour Party. The political allegiance of *New Scientist* readers, and of scientists and technologists generally, remains unknown. It is as yet impossible to surmise the effect of Wilson's intense campaign to win the technical intelligentsia at the last election, although it seems likely that it had some impact. It is *New Society*, the most recent of these periodicals, which offers perhaps the most interesting insight into the mind of the British intelligentsia today. It may be surmised that the readers of this weekly include a certain overlap from both the literary and the technical intelligentsias. A very detailed and extensive inquiry into the attitudes of some 7,000 of them[1] produced a desolate image of mediocrity, prejudice and confusion. It could not even be said that a lucidly and coherently reactionary outlook was revealed; simply a miserable, chaotic medley of contradictory fears and postures. These intellectuals were in favour of restrictions on immigration, and against capital punishment; in favour of limitations on the right to strike and against the independent deterrent; in favour of punitive laws against homosexuality and for divorce by consent; in favour of greater financial differentials for 'training and skill', and for welfare benefits to 'those in need'; in favour of the 'urgent reform' of the Trade Unions and against the public schools. Eighty per cent refused to believe even in the possibility of a classless society. Their social ideal appeared to be New Zealand. It would be hard to imagine a more devastating portrait of what the Russians call *meshchantsvo* – petty, null philistinism.

This is the size of the problem facing the Labour Party. How can it begin the work of transforming this complex of attitudes? Nothing is less easy than to influence heterogeneous, diffuse congeries of intellectuals, spaced out in widely different roles and positions in society. Clearly no one blanket solution would be viable. But a general line of action, which is applicable in different ways in different situations, is perhaps discernible. It is to work through the existing professional organizations of each group, and try to politicize them from within. When this is not possible, a separate Labour association should be formed, with as wide and active a membership as possible. The aim of this strategy should in no way be to tie each group

[1] *New Society*, 9 May, 16 May, 23 May, 1963.

to the wheels of the Labour Party's chariot. 'Politicization' of this kind is wholly sterile. The aim of the strategy should rather be twofold: in the first place, to achieve the maximum free ventilation and discussion of socialist *ideas* within each group; and in the second place, to formulate and press advanced demands for the democratic transformation of each profession concerned. This is the only way in which politicization will be acceptable and meaningful: it alone will allow the socialists within each profession to exercise a genuine force of attraction over the whole group, as the source of concrete solutions to the common problems which face them all. A few examples can serve as illustration.

In most countries, whether capitalist, communist or Third World, students have in recent years played a dynamic and progressive role in public life. Mass demonstrations, strikes, occupation of university premises, have occurred in a wide range of societies, including even the United States (Berkeley affair, etc.). Nothing could be more natural and healthy than this. Britain, however, remains an outstanding exception. The majority of British students, as a recent survey amply attests, remain listless and conformist, showing only the feeblest flicker of interest in politics or society. Zweig found that 'Politics is regarded as a dull business. It is not a field which excites the imagination or engages the emotions of the Oxford student. . . . As in Oxford, the political interest of Manchester students are both shallow and narrow. The area of genuine political conviction is small . . .'[1] The National Union of Students (N.U.S.) is made in the image of the student body as a whole. Some 220,000 strong, the N.U.S. confines itself to a grey, docile routine: it provides a cheap travel bureau, makes narrowly corporate demands for higher grants (never backed by any action), and issues *bien-pensant* resolutions on South Africa. As a force in national life, it is non-existent. Yet the tradition in recent years has been a leadership that is informally 'Labour' (usually right-wing Labour). But this has had no serious incidence on the Union itself. The contrast with, say, the French student union U.N.E.F. is dismaying. U.N.E.F.

[1] *The Student in the Age of Anxiety*, pp. 46 and 116.

for long periods led the opposition in France to the Algerian War, drawing the Trade Unions behind it in repeated mass actions, and in doing so showing political courage and responsibility of the highest order, under very adverse circumstances. Today it has taken the lead in pressing for a radical reorganization of the traditional syllabuses and faculty divisions in French universities.

In Britain, it is clear that the issue on which a serious student union would mobilize the whole student body, using strike action if necessary, is that of university democracy. This should be the crux of socialist action amongst students, whether in the N.U.S. or out of it. The utter lack of the most elementary democracy in British universities today passes belief. Argentina – indeed all Latin-America – is regarded as a 'backward' area in England. Yet for *nearly fifty years*, since the Statute of Cordoba in 1918, Argentinian and other Latin-American students have enjoyed wide rights of democratic self-government in their universities, including election of senior university officials, jointly with the teaching staff. These rights are protected by law. In this perspective, the wretchedly mean and provincial horizons of the N.U.S. are evident. A tremendous potential of energy and enthusiasm could be generated by a coherent campaign to democratize British universities: this should be the primary task of socialist students. The short length of university courses and the paucity of graduate students (both products of the inveterate dilettantism of traditional English culture) pose real organizational problems. But these are not insuperable. If the N.U.S. were to prove incapable of change, the specifically Labour student organization, N.A.L.S.O. (National Association of Labour Student Organizations), which now has some 7,000 members, should be the spearhead of the campaign. For this purpose, and for the general work of socialist discussion and persuasion, the Labour Party would have to disburse more than the pittance which it allows N.A.L.S.O. at present.

Schoolteachers offer another obvious field for this type of action. The overwhelming majority of teachers are from working-class and lower-middle class backgrounds; but by a two-thirds majority they favour the Conservative Party.[1] Their professional attitudes, however, often cut right across their political attitudes – as Selwyn Lloyd discovered in 1962. There are, in fact, few more patently exploited and frustrated groups in the community. At present, their anger and mortification is wasted; it usually finds expression only in a disgruntled, rancorous resignation – rather than in effective, militant action. The National Union of Teachers, with some 240,000 members, conducts a worthy but colourless struggle to secure teachers higher pay, smaller classes, better arbitration machinery, etc. Since its demands are never backed by serious action, they are rarely effective. Here too, the example of the French Teachers Union is instructive: by regularly threatening – and implementing – strike action, it has won a far higher social status for teachers in France than they enjoy in Britain. Inside the N.U.T., a somewhat similar situation to that in the N.U.S. prevails. The current leadership has some affinities with the Labour Party – its President is the son of a Labour M.P. – but these again have no relevance in the Union. An attempt in 1922 to affiliate the N.U.T. to the Labour Party was defeated by 30,000 to 15,000 votes. It is noticeable, however, that there are a considerable number of teachers in the Parliamentary Labour Party, and almost none in the Conservative Parliamentary Party.

Politicization of the N.U.T. runs counter, of course, to a cherished belief in the 'non-party' character of the teaching profession. This obstacle can only be overcome, here as elsewhere, if 'politics' becomes, not an abstract allegiance to a party, but a concrete programme for the transformation and liberation of the teachers' situation. Political loyalty can only follow, not precede this demonstration; and the demonstration will always be more important. Concurrently, a determined effort should be made to expand the small Socialist Educational Association (some 300 members – formerly the National Association of Labour Teachers) which at present represents the only foothold of the Labour Party in the teaching world.

At the other extreme, professions like law and medicine offer

[1] See A. Tropp, *The Teachers*.

no chance of the Labour Party ever winning a majority to socialist or progressive ideas. The almost exclusively bourgeois background of lawyers and doctors, and the immensely lucrative possibilities of their work, ensure that these groups will remain bastions of reaction. In cases like these, where there is no possibility of winning an appreciable proportion of the members of the profession, it is nevertheless extremely important to maintain a vigorous and vocal minority organization linked to the Labour Party, which can make the party a felt presence even in these fastnesses of the dominant class. Both the legal system and the health service are badly in need of radical reform; the role of the League of Labour Lawyers (present membership 300 only) and the Socialist Medical Association (present membership 750) should be to press continuously and eloquently for it.

Finally, there are cases where no Labour organizations of any kind exist at present, and where the most urgent task is to create them. Two obvious examples are university teachers and scientists. The first are perhaps the most important single group of intellectuals in the country: it is absurd that there should be no Socialist Association among them. The last public initiative in recent years of any Labour group of university staff was a letter to the Press by a number of academics in 1961, declaring in emotional terms – without any argument – full confidence in the person of the late leader of the Labour Party. This episode can be taken as a token of the low ebb of political discussion and communication among the many university teachers who are undoubtedly Labour supporters. Steps to remedy this situation are essential. Even more disconcerting perhaps, is the complete absence of a Socialist Scientists Association – given the enormous emphasis placed on the scientific and technical intelligentsia by the Labour Party since Wilson became its leader. Yet this is a potentially far more rewarding and important field than law or medicine, where Labour-linked organizations already exist. Such an association, grouping all scientists and technologists who are members of the Labour Party, is both eminently possible and necessary.

To sum up: the main strategic aim must be to make socialism an active, living *presence* in every intellectual group,
through a radius of professional organizations which permanently contest the social order by proposing solutions which
can be seen to be humanly and culturally in advance of what it
offers. Each one of these organizations, which should have full
professional autonomy, could become a pole of attraction in
its own field. If this was achieved, the adumbration of a
socialist hegemony would have begun.

4. *Women*

Finally, it is absolutely necessary to consider the problem posed
to the Labour Party by women. No discussion of socialist
strategy in Britain would be serious without this. For the problem of feminine conservatism is one of the greatest single
stumbling blocks to the Labour Party. *If women had voted the
same way as men, the Labour Party would have been un-
interruptedly in power since 1945*. The figures below show
precisely how damaging the huge deficit in women's votes
has been to the Labour Party at every successive election: [1]

	1959	1955	1951	1950	1945
MEN					
Conservative	$45\frac{1}{2}$	$46\frac{1}{2}$	47	41	$36\frac{1}{2}$
Labour	$47\frac{1}{2}$	51	50	47	55
Liberal	7	$2\frac{1}{2}$	3	12	$8\frac{1}{2}$
Conservative Lead	—	—	—	—	—
Labour Lead	2	$4\frac{1}{2}$	3	6	$18\frac{1}{2}$
WOMEN					
Conservative	51	55	50	$44\frac{1}{2}$	$43\frac{1}{2}$
Labour	43	$42\frac{1}{2}$	46	$43\frac{1}{2}$	$46\frac{1}{2}$
Liberal	6	$2\frac{1}{2}$	4	12	10
Conservative Lead	8	$12\frac{1}{2}$	4	1	—
Labour Lead	—	—	—	—	3

[1] *Gallup Political Index*, January, 1964.

	1959	1955	1951	1950	1945
AGGREGATE					
Conservative	49	50½	48	42½	40
Labour	45	47	48½	45½	50½
Liberal	6	2½	3½	12	9½
Conservative Lead	4	3½	—	—	—
Labour Lead	—	—	½	3	10½

(*Percentages*)

This problem, although so politically crucial, is seldom discussed. The reason for this is undoubtedly to be found in the vast silence which in contemporary Britain lies over the whole subject of women's condition. The premature death of the suffragette movement, with only the most minimal goals achieved, left women in a position of social inferiority, which, forty years later, remains in almost every major aspect unchanged. Education, work, status, income – every one is weighted against women today. They are, on average, more ignorant, worse paid, less respected, and employed in duller work than men. An immense burden of mystification adapts them to their predetermined roles, and renders them the most passive, most prejudiced, most ill-informed citizens in society. In effect, the whole horizontal class system is cross-structured by a deep vertical system of sexual inequality and infantilism. Women are, then, inevitably far more subject than men to the magical aspects of Conservatism – the mystique of deference, the worship of ceremony and hierarchy.

What can be done to change this? The first step is simply to see the existence of the problem, which the Labour Party has not yet done. Next, it is clear that the Labour Party must stand – and be seen to stand – for the elementary rights of women in our society: equal pay for equal jobs (this requires ratification of the I.L.O. convention which Britain has so far shamefully failed to do), equal pensions, and equal educational facilities. This in itself would have some effect. At the same time, it is indispensable to back policy initiatives with organizational effort. The most promising avenue here is, again, unionization. This is more likely to change the consciousness of women than any other single move. It should be noted that between 1958 and 1962 the number of women in Trade Unions rose 10 per cent – from 1,800,000 to 2,000,000. This increase is commendable, but it needs to be greatly accelerated – for it is in any case one of the major priorities for the Trade Union movement today. A real campaign for equal pay and equal jobs might be a critical fulcrum for recruitment. Since most women work in white-collar jobs, this would merge into the drive for white-collar unionization. Simultaneously, political organization must extend and clinch industrial organization. This involves, at the very least, setting up a full-scale National Labour Women's Organization. Such a step is not ideal, since the very notion of a separate women's organization is from one point of view retrogressive – and would be resented as such by many women. But the hard facts of women's political loyalties have to be faced. In most cases, the discrepancy between the male and female votes for the Labour Party probably occurs within the same family. Where wives vote Conservative and husbands Labour, the chance of a specifically feminine organization countervailing this specifically feminine bias is clearly real, and should not be lost.

Lastly, and most fundamentally, it must be recognized that the root of the problem does not lie in the immediate economic interest of women, but in the whole *ideology* which suffuses their lives. It is this which determines their attitudes and expectations, far more than any self-interest. A large number of women – over 50 per cent – are still housewives, whom it is hardly possible to reach by economic appeals for equal pay, etc., in any case. Social services – crèches, laundries, domestic help – must be substituted where possible, but even this misses the true problem, which involves women's image of themselves and their dignity in society. In the long run, only a creative counter-ideology, which offers a new vision of women's social role and purpose, as an integral part of a new vision of culture and society, will liberate women from their present condition. The problem of women's conservatism will disappear when, and only when, this ideology exists.

5. *Political Imperatives*

The strategy suggested above follows from the initial analysis attempted in this essay of the requirements for a hegemonic socialist party. It can be described as a systematic effort to *marry the structure of the socialist movement to the contours of civil society*. As will have been seen, this conception involves an organic unity between the 'political' and 'industrial' wings of the movement, in which each is intimately and dialectically related to the other. The Labour Party must regard the vitality and growth of the Trade Unions as the direct precondition of its own success, and as therefore a priority for itself. Equally, the Trade Unions can only hope to realize the potential for qualitative social change which they necessarily embody, if the Labour Party is capable of assuming the political and cultural leadership of society. *In effect, socialist strategy must aim at entering and inhabiting civil society at every possible point, establishing an entire alternative system of power and culture within it.* Ideally, the network of socialist institutions should be as dense as the sociogram itself. This will never be achieved in a capitalist society, of course: but it is the direction in which political energy should tend.

The purpose of this strategy is not to create a myriad of reflecting mirrors for the narcissism of the party. Any attempt to impose an external discipline on these associations would destroy their whole *raison d'être* – which is not simply to 'extend the influence' of the party, but rather the reverse, to give the party an authentic universality by linking it to the whole social life of the community. Thus, the autonomy of these organizations must be respected as absolutely as that of the Trade Union movement itself. The analogy, indeed, can be taken farther. These newly formed organizations should be represented in the federal constitution of the Labour Party as Trade Unions and socialist societies have been since its foundation.

This discussion has been primarily concerned with the external dimensions of the Labour Party. Its conclusions can be completed by some brief indication of changes needed in its internal articulation. In the main, these follow obviously enough from the preceding critique of the Labour Party as a political organization. The party must be seen, from one point of view, as an end in itself – a prefiguration of the socialist society it promises to create, not simply as a means to the end of winning elections. There must thus be a far greater emphasis on recruitment of membership, on the expansion of the party's mass basis. A preliminary target should be at least to equal Conservative Party membership. Side by side with this, should go an all-out attempt to create a comparable mass youth organization. Hitherto, the Labour Party has each time denounced the capture of its youth movement by a small and irresponsible minority, which has wrecked it as a serious organization. The solution for it, then, is not to retreat towards a third dissolution of its youth movement, but to build a genuinely wide and representative movement, *far larger* than the present Young Socialists. An unrepresentative minority would have as little chance of capturing this as it would the parent party itself. Such a drive would require infinitely greater determination and enthusiasm than has ever been shown before. It would have to be accompanied, moreover, by a resolute break with the repressive heritage of the past – whether at the level of branch dances, or national politics. A seat on the National Executive Committee, in accordance with the normal practice of most political parties, is also a necessity. The safeguard that this autonomy would be used constructively would lie in the scale and solidity of the youth movement itself. A corollary of this emphasis should be legislation granting the vote at 18, not 21 – a move which would both increase democracy and the electoral potential of the party, since the young tend to be markedly more Labour than the old in Britain.

Next, the whole financial basis of the party should be overhauled. This alone would permit a start to be made on an imaginative Labour Press. Duverger commented in 1951: 'It is a strange paradox that the parties based on the poorest classes should have adopted the highest subscriptions . . . Devotion to the party is greater among the working classes than amongst

the middle classes and this makes it easier to set the sub-
scription high.'[1] It has been seen how untrue the latter remark
is in Britain, and the evidence of party subscriptions bears this
out. Current collection of Labour Party dues runs at the sorry
figure of 50 per cent of the nominal sum required – yet another indication of the low quality of party administration and
morale.[2] The experience of both British Trade Unions and
European parties should be consulted, in a systematic effort to
maximize the revenue of the party. Advanced accounting techniques are probably indispensable for greater efficiency –
moderate-sized Trade Unions are now using computers to
handle subscriptions. But it is clear that the problem of dues
is in the first place a problem of communication and morale
within the party and the labour movement as a whole. From a
purely economic point of view, an increase in Trade Union
affiliations is much more important, of course; but this, too,
is only likely to follow a revitalization of democracy and discussion within the party and the Trade Unions.

Not only the financial, but the research apparatus of the
party should be radically renovated. The Labour Party must
finally learn that market research is not sociology.[3] A coherent, long-term strategy requires theoretically adequate,
serious sociological research behind it. The only place where
this is available in Britain today is the universities – and it
should be to them that the party should turn for depth studies
on the class structure. This in itself would constitute a major
step forward in the political planning of the party.

Finally, this discussion can end on a symbolic note. There
is one extremely small measure which the Labour Government
could take here and now, at no cost whatever, which would
make a disproportionately large difference at the next electoral
contest. This is simply to declare polling day a national holiday.
To do so would merely follow the most elementary democratic practice. The present ludicrous system of voting on an

[1] *Political Parties*, p. 73.
[2] See Martin Harrison, *The Trade Unions and the Labour Party*.
[3] Lockwood and Goldthorpe's paper, already referred to, shows
very precisely the difference between the two.

ordinary work-day regularly subtracts crucial thousands of votes from the Labour Poll, as working-class supporters come home too tired to venture out again – while Conservative voters often have all day, or private transport, in which to vote. The extreme narrowness between the two parties' polls at present, and the experience of the last election, in which turn-out was less than in 1959 – costing the Labour Party the comfortable majority it expected, underlines the importance of this infinitesimal reform. The Labour Party's supine acceptance of the handicap which this absurd middle-class totem imposes on it, is a miniature but eloquent symbol of its lack of hegemonic will or ability. Termination of this anachronism would be a first, minuscule proof of change.

D. IDEOLOGY

The whole strategy discussed above depends on one immense precondition: a socialist ideology. Without this, the entire range of possible actions and initiatives has no meaning. For by definition, there is no possibility whatever of ending capitalist hegemony in Britain by purely political or organizational moves. This hegemony rests on a total vision of the world – and can only be replaced by another vision of the world. Socialist hegemony requires, in fact, a rich and complex cultural synthesis – a concrete, universal theory of man and history which in every field visibly outdistances the shrunken social thought of capitalism. Only a synthesis of this scale and generosity will have the necessary attractive force to win the allegiance and ardour of men in the affluent societies of the West. This is why any consideration of socialist strategy in Britain today must as yet be academic. For if any one thing is clear about the Labour Party, it is that it is not the carrier of a socialist ideology. It is not, in fact, in any meaningful sense whatever a socialist party. Until it becomes one, it will never be capable of playing a hegemonic role in British politics.

Having registered this, what remains to be said? The problem of socialist ideology today is so large that it can only be touched on here. It may, however, be possible to indicate some elements of the necessary synthesis in Britain. It will be remembered that a hegemonic party was described as being characterized by its integration of national cultural traditions which constitute, in however limited or repressed a form, a criticism of the existing social order. In Britain, these traditions are perhaps particularly numerous and strong – in part because of the absence of a coherent vision of the world to supersede them. Any socialist ideology in Britain which does not incorporate these traditions as constituent elements will inevitably fail; it will remain abstract and external, unable to affect popular sensibility or imagination. What are the traditions that are vital in this way? There are three main currents which distinguish the British Left today.[1] In the first place, and most fundamentally, there is the deep working-class consciousness which has produced its own corporate culture and an ineradicable sense of antagonistic identity within capitalist society. This class-consciousness, for all its limitations, has nurtured the ideal of solidarity as few others. It provides the basis of the Labour Left. Secondly, there is the long and important legacy of classical English liberalism. This tradition has been singularly confiscated and corrupted in this century, above all in the service of the Cold War. But it remains alive and vigorous in a significant section of the middle class: it is appropriate that its main contemporary manifestation, the Campaign for Nuclear Disarmament, should be a reaction against the Cold War. Thirdly, there is the complex lineage of moral and aesthetic criticism, which descends from the Romantics to Arnold and Morris, and Lawrence and Leavis in the twentieth century – the subject of *Culture and Society*. This is the major creative tradition of British social thought since industrialization.

These three currents mingle in the mainstream of the British Left. The Labour Party, however, reflects only two of them: it is almost entirely cut off from the tradition of *Culture and Society*. The reason for this is easy to see. Its dominant

[1] I have discussed these at greater length in 'The Left in the Fifties', *New Left Review*, January–February, 1965.

ideological heritage, Fabianism, is a direct descendant of utilitarianism and as such is radically incompatible with the whole anti-utilitarian tradition in English culture. Fabian supremacy in the Party ensures the virtual exclusion of the inheritors of Morris and Arnold. It also gravely distorts the relationship between the working-class and liberal traditions which are represented inside the party, creating a negative dialectic between the two, in which each accentuates the vices of the other. In the shadow of Fabianism, liberalism could appear to take on the narrow and dogmatic mask of Hugh Gaitskell, and the working-class ideal of solidarity could seem to degenerate into the brutal authoritarianism of Arthur Deakin. It was no accident that in the late fifties and early sixties, the Liberal Party should have been markedly more progressive than the Labour Party on a range of important issues – civil liberties, Pilkington Report, etc. One of the encouraging results of the new phase inside the Labour Party has been the release of the generous, creative potential of each of these traditions – personified perhaps in men like Benn on the one hand, and Cousins on the other, in the present Government.

What are the possibilities of a fusion of these three main traditions of the British Left in a new Labour ideology? Setting aside for the moment the political difficulties involved, it can be argued that there is one common strand in all of them, which, moreover, could potentially touch one of the deepest chords in the British experience. This strand is the simple idea of *democracy*, understood in its largest and most explosive sense. Already, there are signs that an attempt will be made on the Left to base a critique of capitalism primarily on the grounds of its lack of democracy. This tendency is by no means only British: it corresponds to a widespread trend in the European socialist movement towards the formulation of political programmes in terms of democratization rather socialization. From one point of view, this trend is absolutely welcome and necessary. It is vitally important to reinstate the idea of democracy where it belongs, in the movement towards socialism. The damaging consequences of the belief in a divorce between the two have been countless in the West. And, indeed, there are many aspects of capitalism which can and should be attacked in the name of democracy. The oligarchic character of British society is notoriously pronounced – in education, in industry, in political institutions. At the same time, democracy is regarded in Britain as a quintessentially national attribute and creation: national pride is largely built upon it. The contradiction between these two facts provides the objective validity for the view that in England the idea of democracy has a profound mobilizing potential. It is almost certain that in the coming years something of this will be seen.

At the same time, the limits of a purely or predominantly 'democratic' ideology must be recognized. In Britain, the Labour Party will never be able to achieve the anodyne political dominance of the Social–Democratic Party in Sweden or the Democratic Party in the U.S.A. British society is far too deeply and dramatically class-divided for this. Political conflict involves a much more extreme social and ideological polarization. Faced with as ancient and redoubtable an opponent as the historic English governing class, and its appointed instrument the Conservative Party, the Labour Party can only triumph in the long-run by generating a tremendous political counter-charge, capable of exploding the colossal weight of centuries of sanctified, sedimented authority and custom. The record of no less than eleven Conservative victories out of fourteen clear-cut elections since 1886, should leave few illusions about this. A simple ideology of democracy is much too slender to dislodge this immense supremacy. Because it involves a kind of perpetual analogy of every problem with that of parliamentary government, it can all too easily be contested in these terms. A good example is offered by the debate over 'industrial democracy' – the description, in this idiom, of workers' control. Once this idea was launched, it was almost immediately countered by proponents of the status quo, with the argument that in industry, government (employers) and opposition (unions) always remain the same, whereas in parliament they alternate. Posed in this way, the fundamental issues involved are completely obscured. In effect, workers' control does include the idea of industrial democracy – in the democratization of decision-making in the factory. But it also includes a good deal more than this: in particular, it is concerned with the restoration of *meaning* to work and the products of work. This is not a problem which can be at all adequately discussed in terms of 'democracy'. Much wider and deeper issues are involved, concerning the whole structure of the human personality in industrialized society. The same is true, to take another example, of the problem of sexual relations, already referred to; this, too, cannot be brought into the limited framework of democracy. Finally, of course, the whole historical question of property cannot be arbitrated by a simple appeal to democracy, which was originally conceived to be inseparable from property; a much broader field of reference is needed. All this amounts to saying what should be obvious in any case: that there is no easy route to socialism, to be achieved merely by invoking the principles of democracy, which capitalism tenaciously claims as its own. In Britain, above all, socialist hegemony requires a much richer and more complex ideology than this.

This does not mean that it must be arcane or esoteric. A truly major system of thought is always recognizable by the fact that it is capable of being articulated at a *great number of different levels* – ranging from the most abstruse and sophisticated to the most familiar and concrete. This is perhaps the only valid idea in Eliot's discussion of culture – but it is a very important one. At one end, it eliminates immediately from the category of major systems of thought, otiose labyrinths like Parsonian sociology, which have no dimension reaching into the language of ordinary discourse. At the other, it reveals the insuperable limitations of all existing socialist ideologies, with the exception of Marxism: these remain one-dimensional in the opposite sense – they never attain sufficient complexity or depth to allow articulation at any other than at an elementary level. The task before socialist thought today is too demanding to be acquitted with either type of solution. It requires a language that can simultaneously mobilize and inspire great masses of people, and inform the most intractable scholarly research.

A hegemonic socialist thought today must have this spaciousness. For its goal is necessarily what Kant called a philosophical anthropology – that is, a total theory of man. The purpose of such a theory is in no way academic. Its aim is to change the world, by providing the critical foundations for a new kind of politics, which is no longer concerned simply with the *conditions* of social existence, but takes as its object the *content* of social existence as well. The difference between this conception and the traditional politics of social-democracy is fundamentary. The evolution of radical political thought in this century in effect coincides with the *extension of its problem-areas*. The sequence of these marks the successive boundaries of ordinary political action and discussion – usually some years in advance. Thus, the traditional areas of political concern for social-democracy were *welfare* and *income distribution* – with more emphasis on the former than on the latter. Until the late fifties, these dominated Labour Party debates absolutely. They formed virtually the sole themes of Crosland's book *The Future of Socialism*. Then, when Galbraith published his work *The Affluent Society*, the problem of *social priorities* came to the forefront of intellectual discussion. It now, five years afterwards, makes up a large part of the Labour Party's official rhetoric. A few years later, the whole problem of *work* – its quality and meaning in a capitalist society – began to be ventilated in Britain (a very neglected section of Galbraith's own book had concerned work – perhaps the most radical part). It had, of course, long been a key topic in continental socialist theory, as could easily be seen when Friedmann's book *The Anatomy of Work* was translated in the early sixties. Discussion of work in Britain has only very recently started to become at all programmatic, in Trade Unions resolutions on workers' control, etc. Just before this, *culture* for the first time entered the arena of immediate political debate, in the writings of Hoggart and Williams. This has still to penetrate Labour Party thinking in any significant way, but the original critique of the capitalist organization of culture has, uniquely in the advanced capitalist world, been given a precise programmatic edge – which found echoes in the eminently 'official' Pilkington Report. Undoubtedly, the next and most urgent area to be opened up is that of *sexuality* – in all its multiple dimensions and implications: sexual inequality, statute of the family, socialization of the child, puritan sanctions, legislative repression, etc. This area poses the most difficult and delicate theoretical problems. So far only Marcuse, in his major work *Eros and Civilization*, has broached them. In Britain, the work of R. D. Laing promises to begin the task of inquiry and critique. The climate in Britain has in the past few years undoubtedly become more propitious for serious discussion of this complex of problems.

Hitherto, all these different areas have remained discrete. No unifying theory has integrated them into a total critique of capitalism. For this, the critical foundations are missing in England. These foundations can only take the form of a philosophical anthropology, a theory of man. For the traditional conception of socialist politics in the West involved a certain, compartmentalized vision of man. It was believed that the whole purpose of politics was to ameliorate the conditions of social existence – to ensure that every member of society had enough money, leisure, shelter and protection to lead the life he wanted. This was, in the traditional view, the liberation of man. We know now how inadequate this view is. Men are not liberated by wage packets or health clinics, although these are indeed indispensable elements in any social liberation. For they are not free in their *activity*, in the *use* of their time. Social-democratic politics rested on the idea that there was an absolute distinction between the communal conditions of existence and the private pursuit of happiness: 'society' and the 'individual'. The truth is that no such clear distinction can be drawn. 'Society' and the 'individual' are both essentialist abstractions, based on the notion that persons and institutions are closed, demarcated *beings*, with fixed boundaries between them. In reality, there are no such separate, autarchic beings – there is instead a continuum of human *actions*, which collide, converge and coalesce to form the whole personal and social world we live in. Man and society exist only as *praxis*, outside themselves in the fluctuating interworld their actions compose together.[1] As Merleau-Ponty once wrote: 'Man is excentric to himself, and the social has its centre only in him.'[2] This is also the import of the fundamental first part of Raymond Williams's *The Long Revolution*, which has been so ignored and misunderstood – precisely because it represents the first attempt in Britain to transcend the limits of positivist social thought, the basis of all social-democratic – and capitalist – politics. It follows that there is ultimately no neutral area, into which the individual can withdraw from society: he is socially at stake in the whole plenitude of his life, in his work, in his art, in his sexuality. In a capitalist society, all these domains of living tend to be confiscated and denied. In different ways, each is alienated in Britain today. For just as power is at stake throughout civil society, so are freedom and fulfilment. The ultimate goal is, therefore, necessarily a new model of civilization, with its own values, its own relations, its own creativity. Socialism is a promulgation of human freedom across the entire existential space of the world.

This is the horizon towards which the socialist movement in the West will in the long run move. For the moment, traditional demands – concerning wages, housing, pensions, schools – dominate politics in Britain, and must be fought for their own sake, as the main issues of the day. As often happens, theoretical debate has in recent years overshot the limits of practical politics, and so inevitably remained somewhat abstract and academic. To this extent, we are in a situation not unlike that of the 1840s, when a rarefied intellectual 'criticism', divorced from political struggle, predominated in Germany. The task now is to join the two, developing and enlarging theory in the light of a new practice. There need be little fear that the advent of affluence and automation in Western Europe will void politics of thought or passion, and so undermine the basis of the socialist movement. Such a belief presupposes a stationary humanity and history. Nothing is less

[1] This is why alienation is not a 'psychological state', as is often maintained: it is the inescapable destiny of freedom in a capitalist society, because of the structure of human action.

[2] 'De Mauss à Claude Levi-Strauss', in *Signes*, p. 155.

conceivable. Socialism as a movement and as a critique is based on human *needs* and these needs evolve with society itself. The great, permanent landmark of real abundance will not be the end of ideology, but the *end of necessity*. The empire of scarcity, and its curse, will be over. Integral human freedom will at last be possible.

Meanwhile, elsewhere in the world, in Asia, Africa and Latin-America, men will still struggle to create a socialism of privation and duress. This must never be forgotten, in the task of creating in the advanced capitalist countries a socialism of liberty and privilege. The aims of both are ultimately the same: they are divided by all the immense distance of different historical time. The last and most vital test of an authentic European socialism is to remember this, and to maintain the fraternity between the two.

DEMOCRACY AND WORKERS' CONTROL

Ken Coates

1

The term 'workers' control' is commonly used to cover two quite distinct concepts. One maintains, in the words of the German socialist Thalheimer, that 'control over production signifies the management of the industries by the workers', and usually appears in discussion as an attempt to outline an ideal norm of administration for socialized industries. In this tradition, one finds that in Britain, throughout the nineteen-thirties, speakers in T.U.C. debates on the popular administration of nationalized industries almost invariably used the term in this sense. But another tradition has evolved a quite different concept which speaks of 'workers' control' in those contexts where militant Trade Unions have been able to wrest some, or most, of the prerogatives of management from the unilateral disposition of managers.

It is misleading to use the same term to speak of two such different conditions. To do so implies that an unbroken continuity of democratic advance stretches between the imposition of a Trade Union veto on dismissals and the ultimate overcoming of capitalist property relations. This is a naïve view, because it completely ignores the deforming power of these property relations in the generation both of ideology and of social forces beyond democratic control. In a climate in which all human relationships are founded on cash-values, the most flagrantly anti-social and irresponsible acts of capital appear as 'natural' events, beyond the scope of social control.

What appears to be 'fair' in such a structure is very remote from what would seem so in a society uncluttered by the domination of institutions of property. Even active Trade Unionists, who will respond most vigorously to changes in their conditions of work when these appear to be unfair, very seldom break through the given standards of our society to form any conception of the incomparably richer and more human standards which a classless society would create. Within the compass of this ideology, generated by it and constantly reinforcing it, lies the power of the state. This power, far from giving expression to democratic initiative, inhibits and frustrates it. Nowhere is this more clearly to be seen than in the field of industrial relations, in which the state has consistently intervened to contain or transmute pressures for democratic control into harmless experiments permitting the sovereignty of property institutions to survive unimpaired.

But even if these things were not true, and the continuous encroachment of democracy in industry were assured, we should still require at some point in its progress the recognition of a qualitatively different set of problems. It seems incorrect to speak of 'workers' control' where ultimate authority is supposed to rest with the workers, because 'control' is a term which implies a more or less involved apparatus of checks, or even vetoes, by one party on the behaviour of another. The demand for workers' control, thus literally interpreted, becomes a demand, explicit or implicit, for a reversal of roles in a class-divided society. The workers wish to limit the scope of the action of other *persons*, of managers or owners, and not merely, as is often implied, to 'control' inanimate objects such as their machines and raw materials. Inanimate objects appear to be at stake, because reification is at work; what the machines do is not the result of any will of their own, but of the outcome of a tussle of wills between people, whose relationships have been refracted through things and camouflaged in the process. Whether at the level of shop control of hire-and-fire, and agreements on 100 per cent Trade Union membership, or at the level of detailed Union inspection of a firm's account books and a workers' veto on investment decisions and the distribution of profits, workers' control in this sense involves a balance of hostile forces, a division of authority between rival contenders.

Once property and its taboos are overcome, this mobile, dual relationship ceases to exist. The new problem becomes one of democratic self-regulation. This is a very different concern from that which faces the labour movement this side of the socialist transformation of private property into common wealth. A recognition of this fact is implied in the interesting experiences of – among others – the Yugoslavs and the Algerians. The Algerians invariably speak of the administrative system of their nationalized concerns as 'auto-gestion', while the Yugoslavs use the term 'self-management' to describe the government of their socialized sector. Following this usage, it seems sensible for us to speak of 'workers' control' to indicate the aggressive encroachment of Trade Unions on management powers in a capitalist framework, and of 'workers' self-management' to indicate attempts to administer a socialized economy democratically. While insisting that there is most unlikely to be a simple institutional continuity between the two conditions, it seems quite clear that workers' control can be a most valuable school for self-management, and that the notion of self-management can be an important stimulus to the demand for control. Between the two, however it may be accomplished, lies the political transformation of the social structure.

2

After resting dormant for two generations, the movement for workers' control in Britain has once again begun to stir, reshape itself, and gather force and insight. Already it has become sufficiently explicit to appear as a demand on Union conference agendas, in the utterances of important Trade Union leaders, and in resolutions approved at the Labour Party Conference and Trade Union Congress in 1963.[1]

[1] See *Report of the Labour Party Conference*, 1963, pp. 189–90 *Trades Union Congress Report*, 1963, pp. 276, 420 and *Trades Union Congress Report*, 1964, pp. 321, 446, 489. The T.U.C. discussions involve 'workers' participation in the nationalized industries'. This is an ambiguous term, which can mean anything from Joint Consultation (as it does, obviously, to many members of the General Council) up to full workers' management of nationalized enterprises.

Numerous articles and papers on it have begun to circulate in the socialist and Trade Union press,[1] and well-attended seminars of academics and Trade Unionists have convened to discuss it.[2] The interest which it arouses is not, naturally enough, very easily visible in the popular press, or through the other means of communication which are among the perquisites of capital. But neither do the formal commitments of the big Trade Unions, or statements by their leading personalities, give an adequate idea of the huge powder-keg of workpeople's

[1] Among other interesting examples is an Editorial by Sid Hill, leader of the National Union of Public Employees (215,000 strong) and member of the General Council of the T.U.C., which appeared in the Winter 1963 issue of the *Public Employees' Journal*.

The most radical and coherent appeal yet has come from Ernie Roberts, Assistant General Secretary of the A.E.U. In a broadsheet issued with the Autumn 1964 issue of *Voice of the Unions*, he puts forward a comprehensive plan for the administration of the steel industry after nationalization. This would have the effect of bringing 'participation' up to the point of workers' management: 'Each shop would have its own elected Shop Committee which would send delegates to a central Works Council. The Shop Committee would also elect its supervision, and the Works Councils would appoint higher management. The Board of the enterprise would have representatives from the State agency, charged with implementing the plan, and representatives from the Works Councils, responsible for details of production.' Unions would negotiate with this Board about the distribution of the surplus and conditions of work, just as they would today. Such a scheme would have the dual effect of popularizing nationalization, which is generally construed as a bureaucratic monster, and, at the same time, ensuring that the nationalized industry did not simply subserve the private sector, but made its own pace. *Voice of the Unions* has announced a campaign in the steel producing areas around this platform: its outcome could be extremely important for the advance of British socialism.

[2] One, at Nottingham, attracted 140 participants drawn from most Unions and a number of universities. Reports of it have appeared in *Tribune* (May, 1964), *New Left Review*, No. 25, pp. 13–16, *Anarchy*, No. 40, June, 1964, and *The Week*, vol. II, No. 4, July, 1964. *Hull Left*, published by Labour Students at Hull University, reproduced a number of papers which had been submitted for the consideration of the seminar.

daily concern about it which could eventually be set off by the lightest, most sensitive of trigger actions.

The basic change in the economic condition of Britain, like that of Western Europe as a whole, is the near-full employment which underpins not only the successes but also all the major problems of neo-capitalism. The social effects of this change have, until recently, been noted simply in the shape of obtrusive and often misleading marks of affluence. Up to the beginning of this decade, affluence was almost universally equated with working-class apathy, enervation, and depoliticization. The election result of October, 1964, has provided its own commentary on this view of things. There is some evidence that the Labour victory was the result of a major renovation of traditional working-class loyalties, resulting in a large working-class poll. By and large the middle strata stayed shy of the Labour Party.[1] This working-class feeling came as no surprise to more thoughtful analysts. The Cambridge sociologists Goldthorpe and Lockwood, in their paper 'Affluence and the British Class Structure',[2] concluded in 1963 that in so far as the traditional communal solidarity of some sections of the British working class has become attenuated, and 'instrumental collectivism' has come to replace it, this in no way underwrites the conservative cause, although it may from time to time assist it. Quite possibly the more calculating, rationalistic assessment of interests implied in the new outlook may result in a radicalization of working-class politics. To the extent that workers expect improved living standards to be accompanied by improved status, a strain is thrown on the received social structure. If that structure cannot adapt to allow recognition of new status, then something will give. That something may not be the aspirations of the workers.

Unquestionably, the main battlefront of the real status-war is not the suburb. There, problems of social standing have little

[1] See the study on the election in the *Observer*, 18 October, 1964.

[2] J. H. Goldthorpe and D. Lockwood, 'Affluence and the British Class Structure.' *The Sociological Review*, vol. XI, No. 2, July, 1963, pp. 133–64.

direct political significance; they are trivialized into the tensions of competing snobberies. The place where status has teeth is beyond all doubt the factory, the office, the enterprise. Here all the brutalizing implications of power, from the petty but often infuriating forms it takes in the workshop to the subtly extended and carefully veiled realities at the summits of industry, work into men's souls. The shape of hierarchy in industry was known and felt all too clearly before the war: but it could not become a political issue in any open way while the disciplinary weight of mass-unemployment existed to grind down any protest. Even the socialist case for nationalization before the war rested almost entirely on grounds of efficiency, and was angled solely at the abolition of unemployment. A job was a goal in such circumstances. Only when stomachs were filled, and relative security established, could people afford to notice the real indignities of their position. Before the war, not only did the worker in work watch his step and count his blessings (the shop stewards' movement disappeared immediately after the First World War, only to show up again in the late thirties, in an aircraft industry whose war contracts provided islands of guaranteed work amid the general insecurity) but the worker out of work, or on short time, aspired above all to a regular job. Post-war workers have not faced these troubles, in the overwhelming majority of cases. Far from being chastened by short-time working, most workers have consistently averaged several hours of overtime[1] a week since the late forties. True, a series of recessions, each one tending to become more pronounced than the last, have served to remind Trade Unionists of earlier days; while areas of limbo have continued to exist in the north, and in Northern Ireland, providing a dismal exception to the normal story. Yet the ordinary worker has come to form expectations based on continuing full employment, and these are by no means limited to simple economic appetites. Above all, he has come to experience, day in, day out, the taste of capitalism working as nearly as possible to its

[1] Many of which have been unnecessary, according to H. A. Clegg, 'Implications of the Shorter Working Week for Management', *British Institute of Management* Pamphlet, 1962.

ideal performance. This is not a sweet taste. Indeed, soothing though it may be to certain directors, for whom things are at their best imaginable, it is becoming increasingly brackish to large numbers of workers.

Their feelings can even be dimly discerned in a book like Ferdinand Zweig's *The Worker in an Affluent Society*.[1] One of his chapters begins: ' "Home and work don't mix." This is a phrase which often circulates among working men. It means that "you should leave home at home and work at work", or, "once you leave work, forget it". As one man said, "when you clock out, clock out your mind" . . . Work matters are rarely mentioned at home . . . Work means tension, and home is for relaxation. Men say "I never mention work at home, otherwise I would never relax . . ." '[2] And, towards the end of the book, he writes 'When I asked "Do you like your job?" a generalization was put forward such as "No one really likes his job"; or to a question "Do you work only for money; does the job give you something else from money?" the answer might be "We all work for money, there is nothing else in the job." '[3]

This is the *quiet* response of workers to the working capitalism they have come to know; it is one of dissociation and it is suitable for interviewers. There is a harder response as well.

Faced with psychological withdrawal, and apprehensive about unnecessarily aggravating aspects of the industrial power structure, some leading industrialists have sought ways of mitigating the feel of subordination which is basic to factory organization as far as employees are concerned.[4] Thus the practice of clocking in, the anomalies of differentials between increasingly routinized clerical workers and shop-floor operatives, the more blatantly inefficient effects of piece-work – all of these have been quite sternly debated not only in the schools of human relations, but among the more perceptive industrial executives themselves. Yet movement is slow. The inertia of British businessmen is perhaps nowhere more recognizable

[1] 1961.
[2] Ibid., p. 84.
[3] Ibid, p. 199.
[4] See, for example, W. Brown's well-known *Piecework Abandoned*.

than in this field, where their own interests might be thought to spell out a certain liberalization. But perhaps this conservative resistance to change is not entirely stupid, since a thaw might produce a greater flow beneath the ice than could be contained within acceptable channels. One thing is very clear: for all the labours of industrial liberals, things are constantly called by their right names on the shop-floor. It is still extremely common for a new recruit to be told upon engagement, by the brisk, sergeant-majorly figure who signs him on, that 'When you start here, it is to work, not think: we pay our own thinkers, and they don't need your help.' Even where the notion that workers are hands, not brains, has been expunged by managerial fiat from the vocabulary of supervision, its reality remains no less painfully obvious. The proliferation of work study and method study techniques serve not only to increase the rate of return per man employed, but also, and perhaps far more damagingly to the man concerned, to strip away with increasing efficiency the last remaining areas of independent decision and initiative which had hitherto survived in the workshop. That such techniques do not necessarily serve to increase productivity[1] seems to present no noticeable obstacle to their advance: it seems clear that they owe at least as much of their popularity to their disciplinary advantages as to their productive merits. The growth and decline of formal means of communication, including suggestion schemes, has done nothing whatever to ameliorate the fact that in modern industry workers are used as mere means to ends formed independently of their will. At best such devices have exposed workers to the unilateral adoption of *their* ideas by others; they provide no long-term assurance that the application of these ideas may not be to their own detriment. The remorseless division of labour which polarizes the factory into a small corps of decision-takers on one side, and an army of subordinates on the other, does not simply alienate the labour force. The concentration of decision-taking power, untempered by

[1] This has been lucidly demonstrated by Georges Friedmann in his masterly *Industrial Society*, 1955, and in *The Anatomy of Work*, 1961.

any effective responsible controls, tends to produce a succession of organizational crises, in which expensive blunders are followed by brutal reshuffles, as the left hand of management vainly gropes after even the rudiments of knowledge about the movements of its right hand.

Were data available, there can be little doubt that the present incidence of managerial waste would stagger everyone. As things are, it is seldom documented, and almost never openly discussed. But unless the Nottingham area is completely exceptional, it must run into millions every year. Its human cost is unmeasurable, because mistakes that are tiny in terms of revenue can be cataclysmic in their effects on people. In one enterprise in Nottinghamshire, workers were recently engaged to build an annexe, which was subsequently discovered to be in the way of other developments, and therefore scheduled for demolition. This, so far, is a common enough story. But on this job, the demolition gangs moved in to start work while the decorators were still at their task, making habitable the barely completed building. So, while the painters were busily finishing their work on the fourth wall, the other three were being removed by the heavy squads. Some of the workers concerned claim that they were compelled to wait because demolition had to be suspended until the painters finished and got out of the way. Countless similar stories will be retailed to anyone who talks to groups of workers about the problem of waste. In the nationalized industries the record is no better: I personally have several times been involved in quite large-scale works which were demolished on completion, and have innumerable experiences of installing expensive machines which did not work, or walking past other expensive machines which had lain idle and forgotten for months on end in very damaging conditions. None of these things would be permitted if workpeople were assured of both an interest in production as a whole, and sufficient powers to uphold it. If this is true where a firm's income is at stake, it is even more true where men's dignity and self-respect are involved. One small example of the kind of tragedy that often happens was recorded in the Nottingham press a year ago. It concerns an engineering plant, in which a man was seriously injured by a jet of steam that had been discharged through a grating as he was walking over it. Inquiries revealed that this discharge was the result of a mistake. Another employee had, more than twenty years previously, been detailed to open a valve at certain fixed times of the day, in order to lower available steam-pressure. Many years ago this operation had been made completely unnecessary, because the plant had been adapted in order to make it safe. But no one had ever informed the worker concerned. Year in, year out, he had continued to perform an un-needed task, which was dangerous to others, until an accident interfered to redress the organization of his work. The feelings of this man, placed in such a situation, are not difficult to imagine. In fact, his workmates reported that he was utterly demoralized by the discovery that he had for years been paid to perform a completely useless and damaging operation. Such instances could be extended indefinitely, but the point should already be clear: the deprivation of responsibility which workers suffer in this sort of situation does not merely damage them personally, as individuals; it is also socially destructive, and constantly undermines the development of productive powers. However vigorously employers seek out means to overcome these difficulties, they are fighting a losing battle. Whilst the product itself remains beyond the control of the workpeople who produce it, their self-protection impels them not merely to suffer such absurd failures of 'organization', but even to conspire to prevent their alleviation. If you are alienated from the product of your work, such forms of ca'canny as are involved in protecting management from attaining accurate self-knowledge, and sometimes more radical forms of resistance as well, are by no means stupid. You are aware that augmented productivity may turn out to be a weapon for use against you, rather than a straightforward development and extension of your powers. On the national scale, crusades for productivity were summed up in the early months of 1963 by special postage stamps exalting additional effort, while the unemployment figures were mounting week by week.

The main device which has been employed to sidetrack the frustrations which the authoritarian control of industry induces in its workpeople, and the recurring problems of production which stem from the necessarily abortive attempt to restrict or abolish the initiative of workers, is that of joint consultation. Born in the First World War, an uncertain changeling, it did not survive very long. Between 1918 and 1939 the dole queues provided most employers with all the consultation they felt they needed. But the Second World War brought about a strange reincarnation. Bevin's elevation to the Ministry of Labour coincided with a bizarre turn of fortune, in which the most militant goading force in the Unions, the Communist party, was soon to come out of opposition, and play a major role in the crusade for war-production. Effective pioneer of the reborn shop-stewards movement, the Communist Party found itself also pioneering at the rebirth of joint consultation. It demanded the setting up of joint production committees and activated their members. Huge conferences of stewards were held in the glare of enthusiastic press publicity to consider ways of expanding production. All of this had the effect of creating a certain ambivalence among shop-stewards, which did not wear off with the war effort. But the rationality of joint consultation was not ambivalent. The new situation of the early forties required new practices by management, if it was to continue managing for long. Seldom has the argument for these been presented with more disarming frankness than by G. S. Walpole in *Management and Men*, published as a guide to joint consultation in 1944:

> What joint consultation does for industry is threefold in character. It provides the higher management with an additional source of information, warning, and advice – particularly valuable because it covers a field in which conventional channels of information and advice are too often biased or ineffective. It also provides the means for transmitting to employees information and explanation without which their attitudes towards their work or their management is liable to be prejudiced. Thirdly, on the psychological side *it canalizes the legitimate aspiration of*

labour to have a voice in the industry to which it con-
tributes so much. (My italics.)[1]

This canalization was furthered and consolidated after the election of the post-war Labour Government by the simple device of writing joint consultation procedures into the nationalization acts governing those industries which Labour took into public ownership. (At the same time, a few eminent Trade Union leaders found themselves on the boards of these new corporations – in this way ended all the declamatory 'workers' control' talk of the T.U.C. during the thirties.) The net effect of such consultation, whether in public or private sectors, will surprise very few people. For private industry, it has recently been summed up by D. Llewellyn Davies, in a study entitled *'Formal Consultation in Practice'.* His view is: 'The general impression gained is that the majority of firms do not fully believe in and practise formal consultation and all that it implies, but use it rather as a forum for company pronouncements and the airing of employee irritants.'[2] Even when the employers *do* 'believe in' consultation, of course, all that this can ever mean is that they may seek employees' opinions before they tell them what to do. Such procedures may provide a certain soothing balm during those honeymoons in which competition leaves management free of the need to make sharp turns in policy, with all the consequent upheavals in working conditions which these so frequently involve. But overall, there is no doubt whatever that in recent years they have become increasingly irrelevant.

As evidence of this, we may consider a number of facts. The growth rate of shop-steward representation in the Amalgamated Engineering Union doubled in the period 1957–61, as compared with the period 1947–56.[3] Anthony Topham, in a valuable study published by *New Left Review*,[4] points out:

[1] G. S. Walpole, *Management and Men*, 1944, p. 43.

[2] Industrial Welfare Society, 1962.

[3] Cf. A. T. Marsh and E. E. Coker, Shop Steward Organization in Engineering', *British Journal of Industrial Relations*, vol. I, No. 2.

[4] 'Shop Stewards and Workers' Control', *New Left Review*, No. 25, May–June, 1964, p. 5.

Associated with this very rapid rate of expansion of stewards, has been a decline of one-third in formal Joint Consultation Committees, and a corresponding rise in 'domestic' (i.e. plant-level) bargaining. Related to this again, the number of work stoppages has increased in federated establishments (in the Engineering Industry – KC) by 23 per cent and the number of working days lost as a result rose by 82 per cent.

Direct workshop representation is, in other words, replacing 'the concessionary management device of joint consultation'. In this atmosphere the 'legitimate aspirations' of workpeople to have a say in the control and direction of the enterprises in which they work are less and less capable of being 'canalized', and more and more likely to erupt into their own consciously formulated demands. Until now these demands have tended to remain close to the present experiences of workers, and, as a result, to take on a partial, regional or local significance. This tendency has been reinforced by the whole post-war tradition of the shop-stewards' movement, which began its evolution towards the present state of affairs during the Attlee Government's 'wage-freeze', which in Britain was paradoxically responsible for the initial growth of the phenomenon of wage-drift (or the widening gap between basic rates of pay, usually nationally negotiated, and actual earnings, including locally negotiated piece-work and bonus increments and overtime), which has recently triggered off such complaints from the National Incomes Commission. As local managements found the need to bid up wages in competition for scarce labour, and shop-stewards discovered both the need to fend for themselves and the possibility of doing it rather well, decentralization of wage-bargaining set in with a vengeance. Socialist militants have frequently registered the results of this with some pleasure, because it tends to feed the image of an activist rank and file and a lethargic bureaucracy dominating the central apparatus of the Unions. This image is by no means without its reference point in reality, but it is often very over-simplified. The price of this decentralization was high, both in terms of apathy (if local strikes are not 'a private solution to public problems', then at least they are often a less-than-public solution of them), and in terms of fragmentation and loss of political consciousness. It is strange that more attention has not been paid to this phenomenon in relation to the Labour Party's crisis during the fifties – it is no coincidence that Labour's revival came after a number of fierce attacks on the Unions by the Conservative administration of 1959–64.

Be that as it may, Topham documents a remarkable change in the character of the shop-stewards. He quotes the findings of Professor Turner[1] on the causes of strikes, as given by strikers themselves: between 1940 and 1960, if one excludes strikes in the mining industry, which is still a separate universe in these matters, the proportion of strikes about wage matters *other than* demands for increases', or about 'working arrangements, rules and discipline', rose from one-third to three-quarters of the total. This gives us a measure, not simply of the extent of the 'drift', but also of the changing mood of the workers. There is additional evidence on this score. In 1960 the T.U.C. General Council published their report on 'Disputes and Workshop Representation'[2] which analysed the results of four separate questionnaires, covering the cost of dispute pay to affiliated Unions between 1956 and 1959, details of both official and unofficial strikes in 1958 and 1959, and details of stoppages in which one Union found its members unable to work because members of other unions were on strike. One hundred and forty seven Unions representing seven and a half million workers replied, and this response proved completely unambiguous: only 32 per cent of strikes during that period had been directly about money, and these included cases in which workers had been resisting attempts by employers to reduce wages; 29 per cent were about dismissals, 20 per cent were caused by disciplinary dismissals of stewards or other members, and 9 per cent concerned redundancies. The remainder were about recognition, non-unionism, breach of agreements, changes in work systems, demarcation and dilu-

[1] H. A. Turner, *The Trend of Strikes*, 1963, p. 8, cited Topham, op. cit., p. 6.
[2] *T.U.C. Report*, pp. 125–6.

tion, bad working conditions or complaints about supervisors. When the Unions concerned were able to differentiate between 'underlying causes' as opposed to stated causes, this had the effect of still further reducing the proportion of disputes over wages. The power of shop-stewards was originally fostered and extended by the growth of local negotiations about wages. The strike-record makes it clear that their power is now firmly rooted, and able to burgeon into very much wider fields.

If one accepts that strikes are still relatively uncommon occurrences in British industry, and moves on to examine the normal working of shop-stewards in less turbulent conditions, this story is sharply confirmed. According to Clegg, Killick and Adams, in their survey *Trade Union Officers*,[1] which contains a comprehensive study of the role of stewards in the working of the Unions, the average steward spends six hours a week of his working time and five of his own on a whole range of Trade Union duties. By far the most important of these concern negotiations with foremen and managers. Following these in importance, as a proportion of stewards' time, comes the item 'consultation with constituents and discussions with other stewards'. Together these took up 69 per cent of the time spent on Union business by stewards covered in the survey.[19] When the same stewards were asked to define the priority of their Trade Union aims,[3] 23 per cent of them thought that first was 'better wages and conditions'. But 21 per cent thought that the main thing was 100 per cent organization, 14 per cent that it was 'creating unity between workers', and 10 per cent that it was 'fullest use by the rank and file of the democratic procedures of the Union'. With the 5 per cent who put 'creating political consciousness' first, this amounts to 50 per cent who saw their main Trade Union aims as turning around the development and consolidation of workpeople's *power*. Of course, this power will lever pence out of the employers: but it also poses them with deeper problems, to which cash offers no immediate solution. Even when one looks at the 19 per

[1] 1961.
[2] Clegg, Killick and Adams, pp. 149–80.
[3] Ibid, p. 262.

cent who put first the priority 'effective consultation with the management', one may suspect that this does not always mean quite what the official propagandists of consultation expect.

The sum of these developments has been calculated and expressed by a whole number of close observers of the industrial landscape, many of whom are very far from being disaffected radicals. Speaking of 'something like a revolution in our industrial relations', Arthur Marsh notes that full employment has extended the Trade Union expectations of craftsmen to all the workers, who, since the war, have 'been able to rely more on the fact that employers have been competing for labour of all kinds, that they have been reluctant to lose workers, and unable and unwilling to back their authority by large-scale or selective dismissals. *Work group sanctions against management have gradually become effective, and "management by consent" generally necessary.*'[1] To this picture, Alan Flanders adds: 'The steward's formal role under our traditional system of collective bargaining was largely that of watchdog and policeman. Earnings drift has rendered that view of their role totally unrealistic. Today they are negotiators in their own right, *rule makers as well as rule enforcers.*'[2]

It would be wrong to find in these signs an omen of immediately impending upheaval. Shop-stewards are – contrary to the Press image of them – responsible men. Their average age is in the forties. They have family responsibilities which weigh as heavily on them as on their workmates. The political implications of their situation do not confront them in clear, lucid prescriptions, but are refracted through a fog of local prejudices, overlapping and at times conflicting group interests, irrational organizational boundaries. At the head of their Unions often stand, not the kind of men who can see over all the territory and pierce its obscurities with the insight drawn from a live movement of many thousands of people, but anxious, timid and purblind intriguers, who try to chart their

[1] Arthur Marsh, *Managers and Shop Stewards*, Institute of Personnel Management, 1963, p. 17.

[2] In a paper on 'The Importance of Shop Stewards'.

paths through an alien countryside (which they imagine they know well) by landmarks which have long since ceased to exist (and which they recreate in their imagination, hazier each time, day by day). Beyond these structural deformities in the vision of the labour movement, lies the mystery of capitalist property relations itself.

But today the problems which capital itself has created are fiercely sharpening the outlines, and settling the fog. Neo-capitalism is forced to 'plan', to rationalize itself, and above all to constrain and discipline its labour force; in doing so, it precipitates new problems and objectives for the Unions. The pace at which this has occurred has noticeably increased in the past few years. Indeed, the election of a Labour Government is only one early result of its gathering force, and by no means the ultimate one. Having created the wage-drift, and reactivated the Trade Unions on a local, fragmented basis, neo-capitalism is now in the process of recentralizing them, and giving them new, more integrated and probing policies. But just as the rise of stewards' power was not the result of an act of will by the employers, even though many of them individually fed it and contributed to it, so this new co-ordination is not likely to fall into the set patterns which would enable the established powers to approve it. To be sure, there are now many strange new advocates of industrial Unions, as the business Press begins to evaluate the effects of 'anarchy' in the Unions on the new planning machinery which is being established. But the Unions have not up to now proved amenable to such schemes: if they are to regroup, and streamline their organizations, then very many of their members will insist that this must be under their own banners, in pursuit of their own objects. Paradoxically, this process has been assisted by the very attacks which have been launched to inhibit Trade Union powers. The effect of pay pauses, National Incomes Commissions, rationalization schemes of the Beeching variety, and even the notorious Rookes versus Barnard judgement which placed the right to strike itself in jeopardy, has been to stimulate political consciousness and to turn Trade Union activists away from narrow sectionalism. Clearly the pursuit of political answers to some of the most urgent problems faced by shop-stewards does not in the least imply any retreat from gains won locally. At the local level, the Unions will remain combative, jealous of their powers, and anxious to develop their strength. New political tasks do not in the least imply that one should let go of control of hire and fire, or give away rest breaks, or abandon any of the powers which have been wrested away from the formerly unchallenged disposition of management. On the other hand, the defence of such gains itself comes to insist that a larger view of the world be taken, and that effective nation-wide resistance be offered to the concerted probes which have recently been undertaken to test whether any of the Unions' gains can be recouped from them. The most serious of these probes is beyond any doubt the sustained pressure for an incomes policy, which has simultaneously taken shape in almost every country in Europe in the last few years, and which threatens *all* the major Union advances in a very direct manner.[1]

The campaign for an incomes policy poses on a new plane the very old problem of how capital can co-exist with a powerful Trade Union movement. Beneath all the trimmings of welfare in which neo-capitalism is bedecked, this basic con-flict has in no way been resolved. Now, however, neo-capital-ism faces many closed doors which were at one time open to its forerunners. Above all, the pre-war disciplinary force of sus-tained unemployment, running into millions, is not an option today. Meanwhile, international competition demands that margins be considered ever more tightly, and basic costs be budgeted over longer periods within narrower limits of fluctua-tion. Hence the overriding concern about inflation, and the constant pre-occupation with the 'stabilization' of wage-costs. Wages must be brought under control if the cutting edge of capital is not to be dulled to a degree intolerable to its masters.

---

[1] Some useful documentation on this appears in *International Socialist Journal*, No. 3, June 1964. The issue includes a general analysis by Vittorio Foa, Deputy Secretary of the Italian C.G.I.L., and reports on the state of play in England, France, Italy and Federal Germany.

Those spokesmen of the labour movement who are closest to the acceptance of neo-capitalism pure and simple have already drawn an appropriate moral from this. They see the role of the Labour Government as being that of rationalizer-extraordinary to a system which is short-winded, queazy and directionless. To liberate the power of efficient and well-directed greed, they will happily treat with the Unions, offering to exchange such meagre cash-benefits as they can afford against a surrender of power. So, well-known Fabians write of a controlled war against wage-drift, which of course involves quite simply an offensive against the powers of shop-stewards:[1] they speak of the 'relegation of collective bargaining machinery to a secondary place in the structure':[2] and they discuss the price which Unions may or may not demand as compensation for loss of powers in this realm.[3] In all this can be discerned a pattern of authoritarian paternalism, which assumes a standard of 'fairness' in income distribution which has only to be announced, and then applied by civil servants, to produce universal harmony and rocketing economic advance. In fact, no such standard is possible: while the overwhelming majority of goods are distributed on the market, and not by means of welfare services, 'fairness' will always be determined in the course of argument and the interplay of rival interests, unless totalitarian edicts are to prescribe its limits. More: far from representing a drag on productivity, this argument is generally a stimulus to it. Certainly, under capitalism, Union demands represent a continual goad to technological advance, indeed, they often pose the most serious questions of organization that are ever faced by an increasingly lethargic economic directorate. This point was made, in a heavy-handed way, by

[1] Cf. W. E. J. McCarthy, 'The Price of Wage Restraint'. *New Society*, 5 March 1964.

[2] Cf. Stewart and Winsbury. 'An Incomes Policy for Labour', *Fabian Tract*, 1963.

[3] McCarthy, op. cit. Others, including, rather terrifyingly, Ray Gunter, who is now Minister of Labour, have allowed themselves to discuss this matter in more brutal terms. A heated controversy on Gunter's views broke out in the A.E.U. Journal in mid-1964.

Charles Babbage as long ago as 1832, and it has lost none of its force with the concentration of industrial power and the growth of bureaucratic forms of administration. Paternalist Fabianism is in great danger when it plays with these types of policy. Its advocates seldom show any awareness of the extent to which all the freedoms that they empirically support, are underpinned by the existence of an independent Trade Union movement. The statification of Union powers clearly demands fierce inroads in the freedom of movement of Unions, above all at local level. In the last analysis, Unions do not exist anywhere else than at local level. If apathy and demoralization set in at the root, the leading Trade Union 'planners', who flit from office to office in Whitehall in order to discuss guesses about production levels and fiats about wages, will become increasingly empty poseurs.[1] Without active and politically alive shop-stewards behind them, they can be discarded by any government commission which tires of them. As for the Labour Party, without enthusiasm in the factories it is a shroud for unattained dreams.

A heavy responsibility rests, then, on Trade Union activists under a Labour Government. Confronted with crisis on a dozen fronts at once, the Labour Government will insistently press for agreement on an incomes policy. This places the Unions between two perils. If they agree, their vital powers are at stake. If they refuse, they must fear the fall of the Government, which cannot be seen as an advantage to the workers. What, then, is to be done?

It is here that the traditional demand for workers' control takes on a new meaning, gathering a hard relevance that can turn it from a concern of a few militants into the central strategic demand of the day. The unions can hardly refuse to negotiate with their own Government on incomes policy. But they can set their own price for starting talks, provided it is reasonable. And the elementary price for beginning a discussion on incomes policy is hard information about what incomes *are*. The employers will enter talks on this matter furnished

[1] As Frank Cousins wisely pointed out to the 1963 T.U.C.: cf. *T.U.C. Report*, 1963, p. 399.

with data which can tell them to the last halfpenny what the incomes of the workpeople are. They know all about wages, because they control the payment of them. But the workers know the next best thing to nothing about the incomes of the employers. A point which is commonly made in discussions of tax problems is almost inevitably forgotten when this matter is at issue: it is that rentier incomes can be camouflaged, split, hidden in themselves, in a thousand and one ways. Professor Titmuss[1] has shown in spellbinding detail some of the devices which can be used to convert personal incomes into capital or to lose them in a variety of separate identities. The same sort of analysis, applied to corporate evasions and manœuvres, would be doubly instructive. Today, complaints are heard on all sides that the balance–sheets which are prepared for public consumption do not even allow shareholders to form any intelligible picture of the real financial health of their companies.[2] Lurking in a hundred special reserves, or depreciation allowances, may lie endless delights in store for those who have the power to manipulate, shunt, dissemble and simply 'lose' the revenue of large firms. Where were the mistakes I discussed above, in the balance-sheets? Were they really mistakes, at all? Did some of the planning snags arise purely for the benefit of the tax men? If such suspicions are merely uninformed socialist prejudices, libellous to boot, no doubt the British Employers' Confederation will be pleased to recommend to its members that they open their accounts to Trade Union inspection, thus allowing the Trade Union movement to judge for itself on what basis it needs to negotiate about incomes policy.

Of course, any incomes policy which the Unions even begin to consider must be redistributive. It must take from the haves, and give to the have-nots. Even the most timid, paternalistic supporters of conformity in the Unions will agree to this. The policy will be judged in the light of its ability to reduce rentier incomes and add to the sector of wages and salaries. But it is

---

[1] *Income Distribution and Social Change*, 1962.
[2] Cf. Harold Rose's Eaton Paper, published by the Institute of Economic Affairs, 'Disclosure in Company Accounts,' (1963).

impossible to uphold even the status quo in this field, once you approach the problem through a centralized decision, unless you have the necessary prior information. If the employers' accounts are not open to them, the Union leaders will be blind-folded. Only fools or men who want to lose play such delicate games as these blindfold. But supposing the General Council tells the Labour Government that before it can negotiate an incomes policy, it must see the books? Then we shall see an immediate strengthening, rather than enervation, of the Trade Unions at local level. The national leadership of Unions can-not effectively inspect the accounts of all the firms with which they have negotiating connections, and even if they could see them all, they could never decipher them. But the shop-stewards *can* unravel their own employers' mysteries, given a modicum of professional advice, which many of them could afford to secure at the drop of a hat. Once the accounts are open in sufficient detail, then depreciation claims come home to shop level, and the experience of the workers concerned will be ever liable to discover any snags or contentious areas which may exist. Questionable allowances will be delimited by such grass roots inspection, and if necessary the inland revenue can be called in to adjudicate. Since no one objects to Pay As You Earn when applied to employees, it is difficult to see on what ground such an innovation can be rejected by employers.

If the Unions stand out for this right before starting talks on incomes policy, they will neither weaken their own powers nor threaten the Labour Government. The ball will be in the employers' court, and if they prove hesitant or petulant about the matter, this will present Labour with an excellent cam-paigning issue. An election fought on such a matter would not be a difficult one for the Left. Of course, if such data are secured by the Unions, it may still not result in an acceptable policy on incomes: and they may be compelled to stand their ground on other issues. But at least they will know the score, talks will be conducted on an almost equal footing (almost, because workers' inspection of the accounts only adds to the *risk* involved in distorting them, and will in any case vary in efficiency and rigour) and judgements will therefore lack the perilous, gambling uncertainty with which they will otherwise undoubtedly be fraught.

This approach would remove some of the shibboleths engendered by the dominance of private property over men's minds. The present pattern of rewards, and the absurd tolerance of the private appropriation of the results of public effort, will come to seem less and less 'natural'. When they see precisely how far 'self-financing' has become the norm in private industry, workers will begin to wonder why the results of their effort cannot be invested in their own name rather than to the credit of some rentier. Clause Four of the Labour Party's constitution will cease to be an inspirational icon. From an intensification of the campaign for workers' control, we shall prepare for the leap towards new political and social forms, to self-management.

3

The transition to socialism in Britain is not necessarily a matter of decades. The weight of the problems of capitalism is so heavy and their effect has so disoriented the political guides and leaders of the system, that it seems clear that it is only the inertia and lack of insight of the Labour Movement that allows the whole system to continue. To develop a strategy of advance is the crucial task of the Left today: but this cannot be done if we are not prepared to discuss socialism itself. The goal will cast its own shape on the path we beat towards it.

To say that duality of power ceases to exist once industry is socialized would be a truism, were the word 'socialized' to refer not merely to the juridical ownership of plant, but also to the product. If socialist, or welfare, forms of distribution were general, many present conflicts would be inconceivable. These conflicts arise essentially between opposed interests, which generate opposed ideals, appealing to property and democracy respectively. Although the antithetical natures of private property and democracy are often obscured, deliberately, by ideologists who offer verbal resolutions of the real contradiction, and as a reflex response by people who are thinking within a climate in which it appears as 'natural', none the less it is constantly reasserted in the struggles which take place every day in almost every enterprise. On workpeople's side, the development of democratic ideas under capitalism is inseparable from the development of solidarity. Yet this solidarity is not to be interpreted, as it has been on many occasions, as a founding charter for monolithic discipline in *socialist* factories. The problem of self-management begins with a recognition that each worker has a complex of interests, often divergent ones, involving him as consumer, as producer and as citizen. These must persist as long as the division of labour itself compels men to adopt fixed roles during formative parts of their lives. Such interests will align him with some other men into shifting groups and lobbies, and oppose him to some other men at every major turn of the decision-making process. Either these interests will achieve open and satisfying expression, or they will be muffled, frustrated, and thwarted, thus producing an inhibiting apathy which will drive them further and further underground, sterilizing the creative force which they represent.

Yet those who have witnessed this process at work in countries in which the democratic process has been paralysed over long periods, frequently identify it with the dehumanization of labour under capitalist relations of production, and then telescope all problems of dehumanization together, locating them all in the problem of the popular administration of industry. This is mistaken. The traditional socialist answer to the search for the source of the de-humanization of labour under capitalism involves an integrated critique of the force of the market and the division of labour which it produces: these phenomena express themselves in forms of property. Unless the constrictions of private property can be overcome, we cannot begin to get to grips with the problem of overcoming the tyranny of the market, and with it the division of labour itself. This means that for a socialist the problem of the market can never be a secondary one. Our strategy can never be limited to moves designed to ameliorate the labour process (desirable in themselves though these may be), because our problem is that of overcoming the compulsion to labour itself, and abolishing with it the whole preformed and viciously mutilating division of labour which aligns men into classes and divides classes into castes, stamping rank on the faces of people and dissolving their common humanity. How far can labour be humanized by democratizing industry? The answer is complex: but some things about it are very simple indeed. If we speak of humanizing labour,[1] we are speaking of developing the' labourer's freedom. This freedom is a capacity for self-realization, or it is nothing. But we are members of one another. Our selves are not contained in our skins, but learnt from the people around us in reciprocal human action. For this reason, the division of labour, having opened doors to freedom, becomes a cruel barrier to it. A democratically-run sand-foundry is a far better place than one run by order: but in a world where some men ride round the moon or sing in Fidelio a foundryman is not a *free* man. To secure an explosion in the amount of free time, in which men can travel, work, design or speculate by turns as their wish takes them, we must liberate a technological and productive explosion which can underpin it. Of course, this requires a planned, co-ordinated effort. But precisely here, in the pursuit of the goal of freedom, we find the commonest alibi for ignoring what remains a vital question, that of self-management.

For self-management is essentially a problem of democratic planning. It would be foolish to assume that this is solved, even at the blue-print stage. Whilst we can learn something important from experiments which have already been made, we have most of the work to do ourselves. Even in Yugoslavia, the problem is so far from being solved that it is not impossible that we may yet regard that country as an object-lesson in pitfalls, rather than the brave pilot which it looked like being in the beginning. The Yugoslav assumption that the encroachment of bureaucracy can only be combated by decentralization and increased sensitivity to the demands of the market, tends to

---

[1] If we do, strictly speaking we are erring. The humanization of *work* involves the *abolition* of labour, as Marx was concerned to point out again and again.

reduce the question of democratic control to one of an increasingly meaningless local autonomy, and gradually replaces a central, conscious, willed network of decisions by impalpable and unseen economic pressures. The market calls out for power to repair the damage done by the market, and a complex of incentives invades even hospitals and schools in a vain attempt to check bureaucracy by increasing differentials. All this feeds the fragmentation of workpeople, and multiplies their apathy. This makes it increasingly difficult to evolve corrective policies. One hopes this pessimistic picture will be falsified. But the Yugoslav experience reinforces the view that the key to the problem of democratic planning involves the discovery of means by which we can institutionalize, and thereby legitimize, conflicts about the priorities of the master plan itself. Such conflicts are bound to be serious even in the most advanced countries, where they are extremely unlikely to be resolved in appeals to charismatic forces and individuals 'above the battle'.

To see these difficulties is not to solve them. The solutions will not be easy, and are unlikely to be reached by a process of speculation. Men will hammer out their institutions on the problems that they face with the forces that they have. It is a very practical process, and it gets into books after it has happened. But we have half a century of warnings about some of the problems of the transition we will soon be entering, and we would be fools to ignore them.

But we can clear the way for action. In less than a generation we *can* see, if we wish it, the beginnings of a new style of men, who will have miles to grow and universes to subdue, but who will never have taken an order, or been afraid of other men, or done an action without knowing why.

WORK AND CONSUMPTION

André Gorz

1. *Oppression*

Irrespective of its level or of how it is organized, working-class education tends to produce men whose knowledge and responsibility have been stunted. The most 'advanced' firms dream of integrating workers from the cradle to the grave so as to limit their horizons to those of the company. At birth, their baby-clothes are supplied; at death, their coffins; in between, their technical education, housing and organized leisure are all taken care of.

From the start it is of primary importance that a worker should not be given (or allowed to get) an education more advanced than his specialized job demands. At a recent employers' conference, a top French industrialist candidly explained that this was 'to avoid problems of adjustment'. The worker must not be allowed to comprehend the work process as a whole, or to grasp the creative essence of the act of work – with all the possibilities of initiative, reflection and decision which this entails, among them that of selling his labour elsewhere.

Industry always demands for its repetitive jobs – from the comptometer operator in a bank or insurance company to the solderer in an electronics firm – a passive and ignorant labour force. Workers are recruited straight from school and they are trained either on the job or in company schools where they acquire, not a trade giving them independence and dignity, but a company qualification which is only of use in the firm which employs them. The company thus asserts not only a kind of ownership right over its employees' lives, but also the right to fix the terms of work at will: qualifications, the price of work, schedules, speeds, piece-rates, etc.

Even for skilled workers in industries which require a higher degree of professional training, the productive process remains opaque and elusive. For the semi-skilled worker, the main contradiction is between the active, potentially creative essence of all work and the passive status to which he is reduced by the standardized, repetitive tasks which the semi-automatic assembly line forces on him, turning him into a harassed adjunct of the machinery and robbing him of all initiative and even of independent thought. However, as a worker's qualifications increase, the dominant contradiction is between the active essence of the work he does, with its scope for technical initiative, and the role of passive operator which the company hierarchy imposes on him.

With the exception of a few industries which are rapidly decreasing in importance and which still depend on simple manual labour, an increasingly high level of technical training is required today. But this greater technical responsibility is not matched by any corresponding measure of control over the conditions to which the worker is subjected – conditions which determine how his technical skills are used. Nor, of course, does he have any control over what is produced. He is responsible for his work, but he is not master of the conditions under which he works. The company demands that he show imagination in his job *and* that he submit passively to the discipline and standards prescribed by the management.

At the confines of a civil society which is formally free, industry maintains a despotic and authoritarian society, under a hierarchy and discipline of military character, which demands of its workers both unconditional obedience and active participation in their own oppression. Whenever the chance arises, this militarized society tends to expand beyond the limits of the company, invading every sphere of civil life, and claiming for itself the right to represent the realities of capitalist society itself. It advances authoritarian principles wherever it can, recommending the suppression of the right of free inquiry, of criticism, of discussion and assembly; its ideal social model is the man who is active, but submissive and narrow-minded, and whose skills, however extensive, are solely employed in the technical field. In fact, the majority of wage-claims are revolts against just this kind of oppression – revolts against the systematic mutilation of the worker's personality, against the stunting of his professional and human faculties, against the subordination of the nature and content of his working life to technological developments which rob him of his powers of initiative, control and even foresight. Wage claims are much more frequently motivated by *rebellion against working conditions* than by a revolt against the economic *burden of exploitation* born by labour. They express a demand for *as much money as possible to pay for the life wasted, the time lost, the freedom alienated* in working under these conditions. The workers insist on being paid as much as possible *not because they put wages* (money and what it can buy) *above everything else* but because, *Trade Union action being what it is at present,* workers can fight the employer only for *the price* of their labour, not for control of the conditions and content of their work.

In short, the worker – even the highly-paid worker – tries to sell himself as dearly as possible because he cannot avoid *having* to sell himself. And conversely, whatever the price he manages to get for his freedom, that price will never compensate him for the human loss he has suffered; however much he squeezes out of his employers, it will never give him control of his working life, never give him the freedom to determine his own situation.

It is evident then, that pure wage claims deflect and conceal much deeper claims – worse than that, they are a dead-end which the workers' movement has reached. For wage disputes by themselves tend to serve the employer's own wishes: to be left with the power to organize the productive process at will, the power to regulate, qualitatively and quantitatively, the content and relations of labour; in compensation for which – and for the additional mutilations they can now impose – the employers are ready to grant wage increases. Wage claims as such accept the fundamental criterion of a profit-motivated economy, namely that everything has a price, that money is the supreme value, that you can do anything and everything with human beings as long as you pay. They leave capitalist management free to pursue the maximization of profit, to rule society unchallenged, in exchange for the choice scraps capital hands down from its boardroom table. Wage claims as such allow industry to manufacture a new proletariat: a lobotomized proletariat, whose eight hours of daily degradation and work against the clock leaves them with only the weary desire to escape – an escape which manipulators of leisure and culture sell them on credit in their homes while they convince them that they are living in the best of all possible worlds.

If the working class is to preserve its vocation as a ruling class, it must attack, first and foremost, working conditions at the place of work. It is there, where the worker – both as producer and citizen – is most directly alienated, that capitalist society can be most directly contested. It is there that the workers can reject oppressive work-relations, subject them through conscious action to organized workers' control, determine the conditions of labour through their persistent will to attain independence, and thus maintain and assert their class consciousness. It is there that they can strive towards the human emancipation of the worker as their supreme goal.

This reconquest of the worker's independence within the productive process 'is the keystone of any Trade Union's assessment of its future,' the Italian trade-unionist Vittorio Foa has written.[1] 'Democracy in an industrial society is at stake. In an advanced capitalist society, the specific organization of labour tends increasingly to dissociate the moment of decision from the moment of execution. It tends to reduce the worker to a docile instrument who cannot participate in the productive process as a whole or in its relations with society. In other words, it tends to subordinate the worker rigidly to the decisions taken by the employers to increase their profits.

[1] Vittorio Foa, *Problemi del Socialismo*, March and June, 1963.

Even the desired aim of improving the distribution of income is made use of to turn the worker, with his own complicity, into a certain sort of consumer in order to increase the system's profits by raising the level of mass consumption. However much the political sphere is enlarged institutionally, the laws of social production tend to become more and more independent of political democracy, and of commonly recognized rights – freedom of thought, of the Press, of association, etc. Experience shows that this fundamental lack of freedom in modern work-relations is a permanent threat to general, public liberties . . . .

'Some theoreticians believe that the subordination of workers is an inevitable result of modern productive organization, whether under capitalism or socialism; this would imply the condemnation of industrial society as such, and the problem could perhaps only be overcome in post-industrial society, when human labour would be completely replaced by machines. We do not accept this inevitability: we have confidence in the ability of the popular will to achieve democracy.

'Others again think that the oppression of the workers springs exclusively from private ownership of the means of production and that, once capital has been publicly expropriated, workers' liberties will be assured. Again, this is not quite the case. Socialist power can expropriate the private capitalist and so create the premises of workers' freedom; but if the organization of production in the firm and in the economy as a whole remains bureaucratized through a rigid schema of centralized decisions, the workers will experience social production as an alien process and will be subordinated to it in some respects as they are in capitalist countries today.

'The key problem of industrial society, with its developed organization of production and labour, is how to achieve a democratization of work. At the stage of advanced capitalism, democracy must find forms which spring from the workers' condition, which are deeply involved in it and which consequently embrace the whole human condition.

'The problem of democracy in industrial society can, therefore, wait neither on post-industrial society nor on socialism.
It must be posed now. And this is precisely what the Trade
Union, in the highest form of its struggle, can do in factories
and whole industries.'

2. Counter-Powers

But what is the highest form of struggle? How should it be
engaged? How can the oppression which the workers undergo at the place of work – and in their whole lives – be overcome? Some well-meaning people believe the answer lies in
fighting for the recognition, at the place of work, of the
citizen's formal liberties (assembly, speech, association, etc.),
for the Trade Union's legal recognition in the firm. By putting
the question the wrong way round they neatly suppose it to be
solved. If indeed Trade Unions were the *concrete* embodiment
of liberty (or the promise of liberation) for the workers; if they
were capable of setting out *mobilizing objectives* geared to the
workers' self-determination of their work condition, then the
problems of Trade-Union recruitment and combativity, and
of the role of the Unions in the firm, would be solved. The
workers would already be busy fighting for control over the
conditions and organization of their work; they would impose
recognition (whether legal or not) of the Trade Union branch
by force.

But the fact is that French trade-unionism, at least, has not
yet succeeded in expressing the struggle against oppression and
for workers' control by means of mobilizing objectives. Of
course, this is a difficult thing to do. It is clear, also, that combat, when there has been any, has been badly managed. The
struggle for the emancipation of the worker at his work has
remained on the level of abstract general ideas. The Unions'
attitude has reflected an old Jacobin failing – of approaching
the problem from a juridical and institutional angle. A case in
point was the Renault dispute, early in 1963, when the Trade
Union *added* a demand for increased Union powers to their
claim for a fourth week of paid holidays. The outcome was

typical. They were granted the week, for which they were ready to fight, but refused any increase in power, for which, understandably, they were not ready to fight. For the workers will fight for the Union when it says what it wants to do, concretely, about immediate, specific labour problems, but not if it asks to be strengthened first in order to act later. They will fight for civil liberties in the factory (and outside) when they know why these are demanded and what they are to be. But not before.

Experience has shown that guaranteeing civil liberties in the place of work does not *in itself* bring the slightest scrap of power or workers' control. Moreover, *as long as such liberties are formal and abstract,* they can just as easily be means for attempting to integrate the Trade Union in the system, to bureaucratize the union and thus to secure its co-operation with paternalistic employers. This is what has happened in the U.S.A., in Sweden and, to some extent, in West Germany. The demand for recognition of the Trade Union and civil liberties within the firm remains an *abstract* claim, incapable of mobilizing the workers, as long as it is not organically bound to claims for concrete powers over the relations of work. Recognition of Trade Union and civil liberties at the place of work is not an end in itself. Its value lies only in the content (i.e. specific workers' powers) it makes possible.

This content entails Trade Union control over every aspect of work relations, so that:

1. The demands of the productive process are subordinated and adjusted to the needs of the workers;

2. The scope given to the employers' arbitrary judgement is restricted;

3. A real workers' *counter-power* is eventually set up, capable of contesting and positively countering the decision-making systems of capitalist management in the company – and by extension in society.

These three interconnected aspects of the demand for workers' control over work-relations are in fact more concrete, from the point of view of mobilization and action, than straightforward wage claims (which are necessarily included

in them). In practice, the content of work-relations is left
entirely to the employers' arbitrary judgement, because of the
opaqueness of the productive process as a whole, and the
workers' ignorance of the economic and technical decisions
which determine their conditions of work. In most cases, the
Trade Union confines itself to negotiating the minimum price
for labour-power, leaving the employer free to exploit the
labour force in whatever way and in whatever conditions are
convenient to him. He can add bonuses to the contractual minimum rates, which are usually completely under his control
and which, by definition, are not part of an industrial agreement. Thus an increase in the basic wage can be made without
any practical effect, or can even be neutralized by intensifying
the rate of work (i.e. by extorting more work); by quickening
the tempo and cutting down on bonuses; by putting in new
machinery which makes the job more complex, without granting any correlated rise in gradings or wages; by the downgrading of workers (whether accompanied or not by a cut in
wages), so that they suffer a loss of professional status, a halt
in the development of their capacities and a loss of independence at work.

Demands for a general wage increase are incapable, in this
situation, of remedying the deterioration in the workers' condition. They are incapable of obtaining a cutback in the rates of
profit and exploitation, they are even incapable of measuring
what impact, if any, wage rises have on the rate of profit. But,
above all, wage claims in big industries are incapable of
covering situations as different as those of semi-skilled workers
earning between £7 and £20 a week, depending on whether
they are men or women and on where they work, of skilled
workers earning between £12 and £30 a week and of technicians whose salary, similarly, can be three times as high in
one town or job as in another.

The extreme differentiation of working conditions and
wages within the same industry and for the same work prevents the working class from mobilizing behind undifferentiated, general demands for minimum, hourly wage rates.
Generalized, undifferentiated watchwords are not enough;

they cannot unite and mobilize the working class which is extremely differentiated within itself. They cannot initiate the offensive against the employers' discretionary powers over economic and technical management, or against the differing growth rates of productivity, wages and profits.

This is why the first priority for the workers' movement today is to work out a new strategy and new objectives which will *indissolubly unite demands affecting wages, management and self-determination*. The only way to *mobilize and unite* a differentiated working class is to *attack the class power* wielded by employer and State. And the only way to attack this class power is to capture a *key sector of the power* of decision and administration from *each employer* (the State included).

In concrete terms the objectives of this attack should not be those of modifying and adapting the workers' condition *within* a given management policy and a given stage of technical development. Any victories of this kind, which would bear only on non-generalizable objectives, would be at the mercy of technical progress and new work patterns; such victories would rapidly be forfeited. On the contrary, the workers' movement should demand *permanent* power, written into contracts, to determine every aspect of work relations and the criteria of payment. Any modification in the production process would have to be negotiated with the workers. The workers' movement would thus be able to influence management policy and steer it in the desired direction. For example:

The Trade Union must be able to control *apprenticeship schemes and schools* and make certain that they train, not robots – half-men, whose horizons have been blocked by the *non-knowledge* they are burdened with – but professionally independent workers, whose training has been many-sided and who can advance in their profession at least as quickly as technology advances.

The Trade Union must be able to control the *organization of work* and the way in which jobs are assigned. This is to ensure that changes of job and organization are such that they develop the faculties and the occupational independence of the workers – instead of restricting or downgrading them. Young workers in particular must not be restricted to degrading, compartmentalized jobs.

The Trade Union must also exert its power over the *division of labour*, at the level both of the firm and of the industry, in terms of technology of production and its foreseeable development. It must be able to impose on the employers, in each company, a level of employment and such departmental arrangements as are necessary to force them to adopt the productive techniques and the division and organization of labour which are best from the workers' point of view. Technical progress must coincide with human progress.

The Trade Union must be able to determine contractually the schedules and speeds of work, piece-rates, job qualifications, time-tables, etc. This implies continuous negotiations and knowledge about technical changes and their repercussions on working conditions, as well as the power to influence them.

Finally, the Trade Union must demand a collective *output bonus*. This is a bonus fixed not in terms of individual productivity or profits, but by the production assured in a given number of hours. This bonus, which must be *added* to the basic wage – for which increases should be demanded simultaneously – is the first step by the workers to determining how company income should be distributed between payment for work, investment and amortization. The aim of this bonus is threefold:

1. The annual bonuses which are at present distributed like gifts or 'anti-strike rewards', as the management pleases, would be removed from the sphere of the employers' arbitrary decision. These bonuses must be included in the field of Trade Union negotiation and be based on objective criteria.

2. The annual bonus should be tied to the real rate of return on collective work, i.e. the progressive rise of production from the same number of hours worked. The Union's right to negotiate bonuses must necessarily be accompanied by the right to

have access to all information on the development of the firm's productivity, on the real or potential rate of profit and, in consequence, on the employers' management policy.

3. On the basis of this information the Trade Union could effectively oppose any worsening of the rate of exploitation and any expansion of the employers' field of initiative. It could ensure that *labour costs, in particular, form a proportion that is at least constant of the total cost of production whatever the state of productivity. In this way it could prevent 'cuts' in the labour force being a profitable operation,* and over-expansion an advantageous one. It could prevent any mistaken commercial policy (especially over-production) or a policy of dumping being carried out at the workers' expense. It could adjust its demands to take account of *all the leeway which increased productivity makes available to the employers.* In the end the Union would be able to negotiate every aspect of the firm's programme over its whole range: investments, reserves, direct and indirect wages, spare time and social expenditure, so that it exercised a power of control and veto over the total administration of the firm.

3. *Administration in Dispute*

The general objectives of this struggle can be differentiated and adapted to suit each local situation, for they include the widest range of specific demands and problems within a single class perspective. The struggle for the recognition and independence of the Trade Union in the firm fits naturally into the framework of these objectives, not as an ultimate goal but as an indispensable instrument of power: to contest, to control, to win the right to self-determination and decision at the point where the workers most directly experience their condition, experience the power of capital and their conflict with society; at the point where they must grasp the reality which crushes them if the transformation of society and the political power of the working class are to have any meaning for them – that is to say, at the place of their work.

Of course, this struggle will not abolish profits in one fell swoop; it will not bring about working-class *power*; it will not, even if it is victorious, abolish capitalism. It will lead on only to new battles and the possibility of new and partial victories. And during each stage, especially at the start, it must end in a compromise. It will start down a road full of ambushes. The Trade Unions will be forced into agreements with the employers; they will not be able to reject the employers' authority *in toto*, or dispute capitalist management in its entirety. They will have to be prepared to 'get their hands dirty'. With every compromise, with every agreement that comes out of the struggle, they will endorse the employers' power.

These facts must not be concealed or minimized. The line of action I have sketched out contains real dangers. Why then should it be preferable to the present tactics? Let us look a bit closer.

'We must not accept a system of management which is based on profit. We must carry the working class to power. We must not endorse the employers' power.' Of course, all socialists agree on this. But workers endorse the employers' power every day, by clocking in on time, by submitting to work which they have no hand in organizing, by taking home pay-packets. They accept the profit system at the same time; for them working-class power is no more than a dream. 'At least they do not soil their hands – or the Trade Union which embodies them does not; they remain free to contest everything *in toto*.' That is quite true. But their contentions, their rejection of the system, do not rise above the level of general intentions and speeches. They are abstract; their purity is sterile. They lack the ability to come to grips with reality. They leave the power of capital intact. They lack positiveness. They end up by falling into all the traps they claim to avoid.

In order, for example, to avoid class-collaboration, the Trade Union often tends not to be interested in agreements covering a factory or industrial sector. Collective agreements are tacitly phased out or allowed to fall into disuse because the Union does nothing about renewing them when they expire. Agreements are not signed after a battle for certain demands because the Trade Union does not intend to recognize the employers' power. Demands are not put in writing because the Trade Union leadership does not want to be compromised; instead it organizes partial actions to express a vague discontent and protest. Then it waits for the employers to come up with an offer. There must be no negotiations with the enemy; interrogations take the place of agreements. The Trade Union keeps its hands clean. What is gained by all this? An easy feeling of independence, that is to say – as far as practical victories over capitalist management are concerned – nothing at all. And what does the employer lose? Precisely the same: nothing. He too keeps his independence to manage the firm the way he sees fit, that is to say: to put in new plant when *he* wants to, to write off and invest according to *his* programme, to fix schedules, work programmes, systems of classification, etc., by whatever criteria work to his best advantage – even to pay his labour force *according to an anticipated budget*. For let us make no mistake about this: the safes of large modern firms are not full of banknotes which the workers must try to wrest from the employers' cupidity. They contain programmes. And these programmes include a safety margin: they are calculated so that *foreseeable* wage claims do not interfere with investment and amortization plans (whose variants are anticipated in terms of the possible economic contingencies) or plans for production.

Modern industry's dominant tendency is no longer the maximum exploitation of the workers by every means possible, the carrot and stick method. The dominant tendency (whose numerous exceptions represent the past, not the future) is to 'integrate' the workers into the system. The modern employer knows that piece-work does not 'pay'; he knows even better that in a big company, where fixed capital is more important than circulating capital, regularity is what matters most. To achieve this, it is fatal to stimulate individual output, because its high-points are followed by slack. Five per cent of the workers achieving 200 per cent to 300 per cent of the norm is worth less than a whole factory working *permanently at an average rate* of 100 per cent – an average made up, for example, by one-third working at 80 per cent, another third at

100 per cent and the remaining third at 120 per cent of the average output.

To obtain this regularity, the employer foresees the unforeseen – notably, wage claims. The tactics of the Trade Union which wants to keep its hands 'clean' hardly bother him at all. These tactics leave him with the power he most needs – the power of decision and administration, the power to determine the very pay rises he is going to be forced to give, to keep them within the limits he has fixed and to abstract these limits from any effective counter-claim.

The Trade Union's 'integration' therefore takes place within the very wage claims it puts forward and the concessions it wins. For these have been foreseen in the firm's programme, they have been integrated in advance in the management plan and, to all practical effect, do not counter it. Similarly, a Trade Union cannot hope effectively to contest a redundancy plan by protest movements following its announcement: the cost to the company of protest strikes will have been taken into account as part of the cost of the operation and the dismissals will take place, as foreseen, after being 'contested'. Thus the Trade Union still lacks any hold over the decisions and data of an employers' policy because, precisely, it rejects them entirely. This rejection is in itself a datum of management policy. In practice, management policy reigns supreme. The employers maintain the initiative. Constantly confronting the Trade Unions with new situations – economic, structural, technical, organizational – which condition vocational prospects, careers, workers' lives and relationships, they unfold them along lines which their strategy has laid down, leaving the Union with the sole choice of 'Yes' or 'No'. But its 'No' is unimportant; no *progress* is visible after all the battles the workers have fought. The same kind of battle is repeated time and again, and the workers always return to their point of departure.

Thus the conflict remains abstract. There is no link which unites day-to-day actions to ultimate aims (the reduction and suppression of exploitation, negotiation of all aspects of wages, guarantee of employment and promotions, a rising standard of living according to needs, the abolition of the dictatorship of profit); on the one hand there are long-term objectives and on the other day-to-day actions and there is hardly any connection between the two.

In contrast, if the Trade Union took the data used to plan management policy, if it anticipated employers' decisions, if at each step it put forward its own alternative solution, if it went into battle for its own solutions, then capitalist management would be disputed far more effectively than by any number of contentious speeches. The Trade Union would be in a position to exercise control over development (technical, productive, professional, etc.) and to direct it towards optimal social, human and economic aims. This supposes, for instance, that instead of fighting *against* dismissals and plans for reorganizing an industrial sector, it should fight *for* a plan of reorganization, reclassification and re-employment whose every aspect would be submitted to permanent Trade Union supervision. Instead of fighting against new machines and the new work patterns they impose, it should fight about the type of machines, the way they are installed, the new work patterns to expect, the classifications to be established, *before* the reorganization takes place. Instead of fighting against increased exploitation, it should fight to bring investment and amortization programmes under its control, ensuring that those which benefited the workers are put into effect.

'In acting like this, isn't the Trade Union accepting a capitalist-type management?' In a sense, yes; but I have already said that it accepts it just as much when it pretends to reject it but actually submits to it. The point is not to submit to it. It must be accepted *in order to change it*, in order to modify its basic data, in order to counter it point by point, and step by step, to force it in the direction the workers want: in brief, to force it into a crisis and make the adversary change his ground. After each partial victory, each reclassification, reorganization, investment or dismissal which the Trade Union prevents or imposes, the workers' power is reasserted; the workers' consciousness is heightened; and the employers' freedom and the sovereignty of capital are whittled away. The essential weakness of the system is revealed – the contradiction between the logic of profits and the needs and demands of men.

Is this class collaboration? Undoubtedly it would be if the Trade Union assumed the responsibilities of management – of 'co-management'. It would be if the Trade Union lost sight of the fact that its goal is not a modicum of improvement at any price but the emancipation of the workers and their right to determine their own condition. If the Trade Union agreed to *participate* in making decisions and guaranteed to apply them, that would be class collaboration. It is precisely this participation, which the advocates of 'co-management' want, that must be refused intransigently. It is not a matter of working out a neo-paternalist management policy with the employers, but of opposing Trade Union policies to those of the employers'. This means fighting for a factory plan, an industrial plan, a regional plan, all of which must be carefully and coherently worked out, all of which must concretely show the opposition between what is desirable and *possible* on the one hand, **and** what is realistic, from the standpoint of short-term financial profitability, on the other.

Obviously the battle will end in an argument or compromise. This will shock only ultra-leftists of the type Lenin censured, when he stressed that there were good as well as bad compromises. In this case, the compromise would be bad if the Trade Union *renounced* its plan and its goals, and rested content with an intermediate solution. But why should it give up anything? The arrangement which ends the battle means simply that everything could not be attained. The Trade Union comes to terms when the employers have adopted a substantial part of its plan. It exercises control over the way the plan is carried out. The battle ends in a partial victory, won after a hard struggle, and in a 'moral' victory which in itself is complete. For, during the course of the struggle, the workers' level of consciousness has been raised, and knowing that all their needs have not been satisfied, they are ready for new battles; they have tasted power. The measures they have imposed on the management tend in the direction of what they set out to achieve (although they have not yet got everything). They have not renounced their goal by coming to terms; on the contrary, they have got closer to it. The Trade Union surrenders none of its independence in coming to an arrangement (any more than when it accepts an 8 per cent rise after asking for 12 per cent). It does not guarantee the employers' plan; on the contrary, it forces the employers to guarantee, under Trade Union supervision, to carry out an essential part of the Trade Union's plan.

This strategy sets in motion Trade Union demands to negotiate every aspect of work relations in order to encroach on the employer's independence of management and, by extension, the power of employers and State. This is not a question of institutionalizing Trade Union power, but of building up a positive, antagonistic, counter-power which leaves Trade Union independence intact. This power, once secured, will make opposition to the employers' decisions permanent and *continuous*. It will enable the Trade Union to anticipate these decisions, in order to shape them before they are taken. It will put the workers on the offensive, not the defensive. It will heighten their level of consciousness and their ability. It will expand their knowledge of the productive process. It will make them state their objectives precisely – objectives set out according to a strategic, programmatic vision which they will use to dispute capitalist plans at every level of the factory, the industry, the region and the national economy itself. It will gear partial, local claims to a total, coherent answer or 'alternative' to neo-capitalism – a perspective which in turn will condition and clarify local choices. And it will encourage and stimulate continual advances in the struggle towards more highly developed objectives.

Thus, far from involving the development of particularism or factory 'patriotism', the demand for workers' power has an aggressive, mobilizing capacity. Its meaning, its opportunity, will come only from localized choices which are made in the context of a total answer to the model of capitalist development. It must have this global vision, for without that it will lack a vital correlation on the political plane (the plane on which

major decisions of national development and economic policy
are taken) – just as political action requires the existence of
mobilized and combative masses, not only to move forward but
also, and above all, as a popular *counter-power* able to respond,
in a decentralized manner and with specific, non-bureaucratic
initiatives, to the obstructive power wielded by private and
public decision-making centres.

It is thus quite natural that the demand for workers' powers
of self-determination and management should lead to the
questioning of the priorities and objectives of the capitalist
model of the economy and society.

THE PURPOSE OF WORK

In discussing the content of work relations, we have all the
time been dealing implicitly with the specific orientation given
to labour power by the functioning of capitalism. The theme
outlined under this heading was that of the *meaning*, or more
exactly the purpose, of work. We noted a *formal* contradiction between the active, potentially creative essence of work,
and the passive commodity status conferred on it by the employer who, by managing the conditions, relations and arrangements of the work process, rules arbitrarily and despotically
over the worker's vocational life. This contradiction, which is
experienced as oppression, goes hand in hand with a contradiction of substance. On the one hand, the *intrinsic* purpose of
work from the worker's point of view is to produce, through his
control over matter, wealth of value to men – and in doing so
to produce man as universal producer. On the other, its *ex-
trinsic* purpose from capital's viewpoint is to create surplus
value by the production of anything, no matter what – the
product's use-value being secondary to profit considerations;
and at the same time to produce workers who submit to the
exploitation of their labour power as an alien and hostile quantum – to produce alienated men. In short, for the worker,
labour has no meaning *except as the means of producing a
world for men*; for capital, it has no meaning *except as the*

means of producing profits, independently of the human utility of the products by which profit is made.

The worker's condition is invidious, then, not only because of the direct oppression exercised over work, but also because of the goals that capitalist exploitation assigns to work, and the consequent denial of meaning to the whole field of production. Every worker can experience this alienation more or less consciously in the form of the contradiction between his pride and love in a job well done and his frustration, shame and despair at having to do a job for reasons (of capitalist accumulation) and products which are often not worth the trouble spent on them. He knows that his work fails to answer real needs or essential priorities, that it does not correspond to the general interest of society.

1. *Some Concrete Alternatives*

The struggle against exploitation only gains its full meaning when it is undertaken as a struggle against the social consequences of exploitation: the false system of priorities, the combined wastage and shortage which advanced capitalism imposes on society as its model of 'consumer affluence'. To fight against the exploitation of work is necessarily also to fight *against the ends for which labour is exploited.*

It is less feasible than ever before to keep these two aspects apart, if the labour movement is to maintain its independence today. There is one logical conclusion to the policy of any working-class organization which, claiming to be non-political, tries to restrict its workers' action solely to the front of consumer demands, in the belief that these constitute the fight against exploitation. It will be bound to accept favourably – or at least without any resistance in principle – the proposals put to it by the capitalist State, which aim at incorporating the Trade Unions into the system. These proposals include long-term plans to limit the rate of profits and gear the level of wages to the increase in national income – proposals which question neither the overall rate of capitalist accumulation, the profit motive, the political and economic power of oligopolies, nor the biases and priorities which the search for maximum profit imposes on economic activity as a whole.

Moreover, to fight against exploitation in the name of consumer demands, without questioning the actual purpose of exploitation (i.e. accumulation) and the type and order of consumption offered by advanced capitalist society, is simply to immobilize the working class in a position of deference to the basic choices, values and ideas of that society. The system is, in fact, strengthened by the very piecemeal gains the Unions manage to win. Using the classic slogan of 'prosperity for all', these gains in wages, holidays and personal spending power, are promptly put to account by the Government or oligopoly which granted them, and by the consumer goods industries which rapidly turn them into sources of extra profits – with or without a rise in prices. As long as such economic demands are purely quantitative rather than qualitative, they fail to make any real impact on the system and hardly even contribute to the strengthening and heightening of class-consciousness.

Before going on to show how the workers can be made tangibly aware of goals for reorientating and transforming consumption and production, the inadequacy of quantitative demands can be illustrated by a few examples. American working-class organizations have lobbied (often in concert with the employers and with a great deal of militaristic and patriotic pleading) to keep open arms-industries manufacturing planes, shells and tanks, which are obsolete and due to be closed down. This blinkered idea of how to assure the *collective* defence of work and jobs can, of course, quite easily co-exist with *individual* revolts by workers against the absurdity of their jobs. On American car assembly lines this revolt can go as far as clandestine sabotage of car-body work, a product which the worker experiences as the hated embodiment, in its social uselessness and individual absurdity, of his oppressive job. Another example of the same sort, less extreme but more complex, is the formidable obstinacy with which miners have fought to prevent pit closures, even when the pits are worked in conditions which are humanly and economically subnormal. Individually they know, and admit, that even if the coal they produce was cheaper and better, their jobs, in the conditions in which they work, would still remain frightful. It is clear from such examples of purely defensive action that workers' spontaneous struggles not only fail to make any headway, but actually stop and die out if they are not provided with some political perspective. Such a perspective must axe their immediate demands on a total, strategic vision of class relations, so that their claims become linked to broader, more long-term aims of social change. The struggle for an 'alternative' to the politics and priorities of advanced capitalism, involves a reformulation of demands to seek qualitatively different solutions. This struggle is effectively forced on the working class by such problems as closures, redundancies, changes in factory siting, the opening of new factories, and retraining. These problems are going to become increasingly frequent under the impact of competition between the oligopolies and the accelerating rate of technological evolution. In the absence of a political perspective, the working-class movement will find it hard to do more than conduct desperate, defensive rear-guard actions.

In fact closures, the siting of new factories, retraining, the lack of new industries, give the labour movement a major opportunity to affirm its role of leadership in society. When neo-capitalist decisions entail serious problems for the working-class, or rather for the entire population of whole zones or regions, it must use the opportunity to point out that the optimum solution in human terms − as well as in terms of economic equibrium and regional development − demands decisions which run contrary to capitalist logic. It must urge 'structural reforms' that will change the relationship of forces, and create a fresh distribution of powers and spheres of influence, together with new centres of democratic decision-making. These constitute militant goals which both foreshadow the socialist transformation of society and tend in its direction. The Italian labour movement offers striking examples of this sort of qualitative demand, which presents an alternative to the politics of neo-capitalist development. Some of these examples have become famous on the Continent.

A big machine plant at Reggio Emilia was written off under the Marshall Plan; whereupon its entire personnel – operatives and technical staff – occupied the works, threw out the management and organized the production of tractors on their own initiative, using plans that had been abandoned. There was a period of some months before the first model could be produced. During this time the factory was kept going with money collected by peasants and townspeople of the district. The enterprise was eventually supported officially by the State, after pressure from the working-class parties. It continued to produce tractors for a time before going on to other products. It is still in existence.

Another example is that of the iron and steel plants on the Italian coast. The C.G.I.L. (the joint Communist and Socialist Confederation of Labour) campaigned for a long time at local and regional level for these plants to be built by the State; strikes and mass demonstrations were held in support of the demand. With national support from the working-class parties, the campaign succeeded in establishing a public corporation to finance some of the plants, which the Government had initially turned down as uneconomic. The struggle for the coastal iron and steel industries was waged on a thoroughly prepared and detailed programme. The way in which the : ate finally set up the scheme was a retreat from this programme

None of these battles ever ends in complete victory for the labour movement. But the sheer fact of having fought and achieved partial victories, which in themselves are often of considerable value, made it possible to raise the class-struggle to a higher and more dramatic level. The struggle allowed the movement to present and demonstrate the possibility of an alternative to neo-capitalist expansion, and made the masses who entered the battle conscious of their power and of capitalism's inadequacy and vulnerability; it made them aware of the necessity of transcending capitalism in a perspective which arose directly from their day-to-day struggles.

The struggle for structural reforms – that is, permanent gains in the advance towards a socialist democracy – is essential if action is to develop which can prise open the contradictions and dynamics of neo-capitalism and *force a crisis upon it*. This involves the formulation of intermediary objectives, extrapolated from immediate demands, which highlight the possibility, superiority and necessity of an alternative to the existing system. Through this struggle, possibilities can be made to appear from within the movement of capitalism which foreshadow the system's supersession. They thereby make the present state of affairs all the more intolerable, its contradictions and inadequacies all the more evident. It is obvious that this struggle cannot be confined to a straightforward political and ideological battle. For the fact is that such political and ideological battles only have an effect if their goals, instead of appearing as visions of a more or less distant future, are geared to potential or actual mass campaigns whose concrete aims they serve to enlarge. In other words, the political alternative to the system must appear at every level as a *concrete and positive possibility* which can be realized through the pressure of broad masses of people:

At the workshop level, in a struggle for workers' power over the organization and relations of work.

At the company level, in a struggle for a working-class counter-power capable of influencing the profit rate, the volume and direction of investment, and the level and quality of technological development.

At the industrial level, in a struggle against over-investment, so pregnant with future crises, or conversely against the failure of advanced capitalism to undertake necessary social development – all of which entails a programme setting out how production should be reorientated, in terms of its quantity, quality and nature.

At the urban level, in a struggle against the oligopolies' grip on the cultural, social and economic aspects of urban life: public transport, land and property, local government, the amenities of leisure, etc.

At the regional level, in a struggle for the new industrial development that is essential for the economic survival and health of the region, the absorption of unemployment and underemployment, and the creation of jobs for workers in declining or obsolete industries due to close down. This struggle must be led by Trade Unions and working-class parties acting in harmony, and must aim to create regional centres of decision which will be independent both of the oligopolies and the centralizing tendencies of the State.

At the level of a national plan, that is to say, at the level of society as a whole, in the drafting of the main lines of an alternative plan which corrects the direction given to the economy by neo-capitalism. Such a plan must establish genuine priorities in accord with social needs, and oppose goals which enrich the nation's human wealth – in education, research, health, public facilities, urban life – and material resources – in land use and regional development – to the goals of the 'Consumer Society' and private accumulation.

2. *Squalor amid Affluence*

It cannot be too often stressed that social, cultural and regional underdevelopment, and the rapid growth of industries producing 'affluent' individual consumer goods, are two sides of the same coin. It is indisputable that communal amenities, social and public services (urban public transport, etc.), education, and regional and rural development are in general scandalously neglected, while consumer goods industries enjoy a spectacular prosperity; but this is not because the former are publicly owned and the latter privately. On the contrary, this discrepancy arises because neo-capitalism assigns the principal role in economic development to the latter. Private accumulation switches the bulk of its surplus-value to investments with the highest short-term returns, with the result that the portion of the surplus which can be devoted to social investment is not large enough.

In addition, the neo-capitalist State subordinates its own investments, whose volumes are already insufficient, to the interests of the oligopolies. This is done in several ways: by advance loans for the oligopolies' expansion, by creating the infrastructure for business development, by helping to find markets for their unregulated output (by financial, fiscal, mili-

tary and price policies). At every opportunity the State uses
public funds to cover the *social costs of private accumulation*
in urban congestion, transport, professional training, public
health. When it lacks funds, it skimps those very public investments in the cultural, social or industrial fields which, because of their relative independence, could counter the course
of capitalist development.

The solution of the structural problems of our society cannot, therefore, lie in the creation of more public organizations;
it must lie solely in the extension of public control over the
main centres of decision-making and private accumulation,
with the aim of socializing the function of investment and
accumulation. This is why, when the State asks workers to
accept wage restraint as part of a deal to maintain the 'balance
between consumption and investment', the answer is straightforward:

1. There is no guarantee, under present conditions, that
savings in consumption will be reflected in higher investment.
On the contrary, wage restraint may have the effect of strengthening the employers' power, guaranteeing the oligopolies extra
profits and benefits of productivity, and discouraging scientific and technological research.

2. Even supposing that increased profits were effectively invested, nothing would guarantee that they were invested in the
areas, products and services where they were socially most
necessary.

3. It is possible to increase the workers' level of consumption (personal and *collective*) *at the same time as* the level of
socially useful investment, provided that the content and
structure of consumption and investment are changed: that
luxury consumption and investment are prohibited and that
speculative and parasitic sources of income (notably in commerce and land) are suppressed. This means cutting down
every kind of waste through the socialization of investment. As
long as the State has not taken over the real economic
centres of power; as long as organized labour is unable to
channel economic development towards the most urgent needs;
as long as the State plays a subordinate role to that of the

oligopolies, guaranteeing them risk-free profits and allowing the social product to be wasted for unnecessary and even anti-economic purposes – as long as these conditions hold good, it is the Trade Unions' right and even duty to refuse point-blank any 'wage restraint' and economic co-management, whose effect can only be to perpetuate capitalism's exploitation of labour and its appropriation and misuse of surplus value. As it is, the oligopolies exercise a powerful influence, more or less overtly, over all areas of society. This is not due simply to the fact that they are, within certain limits, able to dictate both the sales price of their products and the purchase price of the goods and services they require. This sector is also able to impose on society its model of production and consumption, to shape the tastes of 'consumers' and persuade them to buy those products which give the highest profit return.

The result is a whole series of distortions and disparities common to all neo-capitalist economies: 'public squalor amid private affluence', to use Galbraith's expression. The megalopolis, so enormously expensive to run and maintain, contrasted with so-called 'peripheral' regions whose decline amounts to depopulation; slums with TV and private cars; backward rural areas with fast motorways; sunless, airless, insanitary cities with cathedrals of commerce; and so on.

Neo-capitalism's grip over all spheres of economic and cultural life is not, of course, direct; it works through a certain number of intermediate mechanisms and is exposed primarily by the *priorities* it affirms, by the subordination and conditioning of living human needs to the inert claims of capital. Certain bourgeois ideologists try to deny this subordination, pointing to the real autonomy which is enjoyed by the State, or by such corporate bodies as the university. And it is true that it would be an over-simplification to speak of a stranglehold in these cases. The State, indeed, plays the role of an enlightened mediator between the oligopolies' crude interests and those of society, and this mediating function may include initiatives which appear to run counter to the immediate interests of neo-capitalism. In the short run, capital's interest lies in limiting to the strict minimum public investment in education, health, sanitation, urban amenities, cultural and sports facilities – for these investments divert resources, which otherwise would increase profits and purchasing power, to social uses from which neither profit nor accumulation will result. Forms of social spending financed by the State are not only a real or potential drain on surplus-value; they also prevent a portion of individual purchasing power from flowing into the hands of private enterprise. They virtually create a monetary circuit closed to the laws of the market and capitalist profit, a sector which is in effect antagonistic to the profit economy.

There is therefore permanent tension between even a capitalist State – in its role of public investor in those sectors of general interest which are unproductive and unprofitable – and private capital. But what so clearly distinguishes neo-capitalism from traditional capitalism is that the former acknowledges the necessity of the State's mediating role, and seeks no longer to restrain, but rather to guide and even develop public initiative in the interests of private accumulation. For it is in neo-capitalism's interest that the system should be made socially tolerable by the redistribution of income; that public health services should prolong the useful life of the labour force; that public education should attend to the future requirements of skilled manpower; that urban public transport, financed by the bulk of the population, should deliver its human consignments to the factories in good condition; that industry's needs should be met at low cost, and at public expense, by the nationalization of power and basic materials. In short, public development is welcome, provided that it is confined *to the public financing of the sources of future neo-capitalist expansion and accumulation;* provided, that is, that it remains subordinate to private enterprise, which must be left with the responsibility of deciding the economy's main orientation.

This means quite simply that the provision of social and cultural needs is never considered as an end in itself, but thought of only from a utilitarian standpoint; it means that the full development of all human faculties (through education, research, communications and culture) is given no priority, no more than urban and land planning. Such activities can only develop to the extent that they are complementary to private enterprise, or at least do not run counter to its interests, do not tempt people to dispute the system. To be sure, university life is free and even Communists can teach there. Neo-capitalist society must, after all, be able to afford the extravagance of philosophers. But information media are controlled either by a paternalist State or else by the distributors of advertising revenue, culture is subjected to the interests of the business world, publishing to the laws of the market and consequent advance censorship.

Economic, cultural and social development is not directed as a priority towards man's development and the fulfilment of his social needs, but *first and foremost* towards the production of those objects which can be sold for maximum profit, no matter what their usefulness or lack of it. Creative work is stunted by considerations of financial profitability or social stability. At the same time millions of working hours are squandered, in the process of neo-capitalist competition, on often minor but always expensive modifications to consumer goods, whose aim is hardly to enhance the product's aesthetic or use-value.

For the process of production is in itself social, and its social repercussions affect all aspects of life: work relations, leisure, education, mass entertainment and consumption, urbanization, etc. The burden of these effects is not borne by any social plan or project designed to humanize this process, imbue it with meaning, and impose social purposes on it. Rather than being mastered by a human society, these social processes in fact master it; they appear as the 'accidental' social by-products of private decisions, and proliferate anarchically: dormitory towns, urban congestion, population drift, every sort of shortage and excess. Instead of production being at the service of society, it is society that is placed at the service of capitalist production – a form of production which excels in offering *individuals* an unending succession of new ways of escaping an unbearable social reality. The large-scale propagation of these *means of individual escape* – the cult of the car, personal housing, camping, passive leisure-pursuits – promptly produces a new and anarchic 'social process' with new deprivations, alienations and conflicting demands.

As a *society*, mature capitalist society remains profoundly barbarous in that it aims not at a civilization based on social existence and social relationships, not at a culture of the individual as a social being, but solely at a civilization of individual consumers. At the same time the homogeneous and stereotyped character of personal consumption fostered by the oligopolies, produces that particular kind of person whose social nature appears accidental and alien to him: the 'mass' individual.

It should not be thought, as do those who yearn nostalgically after the age of the artisan, that it is mass production itself that turns social individuals into 'mass' individuals; this process is by no means the inevitable consequence of large-scale production. It is on the contrary, the consequence of production which is social in *form* but not in its *aims*. It is one thing to mass-produce agricultural machinery, ball-point pens for schools, or cheap work-clothes and satchels designed to meet social needs which are apprehended as such, and which socialized production is called on to satisfy. It is a quite different thing to work for a private firm instead of for society, producing objects which will not meet any social need, but which will be temptingly dangled in front of individual buyers as symbols of their liberation from social pressures.

For this, fundamentally, is the mystification on which so-called 'affluent' capitalism is founded. Production, social in form, scale and consequence, does not allow itself to be apprehended as such: it denies the social character of 'demand' (whether expressed in terms of money or not), of labour, of needs which human beings have in common and which social production enriches and develops. What it offers instead is a set of consumer-needs radically and artificially divorced from work and from the conditions of production which caused these needs in the first place. Not without reason: for in his role as consumer, the individual is urged to escape from his condition as social producer, to assemble round himself a *private* microcosm over which he can reign as a solitary monarch.

The ideology implied by the model of 'affluent' consumption is not so much a life of ease, as the life of the monad immured in his isolated, self-sufficient universe: in a home fitted out with 'all modern conveniences' (i.e. in a closed universe independent of exterior services), in which he can watch the world as a show on television, from which he emerges to take the wheel of his private car and drives off to enjoy the sights of a countryside 'unspoilt by man' – while he curses the 'State' for not building enough motorways to speed up this flight: curses the State, not the profit economy which makes this flight virtually compulsive. The denial of the social origin and nature of human needs, and of the necessarily social character of their satisfaction; the assertion of the possibility of a purely individual liberation by the acquisition of the means of escape (the social character of whose production is painstakingly concealed): these are the basic mystifications of the 'affluent' society.

In this implicit rejection of individual responsibility for society, which casts the social out into the realm of the 'accidental', lies the root cause of 'massification' – that powerless, anarchical solitude of separated individuals, suffering their social existence as a statistical, external reality, and manipulated in their individual behaviour-patterns by the technicians of 'hidden persuasion'.

3. *Consumers made to Order*

A number of highly perceptive observations have been made, especially by the Catholic Left in Italy, on the alienation of the individual in his role as passive consumer. Although these do not always go to the root of the problem, they are worth summarizing.

Up till now the existence of a wide range of unsatisfied primary needs has given the capitalist mode of production a natural basis and a human purpose in the furthering of life, both in appearance and in an objective sense. The greater part of market demand actually related to products that were necessary to the maintenance of life so that, independently of its own internal logic, capitalist production was objectively based on primary and autonomous needs. Because existing demand gave the system this natural basis, it was possible to believe that the economy was at the consumer's service and even that it had a rational justification, in human terms, as a scientific method of developing and using scarce resources. In fact, this natural basis of demand served to *conceal* the *intrinsic* goal of capitalist production, namely the accumulation of surplus as the system's specific driving force and as an end in itself. But what was hidden as long as demand related in the main to goods necessary to the maintenance of life, became abundantly clear the moment primary needs were largely satisfied, or at least were no longer responsible for increasing demand. The growth of production could no longer be justified as the natural basis, the vital necessity, for the maintenance of life.

From the moment when men are freed from primary needs, they have, in theory, the possibility of *choosing* the kind of wealth to be produced. They can choose to produce for consciously creative human ends and no longer merely for those imposed by nature. They can subordinate the mode and organization of production, as well as production itself, to the overriding aim of producing a 'completely human' mankind. They can make creation – both in producing and consuming – the essential activity of life, instead of a subordinate element as it necessarily had had to be until then.

However, for reasons which we shall shortly examine, neo-capitalism has succeeded in preventing this momentous change: production has not been subordinated to creative activity. Indeed neo-capitalism has stifled all creative activity, and, as in the period of general scarcity, has retained the old subordinations, particularly that of consumption to the imperatives of the productive process. As Marx foresaw, advanced capitalism has found itself confronted with the problem of moulding human subjects into the shapes required by the objects it has to sell, of no longer adjusting supply to demand, but demand to supply.

It has resolved this problem by conditioning people to what

is most profitable to produce – not only in respect of their personal needs, but also in the way they see the world, the way they conceive the State, society, civilization and its co-existence with other societies and civilizations. Neo-capitalism subjects society to the service of private accumulation, through the individual consumer as much as through the public consumer (State expenditure). It seeks to extend its grip over every aspect and sphere of civil life, to dominate people in their work, their leisure, their homes, their schools, their sources of news, their manner of renewing their own capacity to work, their human relationships. . . . It demands nothing more nor less than production for production's sake, that is to say, accumulation for accumulation's sake, and the manipulation of society into a state of compulsive consumption. Inevitably, it also demands a type of personality that can be moulded into a condition of passive consumption: 'mass' individuals, on whom it strives to impose aims, desires and longings which are no more than its own instruments.

But to show all this much is only to touch the surface of a phenomenon whose roots lie in the capitalist relations of production. As Bruno Trentin has said in his *Tendenze del Capitalismo Italiano*, the "alienated consumer" is the person who in his consumer needs, reflects his alienation as an agent of production.' He is the worker (manual, intellectual or white-collar) who is atomized, residentially dispersed, pacified, subjugated by the factory's military discipline, cut off from what he produces, called on to sell his time and meekly carry out a prefabricated task without worrying about the purpose of his work. This consumer, whom capitalist production requires in order to subordinate consumption to its own ends, is not wholly created, as is often implied, by advertising, fashion, and the propaganda of 'human relations'. In fact capitalism has *already* produced him by the way its productive and work relations are organized, by the way the producer is cut off from his product, the worker from his work; by the way this work is reflected back to him as a predetermined, alien quantity of time and effort which awaits him at his job and requires only his active passivity.

It is precisely because the worker is not 'at home' in 'his' work; because, denied him as a creative, active function, this work is a calamity, a *means* solely of satisfying needs, that the individual is stripped of his creative, active needs and can find his own power only in the sphere of non-work – the satisfaction of the passive needs of personal consumption and domestic life. It is on the basis of their initial pre-conditioning, that neo-capitalism is able to play upon passive, individual consumer-needs, offering ever more complex and sophisticated ways of satisfying them, developing the need to *escape*, and selling the means of forgetting, of distraction from the pressures of industrial organization. It sells the means of a *make believe* human existence – since there is no question of actually *making* such an existence – through the possession of pre-packaged symbols of humanity. The further it goes in this direction, the more it numbs a stunted, mass-produced humanity with satisfactions that leave the basic dissatisfaction untouched, but still distract the mind from it: the more it hopes that these men, preoccupied with various means of escape and oblivion, will forget to question the basis of the whole system: the alienation of labour. Capitalism civilizes consumption and leisure to avoid having to civilize social relationships, productive and work relationships. Alienating men in their work, it is better equipped to alienate them as consumers; and conversely, it alienates them as consumers the better to alienate them in work.

It is impossible to break this vicious circle by confining politics to a quantitative level of consumer demands. Conversely, it is impossible to dispute the model of consumption offered by neo-capitalism – except by abstractly invoking a scale of spiritual values redolent of medieval and archaic nostalgia – without attacking the root of 'spiritual impoverishment': the alienation of labour.

This task is evidently not a simple one: the subordination of consumption to production, the subjection of all aspects of life to private accumulation, provokes no spontaneous revolt. It can even appear to be a circular argument: since the priorities of the neo-capitalist world of consumption correspond to *real needs* within the framework of existing production and work relations, it may seem impossible to question the former as long as the latter have not been transformed.

This circularity is, all the same, more apparent than real. For it is not a question (as some Christian theoreticians have maintained) of playing down the immediate satisfactions offered to alienated workers by 'consumer society' – by promising them fuller, more substantial satisfactions for tomorrow. The question of the purpose of work and of an alternative social and consumption model, must not be expressed as a choice between 'frivolous affluence' and 'virtuous austerity'. It must be expressed in terms of essentially *political* choices, which are both oriented towards the future, and which arise directly from demands here and now.

A principal aim of these political choices must be to break down the wall that separates the producer from his product, that sets the worker, in his role of mystified consumer, against himself as an alienated producer. Workers' immediate demands over wages, schedules, work rates and gradings give the Trade Unions an opportunity of posing the problem of *the social and individual usefulness* of the production to which the work is geared. They allow them to question the worth (or worthlessness) of proposed innovations, the product's real quality, the orientation that should be given to production, in terms both of needs that are felt and of the existing level of technical and scientific potential. The aim of this action should be the eventual establishment of a working-class power at the level of the company, industry and finally the national economy, capable of countering the mystifications of advertising and fashion by an independent appreciation of the use-values of products. This counter-power could also set a true value on actual cost-prices, profit-margins and the resources wasted in companies or whole industries through over-lapping, competing or simply useless research and output. It would thereby be able to oppose to the neo-capitalist model of consumption (and production) an order of priorities based on needs that were actually experienced – including, of course, needs entailed by leisure, working conditions and way of life.

Only combined Trade Union and political research and action, aimed at re-unifying the producer and the consumer whose functions have been separated by capitalism, can expose the parasitic logic of the system. Only in this way will the outlines of a new social model emerge, a model of consumption and of life *in the light of which* neo-capitalism's model can be seen in all its absurdity, and an alternative created which is far better than any spontaneous rebellion: the conscious will to change the system.

The only effective form of political commitment, the only way of awakening in workers an awareness of their stifled needs, is to dispute neo-capitalist society with a positive socialist model of the human and material possibilities that are denied, oppressed or excluded by capitalism. For we are now in a phase of capitalist development in which *immediate* needs no longer constitute an automatically revolutionary critique of the system. As productive forces develop, revolutionary needs do not disappear, but are repressed by society's persuasion and pre-conditioning. Deprived of any means of satisfaction and therefore of any means of being consciously apprehended, these needs can only be liberated by reflection and a vision of the future which, by affirming the possibility of their satisfaction, reveals their existence. While such a model must necessarily constitute a *total response* to capitalism, it must not be offered as a Utopia or as a 'maximum' demand that projects socialism to a *hereafter* beyond capitalism and erects a great wall of China between the two. It must, on the contrary, be presented as the *meaning*, the strategic horizon, of day-to-day struggles and tactical demands. It cannot exclude compromises or partial objectives, as long as these make sense and the sense is clear.

A strategy of intermediary goals, leading to a peaceful institution of socialism must be based on a dialectical progression. No single one of these partial objectives, no partial socialization of the economy, no partial power won by the working class will ever in itself constitute a revolution; nor will the sum total of partial successes. A strategy of intermediary objectives is not a strategy of 'nibblings' or 'progressive take-over' of the centres of decision, a war of protracted siege and attrition. On the contrary, each partial victory, and even the sum of these victories, will not add up by any logic of their own into a miraculous 'qualitative leap'. They will not automatically tip capitalism over into socialism as the last drop of water makes the glass overflow. Should the strategy of intermediate goals become entangled in this illusion, it would fully merit the pejorative title of 'reformist' and 'social democrat'.

On the contrary, intermediate objectives, and the structural reforms that they entail, can only form a strategy, can only avoid absorption by the capitalist system *on condition* that they are presented from the beginning as successive approximations and as stages towards a socialist society which constitutes their *meaning*; a meaning which must be particularized and illustrated at each stage, a meaning in the light of which each intermediate goal must be seen as leading towards new victories, on pain of seeing all past victories rendered null and void.

The struggle for the extension of social control and the expansion of the socialized sector will only sharpen the contradictions and deepen the crisis of capitalism *on condition* that these objectives are planned not as ends but as means (which are in their way still ends, but provisional ones), prefigurations of what a socialist society can and must be. Given this condition, each single battle will prepare and herald fresh engagements, will raise the level of consciousness and struggle, will embed socialist ideals in the actual sensibility of people, and convince them that the way to defend past victories is to gain greater ones tomorrow. All this clearly presupposes a leadership with an overall perspective, capable of devising a concrete 'global alternative' to capitalism, in the light of which each reform that is won will derive its meaning. The advance towards socialism will be made in this way, or not at all.

If this total perspective is missing, the sum total of reforms, however progressive they may be, will be reabsorbed by capitalism in a mixed economy of the Scandinavian type, leaving the power of capital intact, and work alienated, while offering 'affluence' to all.

If, on the other hand, what is missing are the intermediate aims that lie between the final goal and the day-to-day activity of the movement, an impasse is equally inevitable. In the absence of intermediate objectives which can specify the final end and the path towards it, socialism will remain only an abstract idea.

GOALS OF TODAY'S WELFARE STATE[1]

Richard Titmuss

One point of view which is strongly held in the West (particularly the far West) is that welfare inhibits economic growth; it discourages thrift and savings; it encourages high absenteeism from work and low productivity; it diminishes family responsibility. An opposing point of view – equally strongly held – believes that welfare has more to do with humanitarian values than economic efficiency; with the social and ethical texture of society; with the exercise of compassion and reason in social relations.

Both these points of view have one thing in common. They are largely assertions and do not rest on any firm basis of fact. The concept of welfare has indeed suffered much in the past from stereotypes of deserving or undeserving recipients of charity; from images of well-meaning but muddle-headed social workers cheerfully ignoring the harsh realities of economic life. We all drag about with us the chains of history – including an outdated one about the social worker – but it is time we recognized the evidence for a third point of view. Briefly, this is to see economic growth and social growth as interdependent in the sense that lagging behind in one has, necessarily, negative consequences on the other. Unbalanced economic growth may, for instance, generate a need for greater public expenditures than would otherwise be the case. The social costs of technological change, if allowed to lie where they fall, may result in larger costs in the future in the shape of physical and psychological handicap, destitution, deprived children, ill-educated workers unable or unwilling to acquire

[1] With some additions and revision this essay embodies the main part of a lecture given at the Hebrew University, Jerusalem, in August, 1964, in opening a Seminar on 'Objectives for Social Services' in Israel'.

new skills, and a general slackening in the sense of social involvement and participation in the life of community.

The case for social growth, in making a positive contribution to productivity as well as reinforcing the social ethic of human equality, depends to a large extent on which forms of welfare are developed, how they are administered, and the education and skills of those who staff these services. We know now from experience in Britain that we did not abolish the spirit of the old and hated poor law by enacting new legislation in 1948. The same people – the same administrators and workers – still had to run the hospitals, public assistance offices and welfare services. They poured into the new social service bottles the old wine of discrimination and prejudice. What was needed was a major effort of training, retraining and separation of functions of administrators, social workers and local officials. This, I believe, is one of the less dramatic but important goals of welfare: a more humane and informed administration of social service. This is a prerequisite to 'reaching the unreachables' in our society. We have to realize that in this matter there is an enormous gap between the best we are capable of and what goes on; that reducing this gap is not simply an affair of spending more money; and that it is in great part the responsibility of public authorities to challenge whatever attitudes and conventions stand in the way of improvement, and to initiate themselves to move to higher standards of service everywhere.

This is one of the major goals in the development of welfare as an aid to economic growth. It means efficient and more effective welfare. Before, however, turning to my next point I must say something about the definition of the term. How do we define welfare? What are the main areas of collective action which may be designated as social policy?

I do not wish at this stage to embark on a long essay on definition. It will be sufficient to indicate the main areas of public (or publicly subsidized) social and welfare services, namely:

1. Education from the primary school to the university.
2. Medical care, preventive and curative.

3. Housing and rent policies.
4. Income maintenance (including children's allowances, old age pensions, public assistance, and schemes for unemployment, sickness and industrial injuries benefits).
5. Special services in kind for dependent groups, the old, deprived children, unsupported mothers and various handicapped classes.

All these services are redistributive in their effects. They cannot be neutral, whether they are provided only for certain groups in the population or on the principle of universality. They change patterns of getting, spending and storing. In terms of total government expenditures they may absorb anything from 10 per cent to 30 per cent of the annual budget.

In looking to the future and asking questions about the major objectives of these services we must first inquire how they are functioning at present in the modern state. Are they in reality achieving what they were intended to achieve? To what extent and in what sectors are they redistributing resources on criteria of need or on criteria of productivity – on Myrdal's principle of Cumulative Causation? In attempting to answer such questions we must also take account of the operations of the income tax system with all its complex indirect subsidies and transfers towards meeting the cost of different types of services and needs; for example, allowances for children, deductions for education, medical care, old age pensions, life assurance, owner-occupied houses and so forth. For those who pay income tax, these are welfare contributions and their general tendency in Britain and other countries is to reduce the progressiveness of the taxation system. They are, in short, redistributive in effect just as the formal welfare services are.

I cannot, of course, try to answer these important questions so far as other countries are concerned. However, from social policy studies in the last few years in Britain and the United States it has become increasingly clear that certain tendencies are at work which conflict with the general model of a 'Welfare State' redistributing resources in favour of the poor and those with the greatest need.

In Britain, for example, we have begun to ask statistical and sociological questions about the utilization of the high-cost sectors of social welfare and the low-cost sectors of social welfare. We have been led to do so by the recognition that the Beveridge principle of universality in welfare – comprehensive systems of education, medical care and pensions for all citizens – does not, by itself alone, solve the problems of the underclass in our societies; the fifth or quarter or more of the population who are badly educated, badly housed, badly fed and who often have greater need for medical care and services of many kinds than the general population.

Universality in welfare is needed – and was needed in Britain – to reduce and remove barriers of social and economic discrimination. Separate services for second-class citizens invariably become second-class services – whether they are organized for 10 per cent or 50 per cent of the population. Moreover, those who staff these services may come to believe that they themselves are second-class workers. Hence, when exercising discretionary powers in giving or withholding benefits and services they may adopt a more punishing attitude to those whom they may disapprove of.

The principle of universality applied in 1948 to the main social welfare services in Britain was needed as a major objective favouring social integration; as a method of breaking down distinctions and discriminative tests between first-class and second-class citizens. But equal opportunity of access by right of citizenship to education, medical care and social insurance is not the same thing as equality of outcome. It is only a prerequisite – though a necessary one – to the objective of equalizing the outcome. Other and more precise instruments of social policy are required in addition to achieve equality of outcome irrespective of race, religion or class.

I will now give a few examples of what we have been learning in the past ten years about the actual functioning of universally provided services in Britain.

1. Under the National Health Service we have learnt that the higher income groups make better use of the Service; they

tend to receive more specialist attention; occupy more of the beds in better equipped hospitals; receive more elective surgery; have better maternity care; and are more likely to get psychiatric help and psychotherapy than members of the so-called working classes – particularly the unskilled.

2. In the field of financial provision for old age (which dominates the budget for national insurance) we have learnt that the State now makes a larger contribution on average to the pensions of the rich than it does to the pensions of the poor. This has come about as a consequence of the combined action of the principle of universality, of tax allowances, subsidized pension schemes sponsored by employers, deductible life assurance and other factors.

3. Under the universal system of family allowances and children's allowances a man earning £20,000 a year with 2 children will receive from the State (pay less tax) £5 a week for the children. At the other end of the scale a man with 2 children and earning £500 a year will receive from the State 8/- a week. The rich father thus gets thirteen times more from the State than the poor man in recognition of the dependent needs of children.

4. In the field of housing the subsidy paid by the State to owner-occupiers of many categories of houses is on average greater than the subsidy received by most tenants of public housing (local government) schemes. This has come about as a consequence of the differential effects of local rate payments, housing subsidies, interest rates, tax deductibles for mortgage interest, and other factors. To arrive at this conclusion for housing (as for pensions and benefits for children) calls for a complex and intensive analysis of many diverse systems of Government intervention.

5. For my last example, I take education. Next to the ownership of land and property, this (and the lack of it) is today the most revolutionary and explosive force in developed and developing economies. Earning power, life chances, achievement, position and class, and even the level of pension in old age depend on education and training, and on society's investment of scarce resources in those who are educated. In highly-

developed countries today the total value of the capital sunk in the education of the population is immense. It has been estimated for the United States that in 1957 the capital sunk in the education of the population represented 40 per cent of the total of physical tangible capital plus intangible educational capital.[1]

This, of course, is not to say that education can be viewed simply as another form of productive capital investment. It confers other benefits: social and spiritual. It enables the educated person to enjoy more freedom and a fuller life. But education does have value as a straightforward commercial investment. The return on higher education as a purely commercial investment for the individual is probably larger today in most Western countries than any other form of investment. If heavily financed by the State, and if proportionately more children from better-off homes benefit, then the system will be redistributive in favour of the rich.[2]

In the past, the spread of the first stages of education to all children – the principle of universality – was a major equalizing and integrating force in our societies. It functioned in this way partly because the problem of earnings and labour forgone was less of a problem. But we are now entering in the West a new era in which secondary and higher education may become one of the major disequalizing and socially disruptive forces. There are three reasons for this.

One is that scarce resources only allow a small proportion of young people access to good secondary and higher education. (The principle of universality cannot be applied to higher education in any country of the world in this century.)

The second is a greatly intensified problem of earnings and labour forgone (associated, of course, with the problem of educational motivation) which leads to the exclusion of working-class children. Immense sacrifices are called for from parents and children living in poor conditions and bad housing if earnings are given up in favour of study.

[1] T. W. Schultz, *The Economic Value of Education*, 1963, p. 51.

[2] This process has been well illustrated in a recent study by Dr Ben-David of the Hebrew University, 'Professions in the Class System of Present-Day Societies', *Current Sociology*, vol. XII, No. 3, 1963–4.

logical development demand more people with higher education there will be, as in Britain, pressures to invest more scarce resources in such education at the expense of education for the masses, and also to concentrate secondary education on those who will go on to higher education. These pressures, we must recognize, are growing stronger in our societies.

These five examples I have given of trends and tendencies in the functioning of social welfare services provide us with some glimpses of the magnitude of the task that lies ahead in redefining the goals of welfare. The major beneficiaries of the high-cost sectors of social welfare are the middle and upper income classes. The poor make more use of certain services (for instance, public assistance) but these tend on a *per capita* basis to be the low-cost sectors.

In addition to these trends, Britain and other Western countries have experienced in the last fifteen years a rapid growth in what we may call 'non-wage income'. This has taken the form of services, fringe benefits, privileges and perquisites which are not generally or wholly subject to tax. The major beneficiaries have been the middle and upper income groups.

In short, we can now say that the advent of 'The Welfare State' in Britain after the Second World War has not led to any significant redistribution of income and wealth in favour of the poorer classes. According to the most recent estimates,[1] 5 per cent of the population of the United Kingdom owned 87 per cent of all personal wealth in 1911–13, 79 per cent in 1936–8 and 75 per cent in 1960. The decline in the concentration of wealth, although insignificant over the period of fifty years, is less marked since 1938 than during the years of mass unemployment and economic depression between 1913 and 1938. The trend towards a somewhat less unequal concentration in the ownership of wealth appears to have slowed down

[1] By J. R. S. Revell of Cambridge University published in J. E. Meade, *Efficiency, Equality and the Ownership of Property*, Allen and Unwin, 1964, p. 27.

in the past twenty-five years. This is all the more remarkable when we consider the effects since 1938 of substantially higher rates of taxation and estate duty, the equalizing forces of the Second World War, full employment and a far greater employment of married women, and the supposedly redistributive effects of 'The Welfare State'. Full employment for nearly twenty years, considered alone, might have been expected to have brought about a markedly less unequal concentration; a much greater proportion of workers have had opportunities of accumulating some savings.

Moreover, it has to be remembered that all these figures are expressed in terms of *individual* holdings. We do know from various studies that since the 1930s there has been an increasing tendency for large owners of property to distribute their wealth among their families.[1] The British fiscal system is almost unique in the Western world in its generous treatment of wealth-holders in allowing them to use family settlements, discretionary trusts, gifts, family covenants and other legal devices for redistributing and rearranging income and wealth. This trend is reflected in the startling fact that in the mid-1950s and within age groups, it was in the young adult age group that the tendency for wealth to be concentrated in a few hands was most marked. If it were possible to measure the distribution of wealth in terms of family holdings it might thus be found that inequality had increased since 1938. There is certainly evidence from the United States, which has experienced a marked increase in individual wealth inequality since 1949, that measurement in terms of family holdings does make a significant difference.[2]

Yet since the end of the 1930s it has been the broad intention of welfare measures to facilitate a more equal distribution of economic resources. Why then, it may be asked, have these unintended consequences of social policy come about? There are, of course, many reasons and I can only mention a few.

[1] Richard M. Titmuss, *Income Distribution and Social Change*, 1963, chapter 5.

[2] R. J. Lampman, *Review of Economic Statistics*, 41, November 1959, pp. 379–92.

For one thing, our conceptual frame of reference was too narrow and too romantic. We have associated 'Welfare' with the 'Poor'; it has given us a nice feeling. Secondly, we too readily assumed that social legislation solves social problems. As every social worker knows (or should know) it does not. Thirdly, we failed to develop in the 1950s techniques of social analysis as we have developed techniques of economic analysis. Fourthly, we have tended to 'compartmentalize' welfare; to put it in a separate conceptual box; to see it as a hindrance to economic growth in the long-run – as it may be in the short-run. Accordingly, therefore, we failed to relate the functioning of services and the measurement of social need with the dynamics of change – economic, technological, social and psychological.

Lastly, we lacked vision and we lacked social inventiveness. We did not see that the task of reaching the poor and minority groups, of redistributing resources in their favour, of getting them to use and benefit from health, education and social services was a far more formidable one than most reformers imagined. We gravely under-estimated the growing strength of the forces working in the other direction – forces stemming from economic and technological change, specialization and the class division of society. And we failed to grasp the importance of the connections between, for instance, bad housing and inability to profit from education; between an inadequate command over language and the need for more social workers to help to interpret and manipulate the resources of a complex society; and between social policies and the inadequacy of the administrative machine (particularly at local levels) to translate policies into effective action.

In short, because we were complacent, because we looked inwards and backwards to the 1930s, our social diagnosis was inadequate. Only now are we coming to see that we need much sharper tools of social study and measurement; more precise social analyses of conditions, needs and the actual functioning of services; more attempts at social planning in alliance with economic planning. How many hospital beds shall we need in 1975? How many more social workers, welfare workers, and other staff will be required? What problems of crime, delinquency and deprivation will confront our societies in ten years' time?

These and similar questions are admittedly difficult ones to answer. But if we wish to redefine the goals of welfare then we cannot escape the responsibility of being more intelligent about what is happening and what is likely to happen in our societies.

We shall not make progress in identifying and measuring the future tasks of welfare unless we relate need and response to the ongoing forces of change. If we accept that two of the major positive goals of welfare are to increase and spread the impact of equalizing factors and to speed up the impact of factors favouring integration then we must base the many practical details of policy and action on a more informed diagnosis of change. From recent advances in the social sciences we can be reasonably sure about the continuation of certain trends, for example.

To achieve economic growth and innovation, modern societies need to apply the lessons of advances in technology and science. This means more division of labour and specialization; more education and specialized training; more specificity in manpower recruitment and deployment; longer hierarchies in occupational positions in the labour force; larger incentives for training and mobility; more and probably larger differentials in rewards. These processes, necessary as they are, tend on balance to generate disequalizing forces and, by demanding higher standards of education, training and acquired skills, they can make more difficult the task of integrating people with different cultural backgrounds and levels of motivation. While we may raise expectations in people's minds about what the future may hold, technology simultaneously raises the barriers to entry. This process, now becoming known in the U.S.A. as 'credentialism', is believed to be partly responsible for the solidifying of a permanent underclass of deprived citizens, uneducated, unattached and alternating between apathetic resignation and frustrated violence.

A second process, built-in among modern societies and

related to technological change, which we also need to understand, is represented by growth of professionalism. In Britain and other countries, the professions are largely recruited from the middle classes; professional workers come from homes and educational institutions where they have little contact with manual workers and people from different cultures. Thus, they bring to their work middle-class values in the processes of giving or withholding medical care, education, legal aid and welfare benefits. Their model of the ideal pupil, student, patient and client is one with middle-class values and a middle-class tongue.[1] This process, subtle and often unconscious, partly explains why in Britain, under universally available welfare services, the middle classes tend to receive better services and more opportunities for advancement. This is understandable; we all prefer the co-operative patient or client; motivated to achievement, anxious to learn, anxious to work. Of all professions in contact with the poor, only social workers in their training learn to understand the significance of this factor in their relationships. They recognize the importance of guarding professionalism against functioning as a disequalizing force.

While I have not attempted any precise description of to-day's welfare goals, I believe that some of them are implicit in the lessons of experience. These I have set within the context of certain general principles of economic management. In doing so I have stated a case for a balance of economic and social growth. We want higher productivity for a higher standard of living and we want a more equal society. We want individual advancement and we want an integrated community of self-respecting human beings. In achieving these goals systems of welfare have a major contribution to make. They will, of course, present us time and time again with conflicting ideologies and conflicting policies.

In the choices that we have to make I would like, in conclusion, as a student of welfare, to offer two personal prescriptions.

The world desperately needs standard-bearers of social inventiveness and personal integrity; examples to look up to; pre-

[1] See B. Bernstein, *Brit. Journal of Sociology*, vol 15, No. 1, 1964.

cepts to learn from. In a world made smaller by modern communications what we do in the field of welfare and how we do it has an influence far outside national boundaries. Men are still moved by the ideas of compassion. So we need pioneers in the art of giving. Secondly, I believe that when conflict in policies presents itself we should take risks in welfare choices. We should trust rather than distrust people and put our faith in the ultimate reasonableness of man.

To me, the 'Welfare State' has no meaning unless it is positively and constructively concerned with redistributive justice and social participation. These goals may collide in the short-run with the need to increase economic productivity and so raise the general standard of living. Although we cannot be sure that this collision is inevitable it is, nevertheless, tempting to argue – tempting to take the safe side – that when we are richer we can afford to be more generous to the less fortunate. But, equally, can we be sure that in the processes of getting richer and of concentrating only on getting richer we shall not, as a society, lose the impetus to create a more equal and socially just community?

TOWARDS A SOCIALIST SOCIETY

Raymond Williams

The New Left has been described as 'the politics of the un-political'. The truth of this description can be accepted in one main sense: that the New Left analysis of contemporary British society neither begins nor ends within the terms of politics as now ordinarily defined. Thus it is possible to see the General Election of 1951, in which the Labour Party gained its highest ever popular vote and yet lost power to the Conservatives, as the decisive post-war political event. A society in any case changing, in its social assumptions and expectations, in the nature of its economy after the losses of the war, and in its world position with the imminent loss of its colonial empire, was submitted, by an electoral irony, to a Conservative interpretation and emphasis, which the elections of 1955 and 1959 endorsed and confirmed. If this were indeed so, we could accept the simple thesis of 'thirteen wasted years' and see the election of 1964 as ending the period of that interpretation and emphasis, and inaugurating a new period of the Left. Yet the irony is persistent. It is to 1945, and its major parliamentary victory, that the Labour memory consistently returns, rather than to 1950 and 1951 when, after years of bitterly contested power, it enjoyed the support of more people than at any time in its history. And 1964 is interpreted as an improvement on 1959, because a Labour Government has taken office, though with slightly less popular support than when it was last decisively defeated. One irony is repaid with another: the Labour victory of 1964 is no more but also no less real than the Conservative victory of 1951. The reality of popular support is discreetly modulated, now as then, by an overriding interest in the prevailing organs of government. A Labour emphasis, perhaps in its turn to be endorsed and confirmed at succeeding elections, can now be given to a society still changing in the same essential directions. A pleasing and probably profitable irony, yet we must watch for the last laugh.

The deliberate incompleteness of British democracy (reflected not only in these curious electoral vagaries but in more fundamental matters, such as the reduction of decision to a crude single vote at intervals of years, and the very centralization of power which allows so rapid a take-over on so slender a basis) is after all a form of defence against the precise political and social values which the Left represents. We can be realistic enough to accept that we must beat the system before we can change it. Many of us, already, have done this in education: coming through the channels of an *élite* system so that we can try to convert it to a democratic system. Yet the analogy is disturbing, in a quite personal way. Almost everything is in fact done to invite us to beat the system by joining it, and for individuals the experience can be heady. Wilson and some others in his Government are of the generation faced with this very particular crisis, which is still quite unresolved. All the pressures are towards this kind of transformation of society, if there is to be any at all: a transformation engineered by political methods directly contrary to the values at which the transformation aims. There is a structural similarity, for all the differences of manners, with the taking of arbitrary power by a revolutionary vanguard, in the name of popular liberation. We have seen enough of the paradoxical results – the reality of change and yet the degeneration of political values – to be both tense and alert, as we take our turn to be tested.

Those of us who are not in politics, in the governing sense, yet who are wholly committed to politics, as the whole process of social change, stand to be tested quite as searchingly as the Government which, in a resigned but yet eager realism, we have worked for and now support. The luxury of detached observation would be wholly disqualifying. To fail to participate, in the resolution of this crisis, would be to deny everything we have done and been. Yet the manner of our participation is quite inescapably defined by our experience. Our definition of what should be done is shaped by the nature and problems of the society, rather than by the nature and problems of the forms of government which are no more than its partial reflection and at worst the deliberate obstacles to recognition of its changes. That is to say, we have now to take consciously the pressures and limits of the actual society, and draw strength from the currents of growth within it and from alliances with all that is creative elsewhere in the world. Less publicly, but in the long run no less decisively, we have to negotiate this actual process, which is being simultaneously negotiated, under extreme pressure, and with all our goodwill and respect, by men working within the procedures of existing power.

1. *The System of Decision in Contemporary Britain*

What is the nature of power in contemporary Britain, and how do its forms relate to the struggle for a participating and educated democracy which is at once our most important history and our most immediate commitment?

(i) *The immediate issue.* Effective power in Britain is now shared between the machinery of State (ministers and civil servants and public authorities rather than Parliament) and the very similar machinery of large private corporations. There can be little doubt that a Labour Government will alter the proportions within this balance of power: state initiative, direction and control, already quite powerful, will become marginally and perhaps significantly more dominant. But just as the current political choice is not (as Conservative propaganda would have it) between State control and free enterprise, which are already in harness, so it is not (as Labour propaganda would have it) between the whims of speculators and an overriding social purpose.

Labour proposes important controls on land use and on regional development; these would be the areas in which the balance of power would shift. The re-nationalization of steel, to which Labour is committed, would make a further important difference. But the effective area of power in Britain would still be that of the combination of State and corporation machinery.

It is probable that, revised in the ways Labour proposes, this combination would become more efficient and the economy would gradually be strengthened. But when this is represented as 'making a new Britain', one can only comment that the new will work essentially like the old: a change of body work, but not a change of motive power.

It is not only a matter of abstract social analysis; the resolution will begin, almost immediately, over a whole range of specific questions. The Trade Unions will be required to enter the political field if Labour policy is to be carried out; on wages and prices, on regional planning, on automation and re-training. It is possible that on such matters Labour will try to set a spurious 'national' interest above the interests of the Unions. There can be no such separation. The Unions can no longer defend their members, in a period of technological and regional reorganization, by piecemeal measures. If they are forced into this merely delaying action, it will be the Labour Government's fault. The question is whether Labour will bring in the Unions at the earliest possible stage of planning, and as much more than the representatives of a 'sectional' interest. The demand for redistribution of the industrial product and for industrial democracy, from the boardroom to the shop floor, is not a sectional demand; it is an expression of principles and objectives for the whole society.

Since 1926, the Unions have tended to withdraw from these general and absolute demands in favour of a defensive particularism. But they are bound to do so, if the power in State and industry is always on the other side. Their position will not be changed by consultation; it can be changed only by their inclusion in the original decision making, as the organs of majority economic power. There they can take part in reshaping the economy, rather than merely reacting to it.

On every issue, a crucial and common choice reveals itself. Even to do as much as it proposes, Labour will have to fight hard against existing interests, and it has been characteristic of all previous Labour Governments that they have done enough to mobilize these interests against them and yet not enough to win. A decisive time will come, again, when the choice between going on and 'consolidating' will have to be made: a choice really of which side Labour is on. I think there is a real chance, this time, that the choice will be to go on, but to put it as higher than a chance would be merely utopian.

(ii) *The general situation.* The progress of democracy in Britain is deeply affected by what is happening in the economy, but also by other factors. The aspiration to control the general directions of our economic life is an essential element of democratic growth, but is still very far from being realized. Beyond this general control lies a further aspiration, now equally distant and confused. It is difficult to feel that we are really governing ourselves if in so central a part of our living as our work most of us have no share in decisions that immediately affect us. The difficulties of a procedural kind in ensuring this share are indeed severe, and because of the variety of institutions in which we work there is no single answer. Yet if the impulse is there, some ways can be found, and steadily improved from experience. Even the smallest human group produces leaders, though not always the same leaders for all projects. The difficulty lies in interpreting just what this leadership means. The majority patterns of our society, especially in work, offer an interpretation which not only fixes leaders, for all sorts of circumstances, but encourages them to believe that it is not only their right but their duty to make independent decisions and to be resolute in carrying them out.

There are still many natural autocrats in our society, and the trouble they cause is beyond reckoning. More dangerous, perhaps, because less easily identified, are those skilled in what was called in the Army 'man management'. The point here, as I remember, is that of course you have to command, but since a leader has to be followed he must be diligently attentive to the state of mind of those he is leading: must try to understand them, talk to them about their problems (not about his own, by the way), get a picture of their state of mind. Then, having taken these soundings, having really got the feel of his people, he will point the way forward.

An exceptionally large part of what passes for political commentary is now a public discussion of a party leader's command of this skill: how will the Prime Minister or the Leader of the Opposition 'handle' this or that 'awkward element'; how will he time his own intervention; if he says this, how can he avoid saying that? The really funny thing about this kind of commentary is that it is public; printed and distributed in millions of sheets; read by almost everybody, including the 'awkward elements'. The delicate art has become public myth, and it is rare to see it challenged. This, evidently, is what democratic leadership is supposed to be.

In fact, of course, it is the tactic of a defensive autocracy (and people do not have to be born into an autocracy to acquire its habits). The true process of democratic decision is that, with all the facts made available, the question is openly discussed and its resolution openly arrived at, either by simple majority vote or by a series of voluntary changes to arrive at a consensus. The skills of the good listener and the clarifier are indeed exceptionally necessary in such a process, but these are crucially different from the stance of the leader who is merely listening to the discussion to discover the terms in which he can get his own way. The intricate devices worked out by democratic organizations, to ensure the full record of facts, the freedom of general contribution, the true openness of decision, and the opportunity to review the ways in which decisions are executed, are indeed invaluable. Yet just because they are intricate, they are easily abused by the man-managers: one even hears boasts about the ways in which this or that committee has been 'handled'. I would only say that I have never seen such handling, reputedly practised as a way of 'avoiding trouble', lead to anything but trouble. For once men are reasonably free, they will in the end assert their interests, and if these have not been truly involved in the decision (as opposed to collected and 'borne in mind') the real situation will eventually assert itself, often with a bitterness that shows how bad the man-managers really are. Our main trouble now is that we have many of the forms of democracy, but find these continually confused by the tactics of those who do not really believe in it, who are genuinely afraid of common decisions openly arrived at, and who have unfortunately partly succeeded in weakening the patterns of feeling of democracy which alone could substantiate the institutions.

It is clear, on balance, that we do not get enough practice in the working of democracy, even where its forms exist. Most of us are not expected to be leaders, and are principally instructed, at school and elsewhere, in the values of discipline and loyalty, which are real values only if we share in the decisions to which they refer. Those who are expected to be leaders are mainly trained to the patterns of leadership I have been discussing, centred on the general development of confidence – but in fact that a leader should be self-confident enough to be capable of radical doubt is rarely mentioned and rarely taught. The necessary practice of the difficult processes of common decision and execution is left, on the whole, to hit or miss, and the result, not unexpectedly, is often both. A weakening of belief in the possibility of democracy is then inevitable, and we prefer to lament the 'general indiscipline' (Trade Union leaders cannot control their members, party leaders are not firm enough; it is all sloppy discussion, endless talk, and then people behaving unreasonably) rather than nourishing and deepening the process to which in any case, in any probable future, we are committed.

The counterpart of this feeling, reinforced by the actual history of democratic institutions in this country, is an approach to Government which in itself severely limits active democracy. A tightly organized party system and Parliament seem to have converted the national franchise into the election of a court. As individuals we cast one national vote at intervals of several years, on a range of policies and particular decisions towards which it is virtually impossible to have one single attitude. From this necessarily crude process, a court of ministers emerges (in part drawn from people who have not been elected at all), and it is then very difficult for any of us to feel even the smallest direct share in the government of our affairs. Approaches through the party organizations, taking advantage of the fact that at least there are alternative courts, are more practicable, but not only is it generally true that inner-party democracy is exceptionally difficult in both large parties, it is also the case that the right not to be tied, not to be precisely committed, is increasingly claimed by both sets of leaders. The general influence of public opinion counts for something, since in the long run the court has to be re-elected. But the period is exceptionally long, given the rate and range of development in contemporary politics. In the four and a half years between the elections of 1955 and 1959 several wholly unforeseen major crises developed, and public opinion in fact violently fluctuated, to be met in general only by the bland confidence of the court in its own premises; that the duty of the Government is to govern, for the Queen's Government must be carried on. It is fair to say that this does not even sound like democracy, and we must be fair to our leaders, conceding them at least consistency, in their obvious assumption that direct popular government is not what democracy is about. It is true that any administration should have reasonable time to develop its policies, but this is not the same thing as the current uncritical belief in the importance of 'strong government': certainly one hopes that a good government will be strong, but a government that is both strong and bad (most people are agreed that we had such governments in the 1930s; I think we have had one or two since) is almost the worst possible public evil. I see no reason why two-year intervals of re-election of at least a substantial part of the House of Commons should not be our immediate objective, since it seems vital for the health of our democracy that more of us should feel directly involved in it. Such a change, coupled with working reforms now being canvassed in Parliament, and with an improvement of the democratic process within the parties, would be a substantial yet reasonable gain. The alternative is not only the rapid extension of man-management, monstrously magnified by the use of modern communications as its general device, but also the unpleasant development of organized pressure-groups, pushing into the anterooms of the court. One further necessary amendment seems to be a fixed date for the periodic elections, for to concede choice of this date to the court itself is psychologically quite wrong: we should not have to wait, within broad limits, for the court to ask our approval; the right of election is not theirs but ours.

These changes in themselves would make only a limited difference, but they would at least go some way towards altering the present atmosphere of British democracy, which seems increasingly formal and impersonal, and powered by little more than the belief that a choice of leaders should be periodically available. The next field of reform is obviously the electoral system, which seems designed to perpetuate the existing interpretations. Its most obvious characteristic is that it exaggerates, sometimes grossly, comparatively slight tendencies in opinion. Post-war electoral history suggests a violent fluctuation of opinion, from a very strong Labour to a very strong Conservative Government. But actual opinion, reckoned in terms of people, has changed much less. What I notice most about current political commentary is that it is preoccupied by results at the level of the court, rather than by the registered opinion of actual persons; and this, however natural it may be to people who like living in anterooms, is quite undemocratic in spirit.

At this critical point, the relative absence of democracy in other large areas of our lives is especially relevant. The situation can be held as it is, not only because democracy has been limited at the national level to the process of electing a court, but also because our social organization elsewhere is continually offering non-democratic patterns of decision. This is the real power of institutions, that they actively teach particular ways of feeling, and it is at once evident that we have not nearly enough institutions which practically teach democracy. The crucial area is in work, where in spite of limited experiments in 'joint consultation', the ordinary decision process is rooted in an exceptionally rigid and finely-scaled hierarchy, to which the only possible ordinary responses, of the great majority of us who are in no position to share in decisions, are apathy, the making of respectful petitions, or revolt. If we see a considerable number of strikes, as the evidence suggests, as revolts in this sense, we can see more clearly the stage of development we have reached. The defensive tactic, once again, is man-management, now more grandly renamed personnel management. This is an advance on simple autocracy, but as an answer to the problems of human relations at work only shows again how weakly the democratic impulse still runs. It seems obvious that industrial democracy is deeply related to questions of ownership; the argument against the political vote was always that the new people voting, 'the masses', had no stake in the country. The development of new forms of ownership then seemed an essential part of any democratic advance, although in fact the political suffrage eventually broke ahead of this. The idea of public ownership seemed to be a solution, but there is some truth in the argument that little is gained by substituting a series of still largely authoritarian State monopolies for a series of private monopolies (something is gained, however, to the extent that the State is itself democratically directed). It is obvious that in a complex large-scale economy, many central decisions will have to be taken, and that their machinery easily becomes bureaucratic and protected from general control. At this level there can be no doubt that the separate democratic management of industry is unworkable. The true line of advance is making this machinery directly responsible to the elected government, probably through intermediate boards which combine representation of the industry or service with elected political representatives. With this framework set, as for example it is to some extent set in educational administration, the development of direct participation in the local decisions of particular enterprises could be attempted. The difficulties are severe, and there is no single solution. It seems to me that a government which was serious about this would initiate a series of varied experiments, in different kinds of concern, ranging from conventional methods such as the reform of company law, promoting actual and contractual membership, with definite investments and rights in the concern, to methods that would be possible in concerns already publicly owned, in which elected councils, either from a common roll or at first representing interests in an agreed proportion, would have powers of decision within the accepted national framework. It is commonly objected that modern work is too technical to be subjected to the democratic process, but it is significant that in certain fields, notably education and medicine, the necessarily complicated processes of involving members in self-government are already much further advanced than in work where the 'service' criterion is not accepted, though in fact it is claimed. Education and medicine are not less technical or specialized, but they have a less obvious class structure, which is undoubtedly important.

The necessary principle is that workers of all kinds, including managers, should be guaranteed the necessary conditions, including both security and freedom, of their actual work, in precise ways that are perfectly compatible with general decisions about the overall direction of the enterprise. Boards of directors elected by shareholders now give such directions, ordinarily with less security and freedom for all kinds of workers, since these are not represented. In publicly owned industries and services, and in reformed companies, the principle of boards elected by the members of the industry or service, to operate within the agreed national framework, is surely not difficult. There would be a long and continuous process of setting-up and improving such machinery, and many serious and largely unforeseen problems would undoubtedly arise. But the basis of the whole argument for democracy is that the substance of these problems would in any case exist, and that participation in the processes of decision leads to more rational and responsible solutions than the old swing between apathy, concession, and revolt.

One other field in which the growth of democracy seems urgently necessary is the ordinary process of decision about the development of our communities. This has been approached, but is still very muddled, and it is unfortunately true that there is even more dissatisfaction, and consequent apathy, about local government than about the national court. Authoritarian patterns at the centre seem to be widely reproduced in our local councils, where much more of the process is in the open and within our ordinary experience, unfortunately in its ordinary course giving far too much evidence of how easily democracy is distorted. Still, the problems here are quite widely understood, and the active struggle against distortion is encouraging. More seriously, behind this struggle is a familiar inertia of old social forms. Housing is an excellent example, because the common provision of homes and estates is so obviously sensible, in principle, and is already extending beyond the mere relief of exceptional need. Why then does such an extension, or further extension, leave many of us quite cold? One answer, certainly, is the way such houses and estates are commonly managed, by supposedly democratic authorities. There are public officials who regard such people as council-house tenants as natural inferiors, and they speak and write accordingly. The remedy, of course, is not to teach them man-management, but to try to develop democratic forms within these areas of public provision. Why should the management of a housing estate not be vested in a joint committee of representatives of the elected authority and elected representative of the people who live on it? While general financial policy obviously rests with the whole community, there is a wide area of decision, on the way the houses are used and maintained, on estate facilities, and on any necessary regulations, which could be negotiated through such channels more amicably and I think more efficiently. If this experiment has been tried, we should know more about it and consider extending it. If it has not been tried, here is an immediate field in which the working of democratic participation could be tested. Labour councils, in particular, ought continually to be thinking in these ways, for there is great danger to the popular movement if its organizations are persistently defensive and negative (as in the ordinary Tenants' Association), and it is Labour which has most to lose if it allows democracy to dwindle to a series of defensive associations and the minimal machinery of a single elected administration. The pressure has been to define democracy as 'the right to vote', 'the right to free speech', and so on, in a pattern of feeling which is really that of the 'liberty of the subject' within an established authority. The pressure now, in a wide area of our social life, should be towards a participating democracy, in which the ways and means of involving people much more closely in the process of self-government can be learned and extended.

(iii) *The response*. Labour has taken power with a very small majority, and this means that the anti-democratic features of the present electoral and parliamentary system are being accentuated, as the condition of government. It is possible to accept this, since there is no immediate alternative, but we must be quite clear about what is actually happening, and must continue to press for the use of this power in the direction of much wider participation. This is necessary within the Labour Party itself, within the machinery of regional and economic planning, and in all cases of reform of social institutions. The necessary energy, for the Labour Government to survive, cannot on any terms be enlisted, but it remains possible that it can be released.

2. *The Character of the Economy*

The Labour Government is faced with an immediate and severe economic crisis, and must be supported in all its urgent efforts to resolve this. Yet it is common ground that the crisis is not incidental but structural, and the nature of a satisfactory long-term solution has still to be argued.

(i) *The immediate issue*. In the past few years a spate of books has diagnosed the evident crisis of British society as primarily a case of being insular and behind the times. There is indeed plenty of evidence of this kind, but its interpretation is usually naïve. Talk of modernization makes sense only in the context of a genuine analysis of the structure of the society. We could have a programme of modernization which would break down old Trade Union and Socialist attitudes, the time wasting inherent in democratic procedures, and the traditional subjection of economic policies to a moral test.

Just such a programme has been widely urged by the Right in England; especially often, perhaps, by American and American-influenced observers whose definition of what is old-fashioned in Britain is what is not like the United States. The tone of the recent Conservative Government was wholly modernizing in this sense. We have not for some years seen the Conservatism of the empire, the gentleman and the Christian and classical pieties. Effective Conservatism, in theory and practice, has idolized the super-administrator, the salesman, the speculator; the institutions it will leave as a legacy are the supermarket, the betting shop, commercial television and the motorway beside the closed railway.

Classically, the whole modernization programme is the bourgeois attack on all institutions and habits of mind that limit or hinder the aggressive and expanding operations of the market, which is seen as the only important social process. It is true that Britain has suffered economically because many of its institutions and habits of mind have worked against an efficient market economy. However, the crucial fact about Britain is that, while some of these habits and institutions are pre-bourgeois (the vestiges and illusions of a rural gentry, which new classes have adopted as their own superficial life-style), at least as many are post-bourgeois, are the political and moral criticisms of a market society, and the necessary bases of a more rational and more humane society of the future.

An indiscriminate rejection of these traditional bearings is now the mark of a particular stage of European capitalism, and it is this operation – perfectly embodied in contemporary Conservatism – which is or ought to be the Labour Party's principal enemy. When, in the rhetoric of the period, Labour itself adopts 'modernization' as a sufficient social policy, it becomes not the party of the working class but the party of the latest wave of middle-class reorganization.

(ii) *The general situation.* It remains very difficult to think about our general economic activity at all. Both its successes and its failures remain obstinately local, and to this kind of description (particular successes announced by their makers, particular failures not announced until they erupt in crisis) the only ordinary alternative is an almost useless measurement of total production, as if some single thing were being produced. Economists have done a good deal to make these questions significant, but in ordinary thinking it is either this success and that failure, or this misleadingly simple general graph. We can only think in real terms if we know what real things are being produced, and ask relevant questions about need and quality. Some part of the production may be truly unnecessary, but the more likely situation is that the balance between various kinds of production will be wrong or even absurd. The usual answer to this kind of question is a particular description, the market, which supposedly regulates questions of need and quality. 'It is needed because it is bought; if it were not bought, it would not be made.' Of course this leaves out one major consideration: whether need and ability to buy are matched. But in any case the description is crude, because it leaves out too much. To match the block figure of production, we are offered another block figure, the consumer. The popularity of 'consumer' as a contemporary term deserves some attention. It is significant because, first, it unconsciously expresses a really very odd and partial version of the purpose of economic activity (the image is drawn from the furnace or the stomach, yet how many things there are we neither eat nor burn), and, second, it materializes as an individual figure (perhaps monstrous in size but individual in behaviour) – the person with needs which he goes to the market to supply.

Why 'consumer', to take the first point? We have to go back to the idea of a market, to get this clear. A market is an obviously sensible place where certain necessary goods are made available, but the image of the place lingers when the process of supply and demand has in fact been transformed. We used to go to markets and shops as customers; why are we regarded now as consumers? The radical change is that increasingly, in the development of large-scale industrial production, it is necessary to plan ahead and to know the market demand. What we now call market research was intended as a reasonable provision for this: demand is discovered so that production can be organized. But in fact, since production is not generally planned, but the result of the decisions of many competing firms, market research has inevitably become involved with advertising, which has itself changed from the process of notifying a given supply to a system of stimulating and directing demand. Sometimes this stimulation is towards this version of a product rather than that, but frequently it is stimulation of a new demand or revival of a flagging demand. In these changing circumstances, the simple idea of a market has gone: the huckster stands level with the supplier. It is then clear why 'consumer', as a description, is so popular, for while a large part of our economic activity is obviously devoted to supplying known needs, a considerable and increasing part of it goes to ensuring that we consume what industry finds it convenient to produce. As this tendency strengthens, it becomes increasingly obvious that society is not controlling its economic life, but is in part being controlled by it. The weakening of purposive social thinking is a direct consequence of this powerful experience, which seeks to reduce human activity to predictable patterns of demand. If we were not consumers, but users, we might look at society very differently, for the concept of use involves general human judgements – we need to know how to use things and what we are using them for, and also the effects of particular uses on our general life – whereas consumption, with its crude hand-to-mouth patterns, tends to cancel these questions, replacing them by the stimulated and controlled absorption of the productions of an external and autonomous system. We have not gone all the way with this new tendency, and are still in a position to reverse it, but its persuasive patterns have much of the power of our society behind them.

An equally important effect of the 'consumer' description is that, in materializing an individual figure, it prevents us thinking adequately about the true range of uses of our economic activity. There are many things of major importance, which we do not use or consume individually, in the ordinary sense, but socially. It is a poor way of life in which we cannot think of social use as one criterion of our economic activity, yet it is towards this that we are being pushed by the 'consumer' emphasis, by the supposed laws of the market, and by the system of production and distribution from which these derive.

It has been widely recognized, in recent years, that a serious state of unbalance between provision for social and individual needs now exists in Britain and seems likely to increase. It is easy to get a sense of plenty from the shop windows, but if we look at the schools, the hospitals, the roads, the libraries, we find chronic shortages far too often. Even when things are factually connected, in direct daily experience, as in the spectacular example of the flood of new cars and the ludicrous inadequacy of our road system, the spell of this divided thinking seems too powerful to break. Crises of this kind seem certain to dominate our economy in the years ahead, for even when late, very late, we begin thinking about the social consequences of our individual patterns of use, to say nothing about social purposes in their own right, we seem to find it very difficult to think about social provision in a genuinely social way. Thus we think of our individual patterns of use in the favourable terms of spending and satisfaction, but of our social patterns of use in the unfavourable terms of deprivation and taxation.

It seems a fundamental defect of our society that social purposes are largely financed out of individual incomes, by a method of rates and taxes which makes it very easy for us to feel that society is a thing that continually deprives and limits us – without this system we could all be profitably spending. Who has not heard that impassioned cry of the modern barricade: but it's my money you're spending on all this; leave my money alone? And it doesn't help much to point out that hardly any of us could get any money, or even live for more than a few days, except in terms of a highly organized social system which we too easily take for granted. I remember a miner saying to me, of someone we were discussing: 'He's the sort of man who gets up in the morning and presses a switch and expects the light to come on'. We are all, to some extent, in this position, in that our modes of thinking habitually suppress large areas of our real relationships, including our real dependences on others. We think of my money, my light, in these naïve terms, because parts of our very idea of society are withered at root. We can hardly have any conception, in our present system, of the financing of social purposes from the social product, a method which would continually show us, in real terms, what our society is and does. In a society whose products depend almost entirely on intricate and continuous co-operation and social organization, we expect to consume as if we were isolated individuals, making our own way. We are then forced into the stupid comparison of individual consumption and social taxation – one desirable and to be extended, the other regrettably necessary and to be limited. From this kind of thinking the physical unbalance follows inevitably.

Unless we achieve some realistic sense of community, our true standard of living will continue to be distorted. As it is, to think about economic activity in the limited terms of the consumer and the market actually disguises what many of us are doing, and how the pattern of economic life is in any case changing. Even now, one person in four of the working population is engaged neither in production nor in distribution, but in public administration and various forms of general service. For a long time this proportion has been steadily rising, and it seems certain that it will continue to rise. Yet it is a kind of economic activity which cannot be explained, though it may be distorted, by such descriptions as the consumer and the market. A further one in thirteen work in transport, and it is significant that the ordinary argument about our transport systems, especially the railways, is unusually difficult and confused, as the problem of finding any criterion more adequate than consumption, any method of accounting more realistic than direct profit and loss in the market, inevitably shows through. As for administration and general services, from medicine and education to art, sport, and entertainment, the argument is almost hopelessly confused. The product of this kind of work, which one in four of us give our time to, is almost wholly in terms of life and experience, as opposed to things. What kind of accounting is adequate here, for who can measure the value of a life and an experience? Some parts of the process can be reduced to more familiar terms: medicine saves working days, education produces working skills, sport creates fitness, entertainment keeps up morale. But we all know that every one of these services is directed, in the end, to larger purposes: doctors work just as hard to save the life of a man past working age; every school teaches more than direct working skills, and so on. To impose an accounting in market terms is not only silly but in the end impossible: many of the results of such effort are not only long-term and indirect, but in any case have no discoverable exchange value. The most enlightened ordinary reaction is to put these activities into a margin called 'life' or 'leisure', which will be determined as to size by the shape of 'ordinary' economic activity. On the other hand, if we started not from the market but from the needs of persons, not only could we understand this part of our working activity more clearly, but also we should have a means of judging the 'ordinary' economic activity itself. Questions not only of balance in the distribution of effort and resources, but also of the effects of certain kinds of work both on users and producers, might then be adequately negotiated. The danger now, as has been widely if obscurely recognized, is of fitting human beings to a system, rather than a system to human beings. The obscurity shows itself in wrong identification of the causes of this error; criticism of industrial production, for example, when in fact we should starve without it; criticism of large-scale organization, when in fact this extension of communication is the substance of much of our growth; criticism, finally, of the pressures of society, when in fact it is precisely the lack of an adequate sense of society that is crippling us.

For my own part I am certain, as I review the evidence, that it is capitalism – a particular and temporary system of organizing the industrial process – which is in fact confusing us. Capitalism's version of society can only be the market, for its purpose is profit in particular activities rather than any general conception of social use, and its concentration of ownership in sections of the community makes most common decisions, beyond those of the market, limited or impossible. Many industrial jobs, as now organized, are boring or frustrating, but the system of wage-labour, inherent in capitalism, necessarily tends to the reduction of the meaning of work to its wages alone. It is interesting that the main unrest of our society – the running battle which compromises any picture of a mainly contented and united country – is in this field of wages.

Whenever there is an important strike, or threat of a strike, we tend to react by defining a different conception of work – service to the community, responsibility to others, pulling together. The reaction is quite right: work ought to mean these things. But it is hypocritical to pretend that it now does, all the way through. While the light comes on when we press the switch, we take for granted just these qualities, but ordinarily fail to acknowledge, with any depth, the needs of the man who made the light possible. If we want to stop strikes, we have to carry the reaction right through, for this system of bargaining for labour necessarily includes, as a last resort, as in all other bargaining, the seller's refusal of his labour at the price offered. Strikes are an integral part of the market society, and if you want the advantages you must take the disadvantages, even to the point of dislocation and chaos. While we still talk of a labour market, as despite long protest many of us continue to do, we must expect the behaviour appropriate to it, and not try to smuggle in, when it becomes inconvenient, the quite different conception of common interest and responsibility. The moral disapproval of strikers is shallow and stupid while the system of work is based on the grounds of particular profit which we there condemn.

What is happening to capitalism in contemporary Britain? We are told that it is changing, but while this is obviously true it can be argued that the patterns of thinking and behaviour it promotes have never been more strong. To the reduction of use to consumption, already discussed, we must add the widespread extension of the 'selling' ethic – what sells goes, and to sell a thing is to validate it – and also, I think, the visible moral decline of the labour movement. Both politically and industrially, some sections of the labour movement have gone over, almost completely, to ways of thinking which they still formally oppose. This development is generally damaging, for the society is unlikely to be able to grow significantly if it has no real alternative patterns as the ground of choice. I remember that I surprised many people, in *Culture and Society*, by claiming that the institutions of the labour movement – the Trade Unions, the co-operatives, the Labour Party – were a great creative achievement of the working people and also the right basis for the whole organization of any good society of the future. Am I now withdrawing this claim, in speaking of moral decline? The point is, as I see it, that my claim rested on the new social patterns these institutions offered. I recognize that the motives for their foundation, and consequently their practice, must be seen as mixed. Sectional defence and sectional self-interest undoubtedly played their part. But also there was this steady offering and discovery of ways of living that could be extended to the whole society, which could quite reasonably be organized on a basis of collective democratic institutions and the substitution of co-operative equality for competition as the principle of social and economic policy.

The situation is complicated by the fact that real changes have occurred in the society, through the pressure of these institutions aided by reforming elements within the existing patterns. The extension of social services, including education, is an undoubted gain of this kind, which must not be underestimated by those who have simply inherited it. But it remains true not only that the social services are limited to operation in the interstices of a private-ownership society, but also that in their actual operation they remain limited by assumptions and regulations belonging not to the new society but the old. The other substantial change, the nationalization of certain industries and services, has been even more deeply compromised. The old and valuable principle, of production for use and not for profit, has been fought to a standstill in just this field. The systems taken into public ownership were in fact those old systems no longer attractive in profit terms (coal, railways), new systems requiring heavy initial investment (airways) and systems formerly municipally or publicly developed (gas, electricity). Some of these systems have been much more successful than is generally allowed, but it remains true, first, that they have not only failed to alter the 'profit before use' emphasis in the general economy but have also been steadily themselves reduced to this old criterion; and, second, that they have reproduced, sometimes with appalling accuracy, the human patterns, in management and working relationships, of industries based on quite different social principles. The multiplication of such effects is indeed uninviting, and the easy identification as types of the supposed new society, has added to the general confusion. In being dragged back to the processes of the old system, yet at the same time offered as witnesses of the new, they have so deeply damaged any alternative principle in the economy as to have emptied British socialism of any effective meaning. The proposal to admit this formal vacuity, by detaching the Labour Party from any full commitment to socialism, then makes sense of a kind, the practical acknowledgement of an existing situation, until perhaps one remembers that the containment and eventual cancellation of any real challenge to capitalist society has been, for more than a century, the work of capitalist society itself.

These are major gains in capitalist ways of thinking, and it is easy to be overwhelmed by them. Meanwhile capitalism can point to its successes in expanding consumption, and to its extension of a huge system of consumer credit which, on its own terms, creates one kind of prosperity. With only the consumer in mind, as a point of economic reference, this is not easily challenged. Again, taking the point about restriction of ownership, capitalism has sought to extend ownership by promoting a wider holding of shares. This reply is characteristic, in that it misses the point of the criticism, and proposes reform in terms of the system criticized. The objection was only in part to restricted individual ownership (which in any case still holds); it was mainly to no social ownership. The extension of shareholding to about one in fifteen adults enables more of us to make money as a by-product of the system of satisfying our general needs (money made, in fact, out of the work of the other fourteen) but it does nothing to ensure that the needs are general or that the distribution of energy and resources is right in common terms. The latest device, of some limited control of this distribution by channelling public money into privately-owned systems, is only a further example of the way in which the very aspirations of the original challenge to capitalism are used as a means of strengthening it. Finally, capitalism (and its ex-socialist apologists) emphasizes the decline in control by shareholders (an ironic comment, of course, on the extension of shares, which is then not a new kind of ownership but simply an extension of playing the market), and the rise in importance of the managers and technicians. In fact the economy, while not controlled by ordinary share-holders, is not controlled by managers and technicians either, but by powerful interlocking private institutions that in fact command what some Labour politicians still wistfully call 'the commanding heights of the economy'. Even if the managerial revolution had occurred (and the real revolution is the passing of power to financial institutions and self-financing corpora-tions) the original challenge would still be lost, for the direction of our common economic life would have been reduced to a series of technical decisions, without anything more than a market reference to the kind of society the economy should sustain.

(iii) *The response.* In its first statement on the economic situation, the Labour Government said:

'The Government next examined the prospects for public expenditure and receipts of all kinds. They found here a lack of balance and absence of proper social and economic priori-ties. . . . The Government have already made a start to put these deficiencies right. This will call for increased expenditure in certain fields, where the economic and social benefits are clear, and reduced expenditure in others, where money is being spent without social or economic benefit'.

As a statement of principle this is very welcome, but it is necessary to point out that it has only been applied to *public* expenditure. The crucial question is whether the same assertion of priorities, in terms of social need, can be made and carried through in our economic life as a whole. The intention to do so is generally evident, but the actual negotiation will be a real crisis of power and principle.

3. *Labour and Culture*

(i) *The general situation.* A sustained inquiry into the social significance of modern systems of communications has been one of the principal distinguishing features of the New Left in Britain. This emphasis, while widely influential, has been criticized as a diversion from 'real politics'. It has most often been seen as a form of the intellectuals' preoccupation with themselves and their own activities, and of a corresponding withdrawal from issues affecting majorities of the population. This criticism, interestingly, has been made by people on the Right as well as on the traditional Left. It can be at once admitted that the particular difficulties of intellectuals in an advanced capitalist society, and the further problems of a new generation of intellectuals from working-class families, have been important factors in the genesis of this inquiry. But it is the purpose of this comment to argue that the inquiry is nevertheless of fundamental importance in any modern critique of capitalism, and in the contemporary formulations of socialist policies. In particular, I shall argue that any separation of communications from 'real politics', or of its issues from issues 'affecting majorities', is, in our actual social situation, puerile.

My first argument can be put in traditional terms. It is becoming clear, from British and American experience, that heavy investment in the field of communications – newspapers, magazines, radio, television, records, publicity and public relations – is characteristic of a particular stage of advanced capitalism. The complex of ideas, information, persuasion and entertainment is in this sense a branch of production employing increasing numbers of people and an increasing proportion of capital. The profits to be earned in these growth industries are often significantly high. It is characteristic of the twentieth-century reorganization of the systems, and of their twentieth-century institution in the case of systems employing new techniques, that in a majority of instances typical modern capitalist methods of organization are adopted. The means of production – presses and studios – are mainly controlled by capitalist organizations and groups, which employ the actual producers – writers, performers, directors. As the scale of necessary capital rises, because of the high cost and, in the early stages, inevitable centralization required to exploit new techniques, there is a very marked tendency towards monopoly and the exclusion of small independent organizations. The growth of monopoly in the means of production is matched by similar developments in the means of distribution. Publishing firms and booksellers, newspaper companies and newsagents, film companies and cinemas, all show this process at varying stages of development. In the case of broadcasting and television, there is, in Britain, a characteristic 'mixed economy' compromise, with some public intervention to maintain sound broadcasting and one television service in a position independent of the general commercial process. The general situation in this whole field, is markedly similar to the organization of the economy as a whole.

Yet the significance of this development is not only a matter of similarity of economic structure. The communications systems have a special relationship to the rest of the economy, of a kind which illuminates their special importance in understanding advanced capitalism. Their products are not sold at cost plus profit, but, while retaining the profit, are sold normally below cost. The average newspaper in Britain can cost as much as 6d. a copy to produce, and as little as 3d. a copy to buy. The difference is made up by revenue from advertising. The majority television service is almost wholly financed by advertising revenue. Thus the communications system in these major sectors, is geared to servicing the capitalist economy as a whole, and, if organized in this way, can survive only while it fulfils this function. This relationship is itself typical of a particular stage in the creation of a consumer economy, shaped by the need to sell goods and services beyond immediate and evident demand, by competition between large groups making comparable products, and by the overriding need to organize the market in conditions of mass production requiring advance planning of outlets. The development of mass advertising in Britain dates from the late nineteenth-century crisis in the British economy, from which large-scale monopoly development and price-fixing schemes also date. Each of these tendencies has grown in step with the others. At the economic level, the system of communications has been reorganized around this basic function of servicing a capitalist economy in its monopoly and consumer-goods stages. At the same time, however, the system of communications has been shaped by the needs and pressures of a capitalist society. There has been the need to retain the realities of class rule within the forms of political democracy with universal suffrage. There has been the further need to contain the effects of general literacy and improved educational opportunities. At different stages these have been directly fought, and in the spheres of education are still being fought. But the degree of involvement of majorities with the process of political decision is, though still limited, already at a stage where it can threaten class rule. The extension of the effective community has been, in recent decades, spectacular: both in its powers of decision, and, in the new scale of international politics and trade, in its need for information. There is no case, in an advanced capitalist society, of the system of communications corresponding, in ownership or policies, to the actual distribution of political opinions or affiliations. Because the organization of communications is either directly capitalist or a compromise between capitalism and the existing capitalist state, with only a limited and difficult minority sector maintained by the parties of opposition to capitalism, the ruling class has an outstanding political advantage: both in the direct propagation of opinions and attitudes and in the more decisive long-term creation and limitation of consciousness. Every working-class party, in the advanced capitalist countries, has experienced this disadvantage, which an increasing reliance on centralized communications only accentuates. At the level of direct instruction in opinion the capitalist organs often fail (though they never entirely fail). But at the level of the structuring of convictions and expectations they often notably succeed. To argue that a concern with this system is a diversion from 'issues affecting majorities' is ludicrous.

It can be observed at this point that for socialists this is not a new situation, even if the scale and the techniques have so remarkably developed. Socialists already know that the structure of the economy will in these ways determine its superstructure. Yet this cultural theory, for all its evident elements of truth, appears inadequate, in its usual formulations, to explain our real experience in communications. One notable mark of its inadequacy is the poverty of socialist theory, to say nothing of its often disastrous practice, in the field of making an alternative communications system. For it is increasingly clear that we make only a partial gain if we merely invert the capitalist subordination of communications to class needs. The limitation of communications to servicing an economy and a political system is factually a crime against humanism. Itself developed as a bourgeois distortion of man, it retains its crippling power even in transformed economic and political systems. One of the deepest failures in the new socialist societies has, understandably, been in this field: that cultural expansion has been limited and directed by a subordination of the communications system to the political and economic system. The bourgeois repudiation of communication as a primary human process, its relegation to a secondary activity derivative from 'real' economic activity, has often been taken over, unexamined, by socialists. The fact that communication, in its highest and most permanent forms, is art, serves now to remind us that this kind of inherited bourgeois subordination is extremely dangerous, in the contemporary struggle of ideas. The relation of art to social experience is, though often complicated, clear and important, but the significance of art is that it is a primary human process, even when affected, like all human activities, by the historical and social matrices of experience. What is true in this respect of art can also be true of many other kinds of communication, and we are in no position to make the necessary critique of communications under capitalism if we miss the essential theoretical point that the alienation of communication processes from the communicators is one of the most damaging consequences of capitalist society: an alienation comparable to that in other kinds of human activity and work. Further, there is a factual alienation of the majority of men, who are assigned a merely passive role in communication: the 'public' for whom the communicators write, or, as so often, whom they seek to manipulate. Socialist theory must break free from this kind of negative conversion of men into 'masses', the material rather than the sources of the communication process. Sophisticated bourgeois accounts of the problems of 'mass society', so common in American writers on communication, are quite evidently forms of acceptance of a class society from which most men, in their full humanity, are both factually and theoretically shut out. It would be disastrous if we allowed socialist communication theory to be distorted by the same assumptions. When we are shaping socialist policies on communications, we must be guided by two principles: first, the restoration of the means of communication to the communicators themselves, by the ending of capitalist organization and the making of new kinds of democratic ownership and control;[1] second, the breaking down of the special class structure of communications, which divides men into fixed classes of active and passive, manipulators and manipulated. We must do this not only for political reasons, though such a struggle is now a central part of the general struggle against capitalism, and also a central part of the struggle to rectify our own errors and to build a humane socialism. We must do it also as part of our necessary definition of the full claims of man, against the distortions of class society. Within a class society, communication is structured and limited by the imperatives of power and capital, and by the consequent pressures to conformity. Yet human communication is always breaking beyond these imperatives, and it is in human communication, as well as in the connected process of work, that the real world we share is learned, interpreted and changed. In this struggle for freedom of communications, through a recognition of primary rather than merely derivative or qualified status, we are making one of the major demands of a humanism which, to be realized, must become socialism. The fight in communications is not a competitor with our other kinds of struggle: for peace, for the ending of poverty and disease. It is at once a necessary part of all these struggles, and one of the permanent conditions and claims of the dignity of man.

(ii) *Cultural Policy*. Labour policy on cultural matters was

[1] I have developed these proposals in my book *Communications*, Penguin, 1963.

set out in the statement called *Leisure for Living*. There is a good deal right but also a good deal wrong with the statement as it stands. It is full of goodwill, but theoretically it is very feeble. Much of the essential case is lost at the beginning if a cultural policy is reduced to, or even presented as, a policy for leisure. In the first place, this ignores the fact that the economic and institutional structures of the arts and entertainment form the working conditions of a quite considerable number of people. Secondly, there is a hollowness about leisure as a concept, as if it were only time to be filled, or the 'free time' which comes after work. It is perfectly clear, in fact, that the uses of leisure relate, often quite deeply, to the nature and conditions of work, and that there is a profound connection between the culture of a society – the whole quality of its arts, entertainments and thinking – and the general social and economic organization. We have seen this clearly in the last twelve years. The economic opportunism and the crudely manipulative ethos of contemporary Conservatism have been as clearly reflected in commercial television and in commercial and political advertising as in any of its more apparently direct social and economic failures. Against that world, which provoked the widespread cultural revolt, especially of the young, during the last ten years, something more and something harder is needed than the kind of policy on leisure which might be appropriate to an enlightened employer, who will also, to keep 'his' workers happy, subscribe to entertainment and sporting and prestige-culture activities. It is a question, at the outset, of a social model. However urgent certain remedial activities may be, within the present system, it will not be enough for a Labour Government to embellish the images we already have. Even a Conservative Government, under pressure, can play the distant patron's role reasonably well: a little help, from special funds, to promising young people; setting the example to others with money (industry, local authorities); keeping the metropolitan institutions going, where foreign visitors can see them, or for State visits; leaving the rest to the market, which governs leisure as it governs work. That kind of policy, even if made a bit more generous, and with an odd bow to 'the provinces', does not need a Labour Party. Nor does the new use of culture as a style in administration – asking the odd sculptor or poet to Chequers, putting an old novelist in the Honours List. What matters, or ought to matter, to the Labour Party, is the quality of the whole way of life of our changing society. It is by that standard that what is done will be judged.

It will need some confidence, and a great deal of consultation and machinery for participation. It will mean getting rid of the twitchy sub-*Express* language of parts of *Leisure for Living*: 'this does not mean that we want to be state nannies' – of course it doesn't, in culture any more than in the social services, but if you pick up their language you'll pick up their attitudes, and the time to stop is now. Or putting words like culture and serious in inverted commas: the nervous tic that is a clear symptom of just what, centrally, is wrong. Fortunately, the right language is also there, or very nearly so: "Good as it would be therefore, to increase the Government grant to the Arts Council (and this we certainly intend to do) it would be even better that this should be done as part of the more purposeful replanning of the economic and social structure of society."

That, in a Labour Government, is the perspective we want.

4. Conclusion

We have been trying to interpret Britain in the sixties; the point now is to change it. The election of a Labour Government creates one kind of political opportunity, but the irony of the general stalemate cuts deeper than we at first supposed. Labour can now only survive, as anything more than a temporary administration, if it makes choices rather than adjustments. We have had the apparent choice, in the past, of making a socialist consciousness or of bidding for an existing kind of parliamentary power. But now political survival and social need point to a single emphasis: the radical attempt to begin changing consciousness by beginning to change our society. In this new situation, theory and practice have a chance of coming together, as they must come together if the first energies are to be maintained. We already know the pressures and limits, and can expect them, in practice, to be very powerful. But to name and understand them, as we meet them in experience, is to gain an energy which now, in these months, can be quickly translated to action. The crisis we have approached theoretically is now open and common, as a public action. The existing framework has been broken to that extent, and it is doubtful if it can ever be put together again, in its old forms. Whether we have the strength and clarity to make a new framework, or must merely endure the present confusion, remains to be tested.